Practice*Planners*

Arthur E. Jongsma

*H*elping therapists help their clients...

Over 250,000 Practice*Planners*® sold . . .

 **WILEY**

Practice*Planners*®   Order Form

Treatment Planners cover all the necessary elements for developing formal treatment plans, including detailed problem definitions, long-term goals, short-term objectives, therapeutic interventions, and DSM-IV diagnoses.

Documentation Sourcebooks provide a comprehensive collection of ready-to-use blank forms, handouts, and questionnaires to help you manage your client reports and streamline the record keeping and treatment process. Features clear, concise explanations of the purpose of each form—including when it should be used and at what point. Includes customizable forms on disk.

The Complete Adult Psychotherapy Treatment Planner, Second Edition
0-471-31924-4 / $44.95

The Child Psychotherapy Treatment Planner, Second Edition
0-471-34764-7 / $44.95

The Adolescent Psychotherapy Treatment Planner, Second Edition
0-471-34766-3 / $44.95

The Chemical Dependence Treatment Planner
0-471-23795-7 / $44.95

The Continuum of Care Treatment Planner
0-471-19568-5 / $44.95

The Couples Psychotherapy Treatment Planner
0-471-24711-1 / $44.95

The Employee Assistance (EAP) Treatment Planner
0-471-24709-X / $44.95

The Pastoral Counseling Treatment Planner
0-471-25416-9 / $44.95

The Older Adult Psychotherapy Treatment Planner
0-471-29574-4 / $44.95

The Behavioral Medicine Treatment Planner
0-471-31923-6 / $44.95

The Group Therapy Treatment Planner
0-471-37449-0 / $44.95

The Family Therapy Treatment Planner
0-471-34768-X / $44.95

The Severe and Persistent Mental Illness Treatment Planner
0-471-35945-9 / $44.95

The Gay and Lesbian Psychotherapy Treatment Planner
0-471-35080-X / $44.95

The Clinical Documentation Sourcebook, Second Edition
0-471-32692-5 / $49.95

The Psychotherapy Documentation Primer
0-471-28990-6 / $45.00

The Couple and Family Clinical Documentation Sourcebook
0-471-25234-4 / $49.95

The Clinical Child Documentation Sourcebook
0-471-29111-0 / $49.95

The Chemical Dependence Treatment Documentation Sourcebook
0-471-31285-1 / $49.95

The Forensic Documentation Sourcebook
0-471-25459-2 / $85.00

The Continuum of Care Clinical Documentation Sourcebook
0-471-34581-4 / $75.00

NEW AND FORTHCOMING

The Traumatic Events Treatment Planner
0-471-39587-0 / $44.95

The Special Education Treatment Planner
0-471-38873-4 / $44.95 p

The Mental Retardation and Developmental Disability Treatment Planner
0-471-38253-1 / $44.95

The Social Work and Human Services Treatment Planner
0-471-37741-4 / $44.95

The Rehabilitation Psychology Treatment Planner
0-471-35178-4 / $44.95

Name_____

Affiliation_____

Address_____

City/State/Zip_____

Phone/Fax_____

E-mail_____

To order, call 1-800-753-0655
(Please refer to promo #1-4019 when ordering.)

Or send this page with payment* to:
John Wiley & Sons, Inc., Attn: J. Knott
605 Third Avenue, New York, NY 10158-0012

❏ Check enclosed   ❏ Visa   ❏ MasterCard   ❏ American Express

Card #_____

Expiration Date_____

Signature_____
*Please add your local sales tax to all orders.

www.wiley.com/practiceplanners

Practice Management Tools for Busy Mental Health Professionals

Homework Planners feature dozens of behaviorally based, ready-to-use assignments that are designed for use between sessions, as well as a disk (Microsoft Word) containing all of the assignments—allowing you to customize them to suit your unique client needs.

Brief Therapy Homework Planner
0-471-24611-5 / $49.95

Brief Couples Therapy Homework Planner
0-471-29511-6 / $49.95

Brief Child Therapy Homework Planner
0-471-32366-7 / $49.95

Brief Adolescent Therapy Homework Planner
0-471-34465-6 / $49.95

Chemical Dependence Treatment Homework Planner
0-471-32452-3 / $49.95

Brief Employee Assistance Homework Planner
0-471-38088-1 / $49.95

Brief Family Therapy Homework Planner
0-471-385123-1 / $49.95

NEW IN THE PRACTICE*PLANNERS*™ SERIES

Progress Notes Planners contain complete prewritten progress notes for each presenting problem in the companion *Treatment Planners*.

The Adult Psychotherapy Progress Notes Planner
0-471-34763-9 / $44.95

The Adolescent Psychotherapy Progress Notes Planner
0-471-38104-7 / $44.95

The Child Psychotherapy Progress Notes Planner
0-471-38102-0 / $44.95

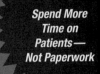
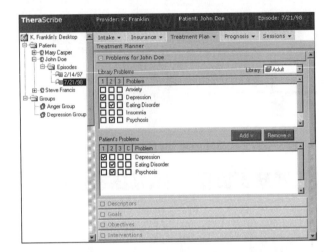

The Child Psychotherapy
Progress Notes Planner

PRACTICE *PLANNERS*® SERIES

Treatment *Planners*

The Chemical Dependence Treatment Planner
The Continuum of Care Treatment Planner
The Couples Psychotherapy Treatment Planner
The Employee Assistance Treatment Planner
The Pastoral Counseling Treatment Planner
The Older Adult Psychotherapy Treatment Planner
The Complete Adult Psychotherapy Treatment Planner, 2e
The Behavioral Medicine Treatment Planner
The Group Therapy Treatment Planner
The Gay and Lesbian Psychotherapy Treatment Planner
The Child Psychotherapy Treatment Planner, 2e
The Adolescent Psychotherapy Treatment Planner, 2e
The Family Psychotherapy Treatment Planner
The Severe and Persistent Mental Illness Treatment Planner
The Mental Retardation and Developmental Disability Treatment Planner
The Social Work and Human Services Treatment Planner

Progress Notes *Planners*

The Child Psychotherapy Progress Notes Planner
The Adolescent Psychotherapy Progress Notes Planner
The Adult Psychotherapy Progress Notes Planner

Homework *Planners*

Brief Therapy Homework Planner
Brief Couples Therapy Homework Planner
Chemical Dependence Treatment Homework Planner
Brief Child Therapy Homework Planner
Brief Adolescent Therapy Homework Planner
Brief Employee Assistance Homework Planner

Documentation *Sourcebooks*

The Clinical Documentation Sourcebook
The Forensic Documentation Sourcebook
The Psychotherapy Documentation Primer
The Chemical Dependence Treatment Documentation Sourcebook
The Clinical Child Documentation Sourcebook
The Couple and Family Clinical Documentation Sourcebook
The Clinical Documentation Sourcebook, 2e
The Continuum of Care Clinical Documentation Sourcebook

Practice *Planners*®

Arthur E. Jongsma, Jr., Series Editor

The Child Psychotherapy
Progress Notes Planner

Arthur E. Jongsma, Jr.

L. Mark Peterson

William P. McInnis

JOHN WILEY & SONS, INC.

New York • Chichester • Weinheim • Brisbane • Singapore • Toronto

Copyright © 2001 by John Wiley & Sons. All rights reserved.

Published simultaneously in Canada.

Library of Congress Cataloging-in-Publication Data:

Jongsma, Arthur E., 1943–
        The child psychotherapy progress notes planner / Arthur E. Jongsma, Jr., William P. McInnis,
    L. Mark Peterson.
            p. cm.
        Includes bibliographical references and index.
        ISBN 0-471-38102-0 (pbk. : alk. paper)—ISBN 0-471-38101-2 (pbk. : alk. paper)
        1. Child psychotherapy.   I. McInnis, William P.   II. Peterson, L. Mark.   III. Title.

    RJ504 .J66 2000
    618.92'8914—dc21

                                                                        00-043466

Printed in the United States of America.

10 9 8 7 6 5 4 3 2 1

CONTENTS

Preface   xi
Introduction   1

Academic Underachievement   4
Adoption   21
Anger Management   33
Anxiety   51
Attachment Disorder   61
Attention-Deficit/Hyperactivity Disorder   76
Autism/Pervasive Developmental Disorder   92
Blended Family   106
Conduct Disorder/Delinquency   118
Depression   134
Disruptive/Attention Seeking   149
Divorce Reaction   165
Enuresis/Encopresis   185
Fire Setting   200
Gender Identity Disorder   208
Grief/Loss Unresolved   217
Low Self-Esteem   229
Medical Condition   240
Mental Retardation   251
Oppositional Defiant   267
Peer/Sibling Conflicts   278
Physical/Emotional Abuse Victim   289
Posttraumatic Stress Disorder   302
School Refusal   314
Separation Anxiety   332

Sexual Abuse Victim   351
Sleep Disturbance   368
Social Phobia/Shyness   376
Specific Phobia   392
Speech/Language Disorders   401

PREFACE

The Child Psychotherapy Progress Notes Planner is another step in the evolution of the Practice Planner series from John Wiley & Sons. This book is written as a companion to *The Child Psychotherapy Treatment Planner* as it provides a menu of sentences that can be selected for constructing a progress note based on the Behavioral Definitions and Therapeutic Interventions from the Treatment Planner.

Our hope and desire is that both students and seasoned clinicians will find this resource helpful in writing progress notes that are thoroughly unified with the client's treatment plan. In our progress note sentences we have tried to provide a range of content that can document how a patient presented and what interventions were used in the session.

The Practice Planner series has continued to expand, especially in the area of Treatment Planners. There are now 16 Treatment Planners published, with several others in the development stage. The original flagship books of this series, *The Complete Psychotherapy Treatment Planner* and the *Child and Adolescent Psychotherapy Treatment Planner,* have both appeared as completely revised books entitled *The Complete Adult Psychotherapy Treatment Planner,* 2d edition, *The Adolescent Psychotherapy Treatment Planner,* 2d edition, and *The Child Psychotherapy Treatment Planner,* 2d edition. Books for specialized patient populations continue to evolve, such as those for the severe and persistently mentally ill population and the mental retardation/developmentally disabled population. All of these Treatment Planners are available with an optional electronic version that can be easily imported into *TheraScribe 3.0* or *3.5; The Computerized Assistant to Psychotherapy Treatment Planning.* The Practice Planners series also includes several psychotherapy Homework Planners that are coordinated with the treatment planners but which can be used independently. Several Documentation Source Books containing useful examples of clinical record keeping forms and handouts round out the Practice Planner series. Future plans include integrating the Progress Notes Planner material into a new version of *TheraScribe* that is currently under development.

We again would like to thank Jennifer Byrne for her tireless dedication to this very tedious project. Her manuscript preparation skills were invaluable to us and her organization skills keep us on track.

Since the publication of the original *Complete Psychotherapy Treatment Planner* by John Wiley & Sons in 1995, Kelly Franklin has been the editor and driving force of this project. We have appreciated her ongoing encouragement, dedication, and support of the Practice Planners series. Beginning with this manuscript, Kelly Franklin is moving into a new e-commerce position at Wiley, and the Practice Planners project has a new editor, Peggy Alexander. We look forward to benefiting from her enthusiasm and fresh ideas, which will provide capable guidance for the future years of development of this series. Welcome aboard, Peggy.

Finally, we would like to take this opportunity to thank our families for their encouragement and tolerance as we all gave many discretionary hours to the writing of this manuscript rather than to relationship building. Thank you Judy, Lynn, and Cherry for your love and encouragement.

ARTHUR E. JONGSMA, JR.
L. MARK PETERSON
WILLIAM P. McINNIS

INTRODUCTION

INTERFACE WITH TREATMENT PLANNER

Progress notes are not only the primary source for documenting the therapeutic process, but also one of the main factors in determining the client's eligibility for reimbursable treatment. Although the books can be used independently, *The Child Psychotherapy Progress Notes Planner* provides prewritten sentences that are directly coordinated with the symptom descriptions in the Behavioral Definition section and with the clinical activity description in the Therapeutic Intervention section of *The Child Psychotherapy Treatment Planner,* 2d ed. (John Wiley & Sons, 2000). By using them together, you'll find these books to be both a time saver and a guidepost to complete clinical record keeping.

ORGANIZATION OF PROGRESS NOTES PLANNER

Each chapter title is a reflection of the client's potential presenting problem. The first section of the chapter, Client Presentation, provides a detailed menu of statements that may describe how that presenting problem has manifested itself in behavioral signs and symptoms. The numbers in parentheses within the Client Presentation section correspond to the number of the Behavioral Definition from the Treatment Planner. For example, consider the following two items from the "Divorce Reaction" chapter of this Progress Note Planner:

3. Emotional Distress around Separations (3)

A. The client has often exhibited a great deal of emotional distress when anticipating a separation from one of his/her parents.

B. The client became visibly upset and began to protest vigorously when asked to separate from his/her parent in today's therapy session.

C. The client has often displayed temper outbursts around separation from one of his/her parents.

D. The client has gradually started to cope more effectively with separations and has not exhibited as much distress when anticipating separation from a parent.

E. The client was able to separate effectively from his/her parent in today's therapy session without exhibiting a significant amount of distress.

4. Emotional Distress around Transfer from Home(s) (3)

A. The client has often exhibited a great deal of emotional distress when making the transfer from one parent's home to another.

B. The parents reported that the client frequently exhibits temper outbursts before and after he/she makes the transfer from one home to another.

C. The client has often begged and pleaded to stay with one parent before making the transfer to the other parent's home.

D. The client has gradually started to cope more effectively with the transfer between homes.

E. The client has consistently been able to make the transition from one parent's home to the other without exhibiting any heightened emotional distress.

In the previous example, the numeral 3 in the two sets of parentheses refers to the third Behavioral Definition from the "Divorce Reaction" chapter in *The Child Psychotherapy Treatment Planner*.

The second section of each chapter, Interventions Implemented, provides a menu of statements related to the action that was taken within the session to assist the client in making progress. The numbering of the items in the Interventions Implemented section follows exactly the numbering of Therapeutic Intervention items in the corresponding Treatment Planner. For example, consider the following two items from the "Divorce Reaction" chapter in this Progress Notes Planner:

2. Explore and Encourage Expression of Feelings (2)

A. Today's therapy session explored the client's feelings associated with his/her parents' separation or divorce.

B. The client was given encouragement and support in expressing and clarifying his/her feelings associated with the separation or divorce.

C. Client-centered therapy principles were utilized to assist the client in expressing his/her thoughts and feelings about the parents' separation or divorce.

D. The client made productive use of today's therapy session and expressed a variety of emotions related to his/her parents' separation or divorce.

E. The client remained guarded in sharing his/her feelings regarding the separation or divorce, despite receiving encouragement and support.

3. Assign Children's Books on Divorce (3)

A. Read *Dinosaur's Divorce: A Guide for Changing Families* (Brown and Brown) to the client in today's therapy session.

B. Read *Divorce Workbook: A Guide for Kids and Families* (Ives, Fassler, and Lash) in today's therapy session to help the client express his/her feelings about the parents' divorce and changes in the family system.

C. Processed the content of the readings in today's therapy session.

D. The reading of the books on divorce helped the client express and work through his/her feelings about the parents' divorce.

E. After reading the book on divorce, the client was able to express his/her thoughts and feelings about the changes that have occurred within the family system.

In the preceding example, the item numbers 2 and 3 correspond directly to the same numbered items in the Therapeutic Interventions section of the "Divorce Reaction" chapter of *The Child Psychotherapy Treatment Planner*. Within the Client Presentation section of each chapter, the statements are arranged to reflect a progression toward resolution of the problem.

The latter statements are included to be used in later stages of therapy as the client moves forward toward discharge.

Finally, all item lists begin with a few keywords. These words are meant to convey the theme or content of the sentences that are contained in that listing. The clinician may peruse the list of keywords to find content that matches the client's presentation and the clinician's intervention.

USING THE CHILD PROGRESS NOTES PLANNER

If the user has not used *The Child Psychotherapy Treatment Planner* to initiate treatment, then relevant progress notes can be found by locating the chapter title that reflects the client's presenting problem, scanning the keywords to find the theme that fits the session, and then selecting the sentences that describe first how the client presented for that session and then which interventions were used to assist the client in reaching his/her therapeutic goals and objectives. It is expected that the clinician will modify the prewritten statements contained in this book to fit the exact circumstances of the client's presentation and treatment. Individualization of treatment must be reflected in progress notes that are tailored to each client's unique presentation, strengths, and weaknesses.

In order to maintain complete client records, the following must be entered in the patient's records: progress note statements that may be selected and individualized from this book; the date, time, and length of a session; those present during the session; and the provider, provider's credentials, and a signature.

All progress notes must be tied to the treatment plan—session notes should elaborate on the problems, symptoms, and interventions contained in the plan. If a session focuses on a topic outside of those covered in the treatment plan, providers must update the treatment plan accordingly.

ACADEMIC UNDERACHIEVEMENT

CLIENT PRESENTATION

1. Academic Underachievement (1)*

A. The client's teachers and parents reported a history of academic performance that is below the expected level, given the client's measured intelligence or performance on standardized achievement tests.

B. The client verbally admitted that his/her current academic performance is below the expected level of functioning.

C. The client has started to assume more responsibility for completing his/her school and homework assignments.

D. The client has taken active steps (e.g., studying at routine times, seeking outside tutor, consulting with teacher before or after class) to improve his/her academic performance.

E. The client's academic performance has improved to his/her level of capability.

2. Incomplete Homework Assignments (2)

A. The client has consistently failed to complete his/her classroom or homework assignments in a timely manner.

B. The client has refused to comply with parents' and teachers' requests to complete classroom or homework assignments.

C. The client expressed a renewed desire to complete his/her classroom and homework assignments on a regular basis.

D. The client has recently completed his/her classroom and homework assignments on a consistent basis.

E. The client's regular completion of classroom and homework assignments has resulted in higher grades.

3. Disorganization (3)

A. The parents and teachers described a history of the client being disorganized in the classroom.

B. The client has often lost or misplaced books, school papers, or important things necessary for tasks or activities at school.

C. The client has started to take steps (e.g., using planner or agenda to record school/homework assignments, consulting with teachers before or after school, scheduling routine study times) to become more organized at school.

D. The client's increased organizational abilities have contributed to his/her improved academic performance.

---

* The numbers in parentheses correlate to the number of the Behavioral Definition statement in the companion chapter with same title in *The Child Psychotherapy Treatment Planner* (Jongsma, Peterson, and McInnis) by John Wiley & Sons, 2000.

4. Poor Study Skills (3)

A. Parents and teachers reported that the client has historically displayed poor study skills.

B. The client acknowledged that his/her lowered academic performance is primarily due to his/her lack of studying.

C. The client has recently spent little time studying.

D. The client reported a recent increase in studying time.

E. The client's increased studying time has been a significant contributing factor to his/her improved academic performance.

5. Procrastination (4)

A. The client has repeatedly procrastinated or postponed doing his/her classroom or homework assignments in favor of engaging in social, leisure, or recreational activities.

B. The client has continued to procrastinate doing his/her classroom or homework assignments.

C. The client has agreed to postpone social, leisure, or recreational activities until completing his/her homework assignments.

D. The client has demonstrated greater self-discipline by completing homework assignments before engaging in social, leisure, or recreational activities.

E. The client has achieved and maintained a healthy balance between accomplishing academic goals and meeting his/her social and emotional needs.

6. Family History of Academic Problems (5)

A. The client and parents described a family history of academic problems and failures.

B. The client's parents have demonstrated little interest or involvement in the client's schoolwork or activities.

C. The client expressed a desire for his/her parents to show greater interest or involvement in his/her schoolwork or activities.

D. The parents verbalized a willingness to show greater interest in and to become more involved in the client's schoolwork or activities.

E. The parents have sustained an active interest and involvement in the client's schoolwork and have implemented several effective interventions to help the client achieve his/her academic goals.

7. Depression (6)

A. The client's feelings of depression, as manifested by his/her apathy, listlessness, and lack of motivation have contributed to and resulted from his/her lowered academic performance.

B. The client appeared visibly depressed when discussing his/her lowered academic performance.

C. The client expressed feelings of happiness about his/her improved academic performance.

D. The client's academic performance has improved since his/her depression has lifted.

8. Low Self-Esteem (6)

A. The client's low self-esteem, feelings of insecurity, and lack of confidence have contributed to and resulted from his/her lowered academic performance.

B. The client displayed a lack of confidence and expressed strong self-doubts about being able to improve his/her academic performance.

C. The client verbally acknowledged a tendency to give up easily and withdraw in the classroom when feeling insecure and unsure of himself/herself.

D. The client verbalized positive self-descriptive statements about his/her academic performance.

E. The client has consistently expressed confidence in his/her ability to achieve academic goals.

9. Disruptive/Attention-Seeking Behavior (7)

A. The client has frequently disrupted the classroom with his/her negative attention–seeking behavior instead of focusing on schoolwork.

B. The parents have received reports from schoolteachers that the client has continued to disrupt the classroom with negative attention–seeking behavior.

C. The client acknowledged that he/she tends to engage in disruptive behavior when he/she begins to feel insecure or become frustrated with schoolwork.

D. The client has started to show greater self-control in the classroom and inhibit the impulse to act out in order to draw attention to himself/herself.

E. The client has demonstrated a significant decrease in his/her disruptive and negative attention–seeking behavior.

10. Low Frustration Tolerance (7)

A. The client has developed a low frustration tolerance as manifested by his/her persistent pattern of giving up easily when encountering difficult or challenging academic tasks.

B. The client's frustration tolerance with his/her schoolwork has remained very low.

C. The client has started to show improved frustration tolerance and has not given up as easily or as often on his/her classroom or homework assignments.

D. The client has demonstrated good frustration tolerance and consistently completed his/her classroom/homework assignments without giving up.

11. Test-Taking Anxiety (8)

A. The client described a history of becoming highly anxious before or during tests.

B. The client's heightened anxiety during tests has interfered with his/her academic performance.

C. The client shared that his/her test-taking anxiety is related to fear of failure and of meeting with disapproval or criticism by significant others.

D. The client has begun to take steps (e.g., deep breathing, positive self-statements, challenging irrational thoughts) to reduce his/her anxiety and feel more relaxed while taking tests.

E. The client reported a significant decrease in the level of anxiety while taking tests.

12. Excessive Parental Pressure (9)

A. The client has viewed his/her parents as placing excessive or unrealistic pressure on him/her to achieve academic success.

B. The parents acknowledged that they have placed excessive or unrealistic pressure on the client to achieve academic success.

C. The parents denied placing excessive or unrealistic pressure on the client to achieve; instead they attributed the client's lowered academic performance to his/her lack of motivation and effort.

D. The client reported that his/her parents have decreased the amount of pressure they have placed on him/her to achieve academic success.

E. The parents have established realistic expectations of the client's level of capabilities.

13. Excessive Criticism (9)

A. The client described the parents as being overly critical of his/her academic performance.

B. The client expressed feelings of sadness and inadequacy about critical remarks that his/her parents have made in regard to his/her academic performance.

C. The client acknowledged that he/she deliberately refuses to do school assignments when he/she perceives the parents as being overly critical.

D. The parents acknowledged that they have been overly critical of the client's academic performance.

E. The parents have significantly reduced the frequency of their critical remarks about the client's academic performance.

14. Lack of Motivation (9)

A. The client verbalized little motivation to improve his/her academic performance.

B. The client has often complained of being bored with or disinterested in his/her schoolwork.

C. The client verbally acknowledged that his/her academic performance will not improve unless he/she shows more interest and puts forth greater effort.

D. The client has shown more interest in his/her schoolwork and has put forth greater effort.

E. The client's renewed interest and motivation have contributed to improved academic performance.

15. Environmental Stress (10)

A. The client's academic performance has markedly declined since experiencing stressors within his/her personal and/or family life.

B. The client's academic performance has decreased since his/her family moved and he/she had to change schools.

C. The client has not been able to invest sufficient time or energy in his/her schoolwork because of having to deal with environmental stressors.

D. The client has begun to manage his/her stress more effectively so that he/she has more time and energy to devote to schoolwork.

E. The client's academic performance has improved since resolving or finding effective ways to cope with environmental stressors.

16. Loss or Separation (10)

A. The client's academic performance has decreased significantly since experiencing the separation or loss.

B. The client verbalized feelings of sadness, hurt, and disappointment about past separation(s) or loss(es).

C. The client has taken active steps (i.e., socialized regularly with peers, studied with peers, participated in extracurricular activities) to build a positive support network at school to help him/her cope with the past separation(s) or loss(es).

D. The client's academic interest and performance has increased substantially since working through his/her grief issues.

INTERVENTIONS IMPLEMENTED

1. Psychoeducational Testing (1)*

A. The client received a psychoeducational evaluation to rule out the presence of a learning disability that could be contributing to his/her academic underachievement.

B. The client was cooperative during the psychoeducational testing and appeared motivated to do his/her best.

C. The client was uncooperative during the psychoeducational testing and did not appear to put forth good effort.

D. The client's resistance during the psychoeducational testing appeared to be due to his/her feelings of insecurity and opposition to possibly receiving special education services.

2. Psychological Testing for ADHD/Emotional Factors (2)

A. The client received a psychological evaluation to help determine whether he/she has ADHD which may be contributing to his/her low academic performance.

B. The client received psychological testing to help determine whether emotional factors are contributing to his/her low academic performance.

C. The client was uncooperative and resistant during the evaluation process.

D. The client approached the psychological testing in an honest, straightforward manner, and was cooperative with the examiner.

3. Obtain Psychosocial History (3)

A. A psychosocial assessment was completed to gather pertinent information about the client's past academic performance, developmental milestones, and family history of educational achievements and failures.

B. The client and parents were cooperative in providing information about the client's early developmental history, school performance, and family background.

C. A review of the client's background revealed a history of developmental delays and low academic performance.

---

* The numbers in parentheses correlate to the number of the Therapeutic Interventions statement in the companion chapter with same title in *The Child Psychotherapy Treatment Planner* (Jongsma, Peterson, and McInnis) by John Wiley & Sons, 2000.

D. The psychosocial assessment revealed a family history of academic underachievement and failures.

E. The psychosocial assessment revealed a history of strong expectations being placed on family members to achieve academic success.

4. Give Evaluation Feedback (4)

A. The examiner provided feedback on the evaluation results to the client, parents, and school officials and discussed appropriate interventions.

B. The psychoeducational evaluation results revealed the presence of a learning disability and the need for special education services.

C. The psychoeducational evaluation results did not support the presence of a learning disability or the need for special education services.

D. The evaluation results supported the presence of ADHD, which may be contributing to the client's lowered academic performance.

E. The evaluation results revealed underlying emotional problems that appear to be contributing to the client's lowered academic performance.

5. Hearing/Vision/Medical Examination Referral (5)

A. The client was referred for a hearing and vision examination to rule out possible hearing or visual problems that may be interfering with his/her school performance.

B. The client was referred for a medical evaluation to rule out possible health problems that may be interfering with his/her school performance.

C. The hearing examination results revealed the presence of hearing problems that are interfering with the client's academic performance.

D. The vision examination revealed the presence of visual problems that are interfering with the client's school performance.

E. The medical examination revealed the presence of health problems that are interfering with the client's school performance.

6. Attend IEPC Meeting (6)

A. The client's Individualized Educational Planning Committee (IEPC) meeting was held with the parents, teachers, and school officials to determine the client's eligibility for special education services, to design educational interventions, and to establish educational goals.

B. The recommendation was made at the IEPC that the client receive special education services to address his/her learning problems.

C. At the IEPC meeting, it was determined that the client is not in need of special education services because he/she does not meet the criteria for a learning disability.

D. The IEPC meeting was helpful in identifying specific educational goals.

E. The IEPC meeting was helpful in designing several educational interventions for the client.

7. Consultation about Teaching Intervention Strategies (7)

A. Consulted with the client, parents, and school officials about designing effective teaching programs or intervention strategies that build on the client's strengths and compensate for his/her weaknesses.

B. The client, parents, and teachers identified several learning or personality strengths that the client can utilize to improve his/her academic performance.

C. The consultation meeting with the client, parents, and school officials identified the client's weaknesses and intervention strategies that he/she can utilize to overcome his/her problems.

8. Refer for Private Tutoring (8)

A. The recommendation was given to the parents to seek private after-school tutoring for the client to boost the client's skills in the area of his/her academic weakness.

B. The client and parents were agreeable to seeking private after-school tutoring.

C. The client and parents were opposed to the idea of seeking private after-school tutoring.

D. The client and parents reported that private tutoring has helped to improve the client's academic performance.

E. The client and parents reported that private tutoring has not led to the desired improvements in the client's academic performance.

9. Private Learning Center Referral (9)

A. The client was referred to a private learning center for extra tutoring in the areas of academic weakness and for assistance in improving his/her study and test-taking skills.

B. The client reported that the extra tutoring and support provided by the private learning center have helped improve his/her performance in the areas of his/her academic weakness.

C. The client reported that his/her performance in the areas of academic weakness has not improved since attending the private learning center.

D. The client reported that his/her study and test-taking skills have improved since attending the private learning center.

E. The client's study skills and test performances have not improved since attending the private learning center.

10. Teach Study Skills (10)

A. The client was assisted in identifying a list of good locations to study.

B. The client was instructed to remove noise sources and eliminate as many distractions as possible when studying.

C. The client was instructed to outline or underline important details when studying or reviewing for tests.

D. The client was encouraged to use a tape recorder to help him/her study for tests and review important facts.

E. The client was instructed to take breaks in studying when he/she becomes distracted and has trouble staying focused.

11. Self-Monitoring Checklists (11)

A. The client was encouraged to utilize self-monitoring checklists to increase completion of school assignments and improve academic performance.

B. The client reported that the use of self-monitoring checklists has helped him/her to become more organized and to complete school assignments on time.

C. The client has failed to consistently use self-monitoring checklists and as a result has continued to have trouble completing his/her school and homework assignments.

D. The client's teachers were consulted about the use of self-monitoring checklists in the classroom to help him/her complete school and homework assignments on a regular, consistent basis.

E. Parents and teachers were instructed to utilize a reward system in conjunction with the self-monitoring checklists to increase the client's completion of school and homework assignments and improve his/her academic performance.

12. Use Assignment Planner or Calendar (12)

A. The client was strongly encouraged to use a planner or calendar to record school and homework assignments and plan ahead for long-term assignments.

B. The client's regular use of a planning calendar has helped him/her complete classroom and homework assignments on a consistent basis.

C. The client has failed to use a planning calendar consistently and has continued to struggle to complete school/homework assignments.

D. The client reported that the use of a planning calendar has helped him/her plan ahead for long-term assignments.

E. The client's ADHD symptoms have contributed to his/her failure to use a planner or calendar on a regular basis.

13. Utilize "Getting It Done" Program (13)

A. The "Getting It Done" program from *The Brief Child Therapy Treatment Planner* (Jongsma, Peterson, and McInnis) was utilized to help the client complete his/her school and homework assignments on a consistent basis.

B. The parents and teachers were encouraged to utilize daily or weekly school reports from the "Getting It Done" program to help them communicate regularly about how well the client is doing at completing his/her school and homework assignments.

C. Regular communication between the parents and teachers has helped the client to complete his/her school and homework assignments on a consistent basis.

D. The client, parents, and teachers were encouraged to utilize the reward system outlined in the "Getting It Done" program to help the client complete his/her school and homework assignments on a regular basis.

E. The reward system has helped motivate the client to complete his/her school and homework assignments.

14. Teach Test-Taking Strategies (14)

A. The client reviewed a list of effective test-taking strategies to improve his/her academic performance.

B. The client was encouraged to review classroom material regularly and study for tests over an extended period of time.

C. The client was instructed to read the instructions twice before responding to questions on a test.

D. The client recognized the need to recheck his/her work to correct any careless mistakes or improve an answer.

15. Utilize Peer Tutor (15)

A. The recommendation was given to parents and teachers that the client be assigned a peer tutor to improve his/her study skills and address areas of academic weakness.

B. The client verbalized a desire and willingness to work with a peer tutor to improve his/her study skills and academic performance.

C. The client expressed opposition to the idea of working with a peer tutor to improve his/her study skills and academic performance.

D. The client reported that peer tutoring has helped to improve his/her study skills and academic performance.

E. The client reported that peer tutoring has not helped to improve his/her study skills and academic performance.

16. Maintain Communication between Home and School (16)

A. The parents and teachers were encouraged to maintain regular communication via phone calls or written notes regarding the client's academic progress.

B. The client's teachers were asked to send home daily or weekly progress notes informing the parents about the client's academic progress.

C. The client was informed of his/her responsibility to bring home daily or weekly progress notes from school, allowing for regular communication between parents and teachers.

D. The parents identified the consequences for the client's failure to bring home a daily or weekly progress note from school.

E. The increased communication between teachers and parents via phone calls or regular progress notes has been a significant contributing factor to the client's improved academic performance.

17. Develop Study and Recreation Schedule (17)

A. The client and parents were assisted in developing a routine schedule to help the client achieve a healthy balance between completing homework assignments and engaging in independent play or spending quality time with family and peers.

B. The client has followed the agreed-upon schedule and has been able to successfully complete homework assignments and engage in independent play or spend quality time with family and peers.

C. The client has failed to consistently complete his/her homework assignments because he/she has not followed the agreed-upon schedule.

18. Encourage Parental Positive Reinforcement (18)

A. The parents were encouraged to provide frequent positive reinforcement to maintain the client's interest and motivation in completing his/her school and homework assignments.

B. The parents were challenged to look for opportunities to praise the client for being responsible or successful at school instead of focusing on times when the client failed to behave responsibly or achieve success.

C. Explored the contributing factors or underlying dynamics that prevent the parents from offering praise and positive reinforcement on a consistent basis.

19. Resolve Family Conflicts (19)

A. Today's therapy session focused on the conflicts within the family system that block or inhibit the client's learning.

B. The family members were asked to brainstorm possible solutions to the conflicts that exist within the family and interfere with the client's academic performance.

C. Today's therapy session dealt with the conflict between the parents over how to address the client's lowered academic performance.

D. The parents resolved their differences over how to respond to the client's learning problems and came up with a mutually agreed-upon plan of action.

E. The parents did not resolve their differences between themselves over how to address the client's learning problems.

20. Encourage Parental Involvement (20)

A. The parents were strongly encouraged to demonstrate regular interest in and involvement with the client's school activities and homework.

B. The parents were encouraged to attend the client's school conferences.

C. The parents were encouraged to read aloud or alongside the client on a regular basis to improve his/her reading skills.

D. The parents were encouraged to use flashcards on a regular basis to improve the client's math skills.

E. The parents were encouraged to work with the client each school night to improve his/her spelling abilities.

21. Identify Rewards to Maintain Motivation (21)

A. The client and parents were helped to develop a list of possible rewards or positive reinforcers that would increase the client's interest and motivation to complete his/her school assignments.

B. The client signed a written contract specifying the positive reinforcers that are contingent on completion of his/her school assignments.

C. The rewards and positive reinforcers have helped to maintain the client's interest and motivation in completing his/her school assignments.

22. Teach Stress-Coping Strategies (22)

A. The client was taught guided imagery and relaxation techniques to help decrease the level of his/her anxiety and frustration when encountering difficult or challenging school assignments.

B. The client was encouraged to utilize positive self-talk as a means of decreasing anxiety and managing frustration when encountering difficult or challenging school assignments.

C. The client was taught cognitive restructuring techniques to decrease his/her anxiety and frustrations associated with schoolwork.

D. The client reported that the use of the positive coping mechanisms (e.g., relaxation techniques, positive self-talk, cognitive restructuring) has helped to decrease his/her level of anxiety and frustration when encountering difficult or challenging school assignments.

E. The client reported experiencing little or no reduction in the level of his/her anxiety or frustration through the use of relaxation techniques, positive self-talk, or cognitive restructuring.

23. Guided Imagery or Relaxation Techniques (23)

A. The client was trained in the use of guided imagery and deep muscle relaxation techniques to help reduce the level of his/her anxiety before or during the taking of tests.

B. The client reported a positive response to the use of guided imagery and deep muscle relaxation techniques to help decrease his/her anxiety before and during the taking of tests.

C. The client appeared uncomfortable during the therapy session when being instructed on the use of guided imagery and deep muscle relaxation techniques.

D. The client was encouraged to continue to practice the use of guided imagery and deep muscle relaxation techniques, even though he/she reports little or no improvement in the reduction of his/her level of anxiety or frustration since the last therapy session.

24. Explore Family Stress (24)

A. A family therapy session was held to explore the dynamics that may be contributing to the client's lowered academic performance.

B. The family members were asked to list the stressors that have had a negative impact on the family.

C. The family members were asked to identify the things that they would like to change within the family.

D. The parents recognized how their marital problems are creating stress for the client and agreed to seek marital counseling.

E. The parents refused to follow through with the recommendation for marital counseling.

25. Use of Systematic Rewards (25)

A. The parents and teachers were consulted about using systematic rewards to reinforce the client's academic progress and accomplishments.

B. A reward system was designed to reinforce the client's completion of school and homework assignments.

C. A reward system was designed to reinforce the client for achieving his/her academic goals.

D. The parents and teachers were strongly encouraged to provide frequent praise for the client when he/she achieves academic success.

E. The parents and teachers were encouraged to utilize a star chart to reinforce the client for his/her academic progress and achievements.

26. Explore Unrealistic Parental Expectations (26)

A. A family therapy session was held to explore whether the parents have developed unrealistic expectations or are placing excessive pressure on the client to perform.

B. The client and parents discussed and identified more realistic expectations about the client's academic performance.

27. Confront Excessive Pressure (27)

A. The parents were confronted and challenged about placing excessive pressure on the client to achieve academic success.

B. Today's family therapy session explored the reasons why the parents have placed excessive pressure on the client to achieve academic success.

C. The client was seen individually to allow him/her to express thoughts and feelings about excessive pressure placed on him/her by parents.

D. A family therapy session was held to provide the client with an opportunity to express anger, frustration, and hurt about parents placing excessive pressure on him/her.

28. Parents Set Firm Limits for Homework Refusal (28)

A. The parents were strongly encouraged to set firm, consistent limits and utilize natural, logical consequences for the client's refusal to do his/her homework.

B. The parents identified a list of consequences to utilize for the client's refusal to do homework.

C. The parents reported that the client has responded positively to their limits or consequences, and has begun to complete his/her homework assignments on a regular, consistent basis.

D. The client has refused to comply with his/her parent's request to complete homework assignments, even though the parents have begun to set firm limits.

29. Teach Avoidance of Unhealthy Power Struggles (29)

A. The parents were instructed to follow through with firm, consistent limits and not become locked into unhealthy power struggles or arguments with the client over his/her homework each night.

B. The client was asked to repeat the rules surrounding his/her homework to demonstrate an understanding of the parents' expectations of him/her.

C. The client and parents were taught effective communication and assertiveness skills to learn how to express feelings in a controlled fashion and avoid becoming locked into unhealthy arguments over homework.

D. Today's therapy session revealed how the client's underlying feelings of insecurity and low self-esteem contribute to his/her argumentativeness and negative attitude about completing homework.

30. Assess Parent's Overprotectiveness (30)

A. A family therapy session was conducted to explore whether the parents' overprotectiveness or infantilization of the client contributes to the client's academic underachievement.

B. The parents were helped to see how their pattern of overprotectiveness or infantilization contributes to the client's academic underachievement.

C. The client and parents were helped to recognize the secondary gain that is achieved through the parents' pattern of overindulging or infantilizing the client.

D. The parents were instructed to expect some resistance (e.g., crying, complaining, exhibiting temper outbursts) when they begin to terminate their pattern of overprotectiveness or infantilization.

E. The parents were encouraged to remain firm and follow through with consistent limits when the client tests them about doing his/her homework.

31. Develop Realistic Expectations (31)

A. The parents were helped to develop realistic expectations of the client's learning potential.

B. The client and parents developed realistic academic goals that were in line with the client's learning potential.

32. Consult School Officials to Improve On-Task Behavior (32)

A. The therapist consulted with school officials about ways to improve the client's on-task behavior.

B. The recommendation was made that the client sit toward the front of the class or near positive peer role models to help him/her stay focused and on task.

C. The teachers were encouraged to call on the client often during the class to maintain the client's interest and attention.

D. The teachers were instructed to provide frequent feedback to the client to maintain his/her interest and motivation to complete school assignments.

E. The recommendation was given to teachers to break the client's larger assignments into a series of smaller tasks.

33. Read *13 Steps to Better Grades* (33)

A. The client was instructed to read *13 Steps to Better Grades* (Silverman) to improve his/her organizational and study skills.

B. The client's reading of *13 Steps to Better Grades* was processed in today's therapy session.

C. After reading *13 Steps to Better Grades,* the client was able to identify several positive study skills that will help him/her remain organized in the classroom.

34. Reinforce Successful School Experiences (34)

A. The parents and teachers were encouraged to reinforce the client's successful school experiences.

B. The client was given the homework assignment of making one positive statement about school each day.

C. All positive statements by client about school were noted and reinforced.

D. The client was helped to realize how his/her negativistic attitude about school interferes with his/her ability to establish peer friendships.

35. Confront Self-Disparaging Remarks (35)

A. The client was confronted about his/her self-defeating pattern of making derogatory comments about himself/herself and giving up easily when encountering difficulty with schoolwork.

B. The client was instructed to use positive self-talk when encountering difficult or challenging tasks at school instead of making disparaging remarks about himself/herself and giving up easily.

C. The client was directed to verbalize at least one positive self-statement around others at school.

36. Record Positive Statements about School (36)

A. The client was assigned the task of making one positive statement daily about school, and either recording the statement in a journal or writing it on a sticky note to place in the kitchen or in his/her bedroom.

B. The client was compliant with the homework assignment to record at least one positive statement daily about his/her school experiences.

C. The client did not cooperate with the homework assignment to record at least one positive statement daily about his/her school experiences.

D. After reviewing the positive statements about school recorded in the journal, the client was encouraged to engage in similar positive behaviors that would help make school a more rewarding and satisfying experience.

37. Increase Motivation (37)

A. The client was assisted in developing a list of possible rewards or positive reinforcements that would increase his/her motivation to improve academic performance.

B. The client signed a written contract specifying the positive reinforcers that are contingent on him/her achieving specific academic goals.

C. Consulted with the parents and teachers about using specific rewards to reinforce the client's improved academic performance.

38. Individual Play Therapy (38)

A. An individual play therapy session was conducted with the client to help him/her work through and resolve painful emotions, core conflicts, or stressors that have impeded his/her academic performance.

B. A psychoanalytic play therapy approach was utilized to explore the core conflicts that are impeding the client's academic performance.

C. The client made productive use of the individual play therapy session to express his/her painful emotions surrounding core conflicts or significant stressors.

D. Client-centered play therapy approaches were utilized to help the client identify and express his/her painful emotions surrounding the core conflicts or significant stressors that impede his/her academic performance.

39. Connect Feelings and Performance (39)

A. Today's therapy session explored underlying, painful emotions that may be contributing to the client's decrease in academic performance.

B. Today's therapy session helped the client develop insight into how his/her lowered academic performance is related to underlying, painful emotions.

C. Role-playing and modeling techniques were used to demonstrate appropriate ways for the client to express his/her underlying painful emotions.

D. The client was helped to identify more effective ways to cope with his/her frustrations or painful emotions instead of giving up and/or refusing to do schoolwork.

40. Teach Self-Control Strategies (40)

A. The client was taught deep breathing and relaxation techniques to inhibit the impulse to act out or engage in negative attention–seeking behaviors when encountering frustration with his/her schoolwork.

B. The client was encouraged to utilize positive self-talk when encountering frustration with his/her schoolwork instead of acting out or engaging in negative attention–seeking behaviors.

C. The client was taught mediational self-control strategies (e.g., "stop, look, listen, and think") to inhibit the impulse to act out or engage in negative attention–seeking behaviors when encountering frustration with schoolwork.

41. Past Periods of Academic Success (41)

A. The client explored periods of time when he/she completed schoolwork regularly and achieved academic success.

B. The client was encouraged to use strategies or organizational skills similar to those that he/she had used in the past to achieve academic success.

C. The client shared the realization that involvement in extracurricular or positive peer group activities increased his/her motivation to achieve academic success.

D. The session revealed that the client was more disciplined with his/her study habits when he/she received strong family support and affiliated with positive peer groups.

E. The client recognized that he/she achieved greater academic success in the past when he/she scheduled routine times to complete homework.

42. Past Successful Coping Strategies (42)

A. The client explored other coping strategies that he/she had previously used to solve other problems.

B. The client was encouraged to use coping strategies similar to those that he/she had used successfully in the past to overcome current problems associated with learning.

C. The session revealed that the client overcame past learning problems when he/she sought extra assistance from teachers, parents, or peers.

D. The client recognized that he/she was more successful in completing school assignments in the past when he/she used a planning calendar to record homework assignments and long-term projects.

43. Identify Resource People within School (43)

A. The client developed a list of resource people within the school whom he/she can turn to for support, assistance, or instruction when encountering difficulty or frustration with learning.

B. After identifying a list of school resource people the client was directed to seek support at least once from one of these individuals before the next therapy session.

C. The client reported that the extra assistance he/she received from other individuals in the school helped him/her to overcome difficulty and learn new concepts or skills.

44. "Reading Adventure" Program (44)

A. The parents were encouraged to use the "Reading Adventure" program from *The Brief Child Therapy Homework Planner* (Jongsma, Peterson, and McInnis) to increase the client's motivation to read on a regular basis.

B. The parents were instructed to use the reward system in the "Reading Adventure" program to reinforce the client for engaging in independent reading.

C. The parents reported that the "Reading Adventure" program has increased the client's interest and enjoyment with reading.

D. The reward system helped the client reach his/her goal of reading for a specific period of time each day or week.

45. Mutual Storytelling Techniques (45)

A. The mutual storytelling technique was used to model appropriate ways for the client to manage frustration related to his/her learning problems.

B. The mutual storytelling technique was used to show how achieving one's academic goals leads to improvements in feelings of self-worth.

C. The mutual storytelling technique was used to show the client the benefits of completing his/her homework before engaging in social or recreational activities.

D. The client found the mutual storytelling technique to be an enjoyable way to learn how to manage frustrations related to his/her learning problems.

E. The client created a story through the use of puppets, dolls, or stuffed animals that reflected his/her feelings of insecurity and frustration about his/her struggles to learn.

46. Art-Therapy Techniques (46)

A. The client was instructed to draw a variety of pictures that reflected how his/her personal and family life would be different if he/she completed homework on a regular basis.

B. After completing his/her drawings, the client verbalized how his/her academic underachievements or failures have negatively impacted his/her self-esteem and family relationships.

C. The completion of the client's drawings led to a discussion about what steps the client can take to improve his/her academic performance.

D. The client's artwork reflected his/her perception of the parents being overly critical or placing excessive pressure on him/her to achieve academic success.

47. Assess Stressors at School through Artwork (47)

A. To help assess possible stressors that may interfere with his/her learning and academic progress, the client was instructed to draw a picture of a school building, then create a story that tells what it is like to be a student at the school.

B. The client created a drawing and story that reflected the stressors that he/she experiences at school.

C. After completing his/her drawing and story, the client was helped to identify more effective ways to cope with the stressors at school that interfere with his/her learning and academic progress.

D. The client's artwork and story reflected how his/her interpersonal conflicts with peers have interfered with his/her learning and academic progress.

E. The client found the art therapy and mutual storytelling techniques to be an enjoyable and beneficial way to learn how to cope with the stressors that interfere with his/her learning and academic progress.

48. Medication Evaluation Referral (48)

A. The client was referred to a physician for an evaluation regarding medication to help stabilize his/her moods.

B. The client was referred to a physician for a medication evaluation to address his/her symptoms of ADHD.

C. The client and parents agreed to follow through with a medication evaluation by a physician.

D. The client was strongly opposed to being placed on medication to help improve his/her impulse control and/or stabilize moods.

ADOPTION

CLIENT PRESENTATION

1. Adoption of Special-Needs Children (1)*

A. The parents have recently adopted a special-needs child/sibset.

B. The parents expressed feeling overwhelmed by the demands of the children.

C. The parents asked for support and resources to assist them in coping with the special needs of the adopted child/children.

D. The parents have gradually adjusted to and are becoming accepting of the special-needs child/children.

2. Relates to Others in a Withdrawing/Rejecting Way (2)

A. The parents indicated that from the beginning the client has shown withdrawing and rejecting behaviors toward them.

B. It has been observed by caregivers and professionals that the client relates in a detached manner with everyone.

C. Evaluations have noted that the client rarely makes any eye contact and physically keeps himself/herself away from others.

D. The client has started to relate more closely with others and is allowing others to get physically closer to him/her.

3. Hoarding or Gorging Food (3)

A. Parents have discovered that the client has stashes of food in various hiding places in his/her bedroom.

B. It has been observed that the client eats quickly to ensure that he/she can get more.

C. The parents reported that the client often eats so much that he/she becomes physically sick.

D. The client has been seen sneaking food at home and school to save for eating at a later time.

E. Parents indicated that the client now eats more normal amounts of food and no longer hides food for later consumption.

4. Aggressive Behaviors (4)

A. Records of the client reflected a long, clear history of aggressive acts toward siblings, peers, and caregivers.

B. Parents indicated that they are dealing on a daily basis with the client's aggressive actions toward siblings, peers, and themselves.

C. School officials have reported intervening with the client on a frequent basis for his/her aggressive actions toward peers.

---

* The numbers in parentheses correlate to the number of the Behavioral Definition statement in the companion chapter with same title in *The Child Psychotherapy Treatment Planner* (Jongsma, Peterson, and McInnis) by John Wiley & Sons, 2000.

D. The client showed little, if any, concern about his/her aggressive behaviors.

E. The client has reduced his/her aggressive behaviors toward siblings, peers, and parents.

5. Frequent Lying (5)

A. Parents reported that the client frequently lies about everything.

B. It has been observed by teachers and caregivers that the client often lies even when there is no obvious reason for doing so.

C. The client's record reflected that he/she often lies about his/her behavior.

D. The client shows little remorse when he/she is caught in a lie.

E. The client's frequency of lying has decreased and he/she is now showing remorse when caught in a lie.

6. Stealing Unneeded Items (5)

A. Records reflected that the client has a history of stealing.

B. On several occasions the client has been caught stealing items that he/she doesn't need.

C. The client acknowledged that he/she does not have a reason or explanation for stealing.

D. The client has stopped his/her stealing of unneeded items.

7. Becomes Friendly Too Quickly (6)

A. Parents reported that the client quickly becomes too friendly and affectionate with any adult.

B. The client has rapidly become very friendly and affectionate with the therapist.

C. The client has been observed becoming very friendly and somewhat affectionate with strangers he/she meets in public places.

D. The client has stopped being so friendly and affectionate with strangers.

8. Parental Frustration with Child's Development and Achievement Level (7)

A. The parents expressed frustration with the child's level of achievement and development.

B. The parents expressed unrealistic expectations of where they felt the child should be in terms of his/her development.

C. The parents expressed disappointment about the child's achievement level and noted that they had expected much more from him/her.

D. The parents have worked to adjust their expectations of the child to more realistic levels.

9. Parents Anxious/Fearful of Client's Adoption Questions (8)

A. The parents have voiced anxiety and fear about the client raising questions about being adopted.

B. The parents have sought advice from numerous experts on how to handle an adopted child's questions regarding his/her background.

C. The parents have looked for ways to avoid, ignore, or shut down the client's inquisitiveness about his/her background.

D. The parents have become more comfortable and less anxious and fearful about the client's questions about his/her background.

E. The parents have developed reasonable responses to the possible future questions of the client regarding his/her adoption and this preparation has reduced their concern in this area.

INTERVENTIONS IMPLEMENTED

1. Build Trust (1)*

A. Initial trust level was established with the client through use of unconditional positive regard.

B. Warm acceptance and active listening techniques were utilized to establish the basis for a nurturing relationship.

C. The client has formed a trust-based relationship and has begun to express his/her thoughts and feelings.

D. Despite the use of active listening, warm acceptance, and unconditional positive regard, the client remains resistant to trust and does not share his/her thoughts and feelings.

2. Conduct Psychosocial Assessment (2)

A. The parents and their children participated in a psychosocial assessment.

B. All parties cooperated fully in the psychosocial assessment, providing in detail all of the information that was requested.

C. Parents were generally cooperative with the psychosocial assessment but the information they provided was lacking in detail.

D. The parents' barriers to providing information were confronted, addressed, and resolved.

3. Conduct Psychological Evaluation (3)

A. A psychological evaluation was conducted with the client to assess his/her behavioral/emotional functioning, cognitive style, and intelligence.

B. The client cooperated fully in all areas of the evaluations.

C. The parent's questions about the need for a psychological assessment were addressed and answered to their satisfaction.

D. The psychological evaluation was only partially completed due to lack of the client's co-operation.

4. Summarize Evaluation Results (4)

A. Assessment results and recommendations were presented and explained to the family.

B. The family's questions regarding the assessment and recommendations were clarified and addressed.

C. The parents were asked to make a verbal commitment to follow through on all of the recommendations that evolved from the assessments.

D. The parents' reluctance to verbally commit to following through on the recommendations was explored, processed, and resolved.

* The numbers in parentheses correlate to the number of the Therapeutic Interventions statement in the companion chapter with same title in *The Child Psychotherapy Treatment Planner* (Jongsma, Peterson, and McInnis) by John Wiley & Sons, 2000.

5. Assess Unresolved Infertility Grief (5)

A. The parents' unresolved grief associated with their infertility was assessed.

B. The grief assessment indicated that the parents have worked through most of the issues related to their infertility.

C. The grief assessment revealed that the parents have many unresolved issues surrounding their infertility, and they were given a referral to a counselor who specializes in these issues.

D. The referral of the parents for grief counseling was monitored for their follow-through and for their overall satisfaction with the service provided.

E. The parents reported many positive outcomes from the grief counseling.

6. Establish a Wellness Plan for Family (6)

A. The purpose and benefits of establishing and following through with a wellness plan were explained to the family.

B. A wellness plan was developed with the family, and the parents were asked to make a verbal commitment to implementing it.

C. The family was monitored for implementation of the wellness plan, with redirection being given as needed.

D. The family has actively participated in each of their quarterly wellness checkups.

7. Refer Parents to Skills-Based Marital Program (7)

A. The possible gains for parents of attending a program to strengthen their marriage were identified and explored.

B. The parents were referred to a skills-based marital program that teaches personal responsibility, communication skills, and conflict resolution (e.g., Prep by Markhum, Stanley, and Blumberg).

C. The parents' follow-through on completing the recommended marriage enrichment program was monitored, and positive gains were reinforced.

D. The parents completed the recommended marital program and indicated they gained many new skills that have improved their marital relationship.

E. The parents' dropping out of the recommended marriage enrichment program was addressed and processed.

8. Conduct Filial-Therapy Sessions (8)

A. The purpose of filial therapy was explained to the parents, and their involvement was solicited and encouraged.

B. Role playing was used with the parents to give them opportunities to practice empathetic responses to the client's angry ones.

C. Filial-therapy sessions were conducted in which both the client and the parents took active roles.

D. In filial sessions, parents responded empathetically to angry feelings expressed by the client.

E. Active participation by the parents and the client in filial-therapy sessions has reduced the client's level of anger and increased his/her bond with the parents.

9. Conduct Psychoanalytic Play Therapy (9)

A. A psychoanalytic play-therapy session was conducted to explore the issues, fixations, and developmental arrests that contribute to the client's acting-out behaviors.

B. The client actively and freely participated in the psychoanalytic play therapy.

C. Transference issues that emerged in the session were worked through to resolution.

D. The feelings expressed in the psychoanalytic play-therapy session were interpreted and connected to the client's acting-out behaviors.

E. The client's participation in the psychoanalytic play therapy has reduced the frequency and intensity of his/her acting-out behaviors.

10. Employ A.C.T. Model of Play Therapy (10)

A. The A.C.T. model of play therapy (Landreth) was conducted to acknowledge the client's feelings, communicate limits, and target appropriate alternatives to acting out or aggressive behaviors.

B. Positive verbal affirmation was given in A.C.T. play therapy when the client displayed or verbalized appropriate alternatives to acting out or aggressive behaviors.

C. The client willingly and actively participated in A.C.T. play therapy.

D. The client's involvement in the A.C.T. play-therapy session has helped him/her to decrease the frequency and intensity of his/her acting out or aggressive behaviors.

11. Conduct Individual Play Therapy (11)

A. Individual play therapy was conducted with the client to help him/her express and work through feelings of loss, neglect, and abandonment.

B. The client actively participated in the play-therapy session.

C. The feelings the client expressed through his/her play were affirmed, reflected, and validated.

D. The supportive environment of the play therapy has helped the client express and work through his/her feelings of loss, neglect, and abandonment.

12. Utilize Theraplay Approach (12)

A. The parents were educated in the Theraplay (Jernberg and Booth) approach to building a relationship with the client.

B. A verbal commitment was elicited from the parents to be active cotherapists using the Theraplay approach.

C. The Theraplay attachment-based approach was used as the focus of therapy to entice the client into a relationship and to steer away from his/her intrapsychic conflicts.

D. The parents were given specific therapeutic assignments to do at home with the client between therapy sessions.

E. The parents' follow-through as cotherapists on assignments was monitored and any needed redirection was given.

F. The Theraplay approach appears to be effective, as the client has started to form a relationship with his/her parents and with the therapist.

13. Connect Painful Feelings to Acting-Out Behavior (13)

A. The client was helped to make key connections between his/her painful feelings of loss, rejection, and abandonment and his/her acting-out and/or aggressive behaviors.

B. Verbal praise and affirmation were given to the client for each connection he/she made between his/her feelings and behaviors.

C. The client's progress in connecting painful feelings and behaviors has helped to reduce the frequency of his/her acting-out behaviors.

14. Use Puppets to Tell Loss Story (14)

A. A story of another's loss, rejection, and/or abandonment was told to the client using puppets and/or stuffed animals.

B. The client was asked to create a story about his/her loss, rejection, and/or abandonment using puppets and/or stuffed animals.

C. The client was given positive affirmation for telling the story of his/her loss, rejection, and/or abandonment.

D. The feelings that the client expressed through his/her story were affirmed and validated.

15. Assign Drawing of Self (15)

A. The client was assisted in drawing an outline of himself/herself on a sheet of paper and then told to fill the outline with objects and pictures that reflect what fuels his/her acting-out behaviors.

B. The completed self-portrait was described and explained by the client and then processed with him/her.

C. Verbal affirmation and validation were given to the client for each connection that he/she made between what was inside him/her and the acting-out behaviors.

D. The client completed the self-portrait exercise and was helped to make the connection between his/her emotions and acting-out behaviors.

16. Use Art Therapy Techniques (16)

A. Expressive art materials (e.g., Playdough, clay, and finger paints) were used with the client to create pictures and sculptures.

B. The client's active involvement in creating pictures and sculptures has helped him/her express feelings of rage, rejection, and loss.

C. The feelings that the client expressed through his/her artwork were identified, reflected, and validated.

D. The client's work with various art materials has helped him/her begin to express and resolve his/her feelings of rage, rejection, and loss.

17. Read Books on Anger Management (17)

A. The client was asked to read with therapist the book *Don't Rant and Rave on Wednesday* (Moser) and/or *A Volcano in My Tummy* (Whitehouse and Pudney) to assist him/her in identifying ways to handle angry feelings.

B. The client processed the various ways suggested in the book to handle angry feelings and identified two that he/she could implement in coping with his/her angry feelings.

C. Ways to implement the identified anger-management strategies were developed with the client and he/she committed to using them in his/her daily life when feeling angry.

D. The client has consistently and effectively used the anger-management strategies he/she gained from reading anger-management stories and has had fewer problems with inappropriately expressing his/her angry feelings.

18. Play Therapeutic Games (18)

A. The "Talking, Feeling, Doing Game" (Gardner) and/or "The Anger Control Game" (Berg) was played with the client to help him/her learn to identify his/her emotions.

B. Feelings and thoughts that were identified by the client during the game(s) were affirmed and validated.

C. The parents were given access to the game(s) and encouraged to play them at home with the client one or two times between sessions.

D. The client's active involvement in playing the therapeutic game(s) has increased his/her ability to identify and express his/her thoughts and feelings.

19. Use Feelings Chart (19)

A. Feelings charts and cards were used with the client to increase his/her ability to identify specific feelings.

B. The client received positive verbal affirmation and reinforcement for identifying specific feelings during his/her sessions.

C. The client's resistance to identifying his/her feelings was gently confronted, addressed, and resolved.

D. Through the client's work with feelings charts and cards, he/she has increased his/her ability to identify, understand, and express feelings.

20. Read *How It Feels to Be Adopted* (20)

A. The client was asked to read *How It Feels to Be Adopted* (Krementz) and make a list of key concepts gathered from the reading.

B. The feelings the client identified with from the adoption book were processed.

C. The client has successfully worked through the feelings of rejection and abandonment and has come to see bioparents as possibly having his/her best interest at heart when they released him/her for adoption.

21. Read Books on Adoption Issues (21)

A. The client was asked to read and process the books *I Feel Different* (Stinson) and *Adoption Is for Always* (Girard).

B. The client identified his/her adoption issues after reading the assigned books on adoption.

C. The client's adoption issues that were clarified by reading the assigned adoption books were processed and resolved.

D. The normalization of the client's feelings about being adopted was reinforced at moments of opportunity in the client's processing of assigned readings.

22. Affirm Health of Family (22)

A. The parents were given verbal affirmation and validation for the health and strength of the family system.

B. The parents were educated on triangulation and undermining of authority by children and their effect on family functioning.

C. Ways to cut off or prevent triangulation and undermining were explored, identified, and developed with the parents.

D. The parents gained an understanding and awareness of triangulation and undermining and how to effectively counter them.

23. Support Group Referral (23)

A. Options for possible support groups were explored with the parents and the client.

B. The parents and the client were given information on the various support groups and asked to make a commitment to attend one.

C. The family questioned their need for support outside of therapy and were noncommittal about even trying one meeting.

D. The client and his/her parents have begun attending a support group and have reported that it has been beneficial to them.

24. Parents Read Books on Adoption (24)

A. The parents were asked to read *Helping Children Cope with Separation and Loss* (Jewett) and/or *Adoption Wisdom* (Russell) to increase their knowledge and understanding of adoption.

B. The key concepts of the parents' readings on adoption were processed and reinforced.

C. The parents' questions about adoption that were raised by their reading were discussed and answered.

D. The parents' failure to read the suggested books on adoption was addressed and processed.

E. The parents increased their knowledge and understanding of adoption from reading and processing the assigned books.

25. Reframe Acting-Out Behaviors (25)

A. The parents were worked with in conjoint sessions to understand the client's acting-out behavior as "opportunities" for them to reparent him/her.

B. The parents' barriers to accepting the acting-out behavior as "opportunities to reparent" were explored, addressed, and resolved.

C. The parents were assisted in developing and implementing new interventions for the client's problem behaviors.

D. The parents were given positive reinforcement for implementing new interventions and for their accepting reparenting opportunities.

E. The parents have reported positive results on client's acting-out behavior as a result of their new intervention techniques.

26. Parents Read Books on Adoption Identity Confusion (26)

A. The parents were encouraged to read *The Whole Life Adoption Book* (Schouler) or *Making Sense of Adoption* (Melina) to advance their knowledge and understanding of adoption's effect on identity.

B. The parents were taught various aspects of development with a special focus on the role of adoption on the developmental tasks of the child.

C. The parents' belief that developmental issues are the same for adopted and nonadopted children was confronted and restructured to a more healthy and realistic view.

27. Educate Parents on Affirming Client's Identity (27)

A. The parents were educated on the importance of affirming the client's entire history.

B. The parents were assisted in listing the possible ways that they could affirm the client's entire history.

C. The parents' list for affirming the client's identity was processed and specific ways were developed to implement each suggestion on the list.

D. The parents were monitored for their implementation of the ways they developed to affirm the client's identity and were given verbal reinforcement for their consistent efforts.

E. The client has responded very positively to the parents' affirmations of his/her entire history.

28. Assign "Life Book" (28)

A. The parents were educated on the key benefits for the client in having a "life book."

B. The parents and the client were given instructions on how to create a "life book" and then assigned to put one together.

C. The parents and the client were monitored in their completing the assignment of creating a "life book."

D. The parents reviewed the completed "life book" with the client in order to give the client perspective and knowledge of his/her history.

29. Play "Three Wishes Game" (29)

A. The client was asked to complete and process the "Three Wishes" game from *The Brief Child Therapy Homework Planner* (Jongsma, Peterson, and McInnis) to help him/her begin to express needs and desires.

B. The completed "Three Wishes" game exercise was processed with the client and verbal validation was given for each expressed need and desire.

C. The client was asked to construct and present a list of his/her needs based on results from the "Three Wishes" game exercise.

D. The client presented his/her needs list and received verbal recognition to each identified need.

E. The client has increased his/her ability to recognize and express needs and desires.

30. Assign *SEALS & Plus* Exercise (30)

A. The client was asked to complete a *SEALS & Plus* (Korb-Khara, Azok, and Leutenberg) exercise directed at assisting him/her in developing self-knowledge, acceptance, and confidence.

B. The client reported that the self-awareness exercise was helpful in building confidence.

C. The client has not followed through on completing the self-awareness exercise.

31. Process Parents' Expectations of Behavior (31)

A. The parents' expectations regarding the client's behavior and adjustment were explored, identified, and processed.

B. The parents' unrealistic expectations were confronted and modified to more realistic standards.

C. The parents' resistance to modifying certain unrealistic expectations were addressed, processed, and resolved.

D. The parents have adjusted their expectations to be more appropriate to the client's developmental level and to the adoption process.

32. Assign Parents One-on-One Play with Client (32)

A. The value of spending time in one-on-one daily play with the client was explored and processed with the parents.

B. The parents were asked to commit to spending consistent one-on-one time playing with the client.

C. A daily schedule of one-on-one time, with each parent playing with the client, was developed and implemented.

D. The parents were monitored, encouraged, and redirected in their follow-through on one-on-one daily playtime with client.

E. The parents reported seeing visible gains in client's bonding through spending daily one-on-one time with him/her.

33. Encourage Verbal Reinforcement/Physical Affection (33)

A. The positive value of providing large doses of genuine verbal reinforcement and physical affection were identified with the parents.

B. The parents explored ways they could give the client large doses of reinforcement or affection, and specific ways were selected for them to implement.

C. The parents were encouraged, supported, and monitored in their efforts to provide the client with large daily doses of genuine verbal reinforcement and physical affection.

D. The parents have consistently provided the client with large doses of reinforcement and affection, which the client has responded to by showing signs of increased attachment.

34. Discourage Negative Bioparent References (34)

A. The potential negative consequences of the adoptive parents making negative references about the client's bioparents were explored, identified, and processed.

B. The parents were given instructions on how to respond to the client's questions about his/her bioparents.

C. The parents were confronted when making any negative references to the bioparents.

D. The parents were sensitized to how negative references about the bioparents adversely affect children who are adopted.

E. The parents have terminated making any negative references about the client's bioparents.

35. Answer Parents' Adoption Questions (35)

A. The parents were given an opportunity to raise adoption-specific concerns and questions.

B. The parents received direction and support for each question or issue they raised.

C. The parents were given permission, encouragement, and reinforcement to ask any question and raise any issue.

D. Open opportunities for the parents to ask questions or raise issues have helped to reduce their anxiety and concerns about adoption.

36. Provide Parents with Education on Discipline (36)

A. The parents were provided with education regarding the 3R method (Giles and Nelson) of discipline.

B. Explored with the parents ways to implement the 3R method of discipline.

C. The parents were asked to read the book *How to Raise Responsible Children* (Glen and Nelson) to increase their knowledge of the 3R system.

D. Role-played scenarios with the parents to provide an opportunity for them to build skills and confidence in using the 3R system.

E. The parents' implementation of the 3R system was encouraged, supported, and monitored.

F. The parents' consistent use of the 3R discipline system has reduced the frequency and intensity of conflict with the client.

37. Assign *The Seven Habits of Highly Effective Families* (37)

A. The parents were asked to read *The Seven Habits of Highly Effective Families* (Covey) to obtain ideas for increasing the family's health and interconnectedness.

B. The parents' suggestions for increasing family health and bonding were processed and ways to implement them were explored and developed.

C. The parents were assisted in implementing the suggestions to increase the family's health and sense of unity.

D. The parents' implementation of the suggestions gained from *The Seven Habits of Highly Effective Families* were encouraged, supported, and monitored for their effectiveness.

E. The parents' implementation of the new ideas gained from *The Seven Habits of Highly Effective Families* has helped to increase the family's health and strengthen their sense of unity.

38. Assign Parents One-on-One Time with Other Children (38)

A. The value of spending one-on-one time with each of their other children was explored with the parents and the benefits were identified and processed.

B. The parents committed to spend one-on-one time with all of the children in the family.

C. A weekly schedule of parents spending one-on-one time with each child was developed and implemented.

D. The parents were monitored, encouraged, and redirected in their follow-through on spending weekly one-on-one time with all of the children in the family.

E. The parents reported seeing less conflict and attention-seeking behaviors from their children since starting to spend one-on-one time with each child.

39. Refer Family to Initiative Weekend (39)

A. The positive benefits of attending an initiative weekend were identified, explained, and processed with the family.

B. The parents were given information on several initiative programs and encouraged to choose one to attend.

C. The family arranged for and attended an initiative weekend.

D. The family initiative weekend experience was processed with positive gains in trust, co-operation, and connections being identified, confirmed, and reinforced.

40. Construct a Genogram (40)

A. A genogram was constructed with the family that included each member's origins and how he/she is connected.

B. The family was actively involved in constructing the genogram.

C. Each family member's origin and present place in the family were identified, affirmed, and validated.

D. The family work on constructing the genogram has helped each member visualize the family and how he/she is connected to it.

ANGER MANAGEMENT

CLIENT PRESENTATION

1. Angry Outbursts (1)*

A. The client has exhibited frequent angry outbursts that are out of proportion to the degree of the precipitating event.

B. The client appeared angry, hostile, and irritable during today's therapy session.

C. The client has recently exhibited several angry outbursts at home and school.

D. The client has started to show greater control of his/her anger and does not react as quickly or intensely when angry or frustrated.

E. The client reported a significant reduction in the frequency and intensity of his/her angry outbursts.

2. Verbally Abusive Language (2)

A. The client has a history of yelling, swearing, or becoming verbally abusive when his/her needs go unmet or when asked to do something that he/she does not want to do.

B. The client began to yell and swear during today's therapy session.

C. The frequency and intensity of the client's screaming, cursing, and use of verbally abusive language has decreased to a mild degree.

D. The client has begun to express his/her feelings of anger in a controlled fashion.

E. The client has consistently demonstrated good control of his/her anger and not yelled or become verbally abusive toward others.

3. Physical Aggression/Violence (3)

A. The client described a history of engaging in acts of physical aggression or violence.

B. The client has recently been physically aggressive or violent.

C. The client has gradually started to develop greater control of his/her anger and has not become involved in as many fights in the recent past.

D. The client has recently exercised good self-control and not engaged in any physically aggressive or violent behaviors.

4. Verbal Threats/Intimidation (4)

A. The client has a history of threatening or intimidating others to meet his/her own needs.

B. The client became verbally threatening during today's therapy session.

C. The client has continued to threaten or intimidate others at home, at school, and in the community.

D. The client reported a mild reduction in the frequency and intensity of his/her verbal threats and acts of intimidation.

---

* The numbers in parentheses correlate to the number of the Behavioral Definition statement in the companion chapter with same title in *The Child Psychotherapy Treatment Planner* (Jongsma, Peterson, and McInnis) by John Wiley & Sons, 2000.

E. The client has recently displayed good anger control and reported that he/she has not threatened or intimidated others.

5. **Destructive Behaviors (5)**

A. The client described a persistent pattern of becoming destructive or throwing objects when angry or frustrated.

B. The client described incidents in which he/she has been destructive of property.

C. The client has started to control the impulse to destroy or throw objects when angry.

D. The client reported that he/she has not thrown any objects or been destructive of property in the recent past.

6. **Blaming/Projecting (6)**

A. The client has a history of projecting the blame for his/her angry outbursts or aggressive behaviors onto other people or outside circumstances.

B. The client did not accept responsibility for his/her recent angry outbursts or aggressive behaviors.

C. The client has begun to accept greater responsibility for his/her anger control problems and blames others less often for his/her angry outbursts or aggressive behaviors.

D. The client verbalized an acceptance of responsibility for the poor control of his/her anger or aggressive impulses.

E. The client expressed guilt about his/her anger control problems and apologized to significant others for his/her loss of control of anger.

7. **Guarded/Defensive (6)**

A. The client appeared guarded and defensive during today's therapy session.

B. The client was difficult to engage in the therapeutic process and was resistant to exploring the factors contributing to his/her problems with anger control.

C. The client's defensiveness has started to decrease and he/she has demonstrated a greater willingness to explore the underlying dynamics contributing to his/her anger control problems.

D. The client was pleasant and cooperative during the therapy session and demonstrated a willingness to discuss the factors contributing to his/her anger control problems.

8. **Passive-Aggressive Behavior (7)**

A. The parents and teachers described a persistent pattern of the client engaging in passive-aggressive behaviors (e.g., forgetting, pretending not to listen, dawdling, procrastinating).

B. The client verbally acknowledged that he/she often deliberately annoys or frustrates others through his/her passive-aggressive behaviors.

C. The client has started to verbalize his/her anger directly toward others instead of channeling his/her angry or hostile feelings through passive-aggressive behaviors.

D. The client expressed his/her feelings of anger in a direct, controlled, and respectful manner.

E. The client has recently demonstrated a significant reduction in the frequency of his/her passive-aggressive behaviors.

9. Oppositional/Rebellious Behavior (7)

A. The client's anger is frequently channeled into his/her oppositional and rebellious behaviors.

B. The client appeared highly oppositional during today's therapy session and seemed to argue just for the sake of arguing.

C. The client has recently been defiant of the rules and regulations established by authority figures at home, at school, and in the community.

D. The client has exhibited mild improvements in his/her willingness to comply with the rules and regulations at home, at school, and in the community.

E. The client reported that recently he/she has been cooperative and compliant with the rules at home, at school, and in the community.

10. Authority Conflicts (7)

A. The client displayed a negativistic attitude and was highly argumentative during today's therapy session.

B. The client becomes entangled in frequent disputes with authority figures and does not back down easily in an argument.

C. The client often talks back to authority figures in a disrespectful manner when he/she is reprimanded.

D. The client verbally recognized the need to control his/her anger and be more respectful of authority figures.

E. The client reported that he/she has consistently interacted with adult authority figures in a mutually respectful manner.

11. Family Conflict (7)

A. The client repeatedly becomes involved in heated arguments and/or physical fights with his/her parents and siblings.

B. The client expressed strong feelings of anger and resentment toward family members.

C. The client expressed his/her anger in a controlled and respectful manner toward family members.

D. The client has begun to demonstrate good control of his/her anger at home.

12. Poor Peer Relationships (8)

A. The client's anger-control problems have been a significant contributing factor to his/her strained interpersonal relationships with peers.

B. The client has often projected the blame for his/her interpersonal problems onto peers and refused to acknowledge how his/her anger-control problems contribute to the conflict.

C. The client has started to recognize how his/her anger-control problems interfere with his/her ability to establish and maintain peer friendships.

D. The client reported that his/her effective anger control has led to improved relations with his/her peers.

13. Lack of Empathy (8)

A. The client displayed little empathy or concern for how his/her angry outbursts or aggressive behaviors impact others.

B. The client has demonstrated a willingness to use intimidation or force to meet his/her needs at the expense of others.

C. The client verbalized an awareness of how his/her rebellious, aggressive, or destructive behaviors negatively affect others.

D. The client verbalized empathy and concern for others in today's therapy session.

E. The client has consistently demonstrated empathy and sensitivity to the thoughts, feelings, and needs of others.

14. Feelings of Depression and Anxiety (9)

A. The client's anger-control problems have often masked a deeper feeling of depression and/or anxiety.

B. The client expressed feelings of depression and anxiety about the struggles to control his/her angry or hostile feelings.

C. The client verbally recognized how he/she often reacts with anger and aggression when he/she begins to feel depressed or anxious.

D. The client expressed feelings of happiness and contentment about his/her ability to control his/her anger more effectively.

E. The client has taken active steps (e.g., expressed feelings of sadness to supportive individuals, faced anxiety-producing situations, socialized with positive peer groups) to reduce his/her feelings of depression and anxiety.

15. Low Self-Esteem (9)

A. The client's angry outbursts and aggressive behaviors have often masked deeper feelings of low self-esteem, insecurity, and inadequacy.

B. The client's persistent anger-control problems have resulted in him/her developing a negative self-image and feelings of low self-esteem.

C. The client verbally recognized how his/her angry outbursts and aggressive behaviors are often associated with feelings of inadequacy and insecurity.

D. The client expressed positive self-statements about his/her improved ability to control his/her anger.

E. The client has taken active steps to improve his/her self-esteem and build a positive self-image.

16. Childhood Abuse (9)

A. The client described a history of physical and verbal abuse that correlates to the onset of his/her anger-control problems.

B. The client was resistant to discussing the past incidents of abuse.

C. The client expressed strong feelings of anger, hurt, and sadness about the past abusive episodes.

D. The client has started to show improved anger control as he/she works through many of his/her thoughts and feelings about the past abuse.

E. The client has demonstrated a significant reduction in the frequency and severity of his/her angry outbursts and aggressive behaviors since working through many of his/her feelings about the past abuse.

17. Separation/Loss (9)

A. The client reported a history of experiencing significant separations or losses in his/her life that correlate to the onset of his/her anger-control problems.

B. The client was guarded and resistant to talking about past separations or losses.

C. The client expressed strong feelings of anger, hurt, and sadness about past separations or losses.

D. The client has started to show improvement in his/her anger control since he/she began exploring his/her thoughts and feelings about past separations or losses.

E. The client has demonstrated a significant reduction in the frequency and severity of his/her angry outbursts or aggressive behavior since working through many of his/her thoughts and feelings surrounding past separations or losses.

INTERVENTIONS IMPLEMENTED

1. Psychological Testing (1)*

A. A psychological evaluation was conducted to determine whether emotional factors or ADHD are contributing to the client's anger-control problems.

B. The client approached the psychological testing in an honest, straightforward manner and was cooperative with any requests presented to him/her.

C. The client was uncooperative and resistant to engage during the evaluation process.

D. The client was resistive during the psychological testing and refused to consider the possibility of having ADHD or any serious emotional problems.

2. Psychoeducational Evaluation (2)

A. The client was given a psychoeducational evaluation to rule out the possibility of a learning disability that may be contributing to his/her anger-control problems in the school setting.

B. The client was cooperative during the psychoeducational evaluation and appeared motivated to do his/her best.

C. The client was uncooperative during the psychoeducational evaluation and did not appear to put forth good effort.

3. Evaluation Feedback (3)

A. The client, parents, school officials, and/or criminal justice officials were given feedback from the psychological testing.

B. The evaluation findings supported the presence of ADHD, which contributes to the client's anger-control problems.

* The numbers in parentheses correlate to the number of the Therapeutic Interventions statement in the companion chapter with same title in *The Child Psychotherapy Treatment Planner* (Jongsma, Peterson, and McInnis) by John Wiley & Sons, 2000.

C. The evaluation findings revealed the presence of underlying emotional problems that contribute to the emergence of the client's anger-control problems.

D. The findings from the psychoeducational evaluation supported the presence of a learning disability and the need for special education services.

E. The evaluation process did not reveal the presence of a learning disability, emotional problems, or ADHD that might be contributing to the client's anger-control problems.

4. Consultation with Criminal Justice Officials (4)

A. Consulted with criminal justice officials about the need for appropriate consequences for the client's destructive or aggressive behaviors.

B. The client has been required to make restitution and/or perform community service for his/her destructive or aggressive behaviors.

C. The client was placed on probation for his/her destructive or aggressive behaviors and instructed to comply with all the rules pertaining to his/her probation.

5. Reinforce Natural Consequences (5)

A. The parents were encouraged and challenged not to protect the client from the natural or legal consequences of his/her destructive or aggressive behaviors.

B. The parents agreed to contact the police or appropriate criminal justice officials if the client engages in any serious destructive or aggressive behaviors in the future.

C. The parents followed through and contacted the police or probation officer after the client engaged in the destructive or aggressive behaviors.

D. The parents failed to contact the police and/or criminal justice officials after the client engaged in some serious destructive or aggressive behaviors.

E. The parents acknowledged that they have often failed to follow through with setting limits because of their desire to avoid conflict and tension.

6. Parental Rules and Boundaries (6)

A. Today's family-therapy session focused on helping the parents to establish clearly defined rules and appropriate parent-child boundaries to manage the client's angry outbursts and acts of aggression or destruction.

B. The parents were helped to identify appropriate consequences for the client's angry outbursts and acts of aggression or destruction.

C. The parents identified appropriate and reasonable rules and expectations that the client must comply with at home.

D. The parents had difficulty in identifying appropriate consequences for the client's angry outbursts and destructive or aggressive behaviors.

7. Establish Clear Rules (7)

A. A family-therapy session was held to discuss the rules for and expectations of the client at home and school.

B. Consulted with the client, parents, and teachers to identify rules and expectations in the school setting.

C. The client was asked to repeat the rules to demonstrate an understanding of the rules for and expectations of him/her.

D. The client voiced his/her agreement with the rules and expectations at home and school.

E. The client verbally disagreed with the rules and expectations identified by his/her parents and teachers.

8. Effective Disciplinary Techniques (8)

A. The parents were instructed on how to properly use time outs to help manage the client's angry outbursts or aggressive behaviors.

B. The parents were instructed on how to discipline the client by removing privileges following his/her angry outbursts or aggressive behaviors.

C. The parents were encouraged to utilize natural, logical negative consequences of the client's aggressive or destructive behaviors.

D. The parents were instructed to have the client pay for some or all of the damages that resulted from his/her destructive behaviors.

9. Assign Readings to Parents (9)

A. The parents were instructed to read one or more of the following books to increase their knowledge about effective disciplinary techniques: *1-2-3 Magic: Training Your Preschoolers and Preteens to Do What You Want* (Phelan), *Family Rules: Raising Responsible Children* (Kaye), and *Assertive Discipline for Parents* (Canter and Canter).

B. The assigned reading regarding effective disciplinary techniques that had been given to the parents was processed in today's therapy session.

C. The parents reported that they have found the assigned reading(s) useful in increasing their knowledge about effective disciplinary techniques.

D. The parents reported that they have begun to utilize the disciplinary techniques they learned from reading the assigned book(s).

10. Build Therapeutic Trust (10)

A. Today's therapy session focused on building the level of trust with the client through consistent eye contact, active listening, unconditional positive regard, and warm acceptance.

B. Listened closely to the client's concerns and reflected his/her feelings.

C. Provided empathy and support for the client's expression of thoughts and feelings during today's therapy session.

D. The client has remained mistrustful and is reluctant to share his/her underlying thoughts and feelings.

E. The client verbally recognized that he/she has difficulty establishing trust because he/she has often felt let down by others in the past.

11. Underlying Feelings and Aggressive Behaviors (11)

A. The session was helpful in identifying how the client's underlying, painful emotions are related to an increase in his/her angry outbursts or aggressive behaviors.

B. Role-playing and modeling techniques were used to demonstrate appropriate ways for the client to express his/her underlying, painful emotions.

C. The client was assisted in identifying more appropriate ways to express his/her painful emotions and meet his/her needs instead of reacting impulsively or aggressively with anger.

12. Teach Self-Control Strategies (12)

A. The client was taught mediational and self-control strategies (e.g., relaxation, "stop, look, listen, and think") to help express anger through appropriate verbalizations and healthy physical outlets.

B. The client was asked to identify appropriate and inappropriate ways to express or control his/her anger.

C. The client was encouraged to utilize active listening skills to delay the impulse or urge to react with verbal or physical aggression.

D. The client identified healthy physical outlets for his/her strong feelings of anger and aggressive impulses.

13. Relaxation or Guided Imagery (13)

A. The client was trained in the use of progressive relaxation or guided imagery techniques to help calm himself/herself and decrease the intensity of angry feelings.

B. The client appeared uncomfortable and unable to relax when being instructed in the use of progressive relaxation and guided imagery techniques.

C. The client reported a positive response to the use of progressive relaxation or guided imagery techniques to help control anger.

14. Replace Irrational Thoughts (14)

A. The client was helped to identify how irrational, distorted thoughts have contributed to the emergence of his/her anger-control problems.

B. The client was helped to replace his/her irrational thoughts with more adaptive ways of thinking to help control anger.

C. The client reported that he/she has experienced a reduction in the frequency and intensity of his/her angry feelings by being able to replace irrational thoughts with more adaptive ways of thinking.

D. The client has continued to struggle to control anger because of his/her reluctance to give up or let go of irrational beliefs.

15. Communication and Assertiveness Skills (15)

A. The client was taught effective communication and assertiveness skills to learn how to express his/her feelings in a controlled fashion and meet his/her needs through more constructive actions.

B. Role-playing techniques were used to model effective ways to control anger and identify appropriate ways to meet his/her needs.

C. The client was encouraged to use "I" messages and assertive versus aggressive statements to effectively verbalize his/her needs to others.

D. The client was helped to differentiate between being assertive and being overly aggressive.

16. Self-Monitoring Checklists (16)

A. The client was encouraged to utilize self-monitoring checklists of anger-provoking situations in the home and at school to help improve his/her anger control.

B. Consulted with the client's teachers about the use of self-monitoring checklists in anger-provoking situations to improve the client's anger control.

C. The parents and school officials were instructed to utilize a reward system in conjunction with the self-monitoring checklists of anger-provoking situations.

D. The use of a journal was recommended to help the client identify factors that trigger strong feelings of anger or contribute to the emergence of his/her aggressive or destructive behaviors.

17. Past Successful Coping Strategies (17)

A. The client explored periods of time in the past when he/she demonstrated good anger control and did not lash out as often, either verbally or physically, toward siblings or peers.

B. The client was encouraged to use coping strategies similar to ones that he/she had used successfully in the past to control his/her anger.

C. The therapy session revealed that the client exercised greater anger control during periods of time when he/she received strong family support and affiliated with positive peer groups.

D. Today's therapy session helped the client realize that his/her involvement in extracurricular or positive peer group activities in the past has helped him/her control anger more effectively.

18. Encourage Parents' Positive Reinforcement (18)

A. The parents were encouraged to provide frequent praise and positive reinforcement for the client's ability to control his/her anger in situations involving conflict or stress.

B. The parents were challenged to look for opportunities to praise the client for controlling his/her anger effectively, instead of focusing primarily on his/her behavioral problems.

C. Explored the reasons why the parents have difficulty offering praise and positive reinforcement.

19. Reward System/Contingency Contract (19)

A. The client and parents identified a list of rewards to be used to reinforce the client for demonstrating good anger control.

B. A reward system was designed to reinforce the client's effective anger control and deter destructive or aggressive behaviors.

C. The client signed a contingency contract specifying the negative consequences for his/her destructive or aggressive behaviors.

D. The client and parents verbally agreed to the terms of the contingency contract.

20. Token Economy (20)

A. A token economy was designed for use in the home to increase the client's positive social behaviors, improve anger control, and deter destructive or aggressive behaviors.

B. The clients and parents agreed to the conditions outlined in the token economy program and agreed to follow through with the implementation at home.

C. A token economy was designed and implemented in the classroom to reinforce the client's positive social behaviors, improve anger control, and deter destructive or aggressive behaviors.

D. The token economy has proven to be successful in improving the client's anger control, deterring aggressive or destructive behaviors, and increasing the client's social skills.

21. Anger Control Exercise (21)

A. The client and parents were given the "Anger Control Exercise" from *The Brief Child Therapy Homework Planner* (Jongsma, Peterson, and McInnis) to reinforce the client for demonstrating good control of his/her anger.

B. The "Anger Control Exercise" was utilized to help the client identify the core issues that contribute to his/her angry outbursts and aggressive or destructive behaviors.

C. The parents were encouraged to utilize the Positive Incident Reports in the "Anger Control Exercise" to reinforce the client for showing good control of his/her anger.

D. The parents were encouraged to utilize the reward system from the "Anger Control Exercise" to reinforce the client for demonstrating good control of his/her anger.

22. Confront Aggressive Behavior (22)

A. The client was firmly and consistently confronted with how his/her angry outbursts and destructive or aggressive behavior negatively affect himself/herself and others.

B. The client was asked to list the negative consequences of his/her angry outbursts and destructive or aggressive behavior for self and others.

C. Role-reversal techniques were used to help the client realize how his/her angry outbursts and destructive or aggressive behavior negatively impact others.

D. The client was asked to write a letter of apology to the victims of his/her destructive or aggressive behavior.

E. The client was asked to undo some of the consequences of his/her aggressive or destructive behavior by performing altruistic or benevolent acts for others.

23. Teach Acceptance of Responsibility (23)

A. The client was consistently confronted and challenged to cease blaming others for his/her anger-control problems and accept greater responsibility for his/her actions.

B. The client was confronted with how his/her pattern of excessively blaming others for his/her anger-control problems places a strain on his/her interpersonal relationships.

C. The client was helped to identify more effective ways to resolve conflict and/or meet his/her needs instead of expressing his/her anger through aggressive or destructive behavior.

D. The client was strongly encouraged to apologize to others for his/her aggressive or destructive behavior.

24. Explore Blaming (24)

A. Today's therapy session explored the underlying factors contributing to the client's pattern of blaming others for his/her anger-control problems.

B. The client was challenged to accept the consequences of his/her anger-control problems instead of blaming others.

C. The client identified how his/her pattern of blaming others is associated with underlying feelings of low self-esteem, inadequacy, and insecurity.

D. The client was assisted in identifying constructive ways to improve his/her self-esteem to help reduce the pattern of blaming others.

E. The parents identified natural, logical consequences that they could use if the client is caught in a lie.

25. Explore Family Dynamics (25)

A. A family-therapy session was held to explore the dynamics within the family system that have contributed to the emergence of the client's anger-control problems.

B. The family members were asked to list the stressors that have contributed to an atmosphere of irritability and aggression.

C. The family members were asked to identify the things that they would like to change within the family.

D. The family's pattern of poor anger management was exposed as a negative modeling influence for the client.

26. Employ Family-Sculpting Technique (26)

A. The family-sculpting technique was utilized within the session to help gain greater insight into the roles and behaviors of each family member.

B. The client and family members used the family-sculpting technique to identify positive changes they would like to see take place in the family.

C. The family-sculpting technique revealed how the client perceives the parents as being distant and unavailable.

27. Filial Therapy (27)

A. A filial play-therapy session (i.e., parental involvement) was held to help facilitate the development of a closer parent-child bond.

B. The parent was instructed to allow the child to take the lead in expressing his/her feelings of anger during the filial play-therapy session.

C. The parent was encouraged to respond empathetically to other underlying feelings (e.g., hurt, sadness, helplessness) beneath the anger.

D. The filial play-therapy sessions have helped the parents gain greater insight into the factors contributing to the client's angry outbursts or aggressive behaviors.

E. The filial play-therapy sessions have helped to develop a closer parent-child relationship.

28. Assign Family Problem-Solving Task (28)

A. The family members were given a problem to solve together in today's therapy session to provide an opportunity to observe the family members' interactions with one another.

B. Processed the family members' interactions with one another after they completed the problem-solving task in the session.

C. The client became angry during the problem-solving task when the parents became critical of him/her.

D. The problem-solving task helped identify the family dynamics that contribute to the client's anger-control problems at home.

E. The family problem-solving task helped reveal how the parents are reluctant or hesitant to impose consequences for the client's angry outbursts or aggressive behaviors.

29. Disengaged Parent Involvement (29)

A. The disengaged parent was challenged to spend more time with the client in leisure, school, or work activities.

B. The client verbalized his/her need to spend greater time with the disengaged parent.

C. Today's therapy session explored the factors contributing to the distant relationship between the client and the disengaged parent.

D. The disengaged parent verbalized a commitment to spend increased time with the client.

E. The client and the disengaged parent identified a list of activities that they would both enjoy doing together.

30. Explore Family Abuse History (30)

A. The client's family background was explored for a history of physical, sexual, or substance abuse that may contribute to the emergence of his/her anger-control problems.

B. The client developed a time line in the therapy session where he/she identified significant historical events, both positive and negative, that have occurred in his/her family.

C. The client was instructed to draw a diagram of the house where the abuse occurred.

D. A diagnostic interview was conducted to assess the extent of the family members' use of drugs and alcohol.

31. Confront Parents' Abusive Discipline (31)

A. The client's parents were confronted and challenged to cease physically abusive or overly punitive methods of discipline.

B. The parents were asked to identify how physically abusive or overly punitive methods of discipline negatively affect the client and siblings.

C. The parents apologized to the client for abusive behaviors and overly harsh methods of discipline.

D. The parents were taught how aggressive discipline promotes client's aggression and poor anger management.

E. The parents were referred to a parenting class.

32. Protect the Client from Abuse (32)

A. The physical abuse was reported to the appropriate protective services agency.

B. Recommendation was made that the abuse perpetrator be removed from the home and seek treatment.

C. Recommendation was made that the client and siblings be removed from the home to ensure protection from further abuse.

D. The client and family members identified necessary steps to take to minimize the risk of abuse occurring in the future.

E. The nonabusive parent verbalized a commitment to protect the client and siblings from physical abuse in the future.

33. Feelings Associated with Neglect or Abuse (33)

A. The client was given the opportunity to express his/her feelings about past neglect, abuse, separation, or abandonment.

B. The client was instructed to draw pictures that reflect his/her feelings about past neglect, abuse, separation, or abandonment.

C. The client was instructed to use a journal to record his/her thoughts and feelings about past neglect, abuse, separation, or abandonment.

D. The empty-chair technique was employed to facilitate expression of feelings surrounding past neglect or abuse.

34. Employ Empty-Chair Technique (34)

A. The empty-chair technique was employed to help the client express his/her anger toward the absent or abusive parent.

B. The empty-chair technique was helpful in allowing the client to express feelings of anger, hurt, or sadness toward the absent or abusive parent.

C. The client appeared uncomfortable with the use of the empty-chair technique and had difficulty verbalizing his/her feelings of anger, hurt, or sadness toward the absent or abusive parent.

35. Conduct Play Therapy (35)

A. An individual play-therapy session was held to provide the client with the opportunity to express his/her feelings about the past neglect, abuse, separation, or abandonment.

B. The client expressed strong feelings of anger and resentment during today's play-therapy session about the past neglect, abuse, separation, or abandonment.

C. The client expressed feelings of sadness, hurt, and disappointment during today's play-therapy session about the past neglect, abuse, separation, or abandonment.

36. Interpret Feelings in Play Therapy (36)

A. The client's feelings of sadness and pain expressed during the play-therapy session were interpreted as related to his/her anger and aggressive behaviors.

B. The client agreed with the interpretation that his/her angry outbursts and/or aggressive behaviors are related to underlying feelings of sadness, hurt, and rejection.

C. The client resisted the interpretation that his/her angry outbursts and/or aggressive behaviors are related to underlying feelings of sadness, hurt, and rejection.

D. The individual play-therapy session helped the client realize how his/her angry outbursts and aggressive behaviors are related to underlying feelings of helplessness, vulnerability, and low self-esteem.

37. Child-Centered Play Therapy (37)

A. A child-centered play-therapy approach was utilized to help the client begin to develop greater anger control.

B. The client was given unconditional positive regard and warm acceptance to facilitate the expression of his/her angry feelings during today's play-therapy session.

C. The client's feelings during the play-therapy session were reflected back to him/her in a nonjudgmental manner.

D. The client's capacity to act responsibly and control his/her anger was reinforced during today's play-therapy session.

E. The child-centered play-therapy approaches have been helpful in identifying the underlying dynamics contributing to the client's anger control problems.

38. Employ A.C.T. Model (38)

A. The A.C.T. model (Landreth) was utilized in today's play-therapy session to help the client identify and express his/her feelings.

B. The A.C.T. model was employed to help the client identify acceptable alternatives to his/her destructive or aggressive behaviors.

C. Limits for the client's destructive or aggressive behaviors were communicated to the client in a neutral and nonpunitive manner.

D. The client responded favorably to the limits imposed in today's play-therapy session on his/her aggressive or destructive behaviors.

39. Psychoanalytic Play-Therapy Approach (39)

A. A psychoanalytic play-therapy approach was employed to help the client work through and resolve the issues contributing to his/her anger control problems.

B. A psychoanalytic play-therapy approach was used to explore the etiology of the unconscious conflicts that have contributed to the emergence of the client's anger-control problems.

C. The psychoanalytic play-therapy session helped reveal how the client's anger-control problems are related to earlier developmental arrests or fixations.

D. The client's transference of strong emotions was interpreted in today's psychoanalytic play-therapy session.

E. The psychoanalytic play-therapy approach has helped the client to work through and resolve the core anxieties contributing to his/her anger-control problems.

40. Use of Puppets, Dolls, and Stuffed Animals (40)

A. A mutual storytelling technique using puppets, dolls, or stuffed animals was implemented to model appropriate ways to manage anger and resolve conflict.

B. The mutual storytelling technique helped the client learn effective ways to manage his/her anger and resolve conflict.

C. The client created a story through the use of puppets, dolls, or stuffed animals that reflected strong feelings of anger and aggression.

41. Storytelling Techniques (41)

A. The client was directed to create stories through the use of puppets, dolls, or stuffed animals to help assess his/her unmet needs and the family dynamics that contribute to his/her anger-control problems.

B. The storytelling technique was helpful in identifying the client's unmet needs.

C. The storytelling technique was helpful in identifying the family dynamics that contribute to his/her anger-control problems.

D. The storytelling technique did not provide insight into the dynamics that have contributed to the client's anger-control problems.

42. Draw a House (42)

A. An art-therapy technique was used to help assess family dynamics; client was instructed to first draw a picture of a house and then create a story describing what it is like to live in that house.

B. The art-therapy technique revealed that the client perceives his/her parents as overly critical and/or punitive in their disciplinary measures.

C. The art-therapy technique revealed that the client perceives his/her home and family relationships as lacking in love and support.

D. The client produced a drawing and a story that reflected a considerable amount of discord within the family system.

E. The art-therapy technique led to a discussion about family dynamics and relationships.

43. Anger-Provoking Situations (43)

A. The client was instructed to draw pictures of three events or situations that commonly evoke feelings of anger.

B. Processed the client's thoughts and feelings reflected in drawings that were related to anger-provoking situations.

C. The client's drawings reflected how he/she often becomes angry when self-esteem is challenged and he/she feels insecure or vulnerable.

D. The client's drawings reflected his/her need for power and control.

44. Art-Therapy Techniques (44)

A. The client was instructed to draw an outline of a human body on a large piece of paper or poster board in the therapy session, then asked to fill in the mural with objects, symbols, or pictures that reflect what he/she feels angry about in his/her life.

B. After filling in a human body outline with pictures that symbolize the objects or sources of anger, the client was able to verbalize his/her feelings of anger in the therapy session and identify more constructive ways to resolve conflict or overcome his/her problems.

45. Music-Therapy Techniques (45)

A. The client shared a song in the therapy session that reflected feelings of anger and was then asked to tell of a time when he/she felt angry about a particular issue.

B. The client shared a song in the therapy session that afterward led to a discussion about how the song reflected his/her feelings of anger and what he/she can do to meet his/her needs or overcome problems.

46. Homework from Therapeutic Workbooks (46)

A. The client was given a homework assignment from the therapeutic workbook *The Angry Monster* (Shore) to help him/her develop more effective ways to control his/her anger.

B. The client was given a homework assignment from the therapeutic workbook *How I Learned to Control My Temper* (Shapiro) to help him/her develop more effective ways to control his/her anger.

C. The client reported that he/she was able to successfully use the anger-management techniques that he/she learned from the therapeutic workbooks.

47. Play "The Angry Monster Machine" Game (47)

A. The Angry Monster Machine game (Shapiro) was played to help the client learn more effective ways to control his/her anger.

B. After playing the therapeutic game, the client was able to identify several constructive ways to channel his/her anger.

C. Playing the The Angry Monster Machine therapeutic game helped to establish rapport with the client and also teach him/her more effective ways to control anger.

48. Assigned Readings (48)

A. The client was assigned to read one or both of the following books to improve his/her anger control: *Sometimes I Like to Fight, But I Don't Do It Much Anymore* (Shapiro) and *The Very Angry Day That Amy Didn't Have* (Shapiro).

B. The assigned anger-control reading(s) were processed with the client in today's therapy session.

C. The client was able to identify effective anger-management techniques after reading the assigned book(s).

D. The client reported that the assigned reading(s) helped him/her realize the benefits of controlling his/her anger both for self and others.

E. The client was strongly encouraged to utilize anger management strategies that he/she learned from reading the assigned book(s).

49. Anger Control Toolkit (49)

A. The *Anger Control Toolkit* (Shapiro, et al.) was used to help teach the client effective anger-management techniques.

B. The client identified the *Anger Control Toolkit* as being helpful in learning more effective ways to control his/her anger.

50. Coping with Anger Target Game (50)

A. The client was instructed to use the Coping with Anger Target game (Shapiro) at home to provide him/her with a healthy physical outlet for his/her anger.

B. The parents were encouraged to remind the client to play the Coping with Anger Target game when they see the client's anger beginning to escalate.

C. The client reported that playing the Coping with Anger Target game helped remind him/her of more constructive ways to manage his/her anger.

D. The parents reported that playing the Coping with Anger Target game helps prevent the client from becoming physically aggressive toward family members and peers.

51. Use "Angry Tower" Technique (51)

A. The Angry Tower technique (Saxe) was used in today's therapy session to help the client identify and express his/her feelings of anger.

B. The Angry Tower technique was helpful in identifying the targets of the client's anger.

C. After playing the Angry Tower game, the client was able to identify constructive ways to express his/her anger toward significant others.

D. The client was encouraged to use the Angry Tower technique at home to channel his/her angry feelings through a healthy physical outlet.

E. The Angry Tower technique was used to help the client express his/her feelings about past separations, losses, or abuse.

52. Participate in Activities or Exercise (52)

A. The client was strongly encouraged to participate in extracurricular activities or engage in regular exercise to provide a healthy outlet for his/her anger and improve self-esteem.

B. The client was assisted in developing a list of extracurricular activities that will provide a healthy outlet for his/her anger and improve self-esteem.

C. The client reported that regular exercise has helped him/her control anger.

53. Perform Altruistic Acts (53)

A. The client was given the homework assignment of performing three altruistic or benevolent acts to increase his/her empathy and sensitivity to the thoughts, feelings, and needs of others.

B. The recommendation was made that the client perform community service as part of his/her probation to increase empathy and concern for the welfare of others.

C. The client reported an increase in positive feelings toward self and others after showing empathy, kindness, and sensitivity to the needs of others.

D. The client's failure to comply with the homework assignment that he/she perform altruistic or benevolent acts reflects his/her lack of empathy and concern for the welfare of others.

54. Group-Therapy Referral (54)

A. The client was referred for group therapy to improve his/her anger control, social judgment, and interpersonal skills.

B. The client was given the directive to self-disclose at least one time during the group-therapy session.

C. The client was encouraged to demonstrate empathy and concern for the thoughts, feelings, and needs of others during the group-therapy session.

D. The group-therapy sessions have helped the client control his/her anger more effectively and demonstrate greater empathy for the thoughts, feelings, and needs of others.

55. Client's Positive Characteristics (55)

A. The client was asked to identify and list his/her positive characteristics to improve his/her self-esteem and frustration tolerance.

B. The client was encouraged to utilize his/her strengths and interests to improve self-esteem and provide opportunities to establish friendships.

C. The client was encouraged to make positive self-descriptive statements to improve his/her self-esteem and anger control.

D. The client was given the homework assignment to make at least one positive self-descriptive statement daily around others.

E. The parents were instructed to show interest and enthusiasm when the client makes positive self-descriptive statements.

56. Record Positive Self-Descriptive Statements (56)

A. The client was given the homework assignment of recording one positive self-descriptive statement daily in a journal to help improve his/her self-esteem and anger control.

B. The client complied with the homework to record one positive self-descriptive statement daily in a journal.
C. The client failed to comply with the directive to record one positive self-descriptive statement daily in a journal.
D. The client reported that his/her self-esteem and anger control has improved since he/she started to record one positive self-descriptive statement daily in a journal.

57. Assess Marital Conflicts (57)
A. The marital dyad was assessed for possible conflict and/or triangulation that places the focus on the client's anger-control problems and away from marital problems.
B. The parents recognized how their marital problems are creating stress for the client and agreed to pursue marital counseling.
C. The parents refused to follow through with the recommendation to pursue marital counseling.

58. Medication Evaluation Referral (58)
A. The client was referred for a medication evaluation to help stabilize his/her mood and improve anger control.
B. The client and parents agreed to follow through with a medication evaluation by a physician.
C. The client was strongly opposed to being placed on medication to help stabilize his/her mood and improve anger control.
D. The client reported that the medication has helped to stabilize his/her mood and decrease the frequency and intensity of his/her angry outbursts.
E. The client reported that the medication has not helped to stabilize his/her moods or decrease the frequency or intensity of his/her angry outbursts.

ANXIETY

CLIENT PRESENTATION

1. Excessive Worry (1)*

A. The client presented for the session upset and worried about recent events.

B. The client was upset and worried to the point where he/she could not be easily settled down by the therapist.

C. The client was able to work on the core issues that have caused him/her to be upset.

D. The client reported that he/she has been significantly less worried and less preoccupied with anxieties in the recent past.

2. Fearful/Urgent (1)

A. The client revealed a strong sense of urgency and sought any possible reassurance for his/her fears.

B. The urgency surrounding the client's fear is overwhelming.

C. The client's sense of urgency is not diminished by reassurance from the therapist.

D. The sense of urgency that surrounds the client's fears is no longer existent, and he/she no longer presses for reassurance.

3. Panicky/Uncontrollable (1)

A. The client shows that he/she is panicky to the point of being uncontrollable around the source of the anxiety.

B. The parents reported that each intervention they have tried has not been able to calm and settle the client once he/she reaches the point of panic.

C. Efforts by the client, the parents, and the therapist have not been successful in calming him/her after the panic reaches the uncontrollable point.

D. The client was responsive to a calm, reassuring voice and able to work through his/her panic state and process the causes for this specific reaction.

E. The problem of the client's symptoms of panic has been resolved, and there have been no reports of a recurrence of this phenomenon recently.

4. Restless/Tense (2)

A. The client was restless and tense, making it difficult for him/her to sit in session or to complete thoughts or activities.

B. The client is becoming less tense and is now able to respond to questions attentively.

C. The client is more relaxed and able to focus throughout the session, even when addressing issues that cause him/her anxiety.

---

* The numbers in parentheses correlate to the number of the Behavioral Definition statement in the companion chapter with same title in *The Child Psychotherapy Treatment Planner* (Jongsma, Peterson, and McInnis) by John Wiley & Sons, 2000.

5. Autonomic Hyperactivity Symptoms (3)

A. The client presented as being very anxious and experiencing a rapid heartbeat and short-ness of breath.

B. The client has been plagued by nausea and diarrhea brought on by his/her anxiety, as all physical reasons have been medically ruled out.

C. The client complained of having a dry mouth and frequently feeling dizzy.

D. The client indicated that he/she has not experienced symptoms of a rapid heartbeat or shortness of breath since he/she started to talk about what makes him/her anxious.

6. Body-Focused/Physical Complaints (3)

A. The client presents with numerous physical complaints and is focused on what is hap-pening to his/her body.

B. Body concerns occupied the entire session and it was difficult to move the client away from these concerns.

C. The client shared mother's concern for his/her health and how mother takes good care of him/her.

D. The client accepted reassurance regarding physical complaints and moved to talking about other anxieties he/she experiences.

E. The client was diverted from body focus and has begun exploring other concerns.

7. Hypervigilant (4)

A. The client presented in a tense, on-edge manner.

B. The client's level of tension and anxiety was so high that he/she was unable to concen-trate on anything and was irritable.

C. The client reported sleep disturbance related to anxious worry.

D. The client's anxiety has diminished and he/she is significantly more relaxed.

8. Specific Fear (Phobia) (5)

A. The client presented as being anxious over the specific stimulus situation to the point of being able to function only on a limited basis.

B. The client reported that the phobic anxiety gradually increased to where it now inter-feres with his/her daily life and family's life as well.

C. The client indicated that he/she has no idea of why the phobic fear has come to dominate his/her daily existence.

D. The client's daily ability to function has increased steadily as he/she has begun to face the phobic fear.

9. Parental Causes for Anxiety (6)

A. The client complained of being worried and anxious about the constant arguing of his/her parents.

B. The parents reported that they restrict the client's freedom and physical activity to pro-tect him/her from the dangers present today.

C. It was observed that the parents' use of excessive guilt and threats of abandonment caused worry and anxiety in the client.

D. The client indicated that he/she now feels less anxious, as the parents have stopped arguing so often.

E. The parents' relaxing their restrictions and control has reduced the client's level of worry and anxiety.

INTERVENTIONS IMPLEMENTED

1. Establish Trust/Express Anxious Feelings (1)*

A. An initial trust level was established with the client through the use of unconditional positive regard.

B. Warm acceptance and active-listening techniques were utilized to establish the basis for a trusting relationship with the client.

C. The client has formed a trust-based relationship and has started to express his/her anxious feelings.

D. Despite the use of active listening, warm acceptance, and unconditional positive regard, the client remains hesitant to trust and share his/her anxious feelings.

2. Talking, Feeling, Doing Game (2)

A. The Talking, Feeling, Doing game (Creative Therapeutics) was played with the client, who readily responded in detail to all questions.

B. The client played the Talking, Feeling, Doing game only after some coaxing and then offered only brief responses to some questions.

C. The client eagerly played the Talking, Feeling, Doing game and was pleased by the therapist's responses. The client would like to play again.

D. Playing the Talking, Feeling, Doing game has been helpful in getting the client to identify, explore, and express his/her feelings.

3. Conduct Play-Therapy Sessions (3)

A. Play-therapy sessions were conducted with the client in which his/her fears, worries, and anxieties were explored and worked through.

B. The client actively participated in play therapy, sharing his/her fears, worries, and anxieties, and exploring ways to cope and resolve these feelings.

C. The parents were updated regularly on what was occurring in the sessions and the progress the client was making.

D. The client's involvement in play therapy has helped him/her make progress in both reducing and resolving his/her fears and anxieties.

4. "Finding and Losing Your Anxiety" (4)

A. The client was asked to complete and process the exercise "Finding and Losing Your Anxiety" from *The Brief Child Therapy Homework Planner* (Jongsma, Peterson, and McInnis).

---

* The numbers in parentheses correlate to the number of the Therapeutic Interventions statement in the companion chapter with same title in *The Child Psychotherapy Treatment Planner* (Jongsma, Peterson, and McInnis) by John Wiley & Sons, 2000.

B. The completed anxiety-resolution exercise was processed with the client and specific fears and anxieties were identified, along with possible strategies for coping with these feelings.

C. From the suggestions in the exercise, the client was assisted in developing and implementing specific strategies for each fear and/or anxiety.

D. The client's implementation of the strategies was monitored for their effectiveness and his/her consistency in follow-through.

E. The strategies developed and implemented by the client from the exercise have seemed to be effective in helping him/her cope with their fears and anxieties.

5. Utilize "Squiggle Wiggle" Game (5)

A. The "Squiggle Wiggle" game (Winnicott) was played with the client to assist him/her in externalizing the source of the anxiety.

B. The client actively participated in the "Squiggle Wiggle" game, explaining in detail the story around his/her anxiety.

C. The client's open participation in the "Squiggle Wiggle" game helped to reveal the source of his/her current anxieties.

D. Due to the client's silliness and passive resistance, the "Squiggle Wiggle" game could not be completed.

E. The client completed the drawing portion of the "Squiggle Wiggle" game, but refused to tell the story of his/her drawing.

6. Draw Anxious Situations (6)

A. The client was asked to draw two or three situations that generally make him/her anxious.

B. The client explained and processed each picture, telling, with detail, what situations cause his/her anxiety.

C. Options for handling the client's anxious feelings were explored for each of the drawings.

D. The client has tried each coping option when he/she encountered anxiety situations in his/her daily life and reported reduced distress.

7. Conduct Psychoanalytic Play-Therapy (7)

A. Using a psychoanalytic play-therapy approach, the client's core conflicts were identified, processed, and resolved.

B. In the psychoanalytic play-therapy session, the client was allowed to take the lead and explore the sources of his/her unconscious conflict and/or core anxieties.

C. Resistance issues that emerged in the psychoanalytic play-therapy session were worked through to resolution.

D. The client's active involvement in the psychoanalytical play-therapy session has helped him/her to work through to resolution his/her unconscious conflicts and core anxieties.

8. Use Child-Centered Play-Therapy Approach (8)

A. A child-centered play-therapy approach was utilized with the client to help him/her work through and resolve his/her anxiety.

B. In the child-centered play-therapy session, the client's feelings were mirrored, reflected, and validated.

C. In session, the client's feelings were reflected back to him/her in an affirming, nonjudgmental manner to promote his/her working through anxieties.

D. The child-centered play-therapy approach has helped the client reduce and resolve most of his/her unconscious conflicts and core anxieties.

9. Explore Messages/Retrain Cognition (9)

A. The client's cognitive messages that cause anxiety were explored and the client was taught their role in the process of creating anxiety.

B. The client was assisted in successfully listing the most frequent, distorted self-talk that precipitates anxiety.

C. The client is having persistent difficulty in identifying and clarifying the distorted cognitive messages that precipitate anxiety.

10. Create New Messages/Expand Coping Skills (10)

A. The client was assisted in identifying and developing positive, realistic cognitive messages to help increase his/her self-confidence.

B. The client was taught specific coping skills to assist him/her in effectively responding to anxious situations.

C. It continues to be very difficult for the client to replace the distorted cognitive messages that precipitate anxiety with positive, realistic messages that would induce calm confidence.

D. The client was asked to continue to work on implementing specific coping skills that would reduce anxiety.

11. Teach Positive Imagery/Relaxation (11)

A. The client was taught deep-muscle relaxation, deep breathing, and positive imagery as a means of coping with his/her anxieties.

B. The client practiced positive imagery and relaxation in role-play situations with the therapist.

C. A verbal contract was agreed upon, with the client to use relaxation and positive imagery when anxiety or fear presents itself.

D. The implementation of deep-muscle relaxation, deep breathing, and positive imagery as coping skills has been very effective in helping the client reduce his/her level of anxiety.

12. Model Positive Cognitive Responses to Anxiety (12)

A. Using puppets, the snip tray, or felts, the client was encouraged to create scenarios that provoke anxiety.

B. The client actively took part in creating and explaining the various scenarios that create anxiety in him/her.

C. For each scenario created by the client, a positive cognitive response was modeled that would help him/her reduce the anxiety of the situation.

D. The positive cognitive responses modeled for the client have been put to successful use by him/her in handling situations that cause him/her anxiety.

13. **My Home and Places Game (13)**

A. The My Home and Places game (Flood) was played with the client, who participated without resistance.

B. As the client played My Home and Places, he/she was able to identify what made him/her anxious.

C. The client played My Home and Places with the therapist under duress and gave only partial and minimal responses.

14. **Sing a Song or Play an Instrument (14)**

A. The client was instructed to sing a song or play a musical instrument to reflect his/her anxiety.

B. The client cooperated with the directive to use a musical expression to his/her anxiety.

C. The client resisted the suggestion to use a musical expression that reflected his/her anxiety.

D. The client was able to effectively convey through music times that he/she felt anxiety.

E. The musical expression of anxiety facilitated the client's resolution of the issue.

15. **List Past/Present Conflicts (15)**

A. The client was asked to make a list of all his/her past and present conflicts to help connect those conflicts with current anxieties.

B. The client processed the list of past and present conflicts with the therapist and was able to make key connections between conflicts and his/her anxiety.

C. The client required assistance in making connections from his/her list of conflicts and the anxiety he/she experiences.

D. The client could identify no past or present conflicts that he/she could connect with current experience of anxiety.

16. **Resolve Past/Present Conflicts (16)**

A. Cognitive restructuring was utilized in assisting the client to resolve key past and present situations.

B. The client was taught assertiveness techniques to use in resolving past/present conflicts.

C. The client was instructed in various conflict-resolution techniques to apply to resolve key past/present conflicts.

D. The client was gently but firmly confronted on his/her resistance to resolving either past or present conflicts.

17. **Connect Anxiety and Wishes (17)**

A. The client participated in an interpretive interview in which he/she expressed his/her suppressed wishes and feelings.

B. The client was assisted in making key connections between his/her anxiety and his/her "unacceptable" wishes or "bad" thoughts.

C. As the client identified and expressed his/her suppressed wishes and censored thoughts, his/her level of anxiety has been reduced.

18. Narrative Approach to Anxiety (18)

A. The client was assigned the task of writing out the story of his/her anxious feelings.

B. The client was instructed to act out the story that he/she created about his/her anxiety.

C. The externalized anxiety story was processed with the client after he/she completed acting it out.

D. The client was assisted in developing effective coping resolutions to the story that could be implemented in his/her daily life.

E. The client was helped to identify ways to implement strategies to reduce his/her fear in daily life.

F. The strategies developed and implemented from the narrative exercise have helped reduce the client's fear in his/her daily life.

19. *My Own Thoughts and Feelings* (19)

A. The client completed and processed exercises from *My Own Thoughts and Feelings: A Growth and Recovery Workbook for Children* (Deatin).

B. The client's completed exercises were processed with emphasis placed on increasing the understanding of and ability to cope with his/her anxious feelings.

C. The client was assisted in selecting and implementing several of the ideas for coping with anxious feelings presented in the *My Own Thoughts and Feelings: A Growth and Recovery Workbook for Children* exercises.

D. The client's implementation and follow-through on the anxiety-coping strategies were monitored, redirected, and validated.

E. The client was encouraged to share with his/her parents what he/she was learning through the exercises; the parents were encouraged to give verbal praise and affirmation for the client's efforts to understand and reduce his/her anxiety.

20. Focus on Anxiety-Producing Situations (20)

A. The client used storytelling techniques, drawing, and viewing pictures of anxiety-producing situations to help him/her talk about and reduce his/her level of anxiety.

B. The client has gradually been able to tolerate more of the anxiety-producing situations and talk more freely about his/her anxiety.

C. The client was given encouragement and support in exploring stories, drawing, and viewing pictures of anxiety-producing situations.

D. The client reported an increased ability to tolerate anxiety-producing situations as they occur.

21. Utilize Mutual Storytelling Technique (21)

A. The client was encouraged to tell his/her story of an anxiety-producing situation utilizing a mutual storytelling technique.

B. The client readily told his/her story about anxiety, which was interpreted for its underlying meaning.

C. The client was told a story that used the same characters and settings as his/her story but wove in healthy ways to handle, cope with, and resolve anxieties.

D. The client verbalized that the mutual storytelling technique was helpful in providing him/her ways to handle and resolve anxieties.

22. **Behavioral Anxiety-Coping Strategies (22)**

A. The client was assisted in selecting anxiety-coping strategies that he/she felt would be helpful in resolving anxiety.

B. Behavioral rehearsal was used to instruct the client in how to implement behavioral anxiety-coping strategies.

C. A contract was developed, agreed upon, and signed by the client to implement the identified behavioral anxiety-coping strategies.

D. The client reported that the implementation of the behavioral anxiety-coping strategies has been helpful in reducing the experience of anxiety significantly.

23. **Develop Schedule for Physical Activity (23)**

A. The client and parents were taught the value of physical activity and its possible anxiety reduction benefits.

B. The client and parents were assisted in developing and implementing a schedule for physical activity that would help reduce the client's level of anxiety.

C. The client and parents were monitored for their implementation and follow-through of the physical activity schedule that would help reduce the client's level of anxiety.

D. The client and parents were confronted about the lack of consistent implementation of the physical activity schedule that would help reduce the client's level of anxiety.

E. The implementation of a daily physical activity schedule has helped reduce the client's anxiety level.

24. **Involve Parents in Treatment Process (24)**

A. The parents were encouraged to take part in an experiential family weekend to assist them in facing fears, building trust, and increasing self-confidence.

B. The parents were assisted in locating and scheduling a family experiential weekend.

C. After the family experiential weekend, the family processed the experience and identified the benefits achieved.

D. The family did not follow through on participating in a family experiential weekend.

25. **Overthinking the Anxiety Situation (25)**

A. The client was encouraged to think for a determined amount of minutes three times each day about the situation that elicits his/her fear or anxiety.

B. A contract was elicited from the client to implement the overthinking coping strategy regularly until the next therapy session.

C. The overthinking exercise has been successfully implemented by the client and has served to reduce the amount of time that the client is preoccupied with anxious thoughts or feelings.

26. **Normal Developmental Anxieties (26)**

A. The parents were taught about the fears and anxieties of various developmental stages.

B. Anxiety and fears were normalized with the parents, and coping strategies were stressed as the way to handle them.

27. Parents Read Books on Child Development (27)

A. The parents were asked to read *Between Parent and Child* (Ginott) and/or *How to Talk So Kids Will Listen* (Faber and Mazlish) to increase their understanding of children.

B. The assigned reading material was processed with the parents to support what they had learned and to answer any questions that emerged from their reading.

C. The parents were confronted about unrealistic expectations or solutions to child development issues.

D. The parents have not followed through with reading the assigned material on child development, and they were encouraged to do so.

28. Parenting Class Referral (28)

A. The parents were encouraged to attend a parenting class or support group.

B. The parents gave a commitment to join a parenting class or support group.

C. The parents reported on their experience within a parent support group.

D. The parents were resistive of a referral to a parenting class and refused to commit to attending such a class.

29. Parents' Response to Client's Fears (29)

A. The parents were taught effective responses to the client's fears.

B. The parents have learned to identify and eliminate detrimental responses that intensify the client's fears/anxieties.

C. The parents made a verbal commitment to implement new responses to the client's fears/anxieties.

D. The parents reported that they have begun to respond more effectively to the client's fears and that this has resulted in a reduction in the client's level of anxiety.

30. Underlying Family Conflicts (30)

A. Family sessions were conducted to look for underlying conflicts that may be present within the family.

B. Family sessions were held and underlying conflicts within the family were identified in specific terms.

C. Attempts were made to hold a family session to look for underlying conflicts, but the family was resistive of the intervention, preferring not to discuss their conflicts.

31. Resolve Family Conflict (31)

A. Positive ways of resolving conflicts were identified and examined by the family.

B. In family sessions, the family was able to resolve key family conflicts.

C. Healthy aspects of the family functioning were affirmed, and the family was encouraged to work toward resolving ongoing family conflicts.

D. The resolution of underlying family conflicts has had a very beneficial effect on reducing the client's level of anxiety.

32. Structure Roles within the Family (32)

A. Family sessions were held in which family roles were explored and adjusted to strengthen the parental team and solidify the sibling group.

B. Separate family sessions were held with the parents and siblings in order to emphasize family hierarchy and to define the sibling group as separate from the parents.

C. As clarity has been added to the family roles, the client's level of anxiety has been reduced.

D. The parents were reinforced for reducing their efforts to control the children unnecessarily.

33. Decrease Parental Control (33)

A. Strategic interventions were developed and implemented in family sessions that were aimed at decreasing parental control and increasing children's freedom of choice.

B. Specific situations were identified in which the parents can reduce their control and offer more choice to the children.

34. Utilize Metaphors and Parables (34)

A. The client was given a metaphor to evoke his/her abilities and to implant hope for a good outcome.

B. Fairy tales and parables were read with the client to get his/her attention and evoke the possibility of a good outcome in his/her anxiety-reduction efforts.

C. Metaphors were used with the client to suggest a good outcome in his/her efforts to cope with anxiety.

D. Metaphors, parables, and fairy tales have helped the client see more possibilities and have more hope in coping effectively with his/her anxieties.

35. Develop Internal Structures for Self-Regulation (35)

A. The client was taught the method of evoking the memory of the therapist to soothe and encourage self when confronted with anxiety-producing situations.

B. Role play and behavioral rehearsal were used to build the client's skill and self-confidence in using the strategy of evoking the memory of the therapist.

C. The client reports successfully using the memory of the therapist as a strategy for coping with anxiety-producing situations.

36. Prescribe a Prediction Task (36)

A. The client was instructed to predict each night the anxiety that would bother him/her the next day, along with key elements that would make it a good day.

B. The experience of predicting the anxiety was processed with the client, and key elements that were part of making for a good day were affirmed and reinforced.

C. A solution was formed from the data gathered by the client about elements that led to good days; this solution was assigned to him/her to implement in order to increase the frequency of good days.

D. The client's active embracing of the prediction task has increased the number of good days he/she has had in managing his/her anxiety.

ATTACHMENT DISORDER

CLIENT PRESENTATION

1. Adoption from Abusive Family (1)*

A. Reports and sources indicated that the client comes from a severely abusive and neglectful biological family.

B. The client's affect and emotional distance were consistent with his/her history of an abusive and neglectful family background.

C. The parents reported that the client seemed to be very unsure and confused in the structured, caring environment of their family.

D. The parents have started to see signs that the client is overcoming his/her abusive and neglectful past and is becoming more a part of their new family.

2. Does Not Initiate/Respond to Social Interactions (2)

A. The parents indicated that from the beginning the client has withdrawn from and rejected their attempts to be warm and affectionate.

B. It has been observed by caregivers and professionals that the client relates in a detached manner to everyone.

C. Parents and teacher have noted that the client does not attempt to form relationships with his/her peers or with adults.

D. The client has begun to initiate some social contacts and has started to respond more warmly to contact with others.

3. Becomes Friendly Too Quickly (3)

A. The parents reported that the client quickly becomes too friendly and affectionate with any adult.

B. The client has rapidly become very friendly and affectionate with the therapist.

C. The client has been observed becoming very friendly and somewhat affectionate with strangers he/she meets in public places.

D. The client has stopped being so friendly and affectionate to strangers.

4. No Bond to Any Caregiver (4)

A. The client has made no appreciative reference to any past caregivers.

B. Reports and evaluations have indicated that the client was not attached to his/her biomother or any other caregiver.

C. It has been observed that the client does not look for or ask for parents when in a setting other than his/her home.

D. The client has started to show signs and indications that he/she is bonding with new parents.

* The numbers in parentheses correlate to the number of the Behavioral Definition statement in the companion chapter with same title in *The Child Psychotherapy Treatment Planner* (Jongsma, Peterson, and McInnis) by John Wiley & Sons, 2000.

5. Resists Care and Help of Others (5)

A. The parents reported that the client resists or rejects any words or gestures of caring from them.
B. The client reported in clear terms that he/she can and prefers to do things for himself/herself without help from others.
C. The client has resisted or rejected all help from his/her teacher.
D. Gradually the client has come to allow others to help him/her and to accept their caring gestures.

6. Hoarding or Gorging Food (6)

A. The parents have discovered that the client has stashes of food in various hiding places in his/her bedroom.
B. It has been observed that the client eats quickly to ensure that he/she can get more.
C. The parents reported that the client often eats so much that he/she becomes physically sick.
D. The client has been seen sneaking food at home and at school to save for a later time.
E. The parents indicated that the client now eats more normal amounts of food and no longer hides food for later consumption.

7. Aggressive Behaviors (7)

A. Records of the client reflect a long, clear history of aggressive acts toward siblings, peers, and caregivers.
B. The parents indicated that they confront the client's aggressive actions toward siblings, peers, and/or themselves on a daily basis.
C. School officials have reported intervening with the client on a frequent basis for his/her aggressive actions toward peers.
D. The client showed little, if any, concern about his/her aggressive behaviors.
E. The client has reduced the frequency and intensity of his/her aggressive behavior toward siblings, peers, and parents.

8. Frequent Lying (8)

A. The parents reported that the client frequently lies about everything.
B. It has been observed by teachers and caregivers that the client often lies even when there is no obvious reason for doing so.
C. The client's record reflects that he/she often lies about his/her behavior.
D. Little remorse is shown by the client when he/she is caught in a lie.
E. The frequency of the client's lying has decreased and he/she now is showing remorse when caught in a lie.

9. Stealing Unneeded Items (9)

A. Records reflect that the client has a history of stealing.
B. The client has been caught on several occasions stealing items that he/she doesn't need.
C. The client indicated that he/she does not have a reason or explanation for his/her stealing.
D. The client has stopped his/her stealing of unneeded items.

10. No Sign of Conscience Development (10)

A. It is reported by caregivers that the client does not show any guilt or remorse for his/her bad behavior.

B. Parents reported that the client blames others for his/her bad behavior and refuses to see it otherwise, even when confronted with solid evidence.

C. Records of the client's behavior indicate that he/she showed little or no remorse when caught lying, cheating, or hurting another person.

D. The client appeared to fail to see anything he/she did as bad or wrong.

E. The client has started to show some concern and regret when caught doing something that is wrong.

11. Clinginess to Primary Caregiver (11)

A. Parents reported that it is impossible to leave the client without him/her becoming emotionally distraught.

B. The client presented as being excessively clingy to his/her parents.

C. The client expressed that he/she becomes very afraid and worried when parents are out of his/her sight.

D. The client's excessive clinginess has made it difficult for parents to get him/her to attend school.

E. The client has gradually started to tolerate being away from his/her parents without becoming emotionally distraught.

12. Experienced Neglect of Emotional/Physical Needs (12)

A. Records of the client's background reflect that he/she was severely emotionally and physically neglected by his/her biomother and other caregivers.

B. Parents reported that to date the client has shown difficulty accepting or responding positively to their caring and supportive actions.

C. The client indicated that he/she remembers always taking care of and looking out for himself/herself.

D. The client has started to respond positively to parents' efforts to meet his/her emotional and physical needs.

13. Frequent Changes in Primary Caregiver (13)

A. Records indicate that the client has had numerous primary caregivers, all of whom have had brief tenures.

B. The client quickly listed many people who have been his/her primary caregivers.

C. The client cannot remember several of his/her primary caregivers.

D. The fact that the client has had numerous primary caregivers has made him/her hesitant to become attached to new parents.

INTERVENTIONS IMPLEMENTED

1. Build Trust (1)*

A. Consistent eye contact, active listening, and empathic responses were utilized to build a level of trust with the client.

B. Trust was actively built with the client through the use of unconditional positive regard.

C. Despite the use of consistent eye contact, active listening, and empathic responses, only a small degree of trust was established with the client.

D. A level of trust has been established with the client such that he/she is now openly expressing his/her thoughts and feelings.

2. Conduct Celebrity-Style Interview (2)

A. A celebrity-style interview was conducted with the client to build a relationship with him/her and to help him/her to learn more about himself/herself.

B. After completing the celebrity-style interview, the client was encouraged to ask any of the same questions of the therapist or any other questions he/she wished answered about the therapist.

C. Important information about the client that become evident from the interview was reflected back to help him/her affirm things about himself/herself.

D. The client was able to identify several specific things he/she had learned about himself/herself from the interview.

3. Conduct Session in Consistent Manner (3)

A. Session structure followed a consistent, predictable form to help the client feel more comfortable and trust the therapist.

B. The session structure was explained to the client and questions he/she had were answered to his/her satisfaction.

C. The client appears to have become very comfortable with the session's structure and has begun to express himself/herself a little more freely.

4. Conduct Psychosocial Evaluation (4)

A. A psychosocial evaluation was conducted with the parents and the client.

B. The parents and client cooperated with all aspects of the psychosocial evaluation, answering all questions in significant detail.

C. The parents and client complied with the psychosocial evaluation but gave just brief information with very little detail.

D. Strengths of both parents and the client that emerged from the psychosocial evaluation were identified and affirmed with them.

5. Arrange for Psychological Evaluation (5)

A. The purpose of the psychological evaluation was explained to the client and parents, and any questions they had regarding it were answered.

---

* The numbers in parentheses correlate to the number of the Therapeutic Interventions statement in the companion chapter with same title in *The Child Psychotherapy Treatment Planner* (Jongsma, Peterson, and McInnis) by John Wiley & Sons, 2000.

B. A psychological evaluation was conducted with the client to determine his/her level of behavioral functioning, cognitive style, and intelligence.

C. The client and parents were told the purpose of the evaluation, and any questions they had regarding it were answered.

D. The client cooperated with all aspects of the psychological evaluation.

E. The psychological evaluation could be only partially completed due to the client's lack of focus and cooperation.

6. Present Assessment Data to Family (6)

A. Data from the psychological and psychosocial evaluations was summarized and presented to the family, along with treatment recommendations.

B. The parents' questions regarding the evaluation findings and treatment recommendations were answered.

C. A verbal commitment to follow through on all the treatment recommendations was asked for and received from the client and parents.

D. The parents' resistance to several of the treatment recommendations was addressed and resolved.

7. Refer Parents to Skills-Based Marital Program (7)

A. The possible benefits of the parents attending a program to strengthen their marriage were identified and explored.

B. The parents were referred to a skills-based marital program that teaches personal responsibility, communication skills, and conflict resolution (e.g., Prep by Markhum, Stanley, and Blumberg).

C. The parents' follow-through on completing the recommended marriage-enrichment program was monitored, and positive gains were reinforced.

D. The parents completed the recommended marital program and indicated that they gained many new skills that have improved their marital relationship.

E. The parents' dropping out of the recommended marriage-enrichment program was addressed and processed.

8. Assess Unresolved Infertility Grief (8)

A. The parents' unresolved grief associated with their infertility was assessed.

B. The results of the grief assessment indicated that the parents have worked through most of the issues related to their infertility.

C. The grief assessment revealed that the parents have many unresolved issues surrounding their infertility and were given a referral to a counselor who specializes in these issues.

D. The referral of the parents for grief counseling was monitored for their follow-through and overall satisfaction with the service provided.

E. The parents reported many positive outcomes from the grief counseling they have completed.

9. Process Parents' Expectations for Client (9)

A. The parents were asked to list the expectations that they currently hold for the client and to indicate which expectation is most important to them.

B. The parents' list of expectations for the client was processed, and each unrealistic expectation was addressed and either modified or discarded.

C. Parents' insistence on holding onto unrealistic expectations for the client was addressed and the negative consequences of doing so were explained.

D. The parents were assisted in forming more realistic expectations and developing ways to help the client meet these expectations.

E. The parents' modified expectations seem to be resulting in a more relaxed relationship with the client.

10. Show Reality of Love Being Last (10)

A. The parents were assisted in identifying and discussing key components of building strong relationships.

B. The parents were helped to express and process their hopes and desires for their relationship with client.

C. The reality was shown of love being the last emotion to be expressed and shown by the client.

D. The reality of love being the last thing expressed in the relationship was reflected to parents when they expressed their frustration with the client's lack of responsiveness to them.

E. The parents have done well in continuing to build their relationship with the client while not yet expecting verbal or behavioral expressions of love.

11. Solicit Parents' Treatment Commitment (11)

A. The possible benefits of their active involvement in the client's treatment was discussed with the parents.

B. Specific ways that the parents could be involved in treatment were explored and identified.

C. The parents were asked to make a verbal commitment to be an active part of the client's treatment, both in counseling sessions and in their home.

D. As their participation decreased, the parents were gently but firmly reminded of their commitment to the treatment process and the benefits of their involvement.

E. The active participation by parents in the client's treatment, both in sessions and at home, has helped to build a bond between them and the client.

12. Reframe Acting-Out Behaviors (12)

A. Through work in conjoint sessions, parents have come to understand the client's acting-out behaviors as opportunities for them to reparent him/her.

B. The parents' barriers to accepting the acting-out behaviors as opportunities to reparent were explored, addressed, and resolved.

C. The parents were assisted in developing and implementing new interventions for the client's problem behaviors.

D. The parents were given positive reinforcement for implementing new interventions and for their acceptance of reparenting opportunities.

E. The parents have reported positive results from their new intervention techniques for dealing with client's acting-out behaviors.

13. Train Parents as Cotherapists (13)

A. The parents were introduced to the concept of being cotherapists in the client's treatment process.

B. The benefits of the parents being cotherapists were identified and processed.

C. The parents were trained and empowered to be involved as cotherapists in the client's treatment.

D. The parents were guided and directed in their roles as cotherapists.

E. Positive verbal affirmation was given to the parents for their consistent commitment to being cotherapists in the client's treatment.

F. The client has shown strong positive gains in his/her ability to develop strong bonds, which has been aided by the parents' involvement as cotherapists.

14. Utilize Theraplay Approach (14)

A. The parents were educated in the Theraplay approach to building a relationship with the client.

B. A verbal commitment was elicited from the parents to be active cotherapists using the Theraplay approach.

C. The Theraplay attachment-based approach was used as the focus of therapy to entice the client into a relationship and to steer away from his/her intrapsychic conflicts.

D. The parents were given specific therapeutic assignments to do at home with the client between therapy sessions.

E. The parents' follow-through as cotherapists on assignments was monitored, and any needed redirection was given.

F. The Theraplay approach appears to be effective, as the client has started to form a relationship with the therapist and parents.

15. Employ A.C.T. Model in Play Therapy (15)

A. A.C.T. model of play therapy was conducted with the client, whereby his/her feelings were acknowledged, limits communicated, and acceptable alternatives to acting-out or aggressive behaviors were targeted.

B. The client actively participated in A.C.T. play-therapy sessions and was open to accepting alternatives to acting-out and aggressive behaviors.

C. The client participated in A.C.T. play-therapy sessions but was resistive of input of limits and targeted behaviors.

D. The A.C.T. approach with the client has been effective in implementing new behaviors to replace his/her previous acting-out and aggressive ones.

16. Conduct Filial Therapy (16)

A. The parents were educated in the filial therapy approach and the possible benefits for the client of their involvement.

B. The client was encouraged in filial therapy sessions to express his/her angry feelings, while parents were coached to respond empathically to the underlying feelings of hurt, fear, and helplessness.

C. The client openly expressed his/her angry feelings, and his/her parents responded appropriately with empathic statements reflecting his/her underlying hurt, fear, and helplessness.

D. The active participation of the client and his/her parents in filial therapy sessions has resulted in a major reduction in the client's angry feelings.

17. Provide Parents with Education Regarding Attachment (17)

A. Education on the nature of attachment and the effect of trauma on it was provided to the parents.

B. The parents were asked to construct a list of questions they had regarding attachment and the effect of trauma.

C. The list of questions constructed by parents about the effects of trauma on attachment were answered and processed.

D. The parents now seem to have a better understanding of attachment.

18. Teach Detachment as a Normal Reaction (18)

A. The client and the parents were introduced to the idea that the client's detachment was a normal reaction to his/her past painful experiences.

B. The client's response to the idea of his/her detachment being a normal reaction to painful experiences was discussed and processed.

C. The client was assisted in seeing the positive aspects of separating his/her current family from past abuse experiences.

D. The client's ability to accept his/her detachment as a normal reaction and to separate past abuse from his/her current family has helped him/her begin to join the new family.

19. Suggest Books for Parents to Read (19)

A. Readings were suggested to the parents to help them better understand the client and give them ideas and encouragement in dealing daily with him/her.

B. The parents were encouraged to implement one or more new approaches to their child that were gained from their reading.

C. The parents' questions that were stimulated by their reading were answered and processed.

D. The parents seemed to gain increased understanding, fresh ideas, and encouragement from the parenting material they read.

20. Empathize with Parents' Frustration (20)

A. The parents were assisted in identifying the frustration they experience in living with a detached child.

B. The parents were encouraged to express the pain and disappointment they feel as a result of living with a detached child.

C. The parents' barriers to identifying and expressing their frustrations, pain, and disappointment were identified, processed, and resolved.

D. After expressing their frustration with living with a detached child, the parents' commitment to keep trying to build a relationship with their child was affirmed and reinforced.

E. The parents' identification and expression of their feelings of frustration has helped them continue to work effectively with the client.

21. "Dixie Overcomes Her Fears" Exercise (21)

A. The client was asked to complete and process the exercise "Dixie Overcomes Her Fears" from *The Brief Child Therapy Homework Planner* (Jongsma, Peterson, and McInnis) to help him/her share fears and gain self-acceptance.

B. The client processed the completed "Dixie Overcomes Her Fears" exercise and was able to specifically identify and share his/her fears and gain self-acceptance.

C. Plans were made with the client to implement several of the ideas that were identified in the "Dixie Overcomes Her Fears" exercise as a way to continue to increase his/her self-acceptance.

D. The client has effectively used the "Dixie Overcomes Her Fears" exercise to continue to share his/her fears and boost his/her self-acceptance.

22. Assign *SEALS & PLUS* Workbook (22)

A. The client was assigned self-esteem exercises from *SEALS & PLUS* workbook (Korb-Khara, Azok, and Leutenberg) to develop self-knowledge, acceptance, and confidence.

B. The client's completed self-esteem workbook exercises were processed with all key points regarding self-knowledge, acceptance, and confidence being verbally affirmed.

C. The client's resistance to completing, sharing, and taking the self-esteem workbook exercise seriously was gently confronted, processed, and resolved.

D. The *SEALS & PLUS* workbook exercise seemed to have noticeably increased the client's degree of self-knowledge, acceptance, and confidence.

23. Assign "Life Book" (23)

A. The parents were educated about the key benefits to the client in having a "life book."

B. The parents and client were given instructions on how to create a "life book" and then were assigned to put one together.

C. The parents and client were monitored on their completion of the assignment of creating a "life book."

D. The completed "life book" was reviewed by parents with the client in order to give the client perspective on and knowledge of his/her history.

24. Educate Parents about Affirming Client's Identity (24)

A. The parents were educated about the importance of affirming the client's entire history.

B. The parents were assisted in listing the possible ways that they could affirm the client's entire history.

C. The parents' list for affirming the client's identity was processed and specific ways were developed to implement each suggestion on the list.

D. The parents were monitored for their implementation of the ways they developed to affirm the client's identity and given verbal reinforcement for their consistent efforts.

E. The client has responded very positively to parents' affirmations of his/her entire history.

25. Assign Parents One-on-One Play with Client (25)

A. The value of spending time in one-on-one daily play was explored and processed with parents.

B. The parents were asked to commit to spending consistent one-on-one time playing with the client.

C. A daily schedule of one-on-one time, with each parent playing with the client, was developed and implemented.

D. The parents were monitored, encouraged, and redirected in their follow-through on one-on-one daily playtime with client.

E. The parents reported seeing visible gains in client's bonding as they have been spending daily one-on-one time with him/her.

26. Encourage Verbal Reinforcement/Physical Affection (26)

A. The positive value of providing large doses of genuine verbal reinforcement and physical affection were identified with the parents.

B. The parents explored ways they could give the client large doses of reinforcement or affection, and specific ways were selected for them to start implementing.

C. The parents were encouraged, supported, and monitored in their efforts to provide the client with large daily doses of genuine verbal reinforcement and physical affection.

D. Parents have consistently provided the client with large doses of reinforcement and affection, to which the client has responded by showing signs of increased attachment.

27. Refer to Initiative- or Adventure-Based Summer Camp (27)

A. The benefits of attending an initiative- or adventure-based summer camp were identified, explained, and processed with the client and parents.

B. The parents were given information on several camps and encouraged to choose one for the client to attend.

C. The parents have made the proper arrangements for the client to attend an initiative-based summer camp.

D. The client's camp experience was processed with the client and parents, and positive gains in self-confidence were identified and reinforced.

28. Conduct Trust Walk (28)

A. A family session was conducted in which the client, family, and therapist took part in a trust walk.

B. The trust-walk experience was processed with the client and family, with barriers to trusting being identified and resolved.

C. The trust-walk experience was repeated with the family and processed, with gains in trust by each member being recognized and affirmed.

D. The trust-walk experience reflected gains that family members have made in increasing their level of trust with each other.

29. Train Client in Meditation and Focused Breathing (29)

A. The client was trained in meditation and focused breathing techniques to calm himself/herself when tension, anger, and frustration are building.

B. Role play and behavioral rehearsal were utilized to give the client the opportunity to practice meditation and focused breathing techniques.

C. The client was helped to identify situations in which he/she could use the stress-reduction techniques and then asked to implement them in these situations as they arise in his/her daily life.

D. The client's use of meditation and focused breathing was monitored, with both redirection and encouragement being given.

E. The client's consistent implementation of meditation and focused breathing has reduced his/her level of tension, anger, and frustration.

30. Read *Don't Rant and Rave on Wednesday* (30)

A. The client was asked to read with the therapist the book *Don't Rant and Rave on Wednesday* (Moser) to assist him/her in identifying ways to cope with angry feelings.

B. The client processed the various ways suggested in *Don't Rant and Rave on Wednesday* to manage angry feelings and identified two he/she could implement in coping with his/her angry feelings.

C. Ways to implement the identified anger-management strategies were developed with the client and he/she committed to using them in his/her daily life when he/she felt angry.

D. The client has consistently and effectively used the anger-management strategies he/she gained from *Don't Rant and Rave on Wednesday* and has had fewer problems with inappropriately expressing his/her angry feelings.

31. Encourage Parents in Maintaining Control (31)

A. The reasons for parental control and sticking with behavior-management techniques were reemphasized with parents.

B. The parents identified times that they have lost control or have given in to the client's demands.

C. The parents were given verbal encouragement and support to maintain firm control of the client's behavior and to stick with effective behavior-management techniques.

D. The parents have responded positively to encouragement and support, have maintained firm control over the client, and have remained consistent in their behavior-management techniques.

32. Design Preventive Safety Measures (32)

A. The need for and value of preventive safety measures to be used if the client's behavior becomes dangerous were explained, emphasized, and reinforced with parents.

B. The parents were assisted in designing preventive safety measures to use if client's behavior ever becomes dangerous to self or others.

C. The parents were trained to identify situations in which they should implement their preventive safety measures.

D. The parents' use of the preventive safety measures was monitored and reviewed at regular intervals in the client's treatment.

E. The parents have used preventive safety measures appropriately with client and have avoided the escalation of his/her dangerous behaviors.

33. Teach Parents to Give Feedback of Expectations (33)

A. The parents were trained in ways to give feedback, structure, and repeated emphasis of expectations to the client to reassure him/her that they are in control.

B. The parents were directed to consistently use feedback, structure, and repeated emphasis of expectations with the client to assert their control and to keep his/her feelings in check.

C. Encouragement was given to the parents for following through with measures that reinforce their control with the client.

D. The parents have consistently used measures that reassure the client that they are in control and that his/her intense feelings will remain in check.

34. Encourage "Cohesive Shared Experiences" (34)

A. The value and benefits of "cohesive shared experiences" (James) were explained, emphasized, and reinforced with the client's parents.

B. The parents were asked to list possible "cohesive shared family experiences" and select two or three they would like to implement.

C. Barriers to "cohesive shared experiences" were explored, identified, and resolved.

D. The family was helped to make specific plans to implement the "cohesive shared family experiences" they identified from their list.

E. The parents' follow-through in implementing "cohesive shared family experiences" was encouraged, supported, and monitored.

F. The parents' implementation and follow-through regarding "cohesive shared family experiences" have further developed the bond between the client and the family.

35. Assign Physical Touching (35)

A. The parents were assisted in identifying the potential benefits that physical touching could have on the client.

B. Barriers to providing increased physical touching to the client were explored, identified, and resolved.

C. The parents were assigned the exercise of 10 minutes of physical touching of the client twice daily for two weeks.

D. The experience of the exercise was processed with the parents, and positive outcomes were identified and reinforced.

E. The parents were encouraged to continue the increased physical touching of the client after completion of the assigned exercise.

36. Develop List of Respite Providers (36)

A. The role of respite care was discussed and processed with the parents.

B. The parents were assisted in developing a list of potential respite-care providers.

C. The parents were assigned to arrange to visit and interview several respite-care providers.

D. The parents have developed a list of potential respite-care providers and have chosen two they would like to use.

37. Encourage Use of Respite Care (37)

A. The parents were helped to develop and implement a plan to use respite care on a regular basis.

B. Barriers to parents' follow-through on the use of respite care were explored, identified, and resolved.

C. The parents' use of respite care was encouraged and monitored for their consistent follow-through.

D. The parents were reminded of the benefits of using respite care.

E. The parents have started to use respite care on a consistent basis, and it has been beneficial for their energy and perspective in dealing with the client.

38. Encourage Parents' Venting of Frustrations (38)

A. Conjoint sessions were conducted in which the parents were given permission and encouraged to vent their concerns and frustrations in dealing daily with the client.

B. The parents were helped to identify difficult situations with the client in which they feel frustrated.

C. The difficult behavior-management situations identified by the parents were processed, and specific suggestions were given to them to try.

D. The parents have openly and freely expressed their frustrations and concerns in working with the client daily and have tried the suggestions given for situations in which they felt ineffective.

39. Educate Parents on Detachment (39)

A. The parents were educated to understand the meaning and purpose of the client's detachment.

B. Issues and questions the parents had concerning detachment were discussed, answered, and resolved.

C. The parents were trained to implement appropriate interventions in dealing with behavior in a therapeutic way.

D. Role play and behavioral rehearsal were utilized to develop parents' skills and build their confidence in implementing new interventions.

E. The parents have used new interventions effectively and consistently with the client on a daily basis, which has helped to foster the client's attachment.

40. Monitor and Adjust Parental Interventions (40)

A. The parents' implementation of interventions designed to increase the client's attachment were monitored as to their effectiveness for the client.

B. The parents were assisted in making adjustments in their interventions so they were more effective in making sure the client's intense feelings did not get acted out.

C. The parents have been open to feedback and have made the suggested adjustments in their interventions with the client to keep his/her intense feelings under control.

41. Assign Parents to Give Client Choices (41)

A. The advantages of offering choices to the client were explored, identified, and reinforced with parents.

B. The parents were asked to give the client as many choices as is reasonable in order to impart a sense of control and empowerment to him/her.

C. The parents' resistance to offering choices to the client was identified, processed, and resolved.

D. The parents' use of choices was monitored, with redirection being given as needed.

E. The parents have effectively given the client choices whenever it was reasonable, and the client has seemed to gain a sense of empowerment and control.

42. Arrange for a Medication Evaluation (42)

A. The need for a psychiatric evaluation for medication was explained to the parents and the client, and any questions they had regarding it were answered.

B. The client was referred for a psychiatric evaluation for medications.

C. The client cooperated fully with all aspects of the psychiatric evaluation.

D. The results of the evaluation were shared and discussed with the client and his/her parents, and any questions they had were answered.

43. Monitor Medication Compliance (43)

A. The client's taking of medication as prescribed was monitored for compliance, effectiveness, and any possible side effects.

B. The client and parents were asked to report any side effects they observed to either the therapist or the psychiatrist.

C. The client and parents were confronted about the client's taking medication on only an inconsistent basis.

D. The overall effectiveness of the medication was communicated to the psychiatrist.

E. The client has taken the medication consistently as prescribed, with no reported or visible side effects.

44. Play "The Good Mourning" Game (44)

A. The Good Mourning game (Bisenius and Norris) was used to introduce the ideas of loss and mourning to the client.

B. The client played The Good Mourning Game with therapist.

C. The questions that the client had about grief and loss after playing the game were discussed and answered.

D. The client refused to play The Good Mourning Game, stating that it was "stupid and boring."

E. The client has gained an introduction to loss and mourning through playing The Good Mourning Game.

45. Assist and Support Grieving Process (45)

A. The client was assisted in recognizing the stages of grieving and where he/she was at in that process.

B. Consistent encouragement, support, and assistance were provided to the client as he/she worked through the stages of grief.

C. Barriers that arose in the client's grieving process were identified, addressed, and resolved.

D. Regular reassurance was given to the client that he/she would make it through the process of grieving the losses.

E. The client has successfully worked through each stage of the grieving process.

ATTENTION-DEFICIT/HYPERACTIVITY DISORDER

CLIENT PRESENTATION

1. Short Attention Span (1)*

A. The parents and teachers reported that the client displays a short attention span and has difficulty staying focused for extended periods of time.

B. The client had trouble staying focused in today's therapy session and often switched from one topic to another.

C. The client remained focused and was able to discuss pertinent topics for a sufficient length of time.

D. The client's attention span has improved in structured settings where he/she receives supervision and greater individualized attention.

E. The parents and teachers reported that the client has consistently demonstrated good attention and concentration at home and school.

2. Distractibility (2)

A. The parents and teachers reported that the client is easily distracted by extraneous stimuli and his/her own internal thoughts.

B. The client appeared highly distractible during today's therapy session and often had to be redirected to the topic being discussed.

C. The client often has to be redirected back to task at home or school because of his/her distractibility.

D. The client appeared less distractible and more focused during today's therapy session.

E. The client has appeared less distractible and more focused at home and school.

3. Poor Listening Skills (3)

A. The client has often given others the impression at home and school that he/she is not listening to what is being said.

B. The client did not appear to be listening well to the topics being discussed in today's therapy session.

C. The client listened well during today's therapy session.

D. The client has recently demonstrated improved listening skills at home and school.

4. No Follow-Through on Instructions (4)

A. The parents and teachers reported that the client does not consistently follow through on instructions.

B. The client's repeated failure to follow through on instructions has interfered with his/her ability to complete school assignments, chores, and job responsibilities in a timely manner.

* The numbers in parentheses correlate to the number of the Behavioral Definition statement in the companion chapter with same title in *The Child Psychotherapy Treatment Planner* (Jongsma, Peterson, and McInnis) by John Wiley & Sons, 2000.

C. The client has generally been able to follow single or simple instructions, but has had trouble following through on multiple, complex instructions.

D. The client has begun to demonstrate improvement in his/her ability to follow through on instructions.

E. The client has recently followed through on instructions from parents and teachers on a consistent basis.

5. Incomplete Classroom/Homework Assignments (4)

A. The client has consistently failed to complete his/her classroom and homework assignments in a timely manner.

B. The client has often rushed through his/her classroom work and does not fully complete his/her assignments.

C. The client has recently demonstrated mild improvements in his/her ability to complete classroom and homework assignments.

D. The client has consistently completed his/her classroom and homework assignments on a consistent basis.

6. Unfinished Chores (4)

A. The client has often failed to comply with parents' requests to complete his/her chores at home.

B. The parents reported that the client often gets sidetracked and does not complete his/her chores.

C. The client has demonstrated mild improvements in his/her ability to finish chores or household responsibilities.

D. The client has been responsible in completing his/her chores on a consistent basis.

7. Poor Organizational Skills (5)

A. The client has displayed poor organizational skills and often loses or misplaces important things necessary for tasks or activities at home and school.

B. The client has a tendency to become more disorganized and impulsive in his/her responding in unstructured settings where there is a great deal of external stimulation.

C. The client has recently taken active steps (e.g., utilizing planner, consulting with teachers about homework, performing homework and chores at routine times) to become more organized at home and school.

D. The client has demonstrated good organizational skills at home and school on a regular basis.

8. Hyperactivity (6)

A. The parents and teachers described the client as being a highly energetic and hyperactive individual.

B. The client presented with a high energy level and had difficulty sitting still for extended periods of time.

C. The client has trouble channeling his/her high energy into constructive or sustained, purposeful activities.

D. The parents and teachers reported a decrease in the client's level of hyperactivity.

E. The client has consistently channeled his/her energy into constructive and purposeful activities.

9. Restless Motor Movements (6)

A. The parents and teachers described the client as being highly restless and fidgety in his/her motor movements.

B. The client was restless and fidgety in his/her motor movements during today's therapy session.

C. The client has frequently annoyed or antagonized peers because of his/her trouble keeping hands to himself/herself.

D. The client exhibited a decrease in the amount of motor activity during today's therapy session.

E. The client has demonstrated greater control of his/her motor movements on a regular basis.

10. Impulsivity (7)

A. The client presents as a highly impulsive individual who seeks immediate gratification of his/her needs and often fails to consider the consequences of his/her actions.

B. The client has considerable difficulty inhibiting his/her impulses and tends to react to what is going on in his/her immediate environment.

C. The client has begun to take steps toward improving his/her impulse control and to delay the need for immediate gratification.

D. The client has recently displayed good impulse control, as evidenced by an improved ability to stop and think about the possible consequences of his/her actions before reacting.

11. Disruptive/Attention-Seeking Behavior (8)

A. The parents and teachers described a history of the client frequently disrupting the classroom with his/her silly, immature, and negative attention–seeking behaviors.

B. The client has often disrupted the classroom by blurting out remarks at inappropriate times.

C. The client has started to exercise greater self-control and recently has not disrupted the classroom as much.

D. The client has demonstrated a significant reduction in the frequency of his/her disruptive or negative attention–seeking behaviors at home and school.

12. Angry Outbursts/Aggressive Behavior (8)

A. The client reported a history of losing control of his/her anger and exhibiting frequent angry outbursts or aggressive behaviors.

B. The client appeared angry and hostile during today's therapy session.

C. The client reported incidents of becoming easily angered over trivial matters.

D. The client has begun to take steps to control his/her anger and aggressive impulses.

E. The client has recently demonstrated good control of his/her anger and has not exhibited any major outbursts or aggressive behavior.

13. Careless/Potentially Dangerous Behavior (9)

A. The client described a history of engaging in careless or potentially dangerous behavior, whereby he/she shows little regard for the welfare or safety of self and others.

B. The client's impulsivity has contributed to his/her propensity for engaging in careless, risky, or dangerous activity.

C. The client verbally recognized a need to stop and think about the possible consequences of his/her actions for self and others before engaging in risky or potentially dangerous behaviors.

D. The client has not engaged in any recent careless or potentially dangerous behaviors.

14. Blaming/Projecting (10)

A. The client has often resisted accepting responsibility for the consequences of his/her actions and has frequently projected the blame for his/her poor decisions or problems onto other people or outside circumstances.

B. The client appeared defensive and made excuses or blamed others for his/her poor decisions and behavior.

C. The client has slowly begun to accept greater responsibility for his/her actions and has placed the blame less often for his/her wrongdoing onto other people.

D. The client admitted to his/her wrongdoing and verbalized an acceptance of responsibility for his/her actions.

15. Conflict with Family Members (10)

A. The client reported a history of becoming entangled in numerous arguments or disputes with family members.

B. The client's family relationships are strained due to his/her impulsivity, hyperactivity, and verbally/physically aggressive behaviors.

C. The client has recently demonstrated a mild reduction in the frequency of his/her arguments with family members.

D. The client and parents reported significant improvement in family relations due to the client's improved impulse control.

16. Low Self-Esteem (11)

A. The client expressed feelings of low self-esteem and inadequacy as a consequence of his/her poor decisions and impulsive actions.

B. The client's defensiveness and unwillingness to accept responsibility for the consequences of his/her actions have reflected deeper feelings of low self-esteem, inadequacy, and insecurity.

C. The client verbalized an awareness of how his/her feelings of inadequacy contribute to an increase in disruptive and impulsive behaviors.

D. The client verbalized positive self-descriptive statements during today's therapy session.

E. The client has taken active steps to improve his/her self-esteem and develop a positive self-image.

17. Poor Social Skills (11)

A. The client historically has had difficulty establishing and maintaining lasting peer friendships because of his/her poor social skills and impulsivity.

B. The client frequently becomes entangled in interpersonal disputes because of his/her failure to pick up on important social cues or interpersonal nuances.

C. The client's interpersonal relationships are strained by his/her intrusive behaviors.

D. The client has begun to take steps (e.g., listen better, compliment others, allow others to go first) to improve his/her social skills.

E. The client has recently demonstrated good social skills and related well to siblings, peers, and adults on a consistent basis.

18. Lack of Empathy/Insensitivity (11)

A. The client has displayed little concern or empathy for the thoughts, feelings, and needs of other people.

B. The client showed little insight or awareness in today's therapy session of how his/her disruptive or impulsive behaviors have negatively affected other people.

C. The client has frequently sought immediate gratification of his/her needs and failed to stop and consider the rights or needs of others.

D. The client verbalized an understanding of how his/her disruptive and impulsive behaviors have had a negative impact on others.

E. The client has recently begun to demonstrate empathy and sensitivity to the thoughts, feelings, and needs of other people.

INTERVENTIONS IMPLEMENTED

1. Psychological Testing to Assess ADHD (1)*

A. A psychological evaluation was conducted to determine whether the client has ADHD.

B. The client was uncooperative and resistant during the evaluation process.

C. The client approached the psychological testing in an honest, straightforward manner and was cooperative with the examiner.

2. Psychological Testing for Emotional or Learning Factors (2)

A. The client received a psychological evaluation to help determine whether emotional factors are contributing to his/her impulsive or maladaptive behaviors.

B. The client received a psychoeducational evaluation to rule out the presence of a possible learning disability that may be contributing to his/her problems with attention, distractibility, and impulsivity in the school setting.

C. The client was uncooperative during the psychoeducational evaluation and did not appear to put forth good effort.

---

* The numbers in parentheses correlate to the number of the Therapeutic Interventions statement in the companion chapter with same title in *The Child Psychotherapy Treatment Planner* (Jongsma, Peterson, and McInnis) by John Wiley & Sons, 2000.

D. The client was cooperative during the psychoeducational evaluation and appeared motivated to do his/her best.

3. Provide Evaluation Feedback (3)

A. The examiner provided feedback on the evaluation results to the client, parents, or school officials and discussed appropriate interventions.
B. The evaluation results supported the diagnosis of ADHD.
C. The evaluation revealed the presence of underlying emotional problems that contribute to the client's problems with inattentiveness, distractibility, and impulsivity.
D. The results of the psychoeducational evaluation supported the presence of a learning disability and the need for special education services.
E. The evaluation process did not reveal the presence of any learning disability, emotional problems, or ADHD that have contributed to the client's problems with attention, distractibility, or impulsivity.

4. Medication Evaluation Referral (4)

A. The client was referred for a medication evaluation to improve his/her attention span, concentration, and impulse control.
B. The client was referred for a medication evaluation to help stabilize his/her moods.
C. The client and parents agreed to follow through with a medication evaluation.
D. The client was strongly opposed to being placed on medication to help improve his/her attention span and impulse control.

5. Monitor Medication Compliance and Effectiveness (5)

A. The client reported that the medication has helped to improve his/her attention, concentration, and impulse control without any side effects.
B. The client reported little to no improvement on the medication.
C. The client has not complied with taking his/her medication on a regular basis.
D. The client and parents were encouraged to report the side effects of the medication to the prescribing physician or psychiatrist.

6. Educate Family about ADHD (6)

A. The client's parents and siblings were educated about the symptoms of ADHD.
B. The therapy session helped the client's parents and siblings gain a greater understanding and appreciation of the symptoms of ADHD.
C. The family members were given the opportunity to express their thoughts and feelings about having a child or sibling with ADHD.

7. Implement Organizational System (7)

A. The parents were assisted in developing an organizational system to increase the client's on-task behavior and completion of school assignments, chores, or work responsibilities.
B. The parents were encouraged to communicate regularly with the teachers through the use of notebooks or planning agendas to help the client complete his/her school or homework on a regular, consistent basis.

C. The client and parents were encouraged to use a calendar or chart to help remind the client of when he/she is expected to complete chores or household responsibilities.

D. The client and parents were instructed to ask the teacher for a course syllabus and use a calendar to help plan large or long-term projects by breaking them into smaller steps.

E. The client and parents were encouraged to purchase a notebook with binders to help the client keep track of his/her school or homework assignments.

8. Develop Routine Schedule (8)

A. The client and parents were assisted in developing a routine schedule to increase the completion of school/homework assignments.

B. The client and parents developed a list of chores for the client and identified times and dates when the chores are expected to be completed.

C. A reward system was designed to reinforce the completion of school, household, or work-related responsibilities.

D. The client and parents signed a contingency contract specifying the consequences for his/her success or failure in completing school assignments or household responsibilities.

9. Encourage Communication between Home and School (9)

A. The parents and teachers were encouraged to maintain regular communication with each other via phone calls or written notes regarding the client's academic, behavioral, emotional, and social progress.

B. Consulted with the teachers about sending home daily or weekly progress notes informing the parents of the client's academic, behavioral, and social progress.

C. The client was informed of his/her responsibility to bring home daily or weekly progress notes, allowing for regular communication between parents and teachers.

D. The parents identified the consequences for the client's failure to bring home the daily or weekly progress notes from school.

10. Teach Effective Study Skills (10)

A. The client was assisted in identifying a list of good locations for studying.

B. The client was instructed to remove noise sources and clear away as many distractions as possible when studying.

C. The client was instructed to outline or underline important details when studying or reviewing for tests.

D. The client was encouraged to use a tape recorder to help him/her study for tests and review important facts.

E. The client was instructed to take breaks in studying when he/she becomes distracted and starts to have trouble staying focused.

11. Consult with Teachers (11)

A. Consulted with the client's teachers to implement strategies to improve school performance.

B. The client was assigned a seat near the teacher or in a low-distraction work area to help him/her remain on task.

C. The client and teacher agreed to use a prearranged signal to redirect the client back to task when his/her attention begins to wander.

D. The client's schedule was modified to allow for breaks between tasks or difficult assignments to help maintain attention and concentration.

E. The teachers were encouraged to obtain and provide frequent feedback to help maintain the client's attention, interest, and motivation.

12. Assign *The ADD Hyperactivity Handbook for Schools* (12)

A. The parents were instructed to read *The ADD Hyperactivity Handbook for Schools* (Parker) to improve the client's school performance and behavior.

B. The reading of *The ADD Hyperactivity Handbook for Schools* was processed with the parents to reinforce what they learned.

C. The parents reported that they learned several helpful tips about how to improve the client's organizational skills from reading *The ADD Hyperactivity Handbook for Schools*.

D. The parents decided to implement a reward system to improve the client's school performance and behavior after reading *The ADD Hyperactivity Handbook for Schools*.

E. The parents reported that reading *The ADD Hyperactivity Handbook for Schools* helped them realize the importance of communicating regularly with the teachers and school officials.

13. Teach Test-Taking Strategies (13)

A. The client reviewed a list of effective test-taking strategies to improve his/her academic performance.

B. The client was encouraged to review classroom material regularly and study for tests over an extended period of time.

C. The client was instructed to read the directions twice before responding to the questions on a test.

D. The client was taught to recheck his/her work to correct any careless mistakes or to improve an answer.

14. Assign *13 Steps to Better Grades* (14)

A. The client was instructed to read *13 Steps to Better Grades* (Silverman) to improve his/her organizational and study skills.

B. After reading *13 Steps to Better Grades,* the client was able to identify several positive study skills that will help him/her remain organized in the classroom.

15. Use "Getting It Done" Exercise (15)

C. The parents and teachers were given the "Getting It Done" program from *The Brief Child Therapy Homework Planner* (Jongsma, Peterson, and McInnis) to help client complete his/her school and homework assignments regularly.

D. The parents and teachers were encouraged to utilize the school contract and reward system outlined in the "Getting It Done" program to reinforce the regular completion of school assignments.

16. Teach Proper Ways to Give Directions (16)

A. The parents were instructed through the use of modeling and role playing to make one request at a time when giving directions to the client.

B. The parents were discouraged from giving multiple directions to the client because of his/her tendency to become sidetracked.

C. The parents were encouraged to repeat the instructions to the client if it appeared that he/she was not listening well or maintaining good eye contact.

D. The parents were encouraged to obtain frequent feedback from the client to help him/her follow through in completing instructions.

E. The parents verbally recognized that the client is more likely to follow through on instructions if he/she is given only one direction at a time.

17. Teach Self-Control Strategies (17)

A. The client was taught mediational and self-control strategies (e.g., relaxation techniques, "stop, look, listen, and think") to help delay the need for immediate gratification and inhibit impulses.

B. The client was encouraged to utilize active-listening skills to delay the impulse to act out or react without considering the consequences of his/her actions.

C. The client was asked to identify the benefits of delaying his/her need for immediate gratification in favor of longer-term gains.

D. The client was assisted in developing an action plan to achieve longer-term goals.

18. Identify Positive Reinforcers (18)

A. The parents identified a list of positive reinforcers or rewards to maintain the client's interest or motivation in completing school assignments or household responsibilities.

B. The parents were encouraged to provide frequent praise and positive reinforcement to maintain the client's interest and motivation in completing his/her school assignments or household responsibilities.

C. The parents were challenged to look for opportunities to praise the client for being responsible, instead of primarily focusing on the times when the client failed to behave in a responsible manner.

19. Establish Parental Rules and Boundaries (19)

A. The family therapy session focused on helping the parents establish clearly defined rules and appropriate parent-child boundaries.

B. The parents were able to identify the rules and expectations that the client is expected to follow at home.

C. The parents were able to identify appropriate consequences for the client's irresponsible or noncompliant behaviors.

D. The parents had difficulty establishing clearly defined rules and identifying appropriate consequences for the client's irresponsible or noncompliant behaviors.

20. Establish Clear Rules (20)

A. Consulted with the client, parents, and teachers to identify the rules and expectations both at home and at school.

B. The client was asked to repeat the rules to demonstrate an understanding of the expectations of him/her.

C. The client verbally disagreed with the rules and expectations identified by the parents and school officials.

21. Facilitate Delay of Gratification (21)

A. The therapy session focused on helping the parents increase the structure in the home to help the client delay his/her needs for immediate gratification in order to achieve longer-term goals.

B. The parents established the rule that the client is unable to engage in social, recreational, or leisure activities until completing his/her chores or homework.

C. The parents identified consequences for the client's failure to complete responsibilities; client verbalized recognition of these consequences.

D. The client and parents designed a schedule of dates and times when the client is expected to complete chores and homework.

22. Develop Reward System/Contingency Contract (22)

A. The client and parents identified a list of rewards to reinforce the desired positive behavior by the client.

B. A reward system was designed to reinforce positive behavior and deter impulsive actions.

C. The client and parents signed a contingency contract specifying the consequences for his/her impulsive behavior.

D. The client and parents verbally agreed to the terms of the contingency contract.

23. Identify Natural Consequences (23)

A. The client and parents developed a list of natural, logical consequences for the client's disruptive and acting-out behaviors.

B. The parents were challenged to not protect the client from the natural, logical consequences of his/her disruptive or acting-out behaviors.

C. The client agreed to accept the natural, logical consequences of his/her disruptive or acting-out behaviors without complaining excessively.

24. Design Token Economy (24)

A. A token economy was designed for use in the home to increase the client's positive social behaviors and deter impulsive, acting-out behaviors.

B. The client and parents agreed to the conditions outlined in the token economy, and they agreed to follow through with the implementation at home.

C. A token economy was designed and implemented in the classroom to improve the client's academic performance and reinforce positive social behavior or good impulse control.

25. Assign Books to Parents (25)

A. The parents were instructed to read *Effective Discipline for Children 2–12* (Phelan) to help them learn effective disciplinary techniques to manage the client's hyperactive and impulsive behaviors.

B. The parents were assigned the reading of *Your Hyperactive Child* (Ingersoll) to educate them about the symptoms of ADHD and learn about effective treatment interventions.

C. The parents were instructed to read *Taking Charge of ADHD* (Barkley) to learn more effective ways to manage the symptoms of ADHD.

D. The reading of the book(s) on managing a child with ADHD was processed with the parents in today's therapy session.

26. Teach Problem-Solving Skills (26)

A. The client was taught effective problem-solving skills (i.e., identify the problem, brainstorm alternate solutions, select an option, implement a course of action, and evaluate) in the therapy session.

B. The client was encouraged to use effective problem-solving strategies to solve or overcome a problem or stressor that he/she is facing in his/her current life.

C. The client was given a directive to use problem-solving strategies at home or school on at least three occasions before the next therapy session.

27. Use *Let's Work It Out* (27)

D. *Let's Work It Out: A Conflict Resolution Tool Kit* (Shore) was used to help teach the client effective problem-solving skills.

E. The client identified the conflict resolution tool kit as being helpful in learning more effective ways to solve problems.

F. The client was given the homework assignment to practice some of the effective problem-solving skills that he/she learned through use of the conflict resolution tool kit.

28. Read Books on Anger Control (28)

A. *The Very Angry Day That Amy Didn't Have* (Shapiro) was read in today's therapy session to help teach the client effective ways to control his/her anger.

B. *Sometimes I Like to Fight, but I Don't Do It Much Anymore* (Shapiro) was read to teach the client effective ways to control his/her anger.

C. The reading of the books on anger control was processed.

D. The client identified the books on anger control as being helpful in learning more effective ways to control his/her anger.

E. The client was instructed to practice the anger management techniques that he/she learned from reading the books on anger control.

29. Play "Stop, Relax, & Think" Game (29)

A. The therapeutic game Stop, Relax, & Think (Shapiro) was played to help the client develop greater self-control.

B. The client identified the therapeutic game as being helpful in teaching self-control strategies.

C. The client was given the homework assignment to practice the self-control strategies that he/she learned from playing the therapeutic game before the next therapy session.

30. Teach Communication and Assertiveness Skills (30)

A. The client was taught effective communication and assertiveness skills to learn how to express feelings in a controlled fashion and meet his/her needs through more constructive actions.

B. Role-playing and modeling techniques were used to teach the client effective ways to control emotions and identify appropriate ways to meet needs.

C. The client was encouraged to utilize "I" messages and positive statements to effectively verbalize needs to others.

31. Confront Impulsive Behavior (31)

A. The client was firmly and consistently confronted with how his/her impulsive behavior negatively affects himself/herself and others.

B. The client was asked to list the negative consequences of his/her impulsive behavior for both self and others.

C. Role-reversal techniques were used to help the client realize how his/her impulsive behavior negatively impacts others.

32. Teach Acceptance of Responsibility (32)

A. The client was consistently confronted and challenged to cease blaming others for his/her impulsive behavior and accept greater responsibility for his/her actions.

B. The client was asked to list how his/her poor decisions and impulsive actions resulted in negative consequences for himself/herself and others.

C. The client was assisted in identifying more effective ways to resolve conflict and/or meet his/her needs instead of acting out in an impulsive manner.

D. The client was instructed to apologize to others for the negative consequences of his/her impulsive actions.

33. Connect Feelings and Behavior (33)

A. The session was helpful in identifying how the client's underlying negative or painful emotions are related to the increase in his/her impulsive or disruptive behaviors.

B. The client verbally recognized how his/her impulsive or disruptive behaviors are connected to underlying feelings of sadness, hurt, disappointment, and so forth.

C. Role-playing and modeling techniques were used to teach appropriate ways for the client to express his/her underlying, painful emotions.

D. The client was assisted in listing more appropriate ways to express his/her painful emotions and meet his/her needs instead of impulsively reacting to situations.

34. Identify Trigger Events to Impulsivity (34)

A. The therapy session explored the stressful events or contributing factors that frequently lead to an increase in the client's hyperactivity, impulsivity, and distractibility.

B. The client identified the stressful events or contributing factors that have contributed to an increase in his/her hyperactivity, impulsivity, and distractibility.

C. Role-playing and modeling techniques were used to teach appropriate ways to manage stress or resolve conflict more effectively.

D. The client and parents were assisted in identifying more effective coping strategies that could be used to manage stress or meet important needs instead of responding impulsively to a situation.

35. Identify Periods of Good Impulse Control (35)

A. The client identified periods when he/she demonstrated good impulse control in the past and engaged in significantly fewer impulsive behaviors.

B. The client was encouraged to use coping strategies similar to those used successfully in the past to control his/her impulses.

C. The therapy session revealed that the client exercised greater self-control and was better behaved during periods of time when he/she received strong family support and affiliated with positive peer groups.

36. Teach Parents to Reinforce Positive Behaviors (36)

A. The parents were instructed to observe and record three to five positive behaviors by the client between therapy sessions.

B. The parents were encouraged to reinforce the client for engaging in positive behaviors.

C. The client was strongly encouraged to continue to engage in positive behaviors to build self-esteem, gain parents' approval, and receive affirmation from others.

37. Assign One-on-One Time with Parents (37)

A. The client and parents acknowledged that there have been many negative interactions between them in the recent past and recognized the need to spend one-on-one time together to provide an opportunity for positive experiences.

B. The client and parents were instructed to spend 10 to 15 minutes of daily one-on-one time together to increase the frequency of positive interactions and help create a closer parent-child bond.

C. The parents were directed to allow the child to take the lead in selecting a task or activity during their one-on-one time together.

D. The client and parents reported that the one-on-one time together has helped them develop a closer relationship.

38. Assign Children's Books on ADHD (38)

A. The client was assigned to read *Putting on the Brakes* (Quinn and Stern) to learn more about ADHD.

B. The client and parents were assigned to read *Sometimes I Drive My Mom Crazy, but I Know She's Crazy About Me* (Shapiro) to help them be more aware and accepting of the symptoms of ADHD.

C. The reading of the book(s) on ADHD was processed.

D. The client reported that he/she learned more effective organizational and study skills after reading *Putting on the Brakes*.

E. The client was able to identify more effective ways to control his/her impulses after reading the children's book(s) on ADHD.

39. Teach Positive Social Behaviors (39)

A. The client was assisted in developing a list of positive social behaviors that will help him/her to establish and maintain meaningful friendships.

B. Role-playing and modeling techniques were used to teach positive social skills that can help the client establish and maintain peer friendships.

C. The parents and teachers were encouraged to reinforce positive social behaviors by the client that will help him/her establish friendships.

40. Encourage Peer-Group Activities (40)

A. The client was encouraged to participate in extracurricular or positive peer-group activities to provide him/her with the opportunity to utilize newly learned social skills and establish friendships.

B. The client was assisted in developing a list of peer-group activities that will provide him/her with the opportunity to establish meaningful friendships.

C. The client agreed that feelings of insecurity and inadequacy have contributed to his/her reluctance to become involved in extracurricular or positive peer-group activities.

41. Group-Therapy Referral (41)

A. The client was referred for group therapy to improve his/her social skills.

B. The client was given the directive to self-disclose at least one time during the group-therapy sessions.

C. The client was encouraged to demonstrate empathy and concern for the thoughts, feelings, and needs of others during the group-therapy sessions.

42. ADHD Parental Support Group Referral (42)

A. The parents were referred to an ADHD support group to increase their understanding and knowledge of ADHD symptoms.

B. The parents verbalized that their participation in the ADHD support group has increased their understanding and knowledge of ADHD.

C. The parents reported that they have learned new strategies for how to deal with the client's impulsive behavior through attending the ADHD support group.

43. Identify Strengths or Interests (43)

A. The client was given a homework assignment to identify 5 to 10 strengths or interests.

B. The client's interests or strengths were reviewed and he/she was encouraged to utilize strengths or interests to establish friendships.

C. The client reported that he/she has been able to establish a greater number of friendships by utilizing his/her strengths and interests.

44. Assign Demonstration of Empathy and Kindness (44)

A. The client was given the homework assignment of performing three altruistic or caring acts before the next therapy session to increase his/her empathy and sensitivity to the thoughts, feelings, and needs of others.

B. The client was encouraged to volunteer in a community service organization or fund-raising activity to demonstrate empathy and concern for others.

45. Play "The Helping, Sharing, and Caring" Game (45)

A. The Helping, Sharing, and Caring game (Gardner) was used to help the client develop positive social skills.

B. The client was able to successfully identify several positive social skills after playing The Helping, Sharing, and Caring Game.

C. The client was given a directive to practice the social skills that were learned while playing the therapeutic game.

46. "Social Skills Exercise" (46)

A. The "Social Skills Exercise" from *The Brief Child Therapy Treatment Planner* (Jongsma, Peterson, and McInnis) was utilized to teach the client self-monitoring techniques to improve his/her social skills.

B. The client's teachers were consulted about using self-monitoring techniques to improve the client's social skills.

C. A reward system was used in combination with the social skills self-monitoring forms to help the client develop positive social skills.

D. The parents and teachers reported that the client has improved his/her social skills through the use of the self-monitoring forms and reward system.

47. Employ Art-Therapy Techniques (47)

A. The client was instructed to draw pictures reflecting the positive and negative aspects of his/her high energy level.

B. The content of the client's drawings was processed in today's therapy session.

C. The art-therapy techniques helped the client identify constructive ways to channel his/her energy.

D. After completing his/her drawings, the client was able to identify positive changes that he/she would like to make in his/her life.

48. Use Puppets, Dolls, and Stuffed Animals (48)

A. Puppets, dolls, and stuffed animals were used to help create a story that modeled effective ways for the client to utilize his/her energy and gain attention from peers.

B. The client created a story using puppets, dolls, and stuffed animals that reflected his/her immature social skills.

C. The client produced a story using puppets, dolls, and stuffed animals that reflected his/her feelings of insecurity about peer relationships.

D. The client was able to identify several positive social skills that were modeled through the use of creative storytelling and/or puppet play.

49. Use "Angry Tower" Technique (49)

A. The Angry Tower technique (Saxe) was utilized to help the client express his/her anger in a controlled, nonharmful manner.

B. The Angry Tower technique was utilized to help identify the targets of the client's anger.

C. The client used the Angry Tower technique to vent strong feelings of anger toward the identified target(s).

D. The client identified the Angry Tower technique as a healthy way to vent his/her feelings of anger.

50. Use Self-Monitoring Checklists (50)

A. The client and parents were encouraged to use self-monitoring checklists to improve the client's attention, academic performance, and social skills.

B. Consulted with the client's teachers about the use of self-monitoring checklists in the classroom to improve attention, concentration, and social skills.

C. The parents and teachers were instructed to utilize a reward system in conjunction with the self-monitoring checklist to improve attention, academic performance, and social skills.

51. Utilize Brain-Wave Biofeedback Techniques (51)

A. The client was trained in the use of brain-wave biofeedback techniques to improve his/her attention span, impulse control, and ability to relax.

B. The client responded favorably to the use of brain-wave biofeedback techniques and was able to relax.

C. The client had difficulty relaxing during the use of the brain-wave biofeedback techniques.

52. Reinforce Transfer of Biofeedback Skills to Everyday Life (52)

A. The client was encouraged to transfer the biofeedback training skills of relaxation and focused cognitive functioning to everyday situations.

B. The client reported that the biofeedback techniques have helped improve his/her attention span, impulse control, and ability to relax.

C. The client has not found the biofeedback techniques useful in improving his/her attention span, impulse control, or ability to relax.

53. Use Heartbeat Audiotapes

A. The client was instructed to utilize the Heartbeat Audiotapes (Lamb) to improve his/her attention and concentration while studying or learning new material.

B. The client reported that the Heartbeat Audiotapes have helped to improve his/her attention while studying.

C. The client reported little to no improvement in his/her ability to concentrate and stay focused through the use of the Heartbeat Audiotapes.

AUTISM/PERVASIVE DEVELOPMENTAL DISORDER

CLIENT PRESENTATION

1. Aloof/Unresponsive (1)*

A. The client presented in an aloof, unresponsive manner.

B. The client showed virtually no interest in the counseling process or in even small interactions with the therapist.

C. All attempts to connect with the client were met with no discernable response.

D. The client has begun to respond in small ways to the therapist's interaction attempts.

2. Detached/Uninterested (1)

A. The client presented in a detached manner with no interest in others outside of self.

B. The parents reported that the client has a history of pervasive disinterest in other people.

C. The client has started to acknowledge others on a somewhat consistent basis.

D. The client has shown more interest in relating with the therapist in sessions.

3. Social Connectedness (2)

A. The client has little to no interest in social relationships.

B. The parents indicated that the client from an early age has not shown interest in friendships or other social relationships.

C. With encouragement, the client has started to interact on a limited basis with a select peer.

D. The client has started to show somewhat more interest in connecting with the therapist, family members, and selected peer(s).

4. Nonverbal/Rigid (3)

A. The client was rigid and nonverbal in his/her interactions during the session.

B. The parents indicated that the client rarely verbalizes unless he/she is disturbed or upset.

C. The client has started to speak with the therapist at intervals in the sessions.

D. The client has begun to initiate verbalizations with the parents and therapist on a regular basis.

5. Lack of Social/Emotional Spontaneity (3)

A. The client exhibited virtually no spontaneity in his/her mood or behavior.

B. The client remains unchanged in his/her emotional presentation when others show emotion.

C. The client has at times shown glimmers of spontaneity.

---

* The numbers in parentheses correlate to the number of the Behavioral Definition statement in the companion chapter with same title in *The Child Psychotherapy Treatment Planner* (Jongsma, Peterson, and McInnis) by John Wiley & Sons, 2000.

6. Language Deficits (4)

A. The parents reported significant delays in the client's language development.

B. The client has developed only a few words, at far below developmental language expectations.

C. The client has engaged in very limited verbalizations with the therapist during sessions.

D. There has been a slight increase in the client's skill and use of language with others.

E. There has been a significant increase in the client's skill and use of language with others.

7. Conversation Deficits (5)

A. The parents reported significant delays in the client's language development.

B. The parents reported that the client has never demonstrated conversational skills with family members.

C. The parents reported that the client has given brief responses to their inquiries on occasion.

D. The parents reported slight improvements in the client's ability to initiate conversations and verbalize single-word responses to their initiatives.

8. Speech and Language Oddities (6)

A. The client presented with a variety of speech oddities such as echolalia and pronominal reversal.

B. The client used metaphorical language as his/her primary speech pattern throughout the therapy session.

C. The client frequently echoed sounds and words he/she heard from the therapist during the session.

D. The parents indicated that the client's language oddities have increased and intensified as he/she has grown older.

E. The parents reported that all their attention and the help of professionals to interrupt and advance the client's speech patterns have been frustrating and nonproductive.

F. The client's speech oddities have decreased as he/she has started to communicate with others in a didactic manner.

9. Inflexible/Repetitive Behavior (7)

A. The parents and school officials reported that the client demonstrates an inflexible adherence to repetition of nonfunctual rituals or stereotyped motor mannerisms.

B. The parents reported that the client becomes upset if his/her behavioral routine is changed or interrupted.

C. The client has started to decrease his/her repetitive behaviors and seems more open to trying some different activities.

D. The client was willing to engage in a new activity during today's therapy session.

E. The client did not exhibit his/her stereotypical motor movements during today's therapy session.

10. Preoccupied/Focused (8)

A. The parents reported that the client appears to be preoccupied nearly all of the time and focused on narrowly selected objects or areas of interest.

B. It has been nearly impossible to intrude on the client's preoccupation or break his/her focus.

C. The client has started to allow others to interrupt his/her preoccupation and focus.

D. The client has recently been less focused and preoccupied with only one thing, and open to new outside stimulants.

11. Impaired Intellectual/Cognitive Functioning (9)

A. The client exhibits marked impairments in his/her intellectual and cognitive functioning.

B. The parents indicated that it is difficult to follow and understand the client's thought process.

C. The client's thinking has often been unaffected by the thoughts and feedback from others.

D. The client has begun to show some positive improvements in his/her intellectual and cognitive functioning.

12. Intellectual Variability (9)

A. The client has demonstrated considerable variability in his/her level of intellectual functioning.

B. The client demonstrated severe deficits in his/her language and verbal comprehension skills, but has shown significant advances in very focused areas.

13. Resistance to Change (10)

A. The client has been resistant to outside stimulation and attempts to engage him/her.

B. Parents and teachers reported that the client is very resistant to any changes in his/her daily schedule, routine, or behaviors.

C. The client has started to tolerate small changes in his/her routine without becoming resistant.

D. The client has recently begun to try new things with the therapist without any show of resistance.

14. Angry/Aggressive (10)

A. The client's mood and behavior are often punctuated by angry and aggressive outbursts.

B. The client has often reacted to others with anger and aggression when they have attempted to interact or connect with him/her.

C. The client has often overreacted with anger and aggression to minor changes in his/her routine or environment.

D. The client has recently started to react with less anger and aggression to changes in his/her routine or environment.

15. Flat Affect (11)

A. The parents reported that the client's affect often appears flat and constricted.

B. The parents reported that the client only becomes animated and spontaneous in his/her emotional presentation on rare occasions.

C. The client has begun to show more affect in interacting with the therapist.

D. The client became animated in his/her emotional presentation when discussing a topic of interest.

16. Self-Abuse (12)

A. The client has exhibited a pattern of self-abusive behaviors such as head banging and hitting self.

B. The parents reported that the client becomes self-abusive when he/she is frustrated.

C. The client demonstrated self-abusive behaviors in today's therapy session.

D. The client has decreased the frequency of his/her episodes of self-abuse.

E. The client did not engage in any self-abusive behavior in today's therapy session.

INTERVENTIONS IMPLEMENTED

1. Assess Cognitive and Intellectual Functioning (1)*

A. An intellectual and cognitive assessment was conducted on the client to determine his/her strengths and weaknesses.

B. The client was uncooperative and resistive in the assessment process.

C. The client was cooperative during the intellectual and cognitive assessment and appeared to put forth satisfactory to good effort.

2. Speech/Language Evaluation Referral (2)

A. The client was referred for a speech and language evaluation.

B. The client was cooperative throughout the entire speech and language evaluation process.

C. Due to client resistance, the speech and language evaluation could not be completed.

D. With urging of the parents and the therapist, the client followed through with the speech and language evaluation with only minimal resistance.

3. Neurological/Neuropsychological Evaluation Referral (3)

A. The client was referred for neuropsychological testing to rule out organic factors.

B. The client was cooperative during the neurological evaluation or neuropsychological testing.

C. With parent encouragement, the client followed through and completed the neurological evaluation.

D. Neuropsychological testing could not be completed as the client was not cooperative.

E. The parents were helped in seeing the need for neuropsychological testing.

---

* The numbers in parentheses correlate to the number of the Therapeutic Interventions statement in the companion chapter with same title in *The Child Psychotherapy Treatment Planner* (Jongsma, Peterson, and McInnis) by John Wiley & Sons, 2000.

4. Evaluation Feedback (4)

A. The parents were asked to sign appropriate releases of information in order for the therapist to consult with each evaluating specialist.

B. Specialists were conferred with to obtain the results of the client's evaluations.

C. The results and recommendations of the evaluations were given and explained to the parents.

D. The parents' questions regarding the evaluation results were encouraged and answered.

E. The parents were encouraged to follow through on all recommendations of each evaluation.

5. Psychiatric Evaluation Referral (5)

A. The client was referred for a psychiatric evaluation.

B. With the parents' assistance, the client followed through with and completed a psychiatric evaluation.

C. A psychiatric evaluation could not be completed as the client was uncooperative and nonverbal.

D. The client was placed on medication to help stabilize his/her moods and decrease the intensity of his/her angry outbursts.

E. The client was placed on a trial of stimulant medication to help increase his/her attention span, decrease distractibility, and lower the level of his/her hyperactivity.

6. Complete an IEPC (6)

A. An Individualized Educational Planning Committee (IEPC) meeting was held to determine the client's eligibility for special education services, to design educational interventions, and to establish goals.

B. The decision was made at the IEPC meeting that the client is eligible to receive special education services under the classification of Autistic Impaired (AI).

C. The decision was made at the IEPC meeting that the client is not eligible to receive special education services.

D. Consulted with the client's parents, teachers, and other appropriate professionals about designing educational interventions to help the client achieve his/her academic goals.

E. The client's academic goals were identified at the IEPC meeting.

7. Design Effective Teaching Program (7)

A. The client's parents, teachers, and other appropriate school officials were consulted about designing effective teaching programs or interventions that build on the client's strengths and compensate for his/her weaknesses.

B. The client's learning strengths and weaknesses were identified in the consultation meeting with his/her parents, teachers, and other appropriate school officials.

C. The client's parents, teachers, and other appropriate school officials were consulted about the ways to maximize the client's learning strengths.

D. The client's parents, teachers, and other appropriate school officials were consulted about ways to compensate for the client's learning weaknesses.

E. The effectiveness of previously designed learning programs or interventions was evaluated and adjustments were made where indicated.

8. Explore Need for Alternative Placement (8)

A. The client's parents, school officials, or mental health professionals were consulted about the need for placing him/her in a foster home, group home, or residential program.

B. After consulting with the client's parents, school officials, or mental health professionals, the recommendation was made that the client should be placed in a foster home.

C. The recommendation was made that the client be placed in a group home or residential program to address his/her intellectual, academic, social, and emotional needs.

D. Placement of the client in a foster home, group home, or residential program was not recommended during the consultation meeting with his/her parents, school officials, or mental health professionals.

9. Speech/Language Therapy Referral (9)

A. The client was referred to a speech and language pathologist.

B. The parents and the client have followed through on referral and have been regularly attending speech therapy sessions.

C. The client has been cooperative in speech and language therapy and those skills are improving.

D. Speech therapy has not been effective, as the client remains uncooperative and resistant.

10. Build Therapeutic Trust (10)

A. Attempts were made to build the level of trust with the client through consistent eye contact, active listening, unconditional positive regard, and warm acceptance.

B. The therapy session was successful in building a basic level of trust with the client.

C. An initial level of trust has been established with the client as demonstrated by his/her increased verbalizations with the therapist.

D. Despite the use of warm acceptance, frequent attention, and unconditional positive regard, the client has remained aloof and detached in his/her interactions with the therapist.

11. Increase Initiation of Verbalizations (11)

A. The client was given frequent praise and positive reinforcement to increase his/her initiation of verbalizations and responses to others.

B. A reward system was designed and implemented to reinforce the client's initiation of verbalizations.

C. A reward system was designed and implemented to increase the client's acknowledgment and responsiveness to others' verbalizations.

D. The use of praise and positive reinforcement has been successful in increasing the client's initiation of verbalizations and responsiveness to others' verbalizations.

E. Despite being given frequent praise and positive reinforcement, the client has continued to initiate verbalizations with others only on rare or infrequent occasions.

12. Facilitate Language Development (12)

A. The speech therapist assisted in designing and implementing a response-shaping program for the client, with positive reinforcement principles.

B. The parents were trained in the response-shaping program and are implementing it with the client in their daily family life.

C. The client has cooperated with the response-shaping program and its positive reinforcement principle, and this has resulted in significant gains in his/her language skills.

D. The client has minimally embraced the response-shaping program and this has resulted in small gains in his/her language development.

13. Support Parental Language Development Efforts (13)

A. Encouragement, support, and reinforcement were given to the parents in their efforts to foster the client's language development.

B. Various modeling methods were demonstrated to the parents to aid them in fostering the client's language development.

C. The parents' efforts in fostering language development in the client have produced noticeable gains.

D. Gains in language development were encouraged and reinforced with the client and the parents.

14. Teach Behavioral Management Techniques (14)

A. Behavioral management techniques (e.g., time-out, response cost, overcorrection, removal of privileges) were taught to the parents to assist them in handling the client's difficult behaviors.

B. Plans were developed with the parents for implementing behavioral management techniques into their day-to-day parenting of the client.

C. Role-playing and behavioral rehearsal techniques were used with the parents to give them opportunity to practice new skills.

D. The parents were verbally reinforced for their consistent use of behavioral management techniques.

E. Behavioral management techniques were reinforced and evaluated for their effectiveness with the client.

15. Design Token Economy (15)

A. The parents were assisted in designing a token economy and the planning of how to implement and administer it.

B. The token economy was monitored for its effectiveness and for the possible need to make adjustments.

C. The parents' effective, consistent implementation and administration of token economy were reinforced with praise and encouragement.

D. The client's embracing of the token economy has produced improvement in his/her social skills, anger management, impulse control, and language development.

E. The client has resisted cooperating with the token economy system.

16. Design Reward System (16)

A. A reward system was designed to help improve the client's social skills.

B. A reward system was designed to help improve the client's anger control.

C. The parents were helped to identify a list of positive reinforcers to be used to improve the client's social skills and anger control.

D. The parents were asked to make a verbal commitment to implement and administer a reward system.

E. The reward system has resulted in slight, moderate, significant (circle one) improvements in the client's social skills and anger control.

17. Stop Self-Abuse with Aversive Techniques (17)

A. Aversive therapy techniques were used with the client to decrease self-abusive and self-stimulating behavior.

B. The parents were trained in aversive techniques and encouraged to implement them in their daily parenting.

C. Role playing was used with the parents to give them opportunity to practice aversive techniques.

D. Self-abusive behaviors have decreased due to the use of aversive techniques.

18. Stop Self-Abuse with Positive Reinforcement (18)

A. The parents were assisted in developing positive reinforcement interventions to manage self-abusive behaviors.

B. Interventions developed by the parents to terminate the client's self-abuse were implemented and monitored for their effectiveness.

C. New interventions of positive reinforcement and response cost have reduced the client's self-abusive behaviors.

D. The parents' effective interventions on self-abusive behavior were affirmed and reinforced.

19. Encourage Structured Family Interaction (19)

A. Family members were encouraged to include structured work and play times with the client in their daily routine.

B. The parents developed and implemented structured work and play times with the client.

C. Structured play and work times have improved the client's social initiation and interest in others.

D. The client was assigned a task to perform in the family to provide him/her with a sense of responsibility or belonging.

E. The client was given praise in today's therapy session for the successful completion of his/her assigned task.

20. Build Trust and Mutual Dependence (20)

A. A task was assigned to the client and the parents to foster trust and mutual dependence.

B. The parents and client were helped to identify a list of activities they could perform at home to build trust and mutual dependence.

C. The parents and family members were strongly encouraged to include the client in outings or activities on a regular basis.

D. A family therapy session was held to explore family members' resistance or objections to including the client in some outings or activities.

E. The level of trust and mutual dependence between the client and parents has increased as they continue to follow through on the recommendation to engage in regular activities together.

21. Involve Detached Parent (21)

A. The detached parent(s) were strongly encouraged to increase their involvement in the client's daily life, leisure activities, or schoolwork.

B. The detached parent was instructed to spend ____ minutes (fill in number) daily with the client in social or physical interaction.

C. The detached parent was given the assignment of helping the client with his/her homework assignments.

D. The detached parent was praised and reinforced for increasing his/her involvement in the client's everyday life.

E. Despite efforts to increase his/her involvement, the detached parent has become only slightly more involved.

22. Educate Family on Developmental Disabilities (22)

A. The parents and family members were educated on the maturation process in individuals with autism and pervasive development disorders.

B. Challenges in the maturation process for the client were identified and processed with the parents and family members.

C. Unrealistic maturation expectations by the parents and family members were confronted and addressed.

D. Realistic hope and encouragement with respect to the client's maturation and development were reinforced in the parents and other family members.

23. Use Respite Care (23)

A. Options for respite care were given and explained to the parents.

B. Advantages to using respite care were identified and the parents were encouraged to use this resource regularly.

C. Resistance on the parents' part to respite care was confronted and resolved.

D. The parents were asked to develop a regular schedule for respite care.

24. Support Group Referral (24)

A. The parents' opinions and feelings about support groups were explored.

B. The client's parents were referred and encouraged to attend a support group for families of individuals with developmental disabilities.

C. The parents attended an autism/developmental disability support group and indicated that they found the experience positive and helpful.

D. Despite encouragement, the parents have continued to be resistive to any involvement in an autism/developmental disability support group.

25. Autism Society of America Referral (25)

A. The parents were encouraged to join the Autism Society of America to expand their knowledge of the disorder and to gain support and encouragement.

B. The parents have received helpful interaction and gained support and encouragement from their contact with the Autism Society of America.

C. The parents remain hesitant and noncommittal in seeking out support services.

26. Encourage Self-Care Skills (26)

A. Various ways to teach the client self-care skills were processed with his/her parents.

B. The parents have committed to actively working with the client on a daily basis to teach and develop his/her self-care skills.

C. The parents' work with the client has produced significant gains in his/her hygiene and self-care skills.

27. Monitor Self-Care Progress (27)

A. The client's progress in developing self-care skills was monitored, and frequent feedback was provided to reinforce his/her progress.

B. Positive feedback on the client's achievement in self-care skills was verbally acknowledged by the client.

C. The parents were encouraged to keep working toward and reinforcing the client's progress in learning and developing self-care skills.

D. The client's resistance toward developing self-care skills has decreased and his/her daily hygiene has visibly improved.

28. Use Operant Conditioning Principles (28)

A. Operant conditioning principles and response-shaping techniques have been used to develop the client's self-help skills and improve his/her personal hygiene.

B. The parents were taught response-shaping techniques to improve the client's self-help skills and personal hygiene.

C. A reward system was designed to improve the client's self-help skills and personal hygiene.

D. The client and parents were assisted in identifying a list of rewards to reinforce the client's self-help skills and personal hygiene.

E. The reward system and response-shaping techniques have helped to improve the client's self-help skills and personal hygiene.

29. Use "Activities of Daily Living" Program (29)

A. The parents were directed to use the reward system in the "Activities of Daily Living" program from *The Brief Child Therapy Homework Planner* (Jongsma, Peterson, and McInnis) to improve the client's personal hygiene and self-help skills.

B. The parents were strongly encouraged to praise and reinforce the client for improvements in his/her personal hygiene and self-help skills.

C. The parents reported that the "Activities of Daily Living" program has helped to improve the client's personal hygiene and self-help skills.

D. The parents reported that the client has demonstrated little to no improvement in his/her personal hygiene and self-help skills since using the "Activities of Daily Living" program.

30. Strengthen Parent-Child Bond through Singing (30)

A. The parents were encouraged to sing songs (e.g., nursery rhymes, lullabies, popular hits, songs related to client's interests) with the client to help establish a closer parent-child bond.

B. The parents were encouraged to sing songs with the client to help increase his/her verbalizations in the home.

C. The parents reported that singing songs with the client has helped them to connect with him/her.

D. The parents reported that singing songs with the client has helped to increase his/her verbalizations at home.

E. The parents reported that they have not been able to connect with the client by singing songs with him/her.

31. Employ Filial Play Therapy (31)

A. Filial play therapy approaches have been employed to help increase the parents' awareness of the client's thoughts, feelings, and needs.

B. The parents' involvement in the play therapy sessions has helped them establish a closer bond with the client.

C. The filial play therapy sessions have helped increase the parents' awareness of the client's thoughts, feelings, and needs.

D. The parents demonstrated empathy and support for the client's expression of thoughts and feelings in today's filial play therapy session.

32. Allow Family Members' Expression of Feelings (32)

A. A family therapy session was held to provide the parents and siblings an opportunity to share and work through their feelings pertaining to the client's pervasive developmental disorder.

B. The family members were educated about the client's symptoms of autism and pervasive developmental disorder.

C. The parents were given the opportunity to express their thoughts and feelings about raising a child with autism or pervasive developmental disorder.

D. The parents and siblings were given support in verbalizing their feelings of sadness, hurt, anger, and disappointment about having a child or sibling with a pervasive developmental disorder.

E. The parents were helped to work through their feelings of guilt about raising a child with a pervasive developmental disorder.

33. Redirect Preoccupation (33)

A. The client's preoccupation with objects and restricted areas of interests were redirected to more productive and socially involved activities.

B. The client's willingness and cooperation in trying new activities were affirmed and positively reinforced.

C. The client has accepted redirection and become actively engaged in several productive activities.

D. The client was reminded and redirected when he/she started again to become preoccupied with objects.

34. Observe Positive Behaviors (34)

A. The parents were instructed to observe and record positive behaviors by the client between therapy sessions.

B. The parents were encouraged to praise and reinforce the client for engaging in any positive behaviors.

C. The client was praised in today's therapy session for his/her positive behaviors.

D. The client was strongly encouraged to continue to engage in the positive and/or adaptive behaviors to help improve his/her self-esteem, gain parents' approval, and receive affirmation from others.

E. The client demonstrated very little responsiveness to the praise he/she was given for positive or adaptive behaviors.

35. Employ Art Therapy Techniques (35)

A. Art therapy techniques were employed to help the client express his/her basic needs or emotions.

B. Art therapy techniques were employed to help the client establish rapport with the therapist.

C. Art therapy techniques were employed to facilitate a closer parent-child relationship.

D. Art therapy techniques helped the client express basic emotions and identify his/her needs.

E. The client was uncooperative and resistant to engage during the art therapy session.

36. Use "Feelings" Poster (36)

A. The Feelings Poster (available from Childswork/Childsplay, LLC) was used to help the client identify and express his/her basic emotions.

B. The parents were encouraged to use the Feelings Poster at home to help the client identify and express his/her basic emotions.

C. The parents were encouraged to use the Feelings Poster at home when the client starts to become agitated or angry, to help prevent an outburst.

D. The parents reported that the Feelings Poster has helped the client identify and express his/her basic emotions.

E. Use of the Feelings Poster has produced little to no improvement in the client's ability to identify and express his/her feelings.

37. Consultation to Increase Client's Social Contacts (37)

A. The parents and teachers were consulted about ways to increase the frequency of the client's social contacts with peers.

B. Recommendation was made that the client be assigned a student aide in the classroom.

C. The parents were encouraged to talk to their minister or church leaders about placing the client in a Sunday school class or other small group.

D. The parents were encouraged to register the client for the Special Olympics to increase his/her social contacts with peers.

E. The parents followed through with the recommendations to increase the frequency of the client's social contacts with peers.

38. Summer Camp Referral (38)

A. The client was referred to a summer camp program for special-needs children to foster his/her social contacts.

B. The parents followed through with the recommendation to enroll the client in a summer camp program.

C. The parents reported that the client's summer camp experience was beneficial in fostering his/her social contacts.

D. The client expressed happiness about attending the summer camp program and verbalized a desire to return next year.

39. Applied Behavior Analysis (39)

A. An applied behavior analysis program was designed to help alter the client's maladaptive behaviors in the home and/or school.

B. An applied behavior analysis program was designed and implemented in the residential setting to alter the client's maladaptive behaviors.

C. The specific target behaviors were clearly defined and operationalized.

D. The antecedents and consequences of the target behaviors were selected.

E. The client's responses to the reinforcement interventions have been observed and recorded.

F. The applied behavior analysis program has helped to decrease the frequency and intensity of the client's maladaptive behaviors.

40. Referral for Vision/Hearing Examination (40)

A. The client was referred for a vision and/or hearing examination to rule out problems that may be interfering with his/her social and speech/language development.

B. The findings from the vision examination did not reveal any problems with the client's vision.

C. The findings from the hearing examination did not reveal any problems with the client's hearing.

D. The vision examination revealed the presence of vision problems.

E. The hearing examination revealed the presence of a hearing loss.

41. Referral for Medical Examination (41)

A. The client was referred for a medical examination to rule out possible health problems that may be interfering with his/her speech/language development.

B. The parents followed through with the recommendation to seek a medical examination to rule out possible health problems that may be contributing to the client's speech/language development.

C. The parents have failed to follow through with seeking a medical examination, and were encouraged to do so to rule out possible health problems that may be interfering with the client's speech/language development.

D. The findings from the medical examination did not reveal the presence of any health problems that may be interferring with the client's speech/language development.

E. The findings from the medical examination revealed that the client's health problems and/or physical condition have interfered with his/her speech/language development.

BLENDED FAMILY

CLIENT PRESENTATION

1. Angry/Hostile (1)*

A. Anger and hostility have dominated the client's manner since the parents have blended their two families.

B. The client was extremely angry and hostile about having to be a part of the new blended family.

C. The client's level of anger and hostility has started to diminish as he/she has accepted being a part of the new blended family.

D. The client has dropped his/her anger and hostility and has become a cooperative member of the blended family.

2. Frustrated/Tense (1)

A. There was a deep sense of frustration and tension present in the client as he/she talked of the blended family situation.

B. The client reported being frustrated and tense about feeling pushed into a new blended family.

C. The client's level of tension has subsided as he/she is feeling more comfortable with the idea of being a part of a stepfamily.

3. Rejected/Betrayed (1)

A. The client reported feeling betrayed and rejected since his/her parents' remarriage.

B. The client has felt a sense of rejection and mistrust from the new stepparent.

C. The feelings of betrayal and rejection within the client have decreased, and he/she is beginning to form a cordial relationship with stepparent.

4. Resistant toward Stepparent (2)

A. The client presented in a defiant manner toward the stepparent.

B. In a defiant way, the client reported he/she will have nothing to do with the new stepparent.

C. The client threatened to make it difficult for the new stepparent.

D. The client has dropped some of the resistance and seems to be warming a little to the new stepparent.

5. Defiant of Stepparent (2)

A. The client showed a pattern of making alliances and causing conflicts in an attempt to have a degree of control over the new stepparent.

B. The client reported no interest in taking direction or accepting limits from the stepparent.

---

* The numbers in parentheses correlate to the number of the Behavioral Definition statement in the companion chapter with same title in *The Child Psychotherapy Treatment Planner* (Jongsma, Peterson, and McInnis) by John Wiley & Sons, 2000.

C. Gradually, the client has begun to give up his/her rebellion toward the stepparent and to accept some direction from him/her.

6. Stepsibling Conflict (3)

A. The siblings have engaged in ongoing conflict with one another.

B. The two sibling groups stated clearly their dislike and resentment for one another.

C. The parents indicated their frustration with the siblings' apparent attempt to sabotage their efforts to form a new family group.

D. The two sibling groups have stopped their open conflicts and started to tolerate and show basic respect for each other.

7. Defiance of Stepparent (4)

A. The client presented a negativistic, defiant attitude toward the stepparent.

B. The client seemed very closed and extremely resistant to the new stepparent.

C. The limited disclosures by the client reflected strong resistance to joining the new blended family.

D. The client has started to be a little open and a little warmer to the idea of being a member of the new blended family.

8. Threats of Moving to Other Parent's House (5)

A. The parents reported feeling like hostages to siblings' threats to move to the other parent's home whenever the children were crossed or told no.

B. The siblings presented as being ambivalent and manipulative regarding where they would like to live and why.

C. The siblings indicated they have changed their minds several times regarding where they want to reside and are presently still undecided.

D. The siblings have decreased their threats of going to the other parent's home and have started to join the new family unit.

9. Ex-Spouse Interference (6)

A. Each spouse reported frequent incidents of interference in their new family by their ex-spouses.

B. Ex-spouse interference has caused ongoing conflict and upheaval in the new family unit.

C. Efforts to keep ex-spouses out of the new family business have been unsuccessful and sabotaged by the siblings.

D. Efforts to keep ex-spouses out of the daily life of the new family have started to be effective and the new family has started to solidify and become connected.

10. Parental Anxiety (7)

A. The client's parents presented with anxiety about the blending of their two families.

B. The parents seemed unsure about how to respond to issues being raised by the new blended family.

C. The parents looked for reassurance and some sense of security about how best to respond to blended family issues.

D. Parental anxiety has decreased as both parties have become more comfortable with working toward forming a new blended family.

11. Lack of Responsibility Definitions (8)

A. The family presented as very chaotic, lacking clear boundaries, rules, and responsibility definitions for members.

B. The parents reported they have struggled in their attempts to establish clear definitions of expectations for responsibility for family members.

C. Siblings indicated that they are not clear about their roles, responsibilities, or expectations in their new family.

D. The family has begun to develop and institute clear areas of responsibility for all members, which has also reduced the chaos and confusion for all.

12. Internal Loyalty Conflicts (9)

A. There seemed to be a great deal of ambivalence and uncertainty within the client about whether to attach himself/herself to the stepparent.

B. The client verbalized loyalty toward the biological, noncustodial parent.

C. The client reported fearing hurting the feelings of the biological, noncustodial parent if an attachment were to be made to the stepparent.

D. Internal conflicts have been resolved, and a sense of loyalty and belonging are beginning to develop between the client and the stepparent.

INTERVENTIONS IMPLEMENTED

1. Build Trust (1)*

A. Warm acceptance and active listening techniques were utilized to establish the basis for a trust relationship with the client.

B. The client seems to have formed a trust-based relationship with the therapist and has started to share his/her feelings.

C. Despite the use of active listening, warm acceptance, and unconditional positive regard, the client and family appear to be hesitant to trust the therapist and share their feelings and conflicts.

2. Employ Cooperative Family Drawing (2)

A. Each family member took part in interpreting and listening to others' interpretations of a drawing that was made through the cooperative effort of all family members.

B. All family members were willing to take part in making the family drawing, but were resistant to interpreting it.

C. The family drawing exercise revealed that the family members have a very difficult time cooperating with each other, as there was resistance to the exercise and bickering within the family during the exercise.

* The numbers in parentheses correlate to the number of the Therapeutic Interventions statement in the companion chapter with same title in *The Child Psychotherapy Treatment Planner* (Jongsma, Peterson, and McInnis) by John Wiley & Sons, 2000.

3. Utilize Child-Centered Play Therapy (3)

A. Child-centered play-therapy sessions were conducted with the client to assist him/her in resolving issues of adjusting to and cooperating with a new stepfamily.

B. A child-centered play-therapy approach was utilized to display trust in the client's capacity to resolve the issues surrounding adjustment to a new family.

C. The client actively participated in the child-centered play-therapy sessions.

D. The client's active involvement in the child-centered play-therapy sessions has helped him/her to begin to resolve the issues of being a part of a new stepfamily.

4. Encourage Expression of Feelings (4)

A. Play-therapy sessions were conducted to provide the client with an opportunity to express the feelings surrounding loss and changes in his/her life.

B. The client was given the opportunity to express feelings about loss and changes in his/her life in today's therapy session.

C. The client was guarded and resistant to expressing any feelings about loss and changes in his/her life in the play-therapy session.

D. The client effectively utilized the play-therapy session as he/she openly expressed feelings connected to loss and/or changes in his/her life.

5. Emphasize Respect and Cooperation (5)

A. The need for respect and cooperation among all family members was emphasized in play, sibling, and family therapy sessions.

B. Respect and cooperation were modeled for the family and emphasized in family therapy sessions.

C. Gentle, respectful confrontation and redirection were utilized when members were disrespectful of each other or uncooperative in sibling and family therapy sessions.

D. Puppets were used in play-therapy sessions to create scenarios that could provide opportunities to emphasize respect and cooperation among family members.

E. Barriers to respect and cooperation were explored, identified, and resolved with the family members.

F. The positive value and benefits of respect and cooperation between family members were identified, emphasized, and reinforced in family therapy sessions.

6. Address Family and Marital Issues (6)

A. Family sessions were conducted that focused on addressing and facilitating relationship building and joining rituals.

B. Each family member was asked to make a list of his/her recent losses to share with other members in a family session.

C. The parents were educated in the dynamics of stepfamilies and how they work.

D. Conflict negotiation skills were taught to family members and practiced in role-play situations particular to stepfamilies.

E. Family members have gained information and understanding about stepfamilies, learning to use negotiation skills and building relationships with each other.

7. List Expectations for New Family (7)

A. Each family member was asked to list his/her expectations for the new family.

B. Each family member's list or expectations regarding the future of the blended family was shared and processed in family session, with common realistic expectations being affirmed and reinforced.

C. Unrealistic expectations of family members were gently confronted and reframed into more realistic and attainable expectations.

8. Remind Family of Instant Love Myth (8)

A. The family was reminded of the myth of "instant love" between new members.

B. Family members' expectations of instant love and connections between blended family members were confronted with the reality that time is necessary for relationships to grow.

C. All the family members have become more realistic regarding the time necessary for meaningful relationships to develop between them.

9. Reinforce Kindness and Respect (9)

A. The family was reminded that new members need not love or like each other but that they need to treat each other with kindness and respect.

B. Family members were confronted when they failed to treat each other with kindness and respect.

C. The parents were taught ways to model respect and kindness for all members and to confront and give consequences for disrespectful interactions.

D. There is a discernable growth of respect and consideration among new family members that is being positively reinforced by the parents.

10. Read *Changing Families* (10)

A. The family was asked to read *Changing Families* (Fassler, Lash, and Ives) to identify and reinforce the recent changes each has experienced in family life.

B. The family members struggled to identify the losses and changes that each had experienced, even after reading *Changing Families*.

C. The family was reminded that change is an opportunity to grow and thrive, not just survive.

D. After reading *Changing Families,* the family members have a better understanding of the difficult process they have gone through recently in forming the blended family.

11. List Losses and Changes (11)

A. Each sibling was asked to make a list of all the losses and changes he/she had experienced in the last year.

B. Each sibling's list of losses was shared with other family members and similarities between the lists were identified.

C. Reviewing each sibling's list of losses enhanced the degree of understanding and the feeling of similarity between the siblings.

12. Assign "Tearing Paper" Exercise (12)

A. The "Tearing Paper" exercise (Dawes) was given and the guidelines were explained to the family.

B. The family actively participated in the "Tearing Paper" exercise and followed the guidelines set for the exercise.

C. The experience of doing the "Tearing Paper" exercise was processed with the family regarding the positive aspects of releasing energy and emotion.

D. The family was given positive verbal feedback for their follow-through and cooperation with cleaning up after the "Tearing Paper" exercise.

13. Play Games to Promote Self-Understanding (13)

A. The family was directed to play either The Ungame (Ungame Company) or The Thinking, Feeling, Doing Game (Gardner) to increase members' awareness of themselves and their feelings.

B. Expressions of self-awareness and identification of feelings were reinforced in family sessions.

C. The family members were very uncomfortable during the playing of therapeutic games together and most of them had significant difficulty in identifying and expressing feelings.

14. Educate Family Regarding Feelings (14)

A. The family was taught the basic concepts regarding identifying, labeling, and appropriately expressing their feelings.

B. Through the use of role playing and modeling, each family member was assisted in identifying, labeling, and expressing their feelings in family sessions.

C. Family members were prompted when they ignored or skipped over their feelings in dealing with family issues.

15. Use Feelings Charts (15)

A. Feelings charts, cards, and felt board were utilize to help the family increase their skills in identifying and expressing feelings.

B. The parents were encouraged to use a feelings chart and cards with children at home as a family activity.

C. Positive verbal recognition and reinforcement were given to the family members when they identified or expressed feelings in sessions.

D. Each family member has shown an increased ability to recognize and appropriately express his/her feelings.

16. Practice Identifying and Expressing Feelings (16)

A. Various feelings exercises were used with the family to help expand their ability to identify and express feelings.

B. Positive affirmation was given to family members when they identified and expressed their feelings appropriately.

C. Each family member was confronted and reminded when they were not identifying and expressing their feelings.

17. Read Books on Blended Families (17)

A. Parents and teens were asked to read all or sections of *Stepfamily Realities* (Neuman) and *Stepfamilies Stepping Ahead* (Stepfamily Association of American) to expand their knowledge of stepfamily dynamics.

B. Parents and teens were encouraged to talk with other stepfamilies and to gather knowledge of their experience, past and present.

C. Parents and teens were asked to make a list of questions they had about stepfamilies and to process this list with the therapist.

D. Reading books on blended families and talking to other people who have experienced successful blending of families has helped members gather information and develop understanding of the blending process.

18. Stepfamily Association Referral (18)

A. The parents were referred to the Stepfamily Association of America in order to gather information on the process of blending families.

B. Information gathered from the Stepfamily Association of America was processed and incorporated into a more realistic view of the reality of stepfamilies.

C. The reality that stepfamilies are not inferior to regular families, just different, was introduced, along with the new information the parents received from the Stepfamily Association of America.

D. The parents have not followed through on obtaining further information from the Stepfamily Association of America and were again encouraged to do so.

19. Read *How to Win as a Stepfamily* (19)

A. The parents were asked to read *How to Win as a Stepfamily* (Visher and Visher).

B. Key concepts from the parents' reading of *How to Win as a Stepfamily* were identified and reinforced.

C. Several ideas learned from reading *How to Win as a Stepfamily* were implemented by the parents in their present situations.

D. The parents have not completed the assignment to read *How to Win as a Stepfamily* and were encouraged to do so.

20. Build Negotiating Skills (20)

A. The family members were taught essential negotiating skills.

B. Role play was utilized to give family members the opportunity to practice new skills in negotiating conflicts.

C. The family members tried out their new negotiation skills in a family session on a present family conflict.

D. The family struggled to stay with negotiating skills in the family sessions, and they often reverted to arguing and attacking each other.

21. "Negotiating a Peace Treaty" Exercise (21)

A. The siblings were asked to complete and process the "Negotiating a Peace Treaty" exercise from *The Brief Adolescent Therapy Homework Planner* (Jongsma, Peterson, and McInnis).

B. Through the use of the "Negotiating a Peace Treaty" exercise, the clients were assisted in identifying their conflicts and exploring a variety of solutions.

C. The siblings were asked to select, commit to, and implement one of the solutions they identified in the negotiation exercise.

D. The siblings' completion of the negotiation exercise revealed how far apart they are in terms of having any common ground.

22. Use Humor to Decrease Tension (22)

A. Humor was injected into sessions when it was appropriate to decrease tension and to model balance and perspective.

B. Each family member was directed to tell one joke daily to other family members.

C. Positive feedback was given to family members who created appropriate humor during a session.

D. The family members have extreme difficulty being light and humorous toward each other, as tension levels are high and teasing is reacted to angrily.

23. "Cloning the Perfect Sibling" Exercise (23)

A. Siblings were asked to complete the "Cloning the Perfect Sibling" exercise from *The Brief Adolescent Therapy Homework Planner* (Jongsma, Peterson, and McInnis).

B. In processing the cloning exercise, siblings were assisted in identifying and affirming the positive aspects of individual differences.

C. Siblings continued to argue and bicker with each other, complaining about unique traits and characteristics.

24. Normalize Conflict as a Stage (24)

A. A brief solution-focused intervention was utilized with the family to "normalize" conflict as a stage.

B. Family members were assisted in identifying the next stage after conflict and how they might begin to move in that direction.

C. The intervention of normalizing the conflict as a stage has, according to family reports, reduced the frequency of conflicts.

D. The family was unwilling to embrace any reframing or normalizing interventions.

25. Read *Stone Soup* (25)

A. *Stone Soup* (Brown) was read and processed with the family.

B. After reading *Stone Soup*, the family members were asked to list all the possible positive things that come about when people cooperate and share.

26. Read *The Sneetches* (26)

A. *The Sneetches* (Dr. Seuss) was read and discussed with the family.

B. The folly of perceiving people as top dog, low dog and insider, outsider was seeded with family members.

C. Family members were asked to list each way they felt better than or superior to new members.

27. Encourage Parenting Role for Biological Parent (27)

A. The parents were educated in the positive aspects of each biological parent taking the main role with their children.

B. The parents were assisted in developing ways to redirect the parenting of the stepchildren.

C. The parents were asked to refrain from all negative references to ex-spouses.

D. Incidents of a parent making negative references to ex-spouses were confronted and processed.

28. Parenting Group Referral (28)

A. The parents were referred to a parenting group designed for stepparents.

B. The parents were assisted in implementing new concepts that were learned from the parenting group.

C. The parents were confronted about their poor attendance at the stepparenting group.

29. Institute Family Meeting (29)

A. The parents were assisted in developing a process for and scheduling a weekly family meeting.

B. Family meetings were monitored and the parents were assisted in solving conflictual issues.

C. The parents were given positive verbal support and encouragement for their follow-through on implementing weekly family meetings.

D. The parents have not followed through on implementing regularly scheduled meetings, and a commitment for this scheduling was obtained from them.

30. Develop Family Rituals (30)

A. The positive aspects of family rituals were taught to the parents.

B. The parents were asked to develop a list of possible rituals for their new family unit.

C. The parents were assisted in selecting family rituals and developing a plan for their implementation.

D. Family rituals were monitored for their implementation and effectiveness.

E. Verbal affirmation and encouragement were given to the parents for their effort to implement and enforce new family rituals.

31. Select Past Family Rituals (31)

A. The family members were asked to make a list of rituals that were followed in their previous family.

B. Rituals from previous families were discussed and key rituals were chosen to implement in the new family.

C. Plans were developed to implement the chosen rituals from previous families.

D. The family members were assisted in establishing the new rituals and making the necessary adjustments to increase their effectiveness.

32. Create Birthday Rituals (32)

A. The family was given the assignment of creating new birthday rituals for the new family.

B. The parents were asked to implement the new birthday rituals at the first opportunity.

C. The value of birthday rituals was reinforced with the parents.

D. A new birthday ritual has been implemented, and the family members have responded very favorably to this recognition of their special status.

33. Teach Patterns of Family Interactions (33)

A. The parents were taught key aspects and patterns of family interaction.

B. Past family interaction patterns were explored and identified, with a special focus on those involving triangulation.

C. The parents were assisted in blocking patterns of triangulation that are occurring within the family.

D. The episodes of triangulation within the family have diminished significantly.

34. Identify Triangulation Interaction with Parents (34)

A. A genogram was developed with the family that identified interaction patterns between members.

B. Triangulation patterns of interaction were identified from the genogram, and plans were developed with the parents to break those patterns.

C. Implementation of plans to break triangulation was monitored and evaluated for effectiveness.

D. The parents were reminded when they were observed creating or using triangulation with the family.

E. The episodes of triangulation within the family have diminished significantly.

35. Marital Therapy Referral (35)

A. The parents were referred to a skills-based marital therapy program.

B. Gains made in marital therapy were affirmed and reinforced with the parents.

C. The parents were asked to identify the gains they achieved in the skills-based therapy program and how they would improve parenting.

36. Identify Individual Parental Needs (36)

A. The parents were assisted in exploring and identifying their individual needs within the relationship and family.

B. The needs of each partner were recognized and affirmed, and plans were developed for meeting these needs on a consistent basis.

C. The parents were confronted when they failed to take care of their individual needs and did not follow through on the plans developed to do this.

D. The importance of meeting individual needs in a relationship was reinforced with the parents.

37. Process Sharing of Affection (37)

A. The ways the parents show affection to each other were explored with them in a conjoint session.

B. The negative aspects of blatant displays of parental physical affection were processed with them.

C. The parents were assisted in identifying appropriate ways to show affection to each other when in the presence of their children.

D. The parents were confronted about blatant displays of affection between them, which reminded them of the negative impact this could have on their children.

38. Draw Family Genogram (38)

A. A genogram was developed with the family that included all members and how they are connected.

B. From the genogram, the family was asked to identify the ways in which they see themselves being connected.

C. Constructing the family genogram revealed that some family members are virtually unconnected to other family members, and ways to reverse this fact were discussed.

39. Initiatives Camp Referral (39)

A. The family was asked to attend an initiatives weekend to build trust, cooperation, and the conflict-resolution skills of each family member.

B. The initiatives experience was processed with the family, and each member identified the positive gains he/she received from the weekend.

C. The family was assisted in identifying how they could continue to use and expand on the gains from the weekend.

40. Coat-of-Arms Exercise (40)

A. The family was asked to create a coat of arms for their new family by drawing a collage on poster board.

B. The experience of creating the coat of arms was processed with the family, and both old and new identities were acknowledged and reinforced.

C. The parents were asked to display the coat of arms in their new home.

41. Complete "Cost-Benefit Analysis" Exercise (41)

A. The family was asked to complete the "Cost-Benefit Analysis" exercise (in *Ten Days to Self-Esteem* by Burns) to evaluate a plus-and-minus system of becoming a blended family.

B. The "Cost-Benefit Analysis" exercise was processed, with emphasis on the positives of joining the family.

C. Family members' resistance to working together and accepting one another was confronted using the positive items identified in the "Cost-Benefit Analysis."

42. Plan One-on-One Time (42)

A. The parents were encouraged to build time into their schedules for one-on-one contact with each child and stepchild.

B. The parents were reminded of the importance of taking the time to build parent-child relationships.

43. Emphasize That Relationships Build Slowly (43)

A. Allowing relationships to build slowly was emphasized to the family in family sessions.

B. Ways to build trust in relationships were explored with the parents to help them slowly build relationships with stepchildren.

C. The parents' exhibiting patience in allowing relationships to build was verbally reinforced.

CONDUCT DISORDER/DELINQUENCY

CLIENT PRESENTATION

1. Failure to Comply (1)*

A. The client has demonstrated a persistent failure to comply with the rules or expectations at home, at school, and in the community.

B. The client voiced his/her opposition to the rules at home and school.

C. The client has started to comply with the rules and expectations at home, at school, and in the community.

D. The client verbalized his/her willingness to comply with the rules and expectations at home, at school, and in the community.

E. The client has consistently complied with the rules and expectations at home, at school, and in the community.

2. Aggressive/Destructive Behaviors (2)

A. The client described a series of incidents where he/she became aggressive or destructive when upset or frustrated.

B. The client projected the blame for his/her aggressive/destructive behaviors onto other people.

C. The client has begun to take steps to control his/her hostile/aggressive impulses.

D. The client has recently demonstrated good self-control and not engaged in any aggressive or destructive behaviors.

E. The client has exhibited a significant reduction in the frequency and severity of his/her aggressive or destructive behaviors.

3. Angry/Hostile (2)

A. The client appeared angry, hostile, and irritable during today's session.

B. The client reported incidents of becoming easily angered over trivial matters.

C. The client has recently exhibited frequent angry outbursts at home and school.

D. The client has recently exhibited mild improvements in his/her anger control.

E. The client has demonstrated good control of his/her anger and has not exhibited any major loss-of-control episodes.

4. Stealing (3)

A. The parents reported that the client has an extensive history of stealing from others at home, at school, and in the community.

B. The parents reported that the client was recently caught stealing.

C. The client has not engaged in any stealing in the recent past.

D. The client has stopped stealing and found more effective ways to meet his/her needs.

* The numbers in parentheses correlate to the number of the Behavioral Definition statement in the companion chapter with same title in *The Child Psychotherapy Treatment Planner* (Jongsma, Peterson, and McInnis) by John Wiley & Sons, 2000.

5. Acting-Out/Antisocial Behaviors (3)

A. The parents reported that the client has an extensive history of engaging in acting-out or antisocial behaviors.

B. The client has continued to act out and engage in antisocial behaviors.

C. The client has a tendency to minimize the seriousness of his/her antisocial behaviors.

D. The client verbalized an awareness of how his/her acting-out and antisocial behaviors negatively impact himself/herself and others.

E. The client and parents reported a significant reduction in the frequency and severity of his/her acting-out and antisocial behaviors.

6. School Behavior Problems (4)

A. A review of the client's history revealed numerous acting-out and rebellious behaviors in the school setting.

B. The client has often disrupted the classroom with his/her silly, immature, or negative attention-seeking behaviors.

C. The client has missed a significant amount of time from school due to truancy.

D. The client has started to exercise greater self-control in the classroom setting.

E. The client has recently demonstrated a significant reduction in the frequency of his/her acting-out or rebellious behaviors at school.

7. Authority Conflicts (5)

A. The client displayed a negativistic attitude and was highly argumentative during today's therapy session.

B. The client has often tested the limits and challenged authority figures at home, at school, and in the community.

C. The client has often talked back to authority figures in a disrespectful manner when reprimanded.

D. The client has recently been more cooperative with authority figures.

E. The client has been cooperative and respectful toward authority figures on a consistent basis.

8. Impulsivity (6)

A. The client presented as a highly impulsive individual who seeks immediate gratification of his/her needs and often fails to consider the consequences of his/her actions.

B. The client has engaged in impulsive/thrill-seeking behaviors in order to achieve a sense of excitement and fun.

C. The client has begun to take steps toward improving his/her impulse control and delaying the need for immediate gratification.

D. The client has recently demonstrated good impulse control and has not engaged in any serious acting-out or antisocial behaviors.

E. The client has ceased engaging in acting-out behaviors because of his/her improved ability to stop and think about the consequences of his/her actions.

9. Lying/Conning (7)

A. The client described a pattern of lying, conning, and manipulating others to meet his/her needs and avoid facing the consequences of his/her actions.

B. The client appeared to be lying in the therapy session about his/her misbehaviors or irresponsible actions.

C. The client was honest in the therapy session and admitted to his/her wrongdoing or irresponsibility.

D. The parents reported that the client has been more honest and accepting of their decisions at home.

10. Blaming/Projecting (8)

A. The client was unwilling to accept responsibility for his/her poor decisions and behaviors, instead blaming others as the cause for his/her decisions and actions.

B. The client has begun to accept greater responsibility for his/her actions and placed the blame less often for his/her wrongdoings onto other people.

C. The client admitted to his/her wrongdoings and verbalized an acceptance of responsibility for his/her actions.

11. Lack of Insight (8)

A. The client has demonstrated little insight into the factors contributing to his/her behavioral problems.

B. The client has begun to show some insight into the factors contributing to his/her behavior problems.

C. During the therapy session, the client demonstrated insight into the factors that contributed to his/her behavioral problems.

12. Lack of Remorse/Guilt (9)

A. The client expressed little or no remorse for his/her irresponsible, acting-out, or aggressive behaviors.

B. The client expressed remorse for his/her actions, but apparently only because he/she had been caught and suffered the consequences of his/her actions.

C. The client appeared to express genuine remorse or guilt for his/her misbehavior.

13. Lack of Empathy/Insensitivity (10)

A. The client displayed little concern or empathy for the thoughts, feelings, and needs of other people.

B. The client has often demonstrated a willingness to ride roughshod over the rights of others in order to meet his/her needs.

C. The client verbalized an understanding of how his/her actions negatively impacted others.

D. The client has demonstrated empathy and sensitivity to the thoughts, feelings, and needs of other people.

14. Detached/Guarded (10)

A. The client appeared guarded and defensive during the therapy session.

B. The client was difficult to engage in the therapeutic process and showed little interest in exploring the factors that have contributed to his/her behavioral problems.

C. The client's defensiveness has started to decrease and he/she has demonstrated a greater willingness to explore underlying emotional conflicts.

D. The client was open and talkative about his/her behavioral problems and significant conflicts.

15. Childhood Abuse (10)

A. The client described a history of abuse that correlates to the onset of his/her behavioral problems

B. The client was resistant to discussing past incidents of abuse.

C. The client verbalized feelings of anger, hurt, and sadness about past abusive episodes.

16. Separation/Loss/Abandonment (10)

A. The client reported a history of experiencing significant separations or losses in his/her life.

B. The client was guarded and reticent to talk about past losses or abandonment issues.

C. The client expressed feelings of sadness, hurt, and disappointment about past separations, losses, or abandonment issues.

D. The client vocalized strong feelings of anger about past separations or losses.

INTERVENTIONS IMPLEMENTED

1. Psychological Testing (1)*

A. A psychological evaluation was conducted to determine whether emotional factors or ADHD are contributing to the client's impulsivity and acting-out behaviors.

B. The client was uncooperative and resistant to engaging in the evaluation process.

C. The client approached the psychological testing in an honest, straightforward manner and was cooperative with any requests.

2. Psychoeducational Evaluation (2)

A. The client received a psychoeducational evaluation to rule out the presence of a possible learning disability that could be contributing to his/her impulsivity and acting-out behaviors.

B. The client was uncooperative during the psychoeducational evaluation and did not appear to put forth good effort.

C. The client was cooperative during the psychoeducational evaluation and appeared motivated to do his/her best.

---

* The numbers in parentheses correlate to the number of the Therapeutic Interventions statement in the companion chapter with same title in *The Child Psychotherapy Treatment Planner* (Jongsma, Peterson, and McInnis) by John Wiley & Sons, 2000.

3. Evaluation Feedback (3)

A. Feedback from the psychological testing was given to the client, parents, school officials, or criminal justice officials, and appropriate interventions were discussed.

B. The evaluation findings supported the presence of ADHD, which contributes to the client's tendency toward impulsive responding.

C. The evaluation findings revealed the presence of underlying emotional problems that have contributed to the emergence of impulsive and acting-out behaviors.

D. The findings from the psychoeducational evaluation revealed the presence of a learning disability and the need for special education services.

E. The evaluation process did not reveal the presence of any learning disability, emotional problems, or ADHD that are contributing to the client's impulsive and acting-out behaviors.

4. Consult with Criminal Justice Officials (4)

A. Consulted with criminal justice officials about the need for appropriate consequences for the client's antisocial behavior.

B. The client was placed on probation for his/her antisocial behaviors and instructed to comply with all the rules pertaining to his/her probation.

C. The client agreed to make restitution and/or perform community service for his/her past antisocial behavior.

D. The client was placed in an intensive surveillance treatment program as a consequence of his/her antisocial behavior.

5. Alternative Placement (5)

A. Consulted with parents, school officials, and criminal justice officials about placing the client in an alternative setting because of his/her antisocial behavior.

B. It is recommended that the client be placed in a juvenile detention facility as a consequence of his/her antisocial behavior.

C. It is recommended that the client be placed in a foster home to help prevent recurrences of antisocial behavior.

D. The recommendation was made that the client be placed in a residential program to provide external structure and supervision for the client.

6. Reinforce Legal Consequences (6)

A. The parents were encouraged and challenged not to protect the client from the legal consequences of his/her actions.

B. The parents agreed to contact the police or appropriate criminal justice officials if the client engages in any future antisocial behavior.

C. The parents followed through and contacted the police or probation officer after the client engaged in antisocial behavior.

D. The parents failed to contact the police and/or criminal justice officials after the client engaged in some antisocial behavior.

7. Parental Rules and Boundaries (7)

A. The family therapy session focused on helping establish clearly defined rules and appropriate parent-child boundaries.

B. The parents were able to identify the rules and expectations that the client is expected to comply with at home.

C. The parents were able to identify appropriate consequences for the client's misbehaviors.

D. The parents had difficulty establishing clearly defined rules and identifying appropriate consequences for the client's misbehaviors.

8. Therapeutic Trust (8)

A. An attempt was made to build trust with the client in therapy sessions through consistent eye contact, active listening, unconditional positive regard, and warm acceptance.

B. The client's concerns were listened to closely and his/her feelings were reflected in a nonjudgmental manner.

C. Thoughts and feelings expressed by the client during the therapy session were supported empathetically.

D. The client's mistrustfulness has contributed to his/her reluctance to share underlying thoughts and feelings during the therapy sessions.

9. Connect Feelings and Behavior (9)

A. The session was helpful in identifying underlying painful emotions that contribute to the client's impulsive or reactive behaviors.

B. The client developed insight into how his/her reactive behaviors are connected to underlying feelings of sadness, hurt, and disappointment.

C. Role-playing and modeling techniques were used to demonstrate appropriate ways for the client to express his/her underlying painful emotions.

D. The client was asked to list appropriate ways to express his/her feelings and meet his/her needs instead of impulsively reacting to situations.

10. Confront Antisocial Behavior (10)

A. The client was firmly and consistently confronted with how his/her antisocial behaviors negatively affect himself/herself and others.

B. The client was asked to list the negative consequences of his/her antisocial behavior and negativistic attitude.

C. Role-reversal techniques were used in the therapy session to help the client realize how his/her antisocial behavior negatively impacts others.

D. The client was asked to write a letter of apology to the victim(s) of his/her antisocial behavior.

11. Teach Acceptance of Responsibility (11)

A. The client was consistently confronted and challenged to cease blaming others for his/her misbehaviors and accept greater responsibility for his/her actions.

B. The client was asked to list how his/her poor decisions and irresponsible behavior resulted in negative consequences for himself/herself and others.

C. The client identified ways to resolve conflict and/or meet his/her needs that were more effective than acting out or behaving in an irresponsible manner.

D. The client was instructed to verbally acknowledge his/her wrongdoing and apologize to others.

12. Explore Blaming (12)

A. The underlying factors contributing to the client's pattern of blaming others for his/her misbehavior were explored.

B. The client was challenged to accept the consequences of his/her actions instead of arguing and blaming others.

C. The client identified how the pattern of blaming others is associated with underlying feelings of low self-esteem, inadequacy, and insecurity.

D. The client has modeled other family members' patterns of blaming others.

E. The parents identified natural, logical consequences (e.g., grounding, removing privileges, or taking away desired objects) that can be used if client is caught in a lie.

13. Teach Self-Control Strategies (13)

A. The client was taught mediational and self-control strategies (e.g., relaxation, "stop, look, listen, and think") to help express anger through appropriate verbalizations and healthy physical outlets.

B. The client was asked to identify appropriate and inappropriate ways to express or control anger.

C. The client was encouraged to utilize active listening skills to delay impulses to react with verbal or physical aggression.

D. The client identified healthy physical outlets for his/her strong feelings of anger and aggressive impulses.

14. Self-Monitoring Checklists (14)

A. The client and parents were encouraged to utilize self-monitoring checklists of anger-provoking situations in the home and school to help improve his/her anger and impulse control.

B. Consulted with the client's teachers about the use of self-monitoring checklists of anger-provoking situations to improve the client's anger and impulse control.

C. The parents and school officials were instructed to utilize a reward system in conjunction with the self-monitoring checklists of anger-provoking situations.

D. The use of a journal was recommended to help the client identify factors that trigger strong feelings of anger or contribute to impulsive behaviors.

15. Utilize *The Angry Monster* (15)

A. *The Angry Monster* workbook (Shore) was utilized to help the client develop more effective anger and impulse control.

B. After using *The Angry Monster* workbook, the client was able to identify several coping strategies to help inhibit his/her impulses and control his/her anger more effectively.

C. The client was given the directive to practice the anger management techniques at home and school that he/she learned from *The Angry Monster* workbook.

D. The client reported that the techniques he/she learned from *The Angry Monster* workbook have helped him/her to inhibit impulses and control anger more effectively.

16. Assign Readings on Anger Control (16)

A. The client was assigned the reading of *The Very Angry Day That Amy Didn't Have* (Shapiro) to help him/her learn more effective ways to manage anger.

B. The client was assigned the reading of *Sometimes I Like to Fight, but I Don't Do It Much Anymore* to teach him/her more effective ways to manage anger.

C. The readings from the assigned anger control book(s) were processed in today's therapy session.

D. The client found the assigned reading(s) helpful in learning more effective ways to control his/her anger.

17. Communication and Assertiveness (17)

A. The client was taught effective communication and assertiveness skills to learn how to express feelings in a controlled fashion and meet his/her needs through more constructive actions.

B. Role-playing and modeling techniques were used in the therapy session to teach effective ways to control emotions and identify appropriate ways to meet needs.

C. The client was encouraged to utilize "I" messages and positive statements to effectively communicate needs to others.

18. Assign "Anger Control" Exercise (18)

A. The client and parents were given the "Anger Control" exercise from *The Brief Child Therapy Homework Planner* (Jongsma, Peterson, and McInnis) to reinforce the client for demonstrating good control of anger.

B. The client and parents were encouraged to use the Positive and Negative Incident Reports from the "Anger Control" exercise to help the client identify the core issues that contribute to his/her angry outbursts and aggressive behaviors.

C. The parents were encouraged to utilize a reward system along with the Positive and Negative Incident Reports to reinforce the client for demonstrating good control of his/her anger.

D. The client and parents signed an Anger Control Contract specifying the rewards for his/her effective anger control and the consequences for his/her poor anger control.

19. Encourage Delay of Gratification (19)

A. Consulted with the parents on how to increase structure in the home to help the client delay his/her needs for immediate gratification in order to achieve longer-term goals.

B. The parents established a rule that the client would be forbidden to engage in recreational or leisure activities until completing his/her chores or homework.

C. The parents identified consequences for client's failure to complete responsibilities; the client verbalized recognition of these consequences.

D. The client and parents designed a schedule of dates and times when the client is expected to complete chores and homework.

20. Establish Clear Rules (20)

A. The client was asked to repeat the rules to demonstrate an understanding of the expectations.

B. Consulted with the client, parents, and teachers to identify rules and expectations in the school setting.

C. The client verbally disagreed with the rules and expectations identified by the parents.

21. Reward System/Contingency Contract (21)

A. The client and parents identified a list of rewards to reinforce desired, positive behaviors by the client.

B. A reward system was designed to reinforce positive behaviors and deter impulsive or aggressive acts.

C. The client signed a contingency contract specifying the consequences for his/her impulsive/acting-out behaviors.

22. Token Economy (22)

A. A token economy was designed for use in the home to increase the client's positive social behaviors and deter impulsive, acting-out behavior.

B. The client and parents agreed to the conditions outlined in the token economy and agreed to follow through with the implementation at home.

C. A token economy was designed and implemented in the classroom to reinforce the client's positive social behaviors and good impulse control.

23. Encourage Parental Praise (23)

A. Parents were encouraged to provide frequent praise and positive reinforcement for the client's positive social behaviors and good impulse control.

B. The parents were challenged to look for opportunities to praise the client instead of focusing primarily on behavioral problems.

24. Assign Readings on Disciplinary Techniques (24)

A. The parents were instructed to read one or more of the following books to increase their knowledge of effective disciplinary techniques: *1-2-3 Magic: Training Your Preschoolers and Preteens to Do What You Want* (Phelan), *Family Rules: Raising Responsible Children* (Kaye), and *Assertive Discipline for Parents* (Canter and Canter).

B. The assigned reading(s) on effective disciplinary techniques were processed in today's therapy session.

C. The parents reported that the assigned reading(s) were helpful in learning about effective disciplinary techniques.

D. The parents reported improvements in the client's behavior after they began implementing the disciplinary techniques that they learned from reading the assigned book(s).

25. Explore Family Dynamics (25)

A. A family therapy session was held to explore the dynamics within the family system that have contributed to the emergence of the client's behavioral problems.

B. The family members were asked to list the stressors that have had a negative impact on the family.

C. The family members were asked to identify the things that they would like to change within the family.

26. Employ Family-Sculpting Technique (26)

A. The family-sculpting technique was utilized within the session to help gain greater insight into the roles and behaviors of each family member.

B. The client and family members were instructed to use the family-sculpting technique to identify positive changes they would like to see happen in the family.

27. Assess Family Problem Solving (27)

A. The client and family members were given a problem to solve in order to provide an opportunity to observe the interactions among family members.

B. After successfully solving the problem within the family therapy session, the family was encouraged to use similar strategies at home to solve real-life problems.

28. Increase Disengaged Parent Involvement (28)

A. The disengaged parent attended the therapy session and was challenged to spend more time with the client in leisure, school, or household activities.

B. The client directly verbalized his/her need to spend greater time with the disengaged parent.

C. The factors contributing to the distant relationship between the client and detached parent were explored.

D. The detached parent verbalized a commitment to spend increased time with the client.

29. Explore Family Abuse History (29)

A. The client's family background was explored for a history of physical, sexual, or substance abuse.

B. The client developed a time line in the therapy session that identified significant historical events, both positive and negative, that have occurred in his/her family.

C. The client was instructed to draw a diagram of the house where the abuse occurred.

D. A diagnostic interview was conducted to assess the extent of the family members' use of drugs and alcohol.

30. Confront Parents' Abusive Discipline (30)

A. The client's parents were confronted and challenged to cease physically abusive or overly punitive methods of discipline.

B. The parents were asked to identify how abusive or overly punitive methods of discipline affect the client and siblings.

C. The parents apologized to the client for abusive behaviors and overly harsh methods of discipline.

31. Protect Client from Abuse (31)

A. The abuse was reported to the appropriate agency.

B. A recommendation was made that the perpetrator be removed from the home and seek treatment.

C. A recommendation was made that the client and siblings be removed from the home to ensure protection.

D. The client and family members identified necessary steps to take to minimize the risk of abuse occurring in the future.

E. The nonabusive parent verbalized a commitment to protect the client and siblings from physical abuse in the future.

32. Explore Feelings about Neglect or Abuse (32)

A. The client was given the opportunity in session to express his/her feelings about past neglect, abuse, separation, or abandonment.

B. The client was instructed to draw pictures that reflected his/her feelings about neglect, abuse, separation, or abandonment.

C. The client was instructed to use a journal to record his/her thoughts and feelings about past neglect, abuse, separation, or abandonment.

D. The empty-chair technique was employed to facilitate expression of feelings surrounding past neglect or abuse.

33. Conduct Play-Therapy Sessions (33)

A. An individual play-therapy session was conducted to provide the client with an opportunity to express his/her feelings surrounding the past neglect, abuse, separation, or abandonment.

B. The client's play reflected feelings of sadness and hurt about the past neglect, abuse, separation, or abandonment.

C. The client's play reflected strong feelings of anger about the past neglect, abuse, separation, or abandonment.

D. The client has been able to express his/her feelings about the past neglect, abuse, separation, or abandonment through the modality of play therapy, but has been unable to express his/her feelings directly to others.

E. The interpretation of the client's feelings reflected in his/her play afterward led to a discussion of his/her thoughts and feelings about the past neglect, abuse, separation, or abandonment.

34. Probe Abandonment Issues (34)

A. The client shared the extent of contact with the absent or uninvolved parent in the past and discussed possible reasons for the lack of involvement.

B. The client was instructed to write a letter to the absent parent to provide the opportunity to express and work through feelings about abandonment or lack of contact.

C. The empty-chair technique was utilized to help the client express his/her feelings toward the absent parent.

35. **Read "The Lesson of Salmon Rock . . . Fighting Leads to Loneliness" (35)**

A. The client and parents were given the homework assignment to read "The Lesson of Salmon Rock . . . Fighting Leads to Loneliness" from *The Brief Child Therapy Homework Planner* (Jongsma, Peterson, and McInnis) to help the client express his/her feelings connected with past separations, losses, or abandonment and recognize the negative consequences of his/her aggressive behaviors.

B. The client and parents reported that "The Lesson of Salmon Rock . . . Fighting Leads to Loneliness" helped him/her identify and express underlying feelings related to past separations, losses, or abandonment.

C. The client verbalized that "The Lesson of Salmon Rock . . . Fighting Leads to Loneliness" helped him/her recognize the negative consequences of his/her aggressive behaviors.

36. **Group Therapy Referral (36)**

A. The client was referred for group therapy to improve his/her impulse control, social judgment, and interpersonal skills.

B. The client was given the directive to self-disclose at least one time during group therapy session.

C. The client was encouraged to demonstrate empathy and concern for the thoughts, feelings, and needs of others during the group therapy session.

37. *Let's Work It Out: A Conflict Resolution Tool Kit* **(37)**

A. The *Let's Work It Out: A Conflict Resolution Tool Kit* (Shore) was used to teach the client more effective ways to resolve conflict with peers.

B. The client identified several effective conflict resolution strategies after using *Let's Work It Out: A Conflict Resolution Tool Kit*.

C. The client was given the homework assignment to use his/her newly learned conflict resolution skills with peers before the next therapy session.

D. The client reported that he/she was able to effectively resolve conflict with a peer after using the strategies that he/she learned from *Let's Work It Out: A Conflict Resolution Tool Kit*.

38. **Teach Honesty (38)**

A. The client was taught the value of honesty as a basis for building trust and mutual respect in all relationships.

B. The client was confronted with how a pattern of lying creates distrust and interferes with his/her ability to establish meaningful relationships.

C. The client verbally committed to being more honest to improve his/her relationships with family members and peers.

D. The client agreed to "undo" his/her lies by telling the truth.

39. **Reinforce Positive Peer Group Activities (39)**

A. The client was strongly encouraged to participate in extracurricular or positive peer group activities to provide a healthy outlet for anger, improve social skills, and increase self-esteem.

B. The client was assisted in developing a list of extracurricular or positive peer group activities that will provide him/her with the opportunity to establish meaningful friendships.

C. The client acknowledged that feelings of insecurity and inadequacy contribute to his/her reluctance to become involved in extracurricular or positive peer group activities.

40. Referral to Big Brothers/Big Sisters (40)

A. The client was referred to the Big Brothers/Big Sisters organization to provide him/her with an opportunity to establish a meaningful relationship with a positive role model.

B. The client reported that he/she was assigned a Big Brother or Big Sister.

C. The client reported that he/she has established a close relationship with his/her Big Brother/Big Sister.

D. The client has demonstrated improvements in his/her anger and impulse control since he/she was assigned a Big Brother/Big Sister.

41. Assign Acts of Kindness (41)

A. The client was given the homework assignment of performing at least three acts of kindness before the next therapy session to increase his/her empathy and sensitivity to the thoughts, feelings, and needs of others.

B. The client was praised and reinforced for demonstrating acts of kindness and showing empathy or sensitivity to the thoughts, feelings, and needs of others.

C. A recommendation was made to the court officials that the client perform community service as a part of his/her probation to increase his/her empathy and concern for the welfare of others.

D. The client's failure to comply with the homework assignment to demonstrate acts of kindness reflects his/her lack of empathy and concern for the welfare of others.

42. Parents Reinforce Positive Behavior (42)

A. The parents were instructed to observe and record positive behaviors by the client between therapy sessions.

B. The parents were encouraged to reinforce the client for engaging in positive behaviors.

C. The client was strongly encouraged to continue to engage in positive behaviors to build self-esteem, earn parents' approval, and receive affirmation from others.

43. Identify Times of Good Impulse Control (43)

A. The client explored periods when he/she demonstrated good impulse control in the past and engaged in significantly fewer acting-out behaviors.

B. The client was encouraged to use similar coping mechanisms that he/she used successfully in the past to control impulses.

C. The client shared the realization that involvement in extracurricular or positive peer group activities helped him/her to stay out of trouble.

D. The session revealed that the client was better behaved during periods of time when he/she received strong family support and affiliated with positive peer groups.

44. Utilize Child-Centered Play Therapy (44)

A. Child-centered play-therapy principles were utilized to reinforce and express trust in the client's capacity to behave responsibly.

B. The client received genuine empathy and unconditional positive regard during today's play-therapy session.

C. The child-centered play-therapy approach has helped the client behave in a more responsible manner.

45. Psychoanalytic Play-Therapy Approaches (45)

A. Psychoanalytic play-therapy approaches were employed to explore the etiology of the unconscious conflicts or core anxieties that contribute to the client's acting-out or aggressive behaviors.

B. The psychoanalytic play-therapy session was helpful in identifying the underlying conflicts or dynamics that have contributed to the emergence of the client's behavioral problems.

C. The interpretation of the client's core anxieties afterward led to an open discussion about the factors contributing to his/her behavioral problems.

D. The client has remained resistant to any interpretations about the significant underlying factors that appear to be contributing to his/her behavioral problems.

46. Utilize "Angry Tower" Technique (46)

A. The Angry Tower technique (Saxe) was utilized to help the client identify and express his/her feelings of anger in a constructive manner.

B. The client identified the Angry Tower technique as being a fun and effective way to express his/her angry feelings.

C. The Angry Tower technique helped identify the target(s) of the client's anger.

D. After playing the Angry Tower game, the client processed whether he/she was willing to express his/her feelings of anger toward significant others.

E. The client was encouraged to express his/her feelings of anger in a direct and controlled manner toward significant others.

47. Play "The Talking, Feeling, Doing" Game (47)

A. The Talking, Feeling, Doing game was utilized to increase the client's awareness of his/her thoughts and feelings.

B. The client verbalized several important thoughts and feelings while playing the Talking, Feeling, Doing game.

C. After playing the Talking, Feeling, Doing game, the client was encouraged to directly verbalize his/her thoughts and feelings to significant others.

48. Employ Mutual Storytelling Technique (48)

A. The mutual storytelling technique using puppets, dolls, and stuffed animals was employed to model appropriate ways to control anger and resolve conflict.

B. The client created his/her own story using puppets, dolls, and stuffed animals that modeled effective ways to control anger and resolve conflict.

C. After using the mutual storytelling technique, the client was able to successfully identify effective ways to control his/her anger and resolve conflict with others.

D. The client identified the mutual storytelling technique as being a useful way to learn effective ways to control his/her anger and resolve conflict.

49. Art Therapy Techniques (49)

A. The client was instructed to draw a picture reflecting how his/her impulsive, acting-out behaviors affect self-esteem.

B. The client was instructed to draw a picture reflecting how his/her impulsive, acting-out behaviors affect others.

50. Symbols of Anger (50)

A. The client was first instructed to draw an outline of the human body on a large piece of paper or poster board, and then asked to draw or fill in the body with objects, symbols, or pictures that reflect things or issues that commonly evoke feelings of anger for him/her.

B. The art therapy technique helped the client identify the issues that evoke strong feelings of anger for him/her.

C. After completing the art therapy technique, the client was helped to identify effective and noneffective ways to express his/her feelings of anger.

51. Draw Emotional Conflict Situations (51)

A. The client was instructed to draw pictures of three events or situations that commonly evoke feelings of anger, hurt, or sadness.

B. The client's thoughts and feelings that were reflected in his/her artwork were processed.

C. After completing his/her drawings, the client verbalized strong feelings of hurt, anger, and sadness about past life experiences or events.

D. After completing his/her drawings about past painful events or life experiences, the client expressed a willingness to share his/her thoughts and feelings with family members or significant others.

52. Assess Marital Conflicts (52)

A. The therapist assessed the marital dyad for possible conflict and/or triangulation that places the focus on the client's acting-out behaviors and away from marital problems.

B. The parents recognized how their marital problems are creating stress for the client and agreed to seek marital counseling.

C. The parents refused to follow through with a recommendation to pursue marital counseling.

53. Assess Parental Substance Abuse (53)

A. The parents were assessed for possible substance abuse problems.

B. The client's parents agreed to seek substance abuse treatment.

C. The client's parents appeared to be in denial about substance abuse problems and refused to seek treatment.

54. Medication Evaluation Referral (54)

A. The client was referred for a medication evaluation to improve his/her impulse control and stabilize moods.

B. The client and parents agreed to follow through with a medication evaluation.

C. The client was strongly opposed to being placed on medication to help improve his/her impulse control and stabilize moods.

55. Monitor Medication Effects (55)

A. The client's response to the medication was discussed.

B. The client reported that medication has helped to improve impulse control and stabilize moods.

C. The client reported little or no improvement from the medication.

D. The client has not complied with taking his/her medication on a regular basis.

DEPRESSION

CLIENT PRESENTATION

1. Sad, Depressed Moods (1)*

A. The parents and teachers reported that the client has appeared sad and depressed for a significant length of time.

B. The client appeared visibly sad during today's therapy session and reported that he/she feels depressed most of the time.

C. The frequency and intensity of the client's depressed moods are gradually beginning to diminish.

D. The client expressed happiness and joy about recent life events.

E. The client's depression has lifted and his/her moods are much more elevated.

2. Flat, Constricted Affect (1)

A. The parents and teachers reported that the client's affect often appears flat and constricted at home and school.

B. The client's affect appeared flat and constricted and he/she reported not feeling any emotion.

C. The client appeared more animated in his/her affective presentation and showed a wider range of emotions.

D. The client has consistently appeared more animated in his/her emotional presentation since the onset of treatment.

3. Preoccupation with Death (2)

A. The parents and teachers reported that the client displays a strong preoccupation with the subject of death.

B. The client displayed a preoccupation with the subject of death during today's therapy session and reported that death is often on his/her mind.

C. The client's preoccupation with the subject of death is gradually beginning to decrease.

D. The client did not talk about the subject of death in today's therapy session.

E. The client's preoccupation with the subject of death has ceased and he/she has demonstrated a renewed interest in life.

4. Suicidal Thoughts/Actions (3)

A. The client reported experiencing suicidal thoughts on a number of occasions.

B. The client made a recent suicide attempt.

C. The client has made suicidal gestures in the past as a cry for help.

D. The client denied that suicidal thoughts or urges are a problem any longer.

---

* The numbers in parentheses correlate to the number of the Behavioral Definition statement in the companion chapter with same title in *The Child Psychotherapy Treatment Planner* (Jongsma, Peterson, and McInnis) by John Wiley & Sons, 2000.

5. Moody Irritability (4)

A. The client has displayed a pervasive irritability at home and school.

B. The client's angry, irritable moods have often masked deeper feelings of depression.

C. The client appeared moody and irritable during today's therapy session.

D. The frequency and intensity of the client's irritable moods are diminishing.

E. The client's moods have stabilized and he/she has demonstrated significantly fewer irritable moods.

6. Isolation from Family and Peers (5)

A. The client has become significantly more isolated and withdrawn from family members and peers since the onset of his/her depression.

B. The client appeared withdrawn in today's therapy session.

C. The client's social isolation is diminishing and he/she is interacting more often with family members and peers.

D. The client was much more talkative and spontaneous in today's therapy session.

E. The client has become much more outgoing and has interacted with his/her family members and peers on a regular, consistent basis.

7. Academic Performance Decline (6)

A. The client has experienced a decrease in his/her academic performance since the onset of depression.

B. The client appeared visibly depressed when discussing his/her lowered academic performance.

C. The client's academic performance has increased since his/her depression has lifted.

D. The client expressed feelings of happiness and joy about his/her improved academic performance.

8. Lack of Interest (7)

A. The client reported experiencing little interest or enjoyment in activities that brought him/her pleasure in the past.

B. The parents and teachers reported that the client has shown little interest or enjoyment in activities at home and school.

C. The client's depression has started to decrease and he/she has shown signs of interest in previously enjoyed activities.

D. The client reported that he/she was recently able to experience joy or happiness in several activities.

E. The client has developed a renewed interest in and zest for life.

9. Lack of Communication about Painful Emotions (8)

A. The client has often suppressed and/or avoided talking about his/her painful emotions or experiences with others.

B. The client avoided talking about any painful emotions or topics during today's therapy session.

C. The client's avoidance of or refusal to talk about his/her painful emotions or experiences has been a significant contributing factor to his/her depression.

D. The client has started to talk about his/her painful emotions or experiences.

E. The client's willingness to talk about his/her painful emotions or experiences has helped to lift his/her depression.

10. Substance Abuse (9)

A. The client's substance abuse has masked deeper feelings of depression.

B. The client acknowledged that he/she has often turned to illegal drug or alcohol abuse to elevate his/her mood and block out painful emotions.

C. The client reported that he/she has experienced an increase in his/her feelings of depression since he/she ceased using drugs or alcohol.

D. The client's moods have stabilized since he/she ceased abusing drugs and alcohol.

E. The client reported that he/she is able to enjoy many activities without drugs or alcohol.

11. Low Energy, Listless, and Apathetic (10)

A. The client's depression has been manifested in part by his/her low energy level, fatigue, listlessness, and apathy.

B. The client appeared tired, listless, and apathetic during today's therapy session.

C. The client reported a mild increase recently in his/her level of energy.

D. The client reported experiencing a return to his/her normal level of energy.

12. Lack of Eye Contact (11)

A. The parents and teachers reported that the client displays very little eye contact during his/her social interactions with others.

B. The client displayed poor eye contact during today's therapy session and acknowledged this to be a common practice.

C. The client has demonstrated satisfactory to good eye contact with individuals around whom he/she feels comfortable, but exhibited poor eye contact with unfamiliar people.

D. The client maintained good eye contact during today's therapy session and stated that he/she is making more eye contact with others also.

E. The parents and teachers reported that the client consistently maintains good eye contact.

13. Low Self-Esteem (11)

A. The client has been troubled by strong feelings of low self-esteem, inadequacy, and insecurity.

B. The client verbalized negative and disparaging remarks about himself/herself.

C. The client's low self-esteem, lack of confidence, and feelings of insecurity are significant concomitant aspects of his/her depression.

D. The client verbalized several positive self-descriptive statements during today's therapy session.

E. The client has taken active steps to improve his/her self-esteem such as reaching out to others and challenging self with new activities.

14. Appetite Disturbance (12)

A. The client reported experiencing a loss of appetite during his/her depressive episodes.

B. The client has lost a significant amount of weight since becoming depressed.

C. The client reported that he/she has often turned to food to feel better about himself/herself during periods of depression.

D. The client reported a significant weight gain since the onset of his/her depression.

E. The client's appetite has returned to a normal level since his/her feelings of depression have decreased.

15. Sleep Disturbance (13)

A. The client reported to having difficulty falling asleep and/or experiencing early morning awakenings since he/she became depressed.

B. The client reported sleeping more than usual during his/her bout of depression.

C. The client reported sleeping well recently.

D. The client's sleep has returned to a normal level.

16. Poor Concentration and Indecisiveness (14)

A. The client reported having difficulty concentrating and making decisions since feeling depressed.

B. The client had trouble concentrating and staying focused during today's therapy session.

C. The client's low self-esteem, lack of confidence, and feelings of insecurity have contributed to his/her difficulty in making decisions.

D. The client reported being able to concentrate and stay focused for longer periods of time now that he/she has ceased feeling depressed.

E. The client's ability to make some constructive decisions has helped to decrease his/her feelings of depression.

17. Feelings of Hopelessness/Helplessness (15)

A. The client has developed a pessimistic outlook on the future and is troubled by feelings of hopelessness and helplessness.

B. The client expressed feelings of helplessness and voiced little hope that his/her life will improve in the future.

C. The client expressed confidence about his/her ability to overcome problems or stress and improve his/her life in the future.

D. The client has experienced a renewed sense of hope and feelings of empowerment.

18. Feelings of Guilt (15)

A. The client expressed strong feelings of guilt about his/her past actions.

B. The client's strong feelings of irrational guilt are a significant contributing factor to his/her depression and inability to move ahead with his/her life.

C. The client made productive use of today's therapy session by exploring his/her feelings of guilt about past actions.

D. The client denied being troubled by any significant feelings of guilt.

E. The client has successfully worked through and resolved his/her feelings of guilt about his/her past actions.

19. Unresolved Grief Issues (16)

A. The client's unresolved feelings of grief have been a significant contributing factor to his/her episode of depression.

B. The client expressed strong feelings of sadness and grief about past separations or losses.

C. The client was guarded and reluctant to talk about his/her past losses or separations.

D. The client's depression has begun to lift as he/she works through his/her feelings of grief about past losses or separations.

E. The client has experienced a significant increase in the frequency and duration of his/her happy or contented mood since working through the issues of grief.

20. Mood-Related Hallucinations or Delusions (17)

A. The client reported experiencing mood-congruent perceptual and/or cognitive disturbance during his/her major depressive episode.

B. The client expressed delusional thoughts during today's therapy session.

C. The client reported that he/she has recently been troubled by depression-related hallucinations.

D. The client denied experiencing any recent hallucinations or delusional thoughts.

E. The client has not experienced any further hallucinations or delusions since his/her mood has stabilized.

INTERVENTIONS IMPLEMENTED

1. Psychological Testing (1)*

A. The client was referred for a psychological evaluation to assess the depth of his/her depression.

B. The client was uncooperative and resistant during the psychological testing.

C. The client approached the psychological testing in an honest, straightforward manner and was cooperative with any requests presented to him/her.

2. Give Psychological Testing Feedback (2)

A. The client and his/her family members were given feedback on the results of the psychological testing.

B. The results from the psychological testing showed that the client is currently experiencing a mild amount of depression.

C. The results from the psychological testing showed that the client is experiencing a moderate amount of depression.

D. The results from the psychological testing showed that the client's level of depression is at a severe level.

E. The results of the psychological testing did not support the presence of a depressive disorder.

---

* The numbers in parentheses correlate to the number of the Therapeutic Interventions statement in the companion chapter with same title in *The Child Psychotherapy Treatment Planner* (Jongsma, Peterson, and McInnis) by John Wiley & Sons, 2000.

3. Explore Self-Defeating Behavior (3)

A. Today's therapy session explored how the client's depression is linked to his/her pattern of engaging in self-defeating behaviors.

B. The client was able to recognize the connection between his/her self-defeating behaviors and periods of depression.

C. The client identified more effective ways to cope with stress or meet his/her needs instead of engaging in self-defeating behaviors.

D. The client resisted the interpretation that his/her depression is linked to a pattern of self-defeating behaviors.

E. Client-centered therapy approaches were used to help the client realize how his/her pattern of self-defeating behaviors is linked to his/her depression.

4. Interpret Acting-Out Behavior (4)

A. The client's acting-out behaviors were interpreted as a sign of his/her depression.

B. The client has gained insight into how his/her acting-out behaviors are related to underlying feelings of depression.

C. The client was helped to identify more effective ways to meet his/her needs and overcome feelings of depression instead of engaging in acting-out behaviors.

D. A psychoanalytic approach was utilized to explore how the client's acting-out behaviors are related to deeper feelings of depression.

E. A brief, solution-focused therapy approach was used to help the client identify effective ways to meet his/her needs and overcome feelings of depression.

5. Confront Acting-Out Behavior (5)

A. The client was confronted with how his/her acting-out behaviors serve as a maladaptive coping mechanism to avoid facing the real issues or conflicts.

B. The client responded positively to the confrontation about his/her acting-out behaviors, and acknowledged that there are more effective ways to cope with stress and meet his/her needs other than through acting out.

C. The client was resistant to the interpretation that he/she is acting out as a means of avoiding dealing with conflict or emotional pain.

D. The client was strongly encouraged to directly communicate his/her unmet needs to significant others and to terminate the acting-out behavior.

E. The client was taught effective communication and assertiveness skills to help him/her deal with conflict and meet his/her needs.

6. "Surface Behavior/Inner Feelings" Exercise (6)

A. The client was given the "Surface Behavior/Inner Feelings" exercise from *The Brief Child Therapy Homework Planner* (Jongsma, Peterson, and McInnis) to show the connection between his/her angry, irritable, and acting-out behaviors and feelings of hurt or sadness.

B. The client successfully completed the homework assignment "Surface Behavior/Inner Feelings" exercise and was able to identify how his/her angry, irritable behaviors are connected to underlying feelings of hurt and sadness.

C. The client did not follow through with completing the homework assignment "Surface Behavior/Inner Feelings" exercise, but was asked to do it again.

D. The client successfully completed the homework assignment "Surface Behavior/Inner Feelings" exercise, and reported that he/she was able to share his/her feelings of hurt and sadness with other trusted individuals.

7. Reinforce Expression of Underlying Feelings (7)

A. The client was reinforced for expressing his/her feelings of anger, hurt, and disappointment.

B. A psychoanalytic therapy approach was utilized to help the client explore his/her underlying feelings of anger, hurt, and disappointment.

C. Client-centered therapy principles were utilized to reflect how the client's statements or actions reflect underlying feelings of anger, hurt, and disappointment.

D. After identifying his/her feelings of anger, hurt, and disappointment, the client was encouraged to directly verbalize these feelings to his/her family members or other close, trusted individuals.

8. Explore Fear of Loss (8)

A. Today's therapy session explored the client's fears of abandonment or the loss of love from significant others.

B. The client was helped to examine whether his/her fears surrounding abandonment of loss of love from others are realistic or unrealistic.

C. The client was taught cognitive restructuring techniques to help challenge and overcome his/her irrational fears about being abandoned or rejected by significant others.

D. Psychoanalytic therapy approaches were employed to explore the client's underlying fears of abandonment or loss of love from significant others.

9. Identify Missing Aspects of Life (9)

A. The client was asked to identify what is missing from life that contributes to personal unhappiness.

B. The client was able to successfully identify the missing aspects of his/her life that contribute to feelings of unhappiness and depression.

C. A plan was developed with the client to attempt to find ways to satisfy those missing aspects of his/her life.

D. The client was encouraged to utilize his/her strengths and seek out the support of others to help cope with the missing aspects of his/her life.

10. Probe Current Life Stressors (10)

A. Today's therapy session probed the aspects of the client's current life situation that are contributing to his/her feelings of sadness.

B. The client made productive use of the therapy session and was able to identify the current life stressors that are contributing to his/her feelings of sadness.

C. Role-playing and modeling techniques were used to help the client identify effective ways to cope with his/her current life stressors.

D. A brief solution-focused therapy approach was utilized to help the client identify effective ways to cope with his/her current life stressors and problems.

E. The client was helped to identify successful strategies that he/she used in the past to overcome similar problems.

11. Explore Emotional Pain from Past (11)

A. Today's therapy session explored the emotional pain from the client's past that contributes to his/her feelings of hopelessness and low self-esteem.

B. The client was given empathy and support in expressing his/her painful emotions about the past experiences that have contributed to current feelings of hopelessness and low self-esteem.

C. The client was encouraged to utilize positive self-talk as a means to offset his/her pattern of negative thinking and overcome feelings of hopelessness.

D. Guided imagery techniques were utilized to help the client visualize a brighter future.

12. Address Family Conflict (12)

A. A family therapy session was held to facilitate a discussion of the conflict that exists in the family.

B. Today's family therapy session was helpful in identifying the core areas of conflict that contribute to the client's depression.

C. The family members were asked to brainstorm possible ways to resolve the conflictual issues affecting the family.

D. The family members were able to agree on solutions to the problem(s) that are contributing to the client's depression.

E. The client and family members were unable to reach an agreement on how to resolve the conflict that is contributing to the client's depression.

13. Expression of Emotional Needs (13)

A. The client was given the opportunity to express his/her emotional needs to family members and significant others.

B. The family members responded with empathy and support to the client's expression of needs.

C. The client and family members were helped to identify ways to meet his/her emotional needs.

D. The client was given a specific task to perform with the family members or significant others to meet his/her emotional needs.

14. Allow Respectful Expression of Feelings (14)

A. The parents were challenged to encourage, support, and tolerate the client's respectful expression of his/her thoughts and feelings.

B. The client and parents were helped to differentiate between respectful and disrespectful ways for the client to express his/her thoughts and feelings.

C. Role-playing and modeling techniques were utilized to identify respectful versus disrespectful ways of expressing thoughts and feelings.

D. The parents were encouraged to ignore mild and occasional verbally aggressive or oppositional behaviors to help the client become more assertive and less depressed.

15. Arrange for Play Therapy (15)

A. Play therapy was begun to provide the client with the opportunity to express feelings about himself/herself and others.

B. The client has made productive use of the play-therapy sessions and has been able to express his/her underlying feelings of depression, anxiety, and insecurity.

C. The client has been able to make productive use of the play-therapy sessions and has expressed his/her underlying feelings of anger through play.

D. The client's play reflected little affect or emotional conflict.

16. Interpret Feelings in Play Therapy (16)

A. The client's feelings were interpreted in today's therapy session and related to how the client feels about situations in his/her present life.

B. The client's play reflected feeling of sadness about previous separations, losses, and traumas.

C. The client's play reflected underlying feelings of insecurity and helplessness relating to his/her inability to overcome problems or conflicts.

D. The client's play reflected underlying feelings of anger about past separations, losses, or traumatic experiences.

E. After interpreting the client's feelings expressed in his/her play, the client was able to openly express his/her feelings about significant life events.

17. Utilize Child-Centered Play Therapy (17)

A. A child-centered play-therapy approach was utilized to explore the factors contributing to the client's depression.

B. The client was given unconditional positive regard and warm acceptance to help build his/her self-esteem.

C. A child-centered play-therapy approach was utilized to help identify the client's inner resources that he/she can use to overcome his/her depression.

D. The client's capacity to cope with his/her problems was reinforced to provide him/her with a sense of hope for the future.

E. The child-centered play-therapy approaches have helped the client discover his/her inner resources and given him/her renewed hope for the future.

18. Psychoanalytic Play Therapy (18)

A. A psychoanalytic play-therapy approach was utilized to explore the etiology of the unconscious conflict in the client that produced feelings of hopelessness, low self-esteem, and depression.

B. The psychoanalytic play-therapy session was helpful in identifying the core conflicts or developmental arrests that have contributed to the client's feelings of hopelessness, low self-esteem, and depression.

C. The psychoanalytic play-therapy session helped reveal the reasons for the client's resistance in openly talking about the core conflicts that contribute to his/her depression.

D. Transference issues were processed in today's psychoanalytic play-therapy session.

E. The psychoanalytic play-therapy sessions have helped the client overcome his/her feelings of low self-esteem and depression.

19. Identify Cognitive Messages of Helplessness (19)

A. The client was helped to identify the negative cognitive messages that reinforce feelings of helplessness and hopelessness.

B. The client was encouraged to utilize positive self-talk as a means of overcoming his/her feelings of helplessness and hopelessness.

C. The client was strongly encouraged to challenge his/her irrational thoughts that contribute to his/her feelings of helplessness and hopelessness.

D. The client was given a homework assignment to identify his/her strengths and weaknesses, to improve self-esteem and overcome feelings of helplessness and hopelessness.

20. Reinforce Positive Cognitive Messages (20)

A. The client was trained in the use of positive cognitive messages to help increase his/her self-confidence and self-acceptance.

B. The client reported that the use of positive cognitive messages has helped to increase his/her confidence and feelings of acceptance about self.

C. The client reported that he/she attempted to use positive cognitive messages, but still continues to be troubled by feelings of insecurity and a lack of confidence.

D. The client failed to follow through with using positive cognitive messages as a means of increasing his/her confidence and feelings of self-acceptance.

21. Assess Potential for Suicide (21)

A. The client acknowledged experiencing suicidal thoughts and/or an urge to harm self, and was referred for an evaluation for inpatient hospitalization.

B. The client was admitted into an inpatient psychiatric unit because of his/her risk for suicide or self-harm.

C. The client reported experiencing brief thoughts of suicide, but denied any intent to harm himself/herself; nonetheless, the client's suicide potential will continue to be closely monitored.

D. The suicide assessment revealed that the client is a low risk to harm himself/herself.

22. Reinforce Statements of Hope (22)

A. The client's statements reflecting a will or reason to live were strongly reinforced.

B. The client was asked to develop a list of resource people who he/she can turn to during periods of despair and hopelessness.

C. The support of parent(s) and/or family members was enlisted to help decrease the client's risk for suicide or self-harm.

D. The client was asked to identify 5 to 10 strengths or interests to help reinforce his/her desire or reason to live.

E. The client's past was explored for periods of time when he/she was able to overcome adversity or stress, so as to reinforce the idea that the client can overcome or cope with current stressors.

23. Contract for No Self-Harm (23)

A. The client verbally agreed to contact the therapist, parent(s), or significant others if he/she experiences suicidal thoughts or an urge to harm self in the future.

B. The client signed a contract agreeing to contact the therapist, parent(s), or significant others if he/she contemplates suicide or experiences an urge to harm self in the future.

C. The client was referred for an evaluation for inpatient hospitalization because of his/her refusal to sign a no-self-harm contract or verbally commit to contacting the therapist, parent(s), or significant others if he/she contemplates suicide or experiences an urge to harm self in the future.

D. The signing of the no-self-harm contract helped the client realize that there are resource people available that he/she can turn to in times of distress or despair.

24. Participate in Social/Recreational Activities (24)

A. The client was strongly encouraged to participate in social/recreational activities to decrease feelings of depression and enrich the quality of his/her life.

B. The client was assisted in developing a list of social or recreational activities that will help to enrich the quality of his/her life and provide an opportunity to establish meaningful friendships.

C. The client reported that his/her recent participation in social or recreational activities has helped to decrease feelings of depression.

D. The client has not participated in any recent social or recreational activities because of his/her depression and feelings of low self-worth.

25. Use Therapeutic Feelings Games (25)

A. Therapeutic feelings games have been used to help the client become more verbal.

B. The Talking, Feeling, Doing game was used to help the client identify and express his/her thoughts and feelings.

C. The therapeutic feelings games have helped the client identify his/her feelings and unmet needs.

D. After playing the therapeutic game, the client was helped to identify constructive ways to meet his/her needs.

E. After playing the therapeutic game, the client was encouraged to express his/her thoughts and feelings directly toward significant others.

26. Assess Need for Medications (26)

A. The client was assessed for the need of psychotropic medication.

B. The client was referred for a medication evaluation because he/she continues to experience a significant amount of depressive symptoms.

C. The client was not referred for a medication evaluation because he/she is not exhibiting any endogenous signs of depression or experiencing any suicidal thoughts.

27. Arrange for Antidepressant Medication (27)

A. A trial of antidepressant medication is indicated based on the client's reported symptoms.

B. The client and parents agreed to follow through with a medication evaluation and arrangements were made for the client to be seen by a physician.

C. The client was strongly opposed to being placed on medication to help stabilize his/her moods and decrease symptoms of depression.

28. Monitor Medication Effects (28)

A. The client's response to his/her medication was discussed.

B. The client reported that the medication has helped to decrease symptoms of depression and stabilize his/her mood.

C. The client reported little to no improvement since starting to take the medication.

D. The client has not complied with taking his/her medication on a regular basis.

E. The client was encouraged to report the side effects of the medication to the prescribing physician or psychiatrist.

F. Contact will be made with the prescribing physician regarding the lack of effectiveness and the need for an adjustment in the prescription.

29. Encourage Academic Effort (29)

A. The client was helped to establish academic goals to help lift his/her depression and improve self-esteem.

B. The client was challenged and encouraged to achieve his/her academic goals to offset feelings of depression and improve self-esteem.

C. The client and parents were assisted in developing a routine schedule of study times to mobilize the client and help him/her achieve academic success.

D. A reward system was designed to reinforce the client for achieving his/her academic goals.

E. The client and parents were encouraged to maintain regular communication with the teachers via phone calls or progress notes to help the client stay organized and achieve academic goals.

30. Arrange for Tutor (30)

A. The client and parents were encouraged to work with a tutor to improve the client's academic performance.

B. The client and parents agreed to follow up with contacting a tutor through an outside learning center.

C. The client and parents were encouraged to consult with teachers or school officials about using peer tutors to improve the client's academic performance.

D. The client reported that tutoring has helped to improve his/her academic performance.

E. The client reported little to no improvement in his/her academic performance while working with a tutor.

31. Monitor Food Consumption (31)

A. The client and parents were instructed to keep a daily log of the client's food consumption.

B. The client was encouraged to eat nutritious, well-balanced meals to cease his/her pattern of weight loss.

C. The client was referred to a nutritionist to receive counseling about his/her diet.

D. Today's therapy session explored the factors contributing to the client's overeating.

E. The client verbally recognized that his/her pattern of overeating is related to unfulfilled dependency needs.

32. Monitor Sleep Patterns (32)

A. Today's therapy session explored the factors that interfere with the client being able to sleep restfully through the night.

B. The client was trained in the use of guided imagery and relaxation techniques to help induce calm before attempting to sleep.

C. The client and parents were asked to track the client's sleep patterns to determine whether he/she should be referred for a medication evaluation.

D. The client and parents were instructed to monitor the client's sleep patterns to help determine whether the medication needs to be changed or the dosage adjusted.

E. The client was administered electromyographic (EMG) biofeedback to reinforce a successful relaxation response to help the client sleep restfully at night.

33. Encourage Parental Affirmation (33)

A. The client's parents were strongly encouraged to express warm, positive, affirming statements of love to him/her on a regular basis.

B. The parents were directed to make at least three positive, affirmative statements toward the client each day.

C. The parents were challenged to look for opportunities to praise and affirm the client, instead of focusing primarily on his/her emotional or behavioral problems.

D. The parents were instructed to observe and record three to five constructive behaviors that the client engaged in, to help the client overcome his/her depression.

E. The client was strongly encouraged to continue engaging in responsible or socially appropriate behaviors, to receive his/her parents' approval, affirmation, and expressions of love.

34. Establish Structured Activity Routine (34)

A. The parents were assisted in establishing a routine of positive, structured activities with the client to help mobilize him/her and decrease symptoms of depression.

B. The client and parents were assisted in developing a list of activities that they would enjoy doing together.

C. The client and parents were instructed to spend 15 minutes of daily one-on-one time together in a structured activity to increase the frequency of positive interactions and improve the lines of communication.

35. Identify Pleasurable Activities (35)

A. The client developed a list of pleasurable interests and activities that could be pursued to help lift feelings of depression.

B. The client was strongly encouraged to participate in extracurricular or positive peer group activities to cease social withdrawal and reduce feelings of depression.

C. The client was instructed to engage in at least one potentially pleasurable activity each day.

D. The client explored past interests or activities that provided him/her with a sense of enjoyment and was encouraged to engage in similar activities in the present to help overcome feelings of depression.

E. The client was assisted in identifying three to five role models, and was encouraged to engage in pleasurable activities or interests associated with his/her role models.

36. Develop Plan to Meet Social/Emotional Needs (36)

A. The client was helped to develop an action plan to meet his/her social and emotional needs.

B. The client explored periods of time in the past when he/she felt less depressed and took active steps to meet his/her social and emotional needs.

C. The client was encouraged to take steps similar to ones that he/she had taken in the past, to meet his/her present social and emotional needs.

D. The client shared the realization that his/her involvement in extracurricular or positive peer group activities in the past had helped him/her to meet social and emotional needs.

E. The therapy session revealed how the client had felt less depressed in the past when he/she received strong family support and affiliated with positive peer groups.

37. Reinforce Social Interactions (37)

A. Behavior rehearsal and role-playing techniques were used to model positive social skills and appropriate ways to initiate and/or sustain pleasant conversations with friends or family members.

B. A reward system was implemented to reinforce the client for initiating pleasant social interactions with peers and/or family members.

C. The client was given the homework assignment to initiate one pleasant conversation each day.

D. The client was given a homework assignment to initiate three phone calls per week to different individuals.

38. Utilize Art Therapy Techniques (38)

A. Art therapy techniques were used to help the client express his/her depressive feelings.

B. The client's artwork was used as a springboard to help explore the causes of his/her depression or other painful emotions.

C. The use of art therapy helped the client express his/her feelings of depression and identify the causes.

D. The client's artwork provided little insight into the sources of his/her depression.

39. Draw Pictures Reflecting Sadness (39)

A. The client was instructed to draw pictures that reflect his/her feelings of sadness and hurt about significant life experiences.

B. The content and feelings expressed in the client's drawings were processed.

C. After completing his/her drawings, the client was given empathy and support in directly verbalizing his/her feelings of sadness and hurt about past life experiences.

D. After completing the drawings, the client was able to talk about how the past experiences have affected his/her life.

E. After completing his/her drawings, the client was able to identify constructive ways to cope with the life stressors or painful events.

40. Family Kinetic Drawing (40)

A. The client was asked to produce a family kinetic drawing to shed possible insight into the family dynamics that contribute to his/her feelings of depression and hopelessness.

B. The family kinetic drawing was helpful in identifying the family dynamics that have contributed to the client's feelings of depression.

C. The client's family kinetic drawing revealed the client's sense of isolation and estrangement from other family members.

D. The client's family kinetic drawing revealed his/her wish to establish closer family relations.

E. The client's family kinetic drawing demonstrated how the client perceives his/her parents as being overly critical and unavailable to meet his/her emotional needs.

41. "Three Ways to Change the World" Exercise (41)

A. The client was given the "Three Ways to Change the World" exercise from *The Brief Child Therapy Treatment Planner* (Jongsma, Peterson, and McInnis) to identify ways to help bring increased feelings of joy, peace, and security into his/her life.

B. The client was given the "Three Ways to Change the World" exercise to identify the stressors or unmet needs that contribute to his/her feelings of depression.

C. The client was given the "Three Ways to Change the World" exercise to help the therapist establish rapport with him/her.

D. The client reported that the "Three Ways to Change the World" exercise was helpful in identifying constructive steps that he/she can take to cope with stress or overcome his/her problems.

E. The client identified the "Three Ways to Change the World" exercise as being a helpful way to identify the core conflicts contributing to his/her depression.

DISRUPTIVE/ATTENTION SEEKING

CLIENT PRESENTATION

1. Negative Attention-Seeking Behaviors (1)*

A. The parents and teachers reported that the client repeatedly attempts to draw negative attention to himself/herself through silly behaviors, immature or regressive actions, loud talking, and making inappropriate noises or gestures.

B. The client behaved in a disruptive manner during today's therapy session by engaging in silly, immature behaviors and making inappropriate noises or gestures.

C. The client has recently begun to exercise greater self-control and has not engaged in as many disruptive, negative attention–seeking behaviors.

D. The client demonstrated good self-control during today's therapy session and did not engage in any disruptive, negative attention–seeking behaviors.

E. The client has demonstrated a significant reduction in the frequency of his/her disruptive or negative attention–seeking behaviors.

2. Impulsivity (1)

A. The parents and teachers reported that the client presents as a highly impulsive individual who seeks immediate gratification of his/her needs and often fails to consider the consequences of his/her actions.

B. The client's impulsivity has been manifested in disruptive behaviors, excessive talking, and blurting out remarks.

C. The client acknowledged that he/she has difficulty inhibiting impulses and tends to react to what is going on in his/her immediate environment.

D. The client has recently started to improve his/her impulse control and delay the need for immediate gratification.

E. The client has consistently displayed good impulse control as evidenced by his/her improved ability to stop and think about the possible consequences of his/her actions before reacting.

3. Disruptive Classroom Behaviors (2)

A. The parents and teachers described the client's history of often disrupting the classroom with his/her silly, immature, and negative attention–seeking behaviors.

B. The client has often disrupted the classroom by blurting out remarks at inappropriate times.

C. The client has recently started to exercise greater self-control and has engaged in fewer disruptive behaviors in the classroom.

---

* The numbers in parentheses correlate to the number of the Behavioral Definition statement in the companion chapter with same title in *The Child Psychotherapy Treatment Planner* (Jongsma, Peterson, and McInnis) by John Wiley & Sons, 2000.

D. The client has demonstrated a significant reduction in the frequency of his/her disruptive or negative attention–seeking behaviors in the classroom.

E. The teachers reported that the client has consistently achieved positive attention through his/her prosocial and responsible behaviors.

4. Off-Task Behaviors (2)

A. The teachers reported that the client has difficulty staying focused in the classroom and has trouble completing school assignments on time because of his/her disruptive behaviors.

B. The client had difficulty staying focused in today's therapy session and often switched from one topic to another.

C. The parents and teachers reported that the client often has to be redirected back to tasks at home and school.

D. The client maintained good attention and concentration during today's therapy session.

E. The client has consistently maintained good concentration and has completed his/her school assignments on a regular basis.

5. Annoying/Antagonistic Behavior (3)

A. The client has repeatedly engaged in annoying or antagonistic behaviors by teasing, mocking, or picking on others.

B. The client's peer and sibling relationships have been strained by his/her annoying or antagonistic behaviors.

C. The parents and teachers reported that the client shows little or no awareness of how his/her annoying or antagonistic behaviors negatively impact his/her sibling and peer relationships.

D. The client has recently started to develop an awareness of how his/her annoying or antagonistic behaviors negatively impact others.

E. The client has demonstrated a significant reduction in the frequency of severity of his/her annoying and antagonistic behaviors.

6. Peer-Sibling Conflict (4)

A. The client has exhibited a recurrent pattern of creating conflict with siblings or peers by failing to follow agreed-upon rules in play or game activities, refusing to share or cooperate, and/or bossing others around.

B. The client's peer and sibling relationships have been strained by his/her immaturity, demandingness, and negative attention–seeking behaviors.

C. The client has started to develop an awareness of how his/her silly, immature, or disruptive behaviors interfere with his/her ability to establish and maintain sibling/peer relationships.

D. The client's sibling and peer relationships have started to improve as he/she has been more cooperative, willing to share, and compliant with rules during play or game activities.

E. The client has established and maintained positive sibling and peer relationships.

7. Excessive Complaining and Demanding (4)

A. The client has displayed a recurrent pattern of complaining and demanding that others do things his/her way.

B. The client was whiny and demanding in his/her interactions with family members during today's therapy session.

C. The client has demonstrated little awareness of how his/her whining, complaining, and demanding behaviors annoy or irritate other people.

D. The client has started to develop an awareness of how his/her excessive complaining and demandingness annoy or irritate other people.

E. The client has demonstrated a significant reduction in the frequency of his/her whining, complaining, and demanding behaviors.

8. Oppositional Behaviors/Noncompliance (5)

A. The parents and teachers reported that the client often stubbornly refuses to comply with reasonable requests at home and school.

B. The client has often tested the limits and defied the rules established by authority figures at home and school.

C. The client presented as obstinate and stubborn in today's therapy session.

D. The client has started to become more compliant with the rules and requests by authority figures at home and school.

E. The client has consistently complied with the rules and requests by authority figures at home and school.

9. Argumentativeness (6)

A. The parents and teachers described the client as being highly argumentative.

B. The parents reported that the client often refuses to back down in an argument and needs to have the last word.

C. The client appeared angry and irritable during today's therapy session, and seemed to argue just for the sake of arguing.

D. The client has recently started to show greater control of his/her anger as he/she does not argue as intently or as long.

E. The client has demonstrated a significant reduction in the frequency and intensity of his/her arguments with family members, peers, or adult authority figures.

10. Blaming/Projecting (6)

A. The parents and teachers reported that the client has difficulty accepting responsibility for his/her disruptive behaviors and often projects the blame for his/her poor decisions onto other people or outside circumstances.

B. The client appeared defensive in today's therapy session and made excuses or blamed others for his/her poor decisions and disruptive behaviors.

C. The client has recently started to accept greater responsibility for his/her actions and place the blame less often for his/her disruptive behaviors onto other people.

D. The client admitted to his/her wrongdoings during today's therapy session and verbalized an acceptance of responsibility for his/her actions.

E. The parents and teachers reported that the client has consistently accepted responsibility for his/her actions at home and school.

11. Lack of Sensitivity (7)

A. The parents and teachers reported that the client shows little sensitivity or awareness of how his/her disruptive or negative attention–seeking behaviors negatively affect other people.

B. The client demonstrated little sensitivity or empathy for the thoughts, feelings, and needs of others when discussing his/her interpersonal problems during today's therapy session.

C. The client has usually sought immediate gratification of his/her needs and failed to consider how his/her actions may affect others.

D. In today's therapy session, the client verbalized an understanding of how his/her disruptive and impulsive behaviors negatively impact others.

E. The client has recently started to verbalize empathy and sensitivity to the thoughts, feelings, and needs of others.

12. Poor Social Skills (8)

A. The client's poor social skills have interfered with his/her ability to establish and maintain peer friendships.

B. The client's poor social skills have been manifested in his/her lack of awareness of important social cues and/or failure to follow expected social norms.

C. The client has become entangled in frequent disputes or arguments with siblings and peers because of his/her failure to pick up on important social cues or interpersonal nuances.

D. The client has started to improve his/her social skills (e.g., listening better, complimenting others, allowing others to go first).

E. The client has demonstrated good social skills and has related well to sibling, peers, and adults on a consistent basis.

13. Inappropriate Touching/Intrusive Behaviors (9)

A. The parents and teachers reported that they have received numerous complaints from peers and siblings about the client's inappropriate touching or intrusions into their personal space.

B. The client was intrusive in his/her interactions with others during today's therapy session.

C. The client has recently started to show greater respect for other people's personal space and has not been as intrusive.

D. The client has demonstrated a significant reduction in the frequency of his/her inappropriate touching or intrusive behaviors.

INTERVENTIONS IMPLEMENTED

1. Psychological Testing (1)*

A. A psychological evaluation was conducted to determine whether emotional factors or ADHD are contributing to the client's disruptive, antagonistic, annoying, or negative attention–seeking behaviors.

B. The client was uncooperative and resistant to engage in the evaluation process.

C. The client approached the psychological testing in an honest, straightforward manner, and was cooperative with any requests presented to him/her.

2. Psychoeducational Evaluation (2)

A. The client received a psychoeducational evaluation to rule out the presence of a possible learning disability that may be contributing to his/her disruptive and negative attention–seeking behaviors at school.

B. The client was uncooperative during the psychoeducational evaluation and did not appear to put forth good effort.

C. The client was cooperative during the psychoeducational evaluation and appeared motivated to do his/her best.

3. Give Evaluation Feedback (3)

A. Feedback from the psychological testing was given to the client, parents, and school officials and appropriate interventions were discussed.

B. The evaluation findings supported the presence of ADHD, which contributes to the client's disruptive, antagonistic, annoying, and negative attention–seeking behaviors.

C. The evaluation findings revealed the presence of underlying emotional problems that have contributed to the emergence of the client's disruptive, antagonistic, annoying, and negative attention–seeking behaviors.

D. The findings from the psychoeducational evaluation revealed the presence of a learning disability and the need for special education services.

E. The evaluation process did not reveal the presence of any learning disability, emotional problem, or ADHD that is contributing to the client's disruptive and negative attention–seeking behaviors.

4. Build Therapeutic Trust (4)

A. An attempt was made in the therapy session to build trust with the client through consistent eye contact, active listening, unconditional positive regard, and warm acceptance.

B. The client's concerns were closely listened to and his/her feelings were reflected in a nonjudgmental manner.

C. Provided empathy and support for the client's expression of thoughts and feelings during today's session, so that he/she can begin to acknowledge and identify his/her disruptive behaviors.

---

* The numbers in parentheses correlate to the number of the Therapeutic Interventions statement in the companion chapter with same title in *The Child Psychotherapy Treatment Planner* (Jongsma, Peterson, and McInnis) by John Wiley & Sons, 2000.

5. Consult with Parents and School Officials (5)

A. Consulted with the parents, teachers, and school officials about designing and implementing interventions to deter the client's impulsivity, improve his/her academic performance, and increase positive behavior in the classroom.

B. Recommendation was made that the client be seated in the front row to deter his/her distractibility and increase on task behaviors.

C. The teachers agreed to call on the client often and to give frequent feedback to him/her.

D. Recommendation was made at consultation meeting that the client would be assigned a teacher's aide to assist with his/her learning problems.

E. The teachers agreed to send home weekly reports informing the parents about the client's academic and social progress.

6. Reinforce and Clarify Parental Rules and Boundaries (6)

A. Today's family therapy session focused on helping the parents establish clearly defined rules and appropriate parent-child boundaries to manage the client's disruptive, antagonistic, annoying, and negative attention–seeking behaviors.

B. The parents were helped to identify appropriate consequences for the client's disruptive, antagonistic, annoying, and negative attention–seeking behaviors.

C. The parents succeeded in identifying appropriate and reasonable rules and expectations for the client to follow at home.

D. The parents had difficulty identifying appropriate consequences for the client's disruptive, antagonistic, annoying, and negative attention–seeking behaviors.

E. The parents acknowledged that because of their desire to avoid conflict and confrontation they have often failed to follow through with setting limits for the client's disruptive, antagonistic, annoying, and negative attention–seeking behaviors.

7. Establish Clear Rules (7)

A. A family therapy session was held to discuss the rules and expectations for the client at home and school.

B. Consulted with the client's parents and teachers to identify rules and expectations in the school setting.

C. The client was asked to repeat the rules to demonstrate an understanding of the rules and expectations of him/her.

D. The client voiced his/her agreement with the rules and expectations at home and school.

E. The client verbally disagreed with the rules and expectations identified by his/her parents and teachers.

8. Teach Delay of Gratification (8)

A. The family therapy session focused on teaching the parents to increase the structure in the home to help the client delay his/her need for immediate gratification.

B. The parents established the rule that the client cannot engage in social, recreational, or leisure activities until completing his/her chores or homework.

C. The parents identified consequences for the client's failure to complete his/her responsibilities; the client verbalized recognition of these consequences.

D. The client and parents designed a schedule of dates and times when the client is expected to complete chores and homework before engaging in pleasurable activities.

E. The parents were encouraged to communicate regularly with the teachers to keep them informed of any large or long-term projects assigned to the client.

9. Encourage Parental Praise (9)

A. The parents were encouraged to provide frequent praise and positive reinforcement for the client's positive social behaviors and good impulse control.

B. The parents were challenged to look for opportunities to praise the client instead of focusing primarily on his/her disruptive or impulsive behaviors.

C. Explored the reasons why the parents have had difficulty offering praise and positive reinforcement to the client.

10. Design a Reward System/Contingency Contract (10)

A. The client and parents identified a list of rewards to reinforce the desired positive behaviors by the client.

B. A reward system was designed to reinforce the client's positive social behaviors and deter disruptive or negative attention–seeking behaviors.

C. A reward system was designed to increase the client's completion of school and homework assignments.

D. The client and parents signed a contingency contract specifying the consequences for his/her disruptive or negative attention–seeking behaviors.

E. The client and parents signed a contingency contract specifying the consequences for his/her failure to complete school or homework assignments.

11. Design and Implement a Token Economy (11)

A. A token economy was designed for use in the home to increase the client's positive social behaviors and deter his/her disruptive or negative attention–seeking behaviors.

B. The client and parents agreed to the conditions outlined in the token economy, and agreed to follow through with the implementation at home.

C. A token economy was designed and implemented in the classroom to reinforce the client's positive social behaviors and deter his/her disruptive or negative attention–seeking behaviors.

12. Teach Self-Control Strategies (12)

A. The client was taught mediational and self-control strategies (e.g., relaxation techniques, "stop, look, listen, and think") to help him/her resist the impulse to act out and engage in negative attention–seeking behaviors.

B. The client was encouraged to utilize active listening skills to delay the impulse to act out and engage in negative attention–seeking behaviors.

C. The client was asked to identify the benefits of delaying his/her impulse to react immediately.

D. The client reported success at using self-control strategies to manage his/her impulsivity.

13. Encourage Use of Self-Monitoring Checklists (13)

A. The client was encouraged to use self-monitoring checklists to improve his/her impulse control and social skills.

B. Consulted with the client's teachers about the use of self-monitoring checklists in the classroom to improve his/her impulse control and social skills.

C. The parents and teachers were instructed to utilize a reward system in conjunction with self-monitoring checklists to improve the client's impulse control and social skills.

D. The client reported that the self-monitoring checklists have helped to improve his/her impulse control and social skills.

14. Assign "Stop, Think, and Act" Exercise (14)

A. The client and parents were assigned the "Stop, Think, and Act" exercise from *The Brief Child Therapy Homework Planner* (Jongsma, Peterson, and McInnis) to help the client develop coping strategies to inhibit the impulse to act out and engage in disruptive or negative attention–seeking behaviors.

B. The client was given the "Stop, Think, and Act" exercise to help him/her develop an awareness of how his/her disruptive behaviors lead to negative consequences for self and others.

C. The client reported that the "Stop, Think, and Act" exercise has helped him/her deter impulses to act out and engage in disruptive behaviors.

15. Connect Feelings and Behavior (15)

A. The therapy session helped the client to identify how his/her underlying painful emotions are connected to his/her annoying or disruptive behaviors.

B. The client developed insight into how his/her disruptive or impulsive behaviors are related to underlying feelings of sadness, hurt, and disappointment.

C. Role-playing and modeling techniques were used to demonstrate appropriate ways for the client to express his/her underlying painful emotions.

D. The client was assisted in listing appropriate ways to express his/her feelings and meet his/her needs versus engaging in disruptive or annoying behaviors.

16. Teach Communication and Assertiveness Skills (16)

A. The client was taught effective communication and assertiveness skills to learn how to meet his/her needs for attention and approval through appropriate verbalizations and positive social behaviors.

B. Role-playing techniques were used to model effective ways to meet the client's needs for attention and approval.

C. The client was encouraged to utilize "I messages" and assertive versus aggressive statements to effectively verbalize his/her needs to others.

D. The client was helped to identify appropriate versus inappropriate times to meet his/her needs for attention and approval.

E. The client was helped to differentiate between being assertive and overly demanding.

17. Confront Annoying and Disruptive Behaviors (17)

A. The client was firmly and consistently confronted regarding how his/her annoying and disruptive behaviors negatively affect himself/herself and others.

B. The client was asked to list the negative consequences of his/her annoying or disruptive behaviors.

C. Role-reversal techniques were used in the therapy session to help the client realize how his/her annoying or disruptive behaviors negatively impact others.

D. The client was instructed to apologize to others for his/her annoying or disruptive behaviors.

18. Teach Acceptance of Responsibility (18)

A. The client was consistently confronted and challenged to stop blaming others for his/her annoying or disruptive behaviors.

B. The client was asked to list how his/her disruptive behaviors result in negative consequences for self and others.

C. The client was helped to identify effective ways to resolve conflict and meet his/her needs versus antagonizing others or acting out in a disruptive manner.

D. The client was directed to verbally acknowledge his/her wrongdoings to family members, teachers, or peers.

19. Explore Blaming (19)

A. Today's therapy session explored the underlying factors contributing to the client's pattern of blaming others for his/her behavioral problems.

B. The client was challenged to accept the consequences of his/her actions versus arguing and blaming others.

C. The therapy session helped the client realize how his/her pattern of blaming others is associated with underlying feelings of low self-esteem, inadequacy, and insecurity.

D. The therapy session revealed how the client has learned to model other family members' pattern of blaming others.

E. The parents identified natural, logical consequences such as time out, removal of privileges, or taking away a desired object if the client is caught in a lie or adamantly refuses to admit to his/her wrongdoing.

20. Assign Observation Recording of Positive Behaviors (20)

A. The parents and teachers were instructed to observe and record positive behaviors by the client in between therapy sessions.

B. The parents and teachers were strongly encouraged to reinforce the client for engaging in positive behaviors.

C. The client was strongly encouraged to continue engaging in positive behaviors, to build his/her self-esteem, earn parents' and teachers' approval, and receive affirmation from others.

21. Identify Periods of Positive Social Behavior (21)

A. The client and parents identified periods of time in the past when he/she had demonstrated positive social behaviors and engaged in significantly fewer disruptive behaviors.

B. The client was encouraged to use coping strategies similar to those that he/she had used successfully in the past to control or delay his/her impulses.

C. The therapy session revealed that the client exercised greater self-control and was better behaved during periods of time when he/she received strong family support and affiliated with positive peer groups.

22. Introduce Idea of Change (22)

A. Introduced the idea that the client can change, by asking the following question: "What will you be doing when you stop getting into trouble?"

B. Processed the client's response to the question: "What will you be doing when you stop getting into trouble?"

C. The client was helped to establish goals for positive behavior changes in the future.

D. The client was helped to develop an action plan to achieve his/her goals or desired behavior changes.

E. The client identified several strengths or resources that he/she could use to accomplish goals and stay out of trouble in the future.

23. Prescribe Symptom Enactment (23)

A. A paradoxical intervention was employed in an attempt to diffuse the power or purpose of the client's negative attention–seeking behaviors.

B. The client was assigned to engage in the annoying or disruptive behaviors for a specific length of time or at a set time each day, to help disrupt established patterns of negative behaviors.

C. The paradoxical intervention helped to decrease the frequency of the client's annoying and disruptive behaviors.

D. The client and parents failed to follow through with the paradoxical intervention and were asked again to do it.

24. Explore Possible Stressors (24)

A. The client explored possible stressors or frustrations that may cause negative behaviors to reappear in the future.

B. The client and family members identified successful coping strategies that could be used in the future when facing similar stressful or frustrating events.

C. Guided imagery techniques were used to help the client visualize how he/she can solve potential problems or cope with stressors that might arise in the future.

D. The client was encouraged to consult with and/or enlist the support of family members or significant others when facing problems or stressors in the future.

25. Explore Family Dynamics (25)

A. A family therapy session was held to explore the dynamics within the family system that contribute to the emergence of the client's disruptive and negative attention–seeking behaviors.

B. The family members were asked to list the stressors that have had a negative impact on the family.

C. The family members were asked to identify the things that they would like to change within the family.

26. Conduct Filial Play Therapy (26)

A. A filial play-therapy session (i.e., parental involvement in session) was conducted to assess the quality of the parent-child relationship.

B. A filial play-therapy session was conducted to help improve the quality of the parent-child relationship.

C. The filial play-therapy sessions have helped to increase the parents' awareness of the factors contributing to the emergence of the client's disruptive or annoying behaviors.

D. The filial play-therapy sessions have helped to increase the parents' sensitivity to the client's needs.

E. The filial play-therapy sessions have helped to strengthen the client's relationship with his/her parents.

27. Increase Disengaged Parent Involvement (27)

A. The disengaged parent attended the therapy session and was challenged to spend more time with the client in leisure, school, or household activities.

B. The client directly verbalized his/her need to spend greater time with the disengaged parent.

C. The factors contributing to the distant relationship between the client and detached parent were explored.

D. The detached parent verbalized a commitment to spend increased time with the client.

E. The disengaged parent was given the homework assignment to engage in a leisure activity or go on an outing with the client before the next therapy session.

28. Explore Family Abuse History (28)

A. The client's family background was explored for a history of physical, sexual, or substance abuse.

B. The client developed a time line where he/she identified significant historical events, both positive and negative, that have occurred in his/her family.

C. The client was instructed to draw a diagram of the house where the abuse occurred.

D. A diagnostic interview was conducted to assess the extent of family members' use of drugs and alcohol.

E. A family genogram was drawn in the session to identify other family members who have been abused.

29. Protect Client from Abuse (29)

A. The alleged abuse of the client was reported to the appropriate agency.

B. The recommendation was made that the perpetrator be removed from the home and seek treatment.

C. The recommendation was made that the client and siblings be removed from the home to ensure protection.

D. The client and family members identified necessary steps to take in the future to minimize the risk of the abuse occurring again.

E. The nonabusive parent verbalized a commitment to protect the client and siblings from physical or sexual abuse in the future.

30. Explore Feelings Associated with Neglect or Abuse (30)

A. The client was given the opportunity in today's therapy session to express his/her feelings about the past neglect, abuse, separation, or abandonment.

B. The client was instructed to draw pictures that reflected his/her feelings about the past abuse, neglect, separation, or abandonment.

C. The client was instructed to use a journal to record his/her thoughts and feelings about the past abuse, neglect, separation, or abandonment.

D. The client was given empathy and support in expressing his/her feelings about the past abuse, neglect, separation, or abandonment.

31. Conduct Child-Centered Play-Therapy Approaches (31)

A. Child-centered play-therapy approaches were utilized to help the client express and work through his/her feelings surrounding the past abuse, neglect, separation, or abandonment.

B. The client was given unconditional positive regard and warm acceptance while expressing his/her feelings through play.

C. The client's feelings that were expressed in his/her play were reflected to him/her in a nonjudgmental manner.

D. The client's play reflected strong feelings of anger, hurt, and sadness about the past neglect and abuse.

E. The client's play reflected strong feelings of anger, hurt, and sadness about the past separation or abandonment.

32. Utilize Empty-Chair Technique (32)

A. The empty-chair technique was used to help the client express and work through his/her feelings of anger and sadness about the past neglect, abuse, separation, or abandonment.

B. The empty-chair technique was helpful in allowing the client to identify and work through his/her feelings of anger and sadness about the past neglect, abuse, separation, or abandonment.

C. The client appeared uncomfortable about the use of the empty-chair technique and was reluctant to share his/her emotions about the past neglect, abuse, separation, or abandonment.

D. The empty-chair technique helped the client vent his/her feelings of anger, sadness, and hurt toward the perpetrator of the abuse.

E. The empty-chair technique helped the client express his/her feelings toward the parent who neglected or abandoned him/her.

33. Encourage Positive Peer Group Activities (33)

A. The client was strongly encouraged to participate in extracurricular or positive peer group activities to provide a healthy outlet for his/her anger, improve social skills, and increase self-esteem.

B. The client was assisted in developing a list of extracurricular or positive peer group activities that will provide him/her with the opportunity to establish meaningful friendships.

C. The client acknowledged that his/her feelings of inadequacy and insecurity contribute to his/her reluctance to become involved in extracurricular or positive peer group activities.

D. The client reported that participation in extracurricular activities has helped provide a healthy outlet for his/her anger.

E. The client reported that participation in positive peer group activities has helped him/her establish meaningful friendships.

34. Assign to Perform Altruistic Acts (34)

A. The client was given the homework assignment of performing three altruistic or benevolent acts before the next therapy session to increase his/her empathy and sensitivity to the thoughts, feelings, and needs of others.

B. The client was given the homework assignment of performing a caring or benevolent act with his/her sibling before the next therapy session.

C. The client was given the homework assignment of performing an act of kindness with a peer at school.

D. Reinforced the client for following through with the homework assignment of showing show empathy or kindness to others.

E. The client's failure to comply with the homework assignment of performing altruistic or benevolent acts reflects his/her lack of empathy and concern for the welfare of others.

35. Group Therapy Referral (35)

A. The client was referred for group therapy to improve his/her social judgment and interpersonal skills.

B. The client was given the directive to self-disclose at least one time during the group therapy session.

C. The client was encouraged to demonstrate empathy and concern for the thoughts, feelings, and needs of others during the group therapy session.

36. Play "You & Me: A Game of Social Skills" (36)

A. The client played "You & Me: A Game of Social Skills" (Shapiro) to help him/her develop positive social skills.

B. After playing "You & Me: A Game of Social Skills," the client was helped to identify several positive social skills.

C. The client was given the homework assignment of practicing one social skill that he/she had learned from playing "You & Me: A Game of Social Skills," on at least three occasions before the next therapy session.

D. The client identified "You & Me: A Game of Social Skills" as being an enjoyable way to learn about positive social skills.

E. "You & Me: A Game of Social Skills" has helped to improve the client's social judgment.

37. Play "The Helping, Sharing, and Caring" Game (37)

A. Played "The Helping, Sharing, and Caring" game (Gardner) with the client during the initial stages of therapy to help establish rapport with him/her.

B. Played "The Helping, Sharing, and Caring Game" with the client in today's therapy session to help increase his/her empathy and concern for the welfare of others.

C. After playing "The Helping, Sharing, and Caring Game," the client was given the homework assignment of performing three acts of kindness with siblings or peers before the next therapy session.

D. The "Helping, Sharing, and Caring Game" has helped the client to become more empathic and sensitive to the thoughts, feelings, and needs of others.

38. Interpret Feelings Shown in Play Therapy (38)

A. An individual play-therapy session was held to explore and interpret the underlying emotions contributing to the client's negative attention–seeking behaviors.

B. The client's play reflected strong feelings of anger.

C. The client's play reflected underlying feelings of sadness, hurt, and disappointment.

D. The client's play reflected underlying feelings of anxiety about his/her behavior being out of control.

E. Interpreted the client's feelings expressed in his/her play and related them to his/her behavior at home and school.

39. Utilize Psychoanalytic Play Therapy (39)

A. A psychoanalytic play-therapy session was held to allow the client the opportunity to work through and resolve the core conflicts or anxieties that contribute to his/her disruptive behaviors.

B. Processed and worked through transference issues that emerged in the play-therapy session.

C. The client's play revealed insight into the underlying issues that contribute to his/her disruptive and negative attention–seeking behaviors.

D. Interpreted the client's feelings expressed in his/her play and related them to his/her present life situation.

E. The psychoanalytic play-therapy sessions have helped the client work through and resolve the issues contributing to the emergence of his/her disruptive behaviors.

40. Implement Mutual Storytelling Technique (40)

A. The client actively participated in the mutual storytelling exercise.

B. A mutual storytelling technique using puppets, dolls, or stuffed animals was employed to model appropriate ways for the client to gain approval and acceptance from his/her peers.

C. The client identified the mutual storytelling technique as being a fun and beneficial way to learn how to gain approval and acceptance from peers.

D. After completing the mutual storytelling technique, the client reviewed appropriate ways to gain approval and acceptance from peers.

E. After completing the mutual storytelling exercise, the client was given the homework assignment of practicing the positive social skills that were modeled in the stories at least three times before the next therapy session.

41. Use Puppets to Assess Unmet Needs/Core Issues (41)

A. The client was directed to create a story using puppets, dolls, or stuffed animals to help assess his/her unmet needs and/or the family dynamics that contribute to the emergence of his/her disruptive or negative attention–seeking behaviors.

B. The story enactment technique was helpful in identifying the client's unmet needs.

C. Reflected the client's feelings that were expressed in his/her story and related them to his/her feelings about a present life situation.

42. Employ Art Therapy Technique (42)

A. An art therapy technique was employed whereby the client was first instructed to draw a picture of a house, then create a story telling what it is like to live in that house.

B. The art therapy technique was utilized to help assess family dynamics.

C. Processed the feelings and content reflected in the client's artwork and story.

D. The client's drawing and story reflected a perceived lack of closeness and support within his/her family.

E. The client's drawing and story reflected his/her perception of his/her family members being critical and rejecting.

43. Utilize "Color-Your-Life" Technique (43)

A. The "Color-Your-Life" technique (O'Connor) was used to improve the client's ability to identify and verbalize his/her feelings instead of acting them out.

B. The client used color in his/her drawing to reflect feelings of sadness about a significant life event.

C. The client used color to reflect his/her strong feelings of anger about a significant life event.

D. After completing the drawing, the client was able to directly verbalize his/her feelings about the significant life event.

E. The parents were encouraged to utilize the "Color-Your-Life" technique at home to help the client identify and verbalize his/her feelings about significant life events.

44. Assign Reading to Client (44)

A. The client and parents were assigned to read the book *How I Learned to Think Things Through* (Shapiro) to help the client learn to increase his/her impulse control.

B. Read the book *How I Learned to Think Things Through* to help the client learn impulse control and to increase his/her ability to stop and think about the possible consequences of negative social behaviors.

C. After reading the assigned book, the client was able to identify effective ways to inhibit his/her impulses.

D. The client was strongly encouraged to practice the coping strategies that he/she learned from reading the assigned book.

E. The client verbalized that the assigned book helped him/her realize how his/her negative social behaviors negatively affect self and others.

45. Assign Readings to Parents (45)

A. The parents were assigned to read one or more of the following books to help increase their knowledge of appropriate disciplinary techniques: *1-2-3 Magic: Training Your Preschoolers and Preteens to Do What You Want* (Phelan); *Family Rules* (Kaye); and *Assertive Discipline for Parents* (Canter and Canter).

B. Processed the assigned reading(s) with the parents in today's therapy session.

C. The parents reported that the assigned book(s) helped increase their knowledge about appropriate disciplinary techniques.

D. The parents reported that the assigned book(s) helped them realize the importance of establishing clear-cut rules for the client so that he/she has a clear understanding of what is expected of him/her.

E. The parents were strongly encouraged to use the disciplinary techniques that they learned from the assigned reading(s).

46. Assess Marital Dyad (46)

A. Today's therapy session assessed the marital dyad for possible conflict and/or triangulation that places the focus on the client's disruptive behaviors and away from the parents' marital problems.

B. The parents recognized how their marital problems are creating stress for the client and agreed to seek marital counseling.

C. The parents refused to follow through with the recommendation to pursue marital counseling.

D. The client shared his/her worries about the parents' marital problems in today's therapy session.

E. The client acknowledged exhibiting more behavioral problems during times when his/her parents are experiencing greater conflict.

47. Medication Evaluation Referral (47)

A. The client was referred for a medication evaluation to improve his/her impulse control and stabilize moods.

B. The client and parents agreed to follow through with a medication evaluation.

C. The client was strongly opposed to being placed on medication to help improve his/her impulse control and stabilize moods.

D. The client and parents reported that the medication has helped to improve the client's impulse control and stabilize his/her moods.

E. The client and parents reported that the medication has not produced the desired changes in behavior.

DIVORCE REACTION

CLIENT PRESENTATION

1. Reduced Contact with a Parent (1)*

A. The client has had infrequent or no contact with one of his/her parents since the separation or divorce.

B. The client was guarded and reluctant to talk about the infrequent or loss of contact with one of his/her parents.

C. The client expressed feelings of sadness, hurt, and disappointment about the infrequent or loss of contact with one of his/her parents.

D. The client verbalized strong feelings of anger about the limited contact with one of his/her parents.

E. The client has worked through many of his/her emotions surrounding the infrequent or loss of contact with one of his/her parents.

2. Loss of Contact with Positive Support Network (2)

A. The client has experienced a loss of contact with his/her previous support network as a result of moving to a new geographic area.

B. The client expressed feelings of sadness about having to move after his/her parents' separation or divorce because it resulted in a loss of contact with his/her previous support network.

C. The client expressed feelings of anger about having to move after his/her parents' separation or divorce.

D. The client has taken active steps to build a positive support network since moving to a new geographic area.

E. The client reported establishing a strong, supportive social network outside of his/her immediate family.

3. Emotional Distress around Separations (3)

A. The client has often exhibited a great deal of emotional distress when anticipating a separation from one of his/her parents.

B. The client became visibly upset and began to protest vigorously when asked to separate from his/her parent in today's therapy session.

C. The client has often displayed temper outbursts around separations from one of his/her parents.

D. The client has gradually started to cope more effectively with separations and has not exhibited as much distress when anticipating separation from a parent.

E. The client was able to separate effectively from his/her parent in today's therapy session without exhibiting a significant amount of distress.

---

* The numbers in parentheses correlate to the number of the Behavioral Definition statement in the companion chapter with same title in *The Child Psychotherapy Treatment Planner* (Jongsma, Peterson, and McInnis) by John Wiley & Sons, 2000.

4. Emotional Distress around Transfer from Home(s) (3)

A. The client has often exhibited a great deal of emotional distress when making the transfer from one parent's home to the other.

B. The parents reported that the client frequently exhibits temper outbursts before and after he/she makes the transfer from one home to the other.

C. The client has often begged and pleaded to stay with one parent before making the transfer to the other parent's home.

D. The client has gradually started to cope more effectively with the transfer between homes.

E. The client has consistently been able to make the transition from one parent's home to the other without exhibiting any heightened emotional distress.

5. Visitation Arrangements (3)

A. The client reported a significant amount of conflict or discord within the family system over the child visitation arrangements.

B. The client expressed dissatisfaction with the current visitation arrangements between himself/herself and the noncustodial parent.

C. The client expressed a desire to spend more time with the noncustodial parent.

D. The client verbalized his/her preference for socializing with peers instead of visiting with the noncustodial parent.

E. The parents have established and maintained consistent, yet flexible, visitation arrangements that have met the client's social and emotional needs.

6. Fear of Abandonment/Separation (4)

A. The client has developed persistent fears about being abandoned or separated from his/her parents.

B. The client expressed his/her fears of abandonment in today's therapy session.

C. The client expressed his/her worries about being separated from his/her parents.

D. The client has developed persistent worries about being separated from the custodial parent, in part because of the limited contact he/she has with the noncustodial parent.

E. The client has successfully worked through and resolved his/her fears and worries about being abandoned or separated from his/her parents.

7. Feelings of Guilt/Self-Blame (5)

A. The client expressed feelings of guilt about having acted in some way to cause his/her parents' divorce.

B. The client has continued to hold on to the unreasonable belief that he/she either behaved in some manner to cause his/her parents' divorce or failed to prevent the divorce from occurring.

C. The client has started to work through his/her feelings of guilt about his/her parents' separation or divorce.

D. The parent(s) verbalized that the client is not responsible for the separation or divorce.

E. The client has successfully worked through his/her feelings of guilt and no longer blames himself/herself for the parents' separation or divorce.

8. Feelings of Grief and Sadness (6)

A. The client has experienced strong feelings of grief and sadness since his/her parents' separation or divorce.

B. The client was visibly sad when talking about his/her parents' separation or divorce.

C. The client has begun to work through his/her feelings of grief and sadness about the separation or divorce.

D. The client's affect appeared more happy and/or contented in today's therapy session.

E. The client reported a significant reduction recently in the frequency and severity of his/her depressed mood.

9. Low Self-Esteem (6)

A. The client's self-esteem has decreased significantly since his/her parents' separation or divorce.

B. The client verbalized feelings of low self-esteem, inadequacy, and insecurity.

C. The client has begun to take steps to improve his/her self-esteem and develop a positive self-image.

D. The client expressed positive self-descriptive statements during today's therapy session.

E. The client has developed a healthy self-image after working through many of his/her feelings surrounding his/her parents' separation or divorce.

10. Social Withdrawal (6)

A. The client has become significantly more withdrawn and isolated since his/her parents' separation or divorce.

B. The client appeared very quiet and withdrawn during today's therapy session and initiated few conversations.

C. The client has gradually started to socialize more often with his/her peers.

D. The client was more communicative and outgoing during today's therapy session.

11. Oppositional, Acting-Out, and Aggressive Behavior (7)

A. The client has exhibited a significant increase in the frequency and severity of his/her oppositional, acting-out, and aggressive behaviors since his/her parents' separation or divorce.

B. The client appeared angry and irritable when discussing the separation or divorce.

C. The frequency of the client's oppositional, acting-out, and aggressive behaviors has gradually started to diminish.

D. The client has recently demonstrated good self-control and has not engaged in a significant amount of oppositional, acting-out, or aggressive behaviors.

12. Parents Critical of Each Other (7)

A. The client reported that his/her parent(s) often make hostile, critical remarks about one another in his/her presence.

B. The client expressed feelings of anger, sadness, and frustration about his/her parent(s)' pattern of making unnecessary, hostile, or overly critical remarks about one another.

C. The client verbalized his/her request for the parents to cease making unnecessary, hostile, or overly critical remarks about each other in his/her presence.

D. The parent(s) acknowledged that their hostile or critical remarks about the other parent are upsetting to the client and his/her siblings.

E. The client reported that his/her parent(s) have ceased making hostile or overly critical remarks about the other parent in his/her presence.

F. The client has successfully worked through many of his/her feelings surrounding the separation or divorce and has demonstrated a significant reduction in the frequency and severity of his/her oppositional, acting-out, and aggressive behaviors.

13. Lack of Consistency by Parents (7)

A. The parent(s) have not set firm, consistent limits with the client's irresponsible or acting-out behaviors since the separation or divorce.

B. The parent(s) acknowledged that their lack of consistency has contributed to an increase in the client's acting-out and irresponsible behaviors.

C. The parent(s) acknowledged that their feelings of guilt about the separation or divorce have contributed to their lack of consistency.

D. The parent(s) have started to take steps to increase the structure in the home and be more consistent in setting limits with the client's irresponsible or acting-out behaviors.

E. The parent(s) reported that the increase in consistency and structure has led to a decrease in the frequency of the client's irresponsible and acting-out behaviors.

14. Overindulgence by Parents (7)

A. The parent(s) have exhibited a pattern of being overindulgent in meeting the client's desires since the separation or divorce.

B. The parent(s) acknowledged that their feelings of guilt about the separation or divorce have contributed to their pattern of overindulgence.

C. The noncustodial parent acknowledged that to avoid any possible conflict or stress he/she is overindulgent with the client on visits.

D. The parent(s) have begun to establish reasonable limits on the fulfillment of the client's wishes.

15. Decline in School Performance (8)

A. The client's school performance has decreased markedly since his/her parents' separation or divorce.

B. The client verbalized that he/she has experienced a loss of interest or motivation to achieve academic success since the separation or divorce.

C. The client has experienced a renewed interest in schoolwork and has begun to take steps to improve his/her academic performance.

D. The client reported completing his/her school or homework assignments on a regular basis.

16. Regressive Behaviors (9)

A. The client has demonstrated an increase in regressive behaviors since his/her parents' separation.

B. The client exhibited regressive behaviors in today's therapy session.

C. The client spoke in a very immature or infantile (i.e., baby talk) manner when discussing his/her parents' separation or divorce.

D. The client did not engage in any regressive behaviors during today's therapy session.

E. The parent(s) reported that the client has demonstrated a significant reduction in the frequency of his/her regressive behaviors.

17. Bed-Wetting (9)

A. The client has regressed and experienced problems with bed-wetting since his/her parents' separation or divorce.

B. The client verbalized feelings of shame and embarrassment about his/her bed-wetting problem.

C. The client has regained effective bladder control at night.

D. The client expressed feelings of happiness about overcoming his/her problems with bed-wetting.

18. Pseudomaturity (10)

A. The client has responded to his/her parents' separation or divorce by displaying an air of pseudomaturity.

B. The client presented with a facade of pseudomaturity and coolly denied being troubled by any painful emotions about his/her parents' separation or divorce.

C. The client has responded to the separation or divorce by often assuming parental roles or responsibilities.

D. The client verbalized an awareness of how his/her willingness to take on many parental roles or responsibilities has prevented him/her from meeting his/her own emotional or social needs.

E. The client has achieved a healthy balance between fulfilling his/her school or household responsibilities and meeting his/her social and emotional needs.

19. Psychosomatic Ailments (11)

A. The client has demonstrated a significant increase in psychosomatic complaints since his/her parents' separation or divorce.

B. The client complained of not feeling well when the issue of his/her parents' separation or divorce was being discussed.

C. The client was resistant to the interpretation that his/her psychosomatic complaints are related to his/her underlying painful emotions about the separation or divorce.

D. The client verbalized an understanding of the connection between his/her psychosomatic complaints and anticipated separations, stress, or frustration related to the parents' marital conflict.

E. The client has demonstrated a significant reduction in the frequency of his/her psychosomatic complaints.

20. Anxiety (11)

A. The client reported a significant increase in his/her feelings of anxiety since his/her parents' separation or divorce.

B. The client appeared nervous, anxious, and tense during today's therapy session.

C. The client's feelings of anxiety have gradually started to decrease as he/she works through his/her feelings about the separation or divorce.

D. The client appeared more relaxed and comfortable in today's therapy session.

E. The client reported a significant reduction in the frequency of his/her anxious moods.

INTERVENTIONS IMPLEMENTED

1. Build Therapeutic Trust (1)*

A. The objective of today's therapy session was to establish trust with the client so that he/she can begin to express and work through his/her feelings related to the parents' separation or divorce.

B. Attempts were made to build the level of trust with the client through consistent eye contact, active listening, unconditional positive regard, and warm acceptance.

C. The therapy session was helpful in building a level of trust with the client.

D. The therapy session was not successful in establishing trust with the client as he/she remained guarded in sharing his/her feelings about the separation or divorce.

2. Explore and Encourage Expression of Feelings (2)

A. Today's therapy session explored the client's feelings associated with his/her parents' separation or divorce.

B. The client was given encouragement and support in expressing and clarifying his/her feelings associated with the separation or divorce.

C. Client-centered therapy principles were utilized to assist the client in expressing his/her thoughts and feelings about the parents' separation or divorce.

D. The client made productive use of today's therapy session and expressed a variety of emotions related to his/her parents' separation or divorce.

E. The client remained guarded in sharing his/her feelings regarding the separation or divorce, despite receiving encouragement and support.

3. Assign Children's Books on Divorce (3)

A. Read *Dinosaur's Divorce: A Guide for Changing Families* (Brown and Brown) to the client in today's therapy session.

B. Read *Divorce Workbook: A Guide for Kids and Families* (Ives, Fassler, and Lash) in today's therapy session to help the client express his/her feelings about the parents' divorce and changes in the family system.

C. Processed the content of the readings in today's therapy session.

D. Reading the books on divorce helped the client express and work through his/her feelings about the parents' divorce.

E. After reading the book on divorce, the client was able to express his/her thoughts and feelings about the changes that have occurred within the family system.

* The numbers in parentheses correlate to the number of the Therapeutic Interventions statement in the companion chapter with same title in *The Child Psychotherapy Treatment Planner* (Jongsma, Peterson, and McInnis) by John Wiley & Sons, 2000.

4. Create Photo Album (4)

A. The client was instructed to gather a diverse collection of photographs covering many aspects of his/her life, and bring them to the next session to create a photo album.

B. In today's therapy session, the client placed his/her collection of photographs in a photo album.

C. Creating the photo album helped the client identify and express his/her feelings about the changes within the family system.

D. While creating the family photo album, the client expressed his/her feelings of sadness about the changes in the family system.

E. While creating the photo album, the client expressed feelings of anger about the changes in the family system.

5. Develop a Time Line (5)

A. The client developed a time line on which he/she recorded significant developments that have positively or negatively impacted his/her family life, both before and after the parents' separation or divorce.

B. The use of the time line was helpful in allowing the client to express his/her thoughts and feelings about the impact of the parents' separation or divorce on his/her life.

C. The use of the time line exercise was not helpful in facilitating a discussion about the impact of the parents' separation or divorce on the client's life.

D. The client was able to identify a number of positive and negative changes that have occurred within the family system since the parents' separation or divorce.

E. The client used the time line to express his/her ambivalent feelings about the parents' divorce and the subsequent changes within the family system.

6. Color-Your-Life Technique (6)

A. The Color-Your-Life technique (O'Connor) was used to help the client express his/her feelings about the parents' separation or divorce.

B. The client used the Color-Your-Life technique to identify and express his/her ambivalent feelings toward both parents as a result of the parents' separation or divorce.

C. The Color-Your-Life technique helped the client identify and express his/her feelings of sadness about the parents' separation or divorce.

D. The Color-Your-Life technique helped the client identify and express his/her feelings of anger about the parents' separation or divorce.

7. Assign "Feelings and Faces" Exercise (7)

A. The "Feelings and Faces" exercise from *The Brief Child Therapy Homework Planner* (Jongsma, Peterson, and McInnis) was utilized to help the client express and work through his/her ambivalent feelings about the parents' separation or divorce.

B. The "Feelings and Faces" exercise was employed to help the client work through his/her feelings of grief about the parents' separation or divorce.

C. The "Feelings and Faces" exercise was utilized to enlist the support of the parents in helping the client to identify and express his/her thoughts and feelings about their separation or divorce.

D. The client identified the "Feelings and Faces" exercise as being a useful way to express his/her feelings about the parents' separation or divorce.

E. The client failed to complete the "Feelings and Faces" exercise and was asked to do it again to help him/her work through feelings about the parents' separation or divorce.

8. Employ Empty-Chair Technique (8)

A. The empty-chair technique was used to help the client express the mixed emotions that he/she feels toward both parents because of their separation or divorce.

B. The empty-chair technique was helpful in enabling the client to identify and express the emotions that he/she feels toward both parents because of their separation or divorce.

C. The client appeared uncomfortable with the use of the empty-chair technique and was reluctant to share the emotions that he/she feels toward both parents because of their separation or divorce.

D. The empty-chair technique was useful in allowing the client to express his/her thoughts and feelings about the custodial and noncustodial parent.

9. Utilize Family Therapy to Facilitate Feelings Expression (9)

A. A family therapy session was held to allow the client and his/her siblings to express feelings and ask questions about the separation or divorce in the presence of the parent.

B. The custodial parent was supportive in allowing the client and siblings to express their feelings and ask questions about the separation or divorce.

C. The noncustodial parent was supportive in allowing the client and siblings to express their feelings and ask questions about the separation or divorce.

D. The custodial parent became defensive when the client and siblings began expressing their feelings and asking questions about the separation or divorce.

E. The noncustodial parent became defensive when the client and siblings began expressing their feelings and asking questions about the separation or divorce.

10. Provide Opportunities at Home to Express Feelings (10)

A. The parent(s) were encouraged to provide opportunities at home to allow the client and siblings to express their feelings and ask questions about the separation or divorce and subsequent changes in the family system.

B. The parent(s) were encouraged to hold family meetings at home to allow the client and siblings an opportunity to express their feelings and ask questions about the separation or divorce and subsequent changes in the family system.

C. The family members were helped to identify healthy and unhealthy ways to express their feelings about the separation or divorce and subsequent changes in the family system.

D. The parent(s) were encouraged to explore the client's feelings about the separation or divorce and subsequent changes in the family system when he/she becomes more withdrawn or demonstrates an increase in emotional outbursts.

E. The client and siblings were asked to identify the specific, positive changes that they would like to see happen in the family.

11. Assess Factors Contributing to Guilt (11)

A. Today's therapy session explored and identified the factors contributing to the client's feelings of guilt and self-blame about the parents' separation or divorce.

B. The client expressed feelings of guilt about how his/her acting-out or rebellious behaviors may have contributed to the parents' separation or divorce.

C. Today's therapy session did not reveal any specific events that have contributed to the client's feelings of guilt and self-blame about the parents' separation or divorce.

D. The client denied being troubled by any strong feelings of guilt about his/her parents' separation or divorce.

12. Teach That Client's Behaviors Did Not Cause Divorce (12)

A. The client was helped to understand that his/her negative behaviors did not cause his/her parents' divorce to occur.

B. The client was gently confronted with the fact that he/she does not have the power or control to bring his/her parents back together.

C. The client has continued to hold on to feelings of guilt about how his/her negative behaviors caused the parents' divorce, despite efforts to inform him/her that he/she is not responsible.

D. The client was helped to realize how his/her negative behaviors will not bring the parents back together.

13. Affirm Client as Not Being Responsible for Separation/Divorce (13)

A. The custodial parent strongly affirmed the client and siblings as not being responsible for the separation or divorce.

B. The noncustodial parent strongly affirmed the client and siblings as not being responsible for the separation or divorce.

C. The parent(s) verbalized responsibility for the separation or divorce.

D. The client and siblings responded positively to the parents' affirmation that they are not responsible for the separation or divorce.

E. The client has continued to be troubled by feelings of guilt about his/her parents' divorce despite the parents' statements that he/she is not responsible.

14. Confront Blaming by Parents (14)

A. The custodial parent was challenged and confronted about making statements that place the blame or responsibility for the separation or divorce on the client or siblings.

B. The noncustodial parent was challenged and confronted about making statements that place the blame or responsibility for the separation or divorce on the client or siblings.

C. The custodial parent verbalized a commitment to stop making statements that place the blame or responsibility for the separation or divorce onto the client or siblings.

D. The noncustodial parent verbalized a commitment to stop making statements that place the blame or responsibility for the separation or divorce onto the client or siblings.

E. The parent(s) have continued to make statements that place the blame or responsibility for the separation or divorce onto the client or siblings, despite challenges to stop making such remarks.

15. List Positive and Negative Aspects of Divorce (15)

A. The client was given a homework assignment to list both the positive and negative aspects of his/her parents' divorce.

B. The client was reassured of the normalcy of feeling a variety of emotions while processing both the positive and negative aspects of his/her parents' divorce.

C. The client expressed his/her emotions about the negative aspects of his/her parents' divorce but was unable to identify any positive aspects.

D. The client's failure to complete the homework assignment of listing both the positive or negative aspects of his/her parents' divorce appeared to be due to his/her desire to avoid dealing with any painful emotions.

16. Reinforce Healthy Coping with Divorce (16)

A. The therapy session focused on empowering the client's ability to cope with his/her parents' divorce.

B. The client was asked to identify a list of behaviors or signs that would indicate he/she has made a healthy adjustment to the parents' divorce.

C. The client was reinforced for the positive steps that he/she has taken to adjust to his/her parents' divorce.

D. The client remains pessimistic and resistant to the idea that he/she can make a healthy adjustment to the divorce.

17. Encourage Parents to Spend Time with Client (17)

A. The parent(s) were given the directive to spend 10 to 15 minutes of one-on-one time with the client and siblings on a regular or daily basis.

B. The client reported that the one-on-one time spent with the parent(s) has helped to decrease his/her feelings of depression.

C. The client and parents reported that the one-on-one time spent together has helped to improve the client's anger control.

D. The client and parents reported that they have spent little time together because of their busy schedules.

E. The client and parents were strongly challenged to spend time together in order to help the client adjust to his/her parents' divorce.

18. Assist Transition from One Parent's Home to the Other

A. Consulted with the client and parent(s) about establishing a routine or ritual to help decrease the client's emotional distress around periods of separation or transfer from one parent's home to the other.

B. The client and parent(s) reported that the client has made a smoother transition from one parent's home to the other by engaging in relaxing or enjoyable activities.

C. The client has continued to find it difficult to make the transition from one parent's home to the other after visits, but has failed to follow through with the recommendation to engage in relaxing or enjoyable activities.

D. The client was helped to identify a list of activities that he/she could engage in to help him/her cope with separations from parents.

E. The client was encouraged to play or interact with siblings or peers to help him/her cope with separations from parents.

19. Connect Painful Emotions to Angry Outbursts (19)

A. The session was helpful in identifying how the client's underlying, painful emotions about his/her parents' divorce are related to an increase in the frequency of his/her angry outbursts or aggressive behaviors.

B. The client verbalized an understanding of how his/her aggressive behaviors are connected to underlying feelings of sadness, hurt, or disappointment about his/her parents' divorce.

C. Role-playing and modeling techniques were used to demonstrate appropriate ways for the client to express his/her underlying painful emotions.

D. The client was asked to list more appropriate ways to express his/her painful emotions about the divorce instead of reacting impulsively with anger or aggression.

20. Use "Surface Behavior/Inner Feelings" Exercise (20)

A. The client was assigned the "Surface Behavior/Inner Feelings" exercise from the *Brief Child Therapy Homework Planner* (Jongsma, Peterson, and McInnis) to help him/her recognize how acting-out behaviors are connected to the emotional pain surrounding the parents' divorce.

B. The client reported that the "Surface Behavior/Inner Feelings" exercise helped him/her realize how his/her acting-out behaviors are related to the emotional pain surrounding parents' divorce.

C. The client failed to complete the "Surface Behavior/Inner Feelings" exercise and was asked to do it again.

21. Teach Appropriate versus Inappropriate Anger Expressions (21)

A. The client was helped to identify appropriate and inappropriate ways to express his/her anger about the parents' separation, divorce, or changes in family.

B. The client was taught mediational and self-control strategies (e.g., relaxation, "stop, look, listen, and think") to help express anger through appropriate verbalizations and healthy physical outlets.

C. The client was encouraged to utilize active listening skills to delay the impulse or urge to react with anger or physical aggression when upset about his/her parents' separation, divorce, or changes in family.

D. The client identified healthy physical outlets for his/her strong feelings of anger and aggressive impulses.

22. Angry Tower Technique (22)

A. The Angry Tower technique (Saxe) was used in today's therapy session to help the client identify and express his/her feelings of anger about the parents' divorce.

B. The Angry Tower technique helped the client directly verbalize his/her feelings of anger about the parents' divorce.

C. The client identified the Angry Tower technique as being an effective way to discharge his/her angry feelings.

D. After playing the Angry Tower game, the client processed whether he/she was willing to express his/her feelings of anger toward the parent(s).

E. The client was encouraged to express his/her feelings of anger in a direct and controlled manner toward his/her parents or significant others.

23. Reinforce Parents' Setting Consistent Limits (23)

A. The parent(s) were strongly encouraged to set firm, consistent limits with the client's acting-out, oppositional, or aggressive behaviors and not allow guilt feelings about the divorce to interfere with the need to impose consequences for such behaviors.

B. The parent(s) acknowledged their failure to follow through with firm, consistent limits with the client's acting-out, oppositional, or aggressive behaviors because of guilt feelings about the divorce.

C. The parent(s) reported that they have begun to set firm, consistent limits and have not allowed their guilt feelings to interfere with the need to impose consequences.

D. The parent(s) reported that the client has demonstrated improvements in his/her behavior since they began to set firm, consistent limits with his/her acting out, oppositional, or aggressive behaviors.

24. Encourage Parents to Establish Clear Rules (24)

A. The parent(s) were helped to establish clearly defined rules and boundaries for the client.

B. The client and parents were helped to identify natural, logical consequences for the client's acting-out, oppositional, or aggressive behaviors.

C. The client was asked to repeat the rules to demonstrate an understanding of the expectations of him/her.

D. The client verbally disagreed with the rules and expectations identified by the parent(s).

25. Assign Readings on Disciplinary Techniques (25)

A. The parent(s) were instructed to read *1-2-3 Magic: Training Your Preschoolers and Pre-teens to Do What You Want* (Phelan) to increase their knowledge of effective disciplinary techniques used to manage the client's acting out, oppositional, and aggressive behaviors.

B. The assigned readings on effective disciplinary techniques were processed in today's therapy session.

C. The parent(s) reported that the assigned reading was helpful in learning about effective disciplinary techniques.

D. The parent(s) reported improvements in the client's behavior after they began implementing the disciplinary techniques they learned from reading the assigned book.

26. Design Reward System for Anger Control (26)

A. The client and parents identified a list of rewards to reinforce the client for demonstrating good anger control.

B. A reward system was designed to reinforce the client for demonstrating good anger control.

C. The client and parents signed a contingency contract specifying the consequences for the client's acting-out, oppositional, or aggressive behaviors.

D. The client and parents verbally agreed to the terms of the contingency contract.

27. Assist Parents in Developing Homework Routine (27)

A. The parent(s) were assisted in establishing a new routine to help the client complete his/her school or homework assignments.

B. The client and parent(s) were helped to develop a routine schedule of times to increase the completion of homework assignments.

C. The parents were strongly encouraged to maintain regular communication with the teachers or school officials via phone calls or written notes regarding the client's academic progress.

D. Consulted with the teachers about sending home daily or weekly progress notes informing the parents of how well the client has been doing at completing his/her school or homework assignments.

28. Develop Reward System to Improve Academic Performance (28)

A. The client and parents identified a list of rewards to reinforce the client for completing his/her school or homework assignments on a regular basis.

B. A reward system was designed to reinforce the client for completing his/her school or homework assignments.

C. The client and parents signed a contingency contract specifying the consequences for the client's failure to complete school or homework assignments.

D. The client and parents verbally agreed to the terms of the reward system and/or contingency contract.

29. Explore Relationship of Physical Complaints to Emotional Conflicts (29)

A. Today's therapy session focused on the relationship between the client's somatic complaints and underlying emotional conflicts associated with the parents' divorce.

B. Today's therapy session attempted to refocus the discussion away from the client's physical complaints onto the underlying emotional conflicts and the expression of feelings associated with the parents' divorce.

C. Today's therapy session explored the secondary gain that is achieved by the client's somatic complaints.

D. The client verbally acknowledged that his/her somatic complaints are associated with the stress and conflict surrounding his/her parents' divorce.

E. The client verbalized an understanding of how his/her somatic complaints are related to unfulfilled dependency needs.

30. Clarify Roles and Responsibilities of Family Members (30)

A. A family therapy session was held to discuss the roles and division of responsibilities for all family members.

B. Today's therapy session was helpful in identifying the rules, roles, and responsibilities of all family members.

C. The family members disagreed over the roles and division of household responsibilities.

D. A reward system was designed to reinforce the client and siblings for completing their household responsibilities.

E. A contingency contract was established to identify the consequences for the family members' failure to complete their household responsibilities.

31. Assignment of Responsibilities by Noncustodial Parent (31)

A. The noncustodial parent was given the directive to assign chore(s) to the client and siblings during their visits.

B. The noncustodial parent was encouraged to schedule times for the client and siblings to complete their homework.

C. The noncustodial parent acknowledged that he/she is reluctant to assign chores or require the children to complete homework because of the desire to avoid upsetting the client or siblings or creating potential conflict.

D. The noncustodial parent was helped to develop a reward system to reinforce the client and siblings for completing chores and homework during visits.

E. The noncustodial parent was helped to identify consequences for the failure of his/her children to complete chores or homework.

32. Encourage Limit Setting by Noncustodial Parent (32)

A. The noncustodial parent was strongly encouraged to set firm, consistent limits on the client's misbehavior and to refrain from overindulging the client's desires during visits.

B. The noncustodial parent was helped to identify logical, natural consequences for the client's misbehavior.

C. The noncustodial parent verbally acknowledged how his/her pattern of overindulgence contributes to the client's immaturity and resistance to take on responsibilities.

D. The noncustodial parent acknowledged his/her reluctance to set limits for the client's misbehavior because of his/her feelings of guilt and desire to avoid conflict during visits.

E. The noncustodial parent reported that the frequency of the client's misbehavior has decreased since he/she began setting firm, consistent limits on the client's acting out.

33. Teach Enmeshed Parent(s) to Set Limits (33)

A. The enmeshed or overly protective parent was helped to see how his/her failure to set limits reinforces the client's immature or irresponsible behaviors.

B. The enmeshed or overly protective parent was helped to identify natural, logical consequences for the client's immature or irresponsible behaviors.

C. The parent(s) were encouraged to offer frequent praise and positive reinforcement for the client's responsible behaviors.

D. A reward system was designed to reinforce the client for behaving in a responsible manner.

34. Identify Age-Appropriate Ways to Meet Needs (34)

A. The client and parent(s) identified age-appropriate ways for the client to meet his/her needs for affiliation, acceptance, and approval.

B. The client was given the homework assignment to engage in a specific, age-appropriate behavior 3 to 5 times before the next therapy session.

C. Role-playing and modeling techniques were utilized to demonstrate age-appropriate ways to gain affiliation, acceptance, and approval from others.

D. The client was taught effective communication skills to help meet his/her needs for affiliation, acceptance, and approval.

35. Challenge Parent(s) to Assume Parental Role (35)

A. The parent(s) were challenged to assert their appropriate authority and take active steps to prevent the overly responsible child from assuming too many parental or household responsibilities.

B. The parent(s) were helped to identify ways to assert appropriate parental authority.

C. The parent acknowledged that he/she has often turned to the older child for help in performing many of the household responsibilities since the separation.

D. The parent reported that he/she has taken positive steps to decrease the amount of responsibilities expected of the overly responsible or parental child in the family.

E. The parent reported that the overly responsible or parental child has resisted giving up some of his/her parental or household responsibilities.

36. Parent(s) Encourage Client's Social Activities (36)

A. The parents were instructed to schedule or allow time for the overly responsible client to engage in positive peer group or extracurricular activities.

B. The overly responsible client identified a list of interests or extracurricular activities that he/she likes to engage in with peers.

C. The overly responsible client was given a homework assignment to engage in 3 to 5 positive peer group or extracurricular activities before the next therapy session.

37. Urge Parent(s) to Stop Criticizing Ex-Spouse (37)

A. In today's therapy session, the parent(s) were challenged and confronted about making hostile or overly critical remarks about the other parent in the presence of the client and siblings.

B. The client's parent(s) verbally recognized how hostile or overly critical remarks about the other parent are upsetting to the client and siblings.

38. Teach Parent(s) to Avoid Placing Client in Middle (38)

A. The parent(s) were challenged to cease the pattern of placing the client in the middle role by soliciting information about the other parent or sending messages through the client to the other parent about adult matters.

B. The parent(s) verbalized an awareness of how placing the client in the middle role is upsetting to him/her.

39. Confront Playing One Parent against the Other (39)

A. The client was challenged and confronted about playing one parent against the other to meet the client's needs, obtain material goods, or avoid responsibility.

B. Today's therapy session explored the reasons for the client's attempt to play one parent against the other.

C. The parent(s) were encouraged to deal directly with the client and set limits on his/her manipulative behaviors.

D. The client was helped to identify more constructive ways to meet his/her needs or obtain material goods than through the manipulation of parent(s).

E. The client acknowledged how his/her pattern of playing one parent against the other is aimed at trying to bring the parents back together.

40. Facilitate Expression of Feelings about Infrequent Contact, Abandonment, or Abuse (40)

A. An individual play-therapy session was held to provide the client with the opportunity to express his/her feelings about the infrequent contact with one of his/her parents.

B. An individual play-therapy session was held to provide the client with the opportunity to express his/her feelings about abandonment issues.

C. The client made productive use of today's therapy session to express his/her feelings of anger, hurt, sadness, and disappointment about infrequent contact or abandonment by the noncustodial parent.

D. The client was given the opportunity to express his/her feelings about the past abuse within the family.

E. The client expressed feelings of anger, hurt, and sadness about the past abuse within the family.

41. Encourage Noncustodial Parent to Maintain Visitation (41)

A. The noncustodial parent was challenged and encouraged to maintain regular visitation and involvement in the client's life.

B. The client asserted his/her wish in today's family therapy session for the noncustodial parent to maintain regular visitation and involvement in the client's life.

C. Today's therapy session explored the factors contributing to the noncustodial parent's failure to maintain regular visitation and involvement in the client's life.

D. The noncustodial parent verbally recognized how the lack of regular visitation has exacerbated the client's adjustment problems to the divorce.

E. The family therapy session focused on developing a regular visitation schedule between the noncustodial parent and the client.

42. Assign Disengaged Parent to Increase Time with Client (42)

A. The disengaged parent was given a directive to spend more quality time with the client and siblings.

B. The disengaged parent was given a homework assignment of performing a specific task with the client.

C. The client and disengaged parent developed a list of tasks or activities that they would like to do together.

D. The client reported that the increased time spent with the previously disengaged parent has helped them to establish a closer relationship.

E. The client reported that his/her relationship with the disengaged parent remains distant, as the two have spent little time together.

43. Hold Family Theraplay Session (43)

A. A family theraplay session (i.e., parental involvement) was held to facilitate the development of a closer parent-child bond.

B. The parent was instructed to allow the child to take the lead in expressing his/her feelings in today's play-therapy session.

C. The parent was encouraged to respond empathetically to the client's feelings and needs.

D. The family theraplay sessions have helped the parent(s) gain greater insight into the factors contributing to the client's adjustment problems.

E. The family theraplay sessions have helped to develop a closer parent-child relationship.

44. Utilize Psychoanalytic Play Therapy (44)

A. Psychoanalytic play-therapy approaches were utilized to help the client work through and resolve issues connected to the parents' separation or divorce.

B. A psychoanalytic play-therapy approach was used to explore the etiology of the unconscious conflicts that contribute to the emergence of the client's emotional and behavioral problems.

C. The psychoanalytic play-therapy session helped reveal how the client's emotional or behavioral problems are related to unresolved issues about the parents' separation or divorce.

D. Transference issues were identified and processed in today's play-therapy session.

E. The psychoanalytic play-therapy sessions have helped the client work through and resolve his/her feelings related to the parents' separation or divorce.

45. Utilize Child-Centered Play Therapy (45)

A. A child-centered play-therapy approach was utilized to help the client begin to express and work through his/her feelings associated with the parents' separation or divorce.

B. A child-centered play-therapy approach was utilized to help the client begin to express and work through his/her feelings associated with the past abuse.

C. A child-centered play-therapy approach was utilized to help the client begin to express and work through his/her feelings associated with abandonment issues.

D. The client was given unconditional positive regard and warm acceptance to facilitate the expression of his/her feelings about separation or abuse issues.

E. The client's feelings during the play-therapy session were reflected back to him/her in a nonjudgmental manner.

F. Child-centered play-therapy sessions have helped the client successfully work through and resolve issues related to the parents' separation or divorce, abandonment issues, or abuse.

46. Employ Mutual Storytelling Technique (46)

A. The mutual storytelling technique using puppets, dolls, and stuffed animals was employed to model appropriate ways to express emotions related to the separation or divorce.

B. The client created his/her own story using puppets, dolls, and stuffed animals that modeled effective ways to express emotions related to the parents' separation or divorce.

C. After using the mutual storytelling technique, the client was able to successfully identify effective ways to express his/her emotions related to the parents' separation or divorce.

D. The client identified the mutual storytelling technique as being a useful way to learn effective ways to express his/her feelings related to the parents' separation or divorce.

47. Art Therapy Techniques (47)

A. The client was instructed to draw pictures reflecting his/her feelings about the parents' divorce or how divorce has impacted his/her life.

B. The client's drawings reflected strong feelings of anger about the parents' divorce.

C. The client's drawings reflected feelings of sadness, hurt, and disappointment about the parents' divorce.

D. The client's drawings reflected feelings of anger, sadness, and loneliness about the family move and/or change in schools.

E. After completing his/her drawings, the client was able to verbalize his/her feelings about the parents' divorce and the impact that the divorce has had on his/her life.

48. Draw Pictures of Mother's and Father's Homes (48)

A. The client was instructed to draw pictures of both the mother's and father's home and then share what it is like to live in or visit each home.

B. The content of the client's drawings was assessed in regard to the quality of his/her relationship with each parent.

C. The client's drawings and verbalizations revealed that he/she has developed a much closer relationship with the custodial parent than the noncustodial parent.

D. The client's drawings reflected a strained and distant relationship with the noncustodial parent.

E. The client's drawings reflected a strained relationship with the custodial parent.

49. Symbols of Divorce (49)

A. The client was instructed to draw an outline of a human body on a large piece of paper or poster board and then fill in the body with objects, symbols, or pictures that reflect his/her feelings about the parents' divorce.

B. The art-therapy technique helped the client express his/her thoughts and feelings about the parents' separation or divorce.

C. The art-therapy technique reflected the client's strong feelings of anger about the parents' divorce.

D. The art-therapy technique reflected the client's feelings of sadness and hurt about the parents' divorce.

E. After completing the art-therapy technique, the client was helped to identify effective ways to express his/her feelings about the parents' separation or divorce.

50. Play "My Two Homes" Game (50)

A. The therapeutic game, My Two Homes (Shapiro), was played to help the client express feelings and learn effective coping strategies to adjust to the divorce.

B. After playing the My Two Homes game, the client was able to identify effective ways to express his/her feelings about the parents' divorce.

C. After playing the My Two Homes game, the client was able to identify coping strategies that can help him/her adjust to the parents' divorce.

D. The client identified the therapeutic game as being helpful in allowing him/her to express feelings about the divorce.

E. The client was encouraged to practice the positive coping strategies that he/she learned from playing the therapeutic game.

51. Read *All About Divorce* (51)

A. The client and parent were assigned to read *All About Divorce* (Fields) at home.

B. The parent was instructed to read the book while the client acted out his/her feelings and concerns about the divorce with dolls.

C. The parent was instructed to read *All About Divorce* and then have the client write down his/her thoughts and feelings about divorce.

D. Reading *All About Divorce* helped the parent develop a greater understanding of the client's feelings about the divorce.

E. Reading *All About Divorce* helped facilitate a closer parent-child bond.

52. Encourage Participation in Positive Peer Group Activities (52)

A. The client was strongly encouraged to participate in school, extracurricular, or positive peer group activities to offset the loss of time spent with his/her parents.

B. The client developed a list of school, extracurricular, or positive peer group activities that will help him/her cope with parents' divorce and establish meaningful friendships.

C. The client reported that the participation in school, extracurricular, or positive peer group activities has helped him/her cope with parents' divorce and feel less depressed or lonely.

D. The client has continued to struggle to cope with his/her parents' divorce, but has not yet taken many steps to become involved in school, extracurricular, or positive peer group activities.

53. Children of Divorce Group Referral (53)

A. The client was referred to a Children of Divorce group to assist him/her in expressing feelings and to understand that he/she is not alone in going through the divorce process.

B. The client was given the directive to self-disclose at least once about his/her parents' divorce during each group therapy session.

C. The client's involvement in the Children of Divorce group has helped him/her realize that he/she is not alone in going through the divorce process.

D. The client's active participation in the Children of Divorce group has helped him/her share and work through many of his/her emotions pertaining to the parents' divorce.

E. The client has not made productive use of the group therapy sessions and has been reluctant to share his/her feelings about the divorce.

54. Identify Supportive Adults (54)

A. The client was assisted in developing a list of supportive adults outside of the family whom he/she can turn to for support and guidance in coping with the divorce.

B. The client was given the homework assignment to seek guidance and support from at least one adult outside of the family before the next therapy session.

C. The client reported that he/she has talked with other significant adult(s) outside of the family who have been helpful in offering support and guidance.

D. The client has taken active steps to develop a network of significant adults outside of the family system whom he/she can turn to for guidance and support when needed.

E. The client has failed to follow through with the recommendation to make contact with significant adults outside of the family because of his/her mistrust and expectation of experiencing further disappointment.

55. Arrange for Psychological Evaluation (55)

A. The client received a psychological evaluation to help rule out the presence of either an affective or anxiety disorder.

B. The findings from the psychological evaluation revealed that the client has developed an affective disorder in response to his/her parents' divorce.

C. The findings from the psychological evaluation revealed that the client has developed an anxiety disorder in response to his/her parents' divorce.

D. The findings from the psychological evaluation did not reveal the presence of an affective disorder.

E. The findings from the psychological evaluation did not reveal the presence of an anxiety disorder.

56. Refer for Medication Evaluation (56)

A. The client was referred for a medication evaluation to help stabilize his/her mood and improve anger control.

B. The client and parents agreed to follow through with the medication evaluation.

C. The client was strongly opposed to being placed on medication to help stabilize his/her mood or improve anger control.

57. Monitor Effects of Medication (57)

A. The client's response to the medication was discussed.

B. The client reported that the medication has helped to stabilize his/her mood and improve anger control.

C. The client reported little to no improvement in his/her mood or anger control since being placed on the medication.

D. The client reported that he/she has consistently taken the medication as prescribed.

E. The client has failed to comply with taking the medication as prescribed.

ENURESIS/ENCOPRESIS

CLIENT PRESENTATION

1. Nocturnal Enuresis/Bedwetting (1)*

A. The parents reported that the client has consistently wet his/her bed and has never achieved bladder control at night.

B. The parents reported the client has regularly wet his/her bed in the recent past, after having previously achieved bladder control at night.

C. The client and parents reported that the client has continued to wet his/her bed at night on a regular basis.

D. The client and parents reported a moderate reduction in the frequency of the client's bedwetting incidents.

E. The client has achieved bladder control at night and is no longer wetting his/her bed.

2. Daytime/Diurnal Enuresis (1)

A. The parents reported that the client frequently wets his/her clothing during the day and has never achieved bladder control.

B. The parents reported that the client has recently regressed and started to wet his/her clothing during the day.

C. The client has continued to wet his/her clothing during the day.

D. The client has not recently wet his/her clothing during the day.

E. The client's diurnal enuresis has been eliminated.

3. Physiologically Caused Enuresis (1)

A. The client's problems with enuresis are related to a known health problem.

B. The client's problems with enuresis are not related to any known physical or organic causes.

4. Encopresis (2)

A. The parents reported that the client has never achieved consistent bowel control.

B. The parents reported that the client has recently regressed and begun to experience problems with encopresis, after having previously achieved bowel control.

C. The client has continued to have problems with encopresis in the recent past.

D. The client denied having any recent encopretic incidents.

E. The client's encopresis has been successfully eliminated.

* The numbers in parentheses correlate to the number of the Behavioral Definition statement in the companion chapter with same title in *The Child Psychotherapy Treatment Planner* (Jongsma, Peterson, and McInnis) by John Wiley & Sons, 2000.

5. Physiologically Caused Encopresis (2)

A. The client's problems with encopresis are related to a known health problem.

B. The client's problems with encopresis are not related to any known physical or organic causes.

6. Feelings of Shame/Embarrassment (3)

A. The client expressed feelings of shame and embarrassment about his/her problems with enuresis and/or encopresis.

B. The client's feelings of shame and embarrassment have contributed to his/her pattern of avoiding situations (e.g., overnight visits with friends) that might lead to further embarrassment.

C. The client's realization that he/she is not alone in having problems with enuresis and/or encopresis has helped to reduce his/her feelings of shame and embarrassment.

D. In today's therapy session the client was able to talk about his/her problems with enuresis and/or encopresis without experiencing any feelings of shame or embarrassment.

E. The client reported that he/she is no longer troubled by feelings of shame and embarrassment about his/her enuresis and/or encopresis.

7. Social Ridicule, Isolation, or Ostracism (4)

A. The client reported that he/she has been teased or ridiculed by peers at school or in the neighborhood because of his/her problems with enuresis.

B. The client reported that he/she has been teased or ridiculed at school and in the neighborhood because of his/her problems with encopresis.

C. The client reported that he/she has often responded to teasing or ridicule from peers by withdrawing and isolating himself/herself.

D. The parents and teachers reported that the client's problems with enuresis and/or encopresis have contributed to his/her being ostracized.

E. The client has increased his/her social contacts and become more outgoing since overcoming his/her problem with enuresis and/or encopresis.

8. Attempts to Hide Feces/Soiled Clothing (5)

A. The parents reported that the client has a persistent pattern of hiding his/her soiled clothing and/or feces.

B. The client acknowledged that he/she has often attempted to hide his/her soiled clothing because of feelings of shame and fear of experiencing further teasing or ridicule.

C. The client reported that he/she has often attempted to hide his/her soiled clothing or feces because of his/her fear of being punished harshly by parents.

D. The client acknowledged that his/her pattern of hiding feces and/or soiled clothing is self-defeating because it only causes him/her to get into more trouble with parents.

E. The client reported that he/she has stopped his/her pattern of hiding feces and/or soiled clothing.

9. Excessive or Harsh Criticism by Parents (6)

A. The client described his/her parent(s) as being very critical and harsh in their approach to his/her problems with enuresis and/or encopresis.

B. In today's therapy session the parent(s) expressed strong feelings of anger about the client's problems with enuresis and/or encopresis.

C. The parent(s) have continued to be critical of the client because of his/her problem with enuresis and/or encopresis.

D. The parent(s) acknowledged the need to cease making critical or hostile remarks about the client's bladder/bowel control problems.

E. The parent(s) have stopped making hostile, critical remarks about the client's bladder/bowel control problems.

10. Rigid Toilet-Training Practices (6)

A. Today's therapy session revealed that the parents have established rigid toilet-training practices.

B. The client expressed feelings of anger and frustration about his/her parent's rigid toilet-training practices.

C. The parents' rigid toilet-training practices have contributed to the client's anxiety and fearfulness about not gaining bladder/bowel control.

D. The client reported to experiencing less anxiety because his/her parents have become more relaxed and flexible in their toilet-training practices.

E. The client has assumed responsibility for his/her toilet-training practices, and the parents have stopped imposing their rigid toilet training practices.

11. Hostile-Dependent Cycle (6)

A. The client has established a hostile-dependent cycle with the parents whereby his/her wetting or soiling angers the parents; the parents respond in a critical or hostile manner; the client subsequently seeks to punish the parents for their strong displays of anger; and so on.

B. The client and parents acknowledged the presence of a hostile-dependent cycle and agreed to take steps to reduce the anger between one another.

C. The client and parents continue to be locked in a hostile-dependent cycle.

D. The client and parents' hostile-dependent cycle has been terminated, and the client has started to assume responsibility for his/her toilet training practices.

12. Low Self-Esteem (6)

A. In today's therapy session the client expressed feelings of low self-esteem and inadequacy about his/her problems with enuresis.

B. In today's therapy session the client expressed feelings of low self-esteem and inadequacy about his/her problems with encopresis.

C. The parents' hostile or overly critical remarks about the client's problems with bladder/bowel control have contributed to his/her feelings of low self-esteem.

D. The parents' overly punitive methods of discipline for the client's problems with enuresis and/or encopresis have caused the client to experience feelings of low self-esteem, inadequacy, and inferiority.

E. The client reported that his/her self-esteem has increased significantly since gaining bladder/bowel control.

13. Fearfulness (7)

A. The client's anxiety and fears about toilet training have contributed to his/her problems with enuresis.

B. The client's anxiety and fears about toilet training have contributed to his/her problems with encopresis.

C. The client recognized that his/her fears about toilet training are irrational or unrealistic.

D. The client's anxiety and fears about toilet training have started to decrease.

E. The client has successfully worked through the core conflicts contributing to his/her anxiety and fearfulness, and he/she has recently demonstrated good bladder/bowel control.

14. Anger/Hostility (7)

A. The client's strong feelings of anger have been channeled into his/her problems with enuresis.

B. The client's strong feelings of anger have been channeled into his/her problems with encopresis.

C. The client has had much difficulty expressing his/her anger directly toward others.

D. The client has started to express his/her feelings of anger more openly and directly, and at the same time has begun to assume greater responsibility for his/her toilet training practices.

E. The client has achieved good bladder/bowel control since resolving the core conflicts that contributed to his/her strong feelings of anger and resentment.

15. Rejection Experiences/Traumatization (7)

A. The client has demonstrated a regression in his/her bladder or bowel control since experiencing a significant rejection experience.

B. The client has developed problems with his/her bladder or bowel control since experiencing the traumatic incident.

C. The client has started to gain effective bladder/bowel control since he/she began working through his/her feelings about the past rejection experience and traumatic incident.

D. The client has worked through his/her feelings about the traumatic incident or rejection experience, and has now achieved full bladder/bowel control.

16. Separation/Loss (7)

A. The client has developed problems with enuresis since experiencing a major separation or loss.

B. The client has developed problems with encopresis since experiencing a major separation or loss.

C. The client has started to assume responsibility for his/her toilet training as he/she works through his/her feelings associated with the past separation or loss.

D. The client has achieved good bladder/bowel control since successfully working through his/her feeling surrounding the past separation or loss.

17. Poor Impulse Control/Lack of Responsibility (8)

A. The client's impulsivity and irresponsibility with his/her toilet training has been a significant contributing factor to his/her problems with diurnal enuresis.

B. The client's impulsivity and irresponsibility with his/her toilet training has been a significant contributing factor to his/her problems with encopresis.

C. The client has started to assume greater responsibility for his/her toilet training practices.

D. The client has developed good bladder/bowel control since improving his/her impulse control and assuming greater responsibility.

18. Smearing of Feces (9)

A. The parents reported that the client has a history of smearing feces when angry or emotionally upset.

B. The client's pattern of smearing feces reflects the presence of a serious psychiatric disorder.

C. The client has smeared feces on the walls or his/her surrounding when in the midst of a psychotic break.

D. The client has recently not engaged in any smearing of feces.

E. The client has eliminated all incidents of smearing of feces.

INTERVENTIONS IMPLEMENTED

1. Refer for Medical Examination (1)*

A. The client was referred for a medical examination to rule out organic or physical causes that may be contributing to the client's enuresis.

B. The client was referred for a medication examination to rule out organic or physical causes that may be contributing to the client's encopresis.

C. The findings from the medical examination did not reveal the presence of any organic or physical causes for the client's problems with enuresis or encopresis.

D. The findings from the medical examination revealed that the client's problems with enuresis and/or encopresis are due to organic or physical causes.

E. The client was encouraged to comply with all the recommendations regarding medical interventions.

2. Refer for Medication Evaluation (2)

A. The client was referred for a medication evaluation to help improve his/her bladder control at night.

B. The client and parents agreed to follow through with a medication evaluation.

C. The parents objected to their child's being placed on medication to help improve his/her bladder control at night.

D. The client was placed on medication to help improve his/her bladder control at night.

3. Monitor Medication Compliance/Effectiveness (3)

A. The client and parents reported that the medication has helped the client gain effective bladder control at night.

* The numbers in parentheses correlate to the number of the Therapeutic Interventions statement in the companion chapter with same title in *The Child Psychotherapy Treatment Planner* (Jongsma, Peterson, and McInnis) by John Wiley & Sons, 2000.

B. The client and parents reported little to no improvement while using the medication.

C. The client has complied with taking the mediation as prescribed.

D. The client has not complied with taking the medication on a regular basis.

E. The client and parents were encouraged to report any side effects of the medication to the prescribing physician.

4. Psychological Testing (4)

A. The client received a psychological evaluation to help determine whether he/she has ADHD or an impulse-control disorder that may be contributing to the bladder/bowel control problems.

B. The client received a psychological evaluation to help determine whether he/she has a serious underlying emotional problem that may be contributing to his/her problems with bladder/bowel control.

C. The client and parents were provided feedback from the psychological testing, which revealed no serious emotional disorders.

D. The findings from the psychological testing revealed the presence of ADHD and/or an impulse-control disorder that contributes to the client's problems with bladder/bowel control.

E. The findings from the psychological testing revealed the presence of serious underlying emotional problems that contribute to the emergence of the client's problems with enuresis and/or encopresis.

5. Teach Bell-and-Pad Conditioning Procedures (5)

A. The client and parents were trained on how to use bell-and-pad conditioning procedures to treat the client's nocturnal enuresis.

B. The bell-and-pad conditioning procedures have helped the client achieve bladder control at night.

C. The client has demonstrated little to no improvement with his/her bladder control at night since using the bell-and-pad conditioning device.

D. Explored the client and parents' resistance to using the bell-and-pad conditioning device on a regular basis.

E. The parents reported that the bell-and-pad conditioning device has not been helpful because the client sleeps through the alarm.

6. Utilize Positive Reinforcement Procedures (6)

A. The parents were educated about the use of positive reinforcement procedures to increase the client's bladder or bowel control.

B. A reward system was designed to reinforce the client for effective bladder control during the day.

C. A reward system was designed to address the client's nocturnal enuresis.

D. A reward system was designed to reward the client for demonstrating good bowel control.

E. The reward system has helped the client to achieve good bladder/bowel control.

7. Teach Urine-Retention Techniques (7)

A. Taught the client and parents about effective urine-retention training techniques to increase his/her awareness of the sensation or need to urinate.

B. The client reported that the urine-retention training exercises have helped increase his/her awareness of the sensation or need to urinate.

C. The urine-retention training techniques have helped the client establish effective bladder control during the day.

D. The urine-retention training exercises helped increase the client's awareness of his/her need to urinate at night, and subsequently resulted in reduced bedwetting incidents at night.

E. The client and parents reported little to no improvement with the use of the urine-retention training techniques.

8. Teach Staggered-Awakening Procedures

A. The parents were trained on how to use staggered-awakening procedures, using a variable interval schedule, to control the client's nocturnal enuresis.

B. The parents were instructed to wake the client up three times each night during the initial stage, twice a night during the second stage, once during the third stage, and then allow the client to sleep undisturbed through the night during the fourth stage.

C. The client and parents reported that the staggered-awakening procedures have helped the client overcome his/her bedwetting problem.

D. The parents were resistant to implementing the staggered-awakening procedures because of the frequent sleep disruptions that it demanded of the client and themselves.

E. The staggered-awakening procedures helped the client manage his/her nocturnal enuresis during the first three stages, but he/she regressed during the final stage, when the parents were not awakening him/her at night.

9. Teach Dry-Bed Techniques (9)

A. The parents were instructed on how to implement a dry-bed training program that involved response inhibition, positive reinforcement, rapid awakening, gradual increase of fluid intake, self-correction of accidents, and decreased critical comments about toilet-training behavior.

B. The parents were encouraged to refrain from making any hostile, critical remarks about the client's toilet-training behaviors during the implementation of the dry-bed training program.

C. The dry-bed training techniques were successful in eliminating the client's problem with nocturnal enuresis.

D. The dry-bed training techniques were not successful in eliminating the client's problem with nocturnal enuresis.

10. Teach Overlearning Method (10)

A. The parents were encouraged to use the overlearning method (e.g., require client to drink specific amount of fluid shortly before bedtime) during the latter stages of treatment to help prevent a relapse of nocturnal enuresis.

B. The client and parents were encouraged to utilize the overlearning method, along with the bell-and-pad conditioning procedures.

C. The parents reported that combining the bell-and-pad conditioning procedures with the overlearning method proved to be successful in eliminating the client's nocturnal enuresis.

D. The overlearning method was not successful in preventing a relapse of the client's nocturnal enuresis.

11. Assign "Dry Bed Training Program" Exercise (11)

A. The parents were encouraged to use the "Dry Bed Training Program" from *The Brief Child Therapy Homework Planner* (Jongsma, Peterson, and McInnis) to help the client assume greater responsibility in managing his/her nocturnal enuresis.

B. The client and parents were required to sign the Dry Night Training Contract, which specifies the rewards the client will receive if he/she does not wet the bed at night.

C. The parents were encouraged to utilize a bell-and-pad apparatus, along with the "Dry Bed Training Program."

D. The client and parents reported that the "Dry Bed Training Program" was successful in eliminating the client's problem with nocturnal enuresis.

E. The client and parents failed to begin the implementation of the "Dry Bed Training Program," and were strongly encouraged to begin using it in the near future.

12. Design Operant Conditioning Program for Encopresis (12)

A. The client and parents were trained on how to implement a systematic operant conditioning program that combines positive reinforcement principles with the use of glycerine suppositories and enemas if the client does not defecate voluntarily each day.

B. The parents reported that the operant conditioning program has proved to be successful in eliminating the client's encopresis.

C. The parents reported that they had difficulty giving the client glycerine suppositories and/or enemas because of his/her emotional outbursts.

13. Assign "Bowel Control Training Program" (13)

A. The client and parents were encouraged to use the "Bowel Control Training Program" from *The Brief Child Therapy Homework Planner* (Jongsma, Peterson, and McInnis) to help the client assume greater responsibility in developing bowel control.

B. The "Bowel Control Training Program" was utilized to help the client recognize the negative social consequences that can occur as a result of his/her encopretic incidents.

C. Bowel Control Incident Reports helped the client identify the emotional and psychosocial factors that contribute to the problem of encopresis.

D. The client and parents reported that the "Bowel Control Training Program" helped him/her overcome the problem with encopresis.

14. Encourage Client Responsibility (14)

A. The client was encouraged and challenged to assume active responsibility for achieving bladder control.

B. The client was encouraged and challenged to assume active responsibility for achieving bowel control.

C. The client was given the responsibility for cleaning his/her soiled underwear or linens.

D. The client was instructed to keep a record of wet and dry days or nights.

E. The client was placed in charge of setting the alarm at night for voiding times.

15. Confront Lack of Motivation (15)

A. The client was challenged and confronted about his/her lack of motivation or compliance with following through with the recommended treatment interventions.

B. The parents were challenged and confronted about their lack of motivation or compliance in following through with the recommended treatment interventions.

C. Explored the factors contributing to the client's and/or parents' resistance to following through with implementing the recommended treatment interventions.

D. After working through their resistance, the client and parents agreed to follow through with recommended treatment interventions.

16. Explore Irrational Cognitive Messages (16)

A. Today's therapy session explored the client's irrational cognitive messages that produce fear or anxiety associated with toilet training.

B. Today's therapy session helped identify the client's irrational cognitive messages that contribute to his/her fear or anxiety about toilet training.

17. Help Client Realize Irrational Fears (17)

A. The client was helped to realize how his/her anxiety or fear surrounding toilet training is irrational or unrealistic.

B. The client was encouraged to replace his/her irrational or unrealistic thoughts with positive, reality-based self-talk to help eliminate his/her fears about toilet training.

18. Identify Negative Social Consequences (18)

A. The client was helped to identify the potential negative social consequences that may result from his/her bladder or bowel control problems.

B. The client verbalized increased motivation to gain bladder/bowel control after listing the potential negative social consequences.

C. The client seemed unconcerned about the potential negative social consequences that may arise from his/her bladder/bowel control problems.

19. Identify Periods of Good Bladder/Bowel Control (19)

A. The client identified periods when he/she demonstrated good bladder control and did not experience any enuretic incidents.

B. The client identified periods of time when he/she demonstrated good bowel control and did not experience any encopretic incidents.

C. The client was encouraged to take the same positive steps that he/she had taken in the past to achieve bladder control.

D. The client was encouraged to take the same positive steps that he/she had taken in the past to achieve bowel control.

E. Today's therapy session revealed that the client demonstrated good bladder/bowel control during periods of time when he/she received strong family support and felt more confident in himself/herself.

20. Teach Effective, Nonabusive Toilet-Training Practices (20)

A. The parents were taught effective, nonabusive toilet-training practices.

B. The parents verbalized their commitment to use nonabusive toilet-training practices.

21. Assess Family Dynamics (21)

A. Today's family therapy session explored the dynamics that contributed to the emergence or reinforcement of the client's enuresis, encopresis, or smearing of feces.

B. The therapy session revealed how the parents' lack of consistency with toilet-training practices has contributed to the client's problems with enuresis or encopresis.

C. Explored the reasons for the parents' lack of consistency with toilet-training practices.

D. The family members were asked to identify the stressors that have negatively impacted the family.

E. The family members were asked to identify the positive changes they would like to see take place within the family.

22. Explore Parent-Child Interactions (22)

A. Today's therapy session explored the parent-child interactions to assess whether the parents' toilet-training practices are excessively rigid.

B. Today's therapy session explored the parent-child interactions to assess whether the parents are making hostile, critical remarks about the client's bladder/bowel control.

23. Confront Parents' Hostile Remarks (23)

A. The parents were challenged and confronted about making critical or hostile remarks about the client's bladder- or bowel-control problems.

B. The parents acknowledged that their critical or hostile remarks only prove to be self-defeating because they contribute to the client's feelings of low self-esteem, shame, and embarrassment.

C. The parents acknowledged that their critical or hostile remarks only serve to anger the client and do not increase his/her motivation to achieve bladder/bowel control.

D. The parents agreed to stop making critical or hostile remarks about the client's bladder- or bowel-control problems.

E. The parents became defensive in today's therapy session when they were confronted about making hostile or critical remarks toward the client.

24. Assess Hostile-Dependent Cycle (24)

A. Explored the parent-child interactions for the possible presence of a hostile-dependent cycle.

B. Today's therapy session revealed the presence of a hostile-dependent cycle whereby the client's wetting or soiling angers the parents, the parents respond in an overly critical or hostile manner, the client then seeks to punish the parents for their strong display of anger, and so on.

C. The client and parents expressed their desire to stop the hostile-dependent cycle.

D. The parents were taught effective, nonabusive toilet-training practices to help stop the hostile-dependent cycle.

E. The client was helped to identify more effective ways to express his/her feelings of anger toward his/her parents.

25. Explore Secondary Gain (25)

A. A family therapy session was held to explore whether the client achieves any secondary gain from his/her problems with enuresis or encopresis.

B. The client and parents were assisted in identifying the secondary gain(s) that are achieved from the client's enuresis or encopresis.

C. The therapy session showed how the client receives increased parental attention for his/her problems with enuresis or encopresis.

D. The client and parents were helped to realize how the client's enuresis or encopresis maintains or reinforces his/her dependency on the parents.

E. The family therapy session failed to identify any secondary gain that is achieved from the client's enuresis or encopresis.

26. Assign Responsibility to Disengaged Parent (26)

A. The disengaged parent was assigned the responsibility of overseeing or teaching the client effective toilet-training practices.

B. The disengaged parent was assigned the responsibility of keeping a record of the client's wet and dry days.

C. The disengaged parent was given the responsibility of awakening the client at various intervals for bladder voiding.

D. The disengaged parent was assigned the responsibility of reminding or teaching the client how to clean soiled underwear or linens.

E. The disengaged parent verbally committed to taking an active role in the client's toilet-training practices.

27. Assign Increased Involvement by Disengaged Parent (27)

A. The disengaged parent was challenged to spend more time with the client in leisure, school, or household activities.

B. The client verbalized his/her need to spend greater time with the disengaged parent.

C. Today's therapy session explored the factors contributing to the distant relationship between the client and the disengaged parent.

D. The disengaged parent verbalized a commitment to spend greater quality time with the client.

E. The client and disengaged parent identified a list of activities that they would enjoy doing together.

28. Conduct Family Play Therapy (28)

A. To assess the quality of the parent-child relationships, the client and parents engaged in "free play" during today's family play-therapy session.

B. A family play-therapy session was conducted to help gain greater insight into the family dynamics that contribute to the development of the client's enuresis or encopresis.

C. The family play-therapy session revealed that the client has developed a strained and distant relationship with his/her parent(s).

D. After engaging in the "free play" during today's therapy session, the client and parent(s) agreed to spend increased time at home in leisure or recreational activities.

E. The family play-therapy sessions have helped to facilitate a closer parent-child bond.

29. Explore History of Separation, Loss, Trauma, or Rejection (29)

A. Today's therapy session explored whether the client's enuresis is associated with past separation, loss, traumatization, or rejection experiences.

B. Today's therapy session explored whether the client's encopresis or smearing of feces is associated with past separation, loss, traumatization, or rejection experiences.

C. The client experienced a regression in his/her bladder or bowel control after experiencing a major separation, loss, or rejection experience.

D. The client experienced a regression with his/her bladder or bowel control after experiencing a traumatic event.

E. The client's problem with smearing feces began after he/she experienced a traumatic event.

30. Encourage Expression of Feelings Related to Painful Event(s) (30)

A. The client was given encouragement and support in expressing his/her feelings associated with the past separation, loss, trauma, or rejection experience.

B. The client was instructed to draw pictures reflecting his/her feelings about the past separation, loss, trauma, or rejection experience.

C. The empty-chair technique was employed to facilitate the expression of feelings surrounding the past separation, loss, trauma, or rejection experience.

D. The client was instructed to use a journal to record his/her thoughts and feelings about the past separation, loss, trauma, or rejection experience.

E. A family therapy session was conducted to allow the client to express his/her feelings about the past separation, loss, trauma, or rejection experience in the presence of the family.

31. Conduct Child-Centered Play Therapy (31)

A. A child-centered play-therapy approach was utilized to help the client express and work through his/her feelings associated with the past separation, loss, trauma, or rejection experience.

B. The client was given unconditional positive regard and warm acceptance in expressing his/her feelings associated with the past painful event(s).

C. The client's feelings expressed in his/her play were reflected back in a nonjudgmental manner and related to his/her feelings about the past painful event(s).

D. Today's therapy session reinforced the client's capacity for self-growth so that he/she can begin to assume greater responsibility with his/her toilet-training practices.

E. The client has begun to assume greater responsibility for his/her toilet-training practices after being able to express feelings about past painful event(s) during the child-centered play-therapy sessions.

32. Employ Psychoanalytic Play Therapy (32)

A. Using a psychoanalytic play-therapy approach, the client was allowed to take the lead in exploring the issues that contribute to his/her bladder- or bowel-control problems.

B. Interpreted the client's feelings that were expressed in his/her play and related them to the client's feelings about the bladder- or bowel-control problems.

C. Processed and worked through the transference issues that emerged in today's psychoanalytic play-therapy session.

D. The psychoanalytic play-therapy sessions have helped identify the core issues or anxieties that contribute to the client's bladder- or bowel-control problems.

E. The psychoanalytic play-therapy sessions have helped the client work through and resolve the issues contributing to the emergence of his/her bladder- or bowel-control problems.

33. Utilize Mutual Storytelling Technique (33)

A. The client actively participated in the mutual storytelling exercise.

B. Using the mutual storytelling technique, the therapist modeled appropriate ways for the client to gain control and/or attention from others.

C. The client was assisted in creating a story through the use of puppets, dolls, or stuffed animals that helped provide insight into the factors contributing to his/her problems with bladder or bowel control.

D. The mutual storytelling technique helped the client identify more appropriate ways to gain control and/or attention from others.

E. The client was encouraged to practice the skills that he/she learned from the mutual storytelling technique to meet his/her needs more appropriately.

34. Teach Communication/Assertiveness Skills (34)

A. The client was taught effective communication and assertiveness skills to learn how to express his/her feelings through more appropriate verbalizations.

B. Role-playing techniques were used to model effective ways for the client to express feelings and meet his/her needs.

C. The client and parents reported that the newly acquired assertiveness and communication skills have helped the client to express his/her feelings more directly and to begin to take greater responsibility for his/her toilet training practices.

D. The client was given the homework assignment to practice his/her newly learned communication or assertiveness skills at home or school.

35. Identify Positive Characteristics (35)

A. To help decrease his/her feelings of shame or embarrassment, the client was asked to identify and list his/her positive characteristics.

B. The parents were strongly encouraged to provide frequent praise and positive reinforcement to help decrease the client's feelings of shame and embarrassment.

C. The client was encouraged to verbalize positive self-statements to offset feelings of shame and embarrassment.

D. To help improve his/her self-esteem and decrease feelings of shame, the client was given the homework assignment of verbalizing three positive self-statements each night with his/her parents.

36. Assign Recording of Positive Self-Statements (36)

A. The client was directed to record one positive self-statement each day in a journal.

B. The client was instructed to verbalize at least one positive self-statement around peers each day.

C. The client reported that recording the positive self-statements helped to increase his/her self-esteem and decrease feelings of shame.

D. The client failed to follow through with the homework assignment of recording the positive self-statements and was instructed to begin doing so.

37. Teach Physical Outlets for Anger (37)

A. The client was encouraged to channel his/her feelings of anger through appropriate physical outlets instead of through inappropriate wetting or soiling.

B. The client was helped to identify appropriate physical outlets for his/her feelings of anger.

C. The client and parents reported that the client has been channeling his/her anger effectively through appropriate physical outlets.

D. The client recognized that he/she has channeled his/her anger through inappropriate wetting or soiling, and verbalized a commitment to cease this behavior.

38. Assign Drawings That Reflect Self-Esteem (38)

A. The client was instructed to draw pictures reflecting how the enuretic or encopretic incidents affect his/her self-esteem.

B. The client's drawings reflected feelings of low self-esteem, inadequacy, and shame.

C. The client's drawings reflected how he/she feels ostracized from peers because of his/her bladder- or bowel-control problems.

D. Processed the content of the client's drawings and related them to how the client feels in everyday life.

E. After completing the drawings, the client was helped to identify constructive ways to build his/her self-esteem.

39. Utilize Strategic Family Therapy Intervention (39)

A. A strategic family therapy intervention was utilized where the therapist did not talk about the enuresis or encopresis, but rather discussed what might surface if the problem were resolved.

B. The strategic family therapy intervention helped bring to light underlying issues that contribute to the client's bladder- or bowel-control problems.

C. The client and family members were helped to identify more effective ways to resolve the core conflicts or problems that contribute to the client's problems with enuresis or encopresis.

40. Employ Paradoxical Intervention (40)

A. A paradoxical intervention was employed, whereby the client was instructed to pick out a specific night of the week when he/she was instructed to deliberately wet the bed.

B. The paradoxical intervention was successful as it allowed the client to control the enuresis by making the unconscious behavior a conscious maneuver.

C. The client and parents failed to follow through with the implementation of the paradoxical intervention, and were instructed to do so before the next therapy session.

41. Assign *Once Upon a Time Potty Book and Doll Set* (41)

A. The parents were directed to use the *Once Upon a Time Potty Book and Doll Set* to increase the preschool client's motivation to develop his/her bladder or bowel control.

B. The parents reported that the client expressed greater interest and motivation to gain bladder/bowel control after using the *Once Upon a Time Potty Book and Doll Set*.

C. The parents reported that the client has displayed little interest or motivation in achieving bladder/bowel control after using the *Once Upon a Time Potty Book and Doll Set*.

FIRE SETTING

CLIENT PRESENTATION

1. Set One or More Fires in Six Months (1)*

A. It has been reported by others that the client has set several fires in the last several months.

B. The client self-reported that he/she remembers setting one or more fires in the last six months.

C. The parents indicated that the client is suspected by them and other authorities of setting several recent fires in the community.

D. There have been no reported incidents of fire setting by the client since he/she has started treatment.

2. Observed Play with Fire (2)

A. The client has consistently been observed playing with fire, fireworks, or other flammable substances.

B. The parents indicated they are tired of and frustrated by the client's constant and continual requests to buy fireworks.

C. Several neighbors have reported to parents and authorities that they have seen the client playing with fire and combustible substances.

D. The client has honored the contract he/she signed not to play with fire or other combustible substances.

3. Enjoys Being around Fire (3)

A. The client indicated that he/she likes to be around fire.

B. The parents reported that the client seeks out any situation where fire is involved.

C. The client talked excitedly about certain fires he/she has recently seen.

D. The parent's have seen a noticeable decrease in client interest in being wherever fire is present.

4. Consistently Possesses Fire Articles (4)

A. The client has consistently been found with lighters, matches, and candles in his/her possession.

B. The parents reported consistently finding matches, lighters, etc. in the client's pockets or hidden in his/her room.

C. The client has been caught stealing lighters from stores.

D. The client has kept his/her agreement not to have any matches, lighters, or candles in his/her possession.

---

* The numbers in parentheses correlate to the number of the Behavioral Definition statement in the companion chapter with same title in *The Child Psychotherapy Treatment Planner* (Jongsma, Peterson, and McInnis) by John Wiley & Sons, 2000.

5. Fascination/Preoccupation with Fire (5)

A. The client seemed to have a preoccupation with anything that has a connection to fire.

B. The client talked of being fascinated with fire and what it could do.

C. The parents indicated that the client has been very fascinated and preoccupied with anything that is related to fire for a long time.

D. The client's talk frequently referenced some aspect relating to fire.

E. It has been observed by the parents and others that the client's fascination and preoccupation with fire has diminished to the point he/she hardly mentions it.

F. The client showed a marked lack of interest now in talking about things related to fire.

6. Fire Experience Does Not Arouse or Gratify (6)

A. The client's talk around his/her experience with fire exhibited no arousal or gratification from the experience.

B. The client strongly denied feeling any gratification or arousal when he/she had involvement with fires.

C. The parents reported that they did not sense any gratification or arousal on the client's part when he/she was playing with fire.

D. There was not visible evidence of gratification or arousal displayed by the client when telling of his/her experiences with fire.

INTERVENTIONS IMPLEMENTED

1. Urge Structure and Supervision of Client (1)*

A. Areas where structure and supervision were lacking with the client were explored and identified with parents.

B. The parents were assisted in developing specific ways to address the identified areas where supervision and structure of the client's behavior were inadequate.

C. The parents were taught the benefits of more effective structure and supervision for both them and the client.

D. The parents were confronted regarding important issues of supervision where they were resistive to making vital changes.

E. The parents have worked to develop more effective ways to supervise and structure the client's behavior and have verbally committed to implementing them.

2. Monitor Parents' Efforts (2)

A. The parents' efforts to more effectively structure, set limits, and supervise the client were monitored for effectiveness, consistency, and follow-through.

B. Verbal encouragement and support were given to the parents' efforts to supervise and structure the client's behavior in new ways.

C. The parents were given redirection when they were being lax or inconsistent in implementing and reinforcing new methods of supervision, limit setting, and structure.

---

* The numbers in parentheses correlate to the number of the Therapeutic Interventions statement in the companion chapter with same title in *The Child Psychotherapy Treatment Planner* (Jongsma, Peterson, and McInnis) by John Wiley & Sons, 2000.

D.   The parents have been very responsive to the encouragement, support, and redirection that were provided and have become effective in structuring, setting limits, and supervising the client's behavior.

3.   Develop Increased Impulse Control (3)

A.   The parents were given several books, tapes, etc. on positive reinforcement to read/view to assist them in finding ways they could use behavior modification techniques to increase the client's impulse control.

B.   The parents were introduced to and educated in using positive reinforcement to increase the client's impulse control.

C.   The parents were trained to use positive reinforcement with the client at the times he/she demonstrates apparent impulse control.

D.   The parents verbally committed to implementing the positive reinforcement methods they had developed.

E.   The parents have implemented positive reinforcement techniques with the client and report some initial increase in the client's impulse control.

4.   Assign Contrasting Fire Collages (4)

A.   The parents and client were given the assignment and provided the materials to create two collages, one emphasizing the positive aspects of fire and the other the destructive aspects.

B.   The family process of creating the collages was observed and assessed to gain insight into key family dynamics and strengths.

C.   The completed collages were presented and discussed by the client and family with key destructive aspects of fire being identified and reinforced.

D.   The client seemed from his/her statements after discussing the collage to have gained an increased awareness of the destructive aspects of fire.

5.   Assign Interview with Nurse/Firefighter (5)

A.   The parents and client were asked to develop a list of questions to ask a nurse of a burn center or firefighter regarding the effects of fire they have seen in their work.

B.   The parents were assisted in arranging an interview for themselves and the client with a firefighter/nurse.

C.   The parents and client reported on their interview experience and processed the information they gathered about the effects of fire.

D.   The client seemed to be affected by the information on the effects of fire on people that he/she obtained from the professional he/she interviewed.

6.   Assign Operant-Based Intervention (6)

A.   The concepts behind operant-based interventions were explained to the parents.

B.   An operant-based intervention for fire setting was given to the parents and a commitment to implement was elicited from them.

C.   The parents' implementation of the intervention was monitored with encouragement and redirection being given as needed.

D.   The parents indicated they have done the intervention consistently for several weeks and are surprised by the decrease in the client's interest in playing with fire.

7. Assign Stimulus Satiation Intervention (7)

A. The purpose behind stimulus satiation was explained to the client's parents and any questions they had were answered.

B. A stimulus satiation intervention was assigned to the parents and ways to implement it were developed and practiced.

C. The parents' implementation of the intervention was monitored, and encouragement and redirection were given as needed.

D. The parents reported a noted decrease in the client's interest in fire as demonstrated by the reduced number of matches he/she now wants to light when they do the intervention with him/her.

8. Assign Fireproofing Exercise (8)

A. The parents were assigned the "Fireproofing Your Home and Family" exercise from *The Brief Child Therapy Homework Planner* (Jongsma, Peterson, and McInnis).

B. The parents processed the experience of doing the fireproofing exercise while positive actions and follow-through on their part were reinforced.

C. The parents' failure to complete the fireproofing exercise was confronted and processed, and barriers were resolved so they could complete it.

D. The parents' action taken in the fireproofing exercise has had a positive impact on decreasing the client's involvement with fire.

9. Assign Father to Teach Safely Building Fire (9)

A. The client's father was ask to teach the client how to safely build a fire while emphasizing the need for strict control and respect for the power of fire.

B. The instruction session was monitored and afterward processed with the client and his/her father.

C. The father was asked to repeat the assignment at home with the client.

D. The father reported that the client now seems to be quite responsible when he/she is around or handles fire.

10. Utilize Family-Systems Approach (10)

A. The family was asked to agree on a number of sessions all members will attend and then make a verbal commitment to following through on that commitment.

B. Family roles, ways of communicating, and unresolved conflicts were explored and probed with the family.

C. Unresolved conflicts that were identified were processed and worked through to resolution.

D. Roles and communication patterns that were identified in the family as ineffective and destructive were confronted and restructured into new roles and patterns of communication that would increase the family's strength.

E. The family members have kept their commitment to change destructive roles and patterns of communication within the family.

11. **"When a Fire Has No Fuel" Exercise (11)**
   A. The family was asked to complete and process the exercise "When a Fire Has No Fuel" from *The Brief Child Therapy Homework Planner* (Jongsma, Peterson, and McInnis).
   B. The family processed the no-fuel exercise and identified key unresolved issues within their nuclear and family of origins.
   C. The family worked to resolve the identified issue within the family and to start new, healthier patterns.
   D. The family has struggled to reach some resolution of the unresolved conflicts that were identified by the exercise.

12. **Assist Family in Identifying Feelings (12)**
   A. The family members were provided with education on how to identify, express, and tolerate their feelings.
   B. The family members were assisted in expanding their skills in identifying and expressing their feelings by taking part in feelings exercises in family session.
   C. Family members were affirmed and given positive verbal reinforcement when they identified and expressed their feelings.
   D. The family members have increased their skills of identifying, expressing, and tolerating their own and others' feelings in healthy, constructive ways.

13. **Explore Client's Feelings (13)**
   A. The client's emotions were probed gently to help him/her become better able to identify and express these feelings.
   B. The client received verbal affirmation and encouragement each time he/she identified and appropriately expressed his/her feelings.
   C. The client was gently confronted when he/she avoided either identifying or expressing his/her emotions.
   D. The client has exhibited skill in both his/her ability to identify and to express his/her feelings.

14. **Assess Unmet Needs (14)**
   A. The client's unmet needs for attention, nurturance, and affirmation were assessed.
   B. The therapist met with and assisted the client's caregivers in identifying and implementing actions they could use to help meet the client's emotional needs.
   C. The caregivers were given support, encouragement, and redirection in their effort to fill some of the client's unmet emotional needs.
   D. The client's acting-out behaviors (i.e., loud talk, showing off) have decreased as he/she has responded positively to the nurturing actions of his/her caregivers.

15. **Assess Family Violence/Instability (15)**
   A. The family was assessed for the level of violence and chaos present and for what connection it has relative to the client's desire for power and control.
   B. The family members were assisted in identifying specific ways they could improve the structure, predictability, and respectfulness within the family.

C. Verbal support, encouragement, and guidance were provided to family members in their efforts to increase the structure, predictability, and respect within their family unit.

D. The increased structure, predictability, and respect within the family have helped to stabilize the client's behavior and improve his/her overall daily functioning.

16. Develop Client-Father Relationship (16)

A. The father was worked with to increase his awareness of the positive value and impact that a closer relationship with the client could have.

B. The father was asked to identify three possible things he could do to relate more with the client, and then select two that he would be willing to implement.

C. The father was assisted in implementing the new ideas he had for expanding his relationship withe the client.

D. The father's time spent with the client was monitored with encouragement, with redirection being given as needed.

E. The father's increased effort to relate more consistently and closely with the client has resulted in a marked decrease in the client's problem behaviors.

17. Facilitate Big Brother/Sister (17)

A. The Big Brother/Sister program and its benefits were presented to the client and his/her mother.

B. The client's mother was given direction and encouragement regarding making a request to the Big Brother/Big Sister program.

C. The mother was assisted in making a referral for the client to the Big Brother/Sister program.

D. The mother and client indicated that having a Big Brother/Big Sister has been a positive experience for the client.

18. Assess for Severe Mental Illness (18)

A. The client was assessed for the purpose of establishing or ruling out the presence of a psychotic process or a major affective disorder.

B. The client cooperated fully with all aspects of the psychological assessment.

C. The results of the assessment ruled out the presence of a psychotic process or a major affective disorder.

D. The assessment established the presence of psychotic process that would require treatment with medications.

E. The assessment established the presence of a major affective disorder that would need to be treated with psychotropic medications.

F. The client was referred for a psychiatric evaluation.

19. Probe Rejection Feelings (19)

A. The client's feelings of hurt and anger over rejection by peers and family were probed and processed.

B. The client was helped to connect his/her feelings of hurt and anger to experiences of rejection in relationships with peers and family.

C. The client's fire setting was interpreted to him/her as an expression of rage around the rejection of peers and family.

D. There have been no incidents of fire setting and a decreased interest in fire since the client started to process and resolve his/her feelings of rage around the rejection that he/she experienced.

20. Assess for Physical/Sexual Abuse (20)

A. The client was assessed for being a victim of physical and/or sexual abuse.

B. The parents were interviewed regarding the possibility of the client's being a victim of physical or sexual abuse.

C. The assessment substantiated that the client has been sexually abused.

D. The assessment substantiated that the client has been a victim of physical abuse.

E. The assessment ruled out that the client had been a victim or physical or sexual abuse.

F. The client's abuse was reported to the appropriate state authorities (CPS).

21. Assess for ADHD (21)

A. An ADHD assessment was conducted on the client.

B. The client was referred for a complete ADHD assessment.

C. The psychological assessment ruled out the presence of ADHD.

D. The psychological assessment concluded that the client is ADHD and needs to have a more complete ADHD workup and treatment.

E. A referral was made to a physician for a medication evaluation to treat ADHD.

22. Facilitate ADHD Recommendations Implementation (22)

A. The recommendations of the ADHD evaluation were presented and reviewed with the family, and any questions they had were answered and explained.

B. The family was assisted in implementing all the recommendations of the ADHD assessment.

C. The family was confronted and redirected when they failed to consistently implement the recommendations.

D. The family's difficulty in implementing one of the recommendations was processed and resolved.

E. The family was given affirmation for its consistent implementation and follow-through on the recommendations of the evaluation.

23. Arrange for Residential Treatment (23)

A. The need for the client to be placed in a residential setting for treatment of his/her serious psychiatric illness was explained to the family and processed with them.

B. Family resistance to the client's need for placement in a residential treatment program was addressed and resolved.

C. The various options in terms of residential treatment programs were discussed with the family.

D. The family was encouraged to tour several programs and make a decision on the program they feel is best for the client.

E. The family was assisted in obtaining a placement for the client in a residential treatment program.

F. Appropriate releases were signed by the parents to help expedite the procurement of a residential placement for the client.

G. The family reported that the client has been accepted and has an admission date for placement in a residential treatment program.

GENDER IDENTITY DISORDER

CLIENT PRESENTATION

1. Desire to Be Opposite Sex (1)*

A. The parents reported that the client frequently expresses the desire to be the opposite sex.

B. The client expressed a desire in today's therapy session to be the opposite sex.

C. The client verbalized positive remarks about his/her gender in today's therapy session.

D. The client reported in today's therapy session that he/she no longer feels the desire to be the opposite sex.

2. Confusion over Sexual Identity (1)

A. The client reported that he/she feels confused about his/her sexual identity.

B. The client has continued to be troubled by confusing thoughts and feelings about his/her sexual identity.

C. The client has started to feel more comfortable about his/her sexual identity.

D. The client verbalized positive remarks about his/her sexual identity in today's therapy session.

E. The client reported that he/she no longer feels confused about his/her sexual identity.

3. Dressing in Opposite-Sex Clothing (2)

A. The parents reported that the client frequently dresses in clothes typically worn by the opposite sex.

B. The client expressed his/her preference to dress in clothes typically worn by the opposite sex.

C. The client has continued to dress in clothes typically worn by the opposite sex.

D. The client reported that he/she no longer experiences a desire to dress in clothes typically worn by the opposite sex.

E. The client has consistently dressed in clothing typically worn by his/her same-sex peers.

4. Assumes Role of Opposite Sex in Play (3)

A. The parents reported that the client often assumes the role of the opposite sex in his/her make-believe play.

B. In today's play-therapy session the client's play reflected his/her strong identification with the opposite sex.

C. The client has gradually started to engage in play activities that are more typical of his/her same-sex peers.

D. The client has consistently engaged in play activities that are typical of his/her same-sex peers.

* The numbers in parentheses correlate to the number of the Behavioral Definition statement in the companion chapter with same title in *The Child Psychotherapy Treatment Planner* (Jongsma, Peterson, and McInnis) by John Wiley & Sons, 2000.

5. Participates in Pastimes Typical of the Opposite Sex (4)

A. The parents reported that the client often insists on participating in games or pastimes that are typical of the opposite sex.

B. The client expressed his/her interest in participating in games or activities that are typical of the opposite sex.

C. The client has started to participate in games or pastimes that are typical of his/her same-sex peers.

D. In today's therapy session the client expressed an interest in participating in games or pastimes that are typical of his/her same-sex peers.

E. The client has consistently participated in games or pastimes that are typical of his/her gender.

6. Prefers Playmates of the Opposite Sex (5)

A. The parents reported that the client often prefers to play with peers of the opposite sex.

B. The client expressed greater interest and enjoyment in playing with opposite-sex peers.

C. The client has started to play more often with peers of his/her gender.

D. The client verbalized a desire to spend more time in play with same-sex peers.

E. The client has consistently played with peers of his/her same gender.

F. The client has established and maintained lasting same-sex peer friendships.

7. Distant Relationship with Same-Sex Parent (5)

A. The client has a distant relationship with his/her same-sex parent.

B. The client expressed feelings of anger and hurt about his/her relationship with the same-sex parent.

C. The client verbalized his/her distrust of the same-sex parent.

D. The client has started to develop a closer, more trusting relationship with the same-sex parent.

E. The client has established a close relationship with the same-sex parent.

8. Enmeshed Relationship with Opposite-Sex Parent (5)

A. The client has established an overly enmeshed relationship with the opposite-sex parent.

B. The client reported that he/she often turns to the opposite-sex parent for nurturance, support, and encouragement.

C. The client's overly enmeshed relationship with the opposite-sex parent, combined with his/her distant relationship with the same-sex parent, has contributed to the confusion surrounding his/her sexual identity.

D. The client has maintained a very enmeshed relationship with the opposite-sex parent.

E. The client has achieved a healthy balance between spending time with the opposite-sex parent and engaging in activities with the same-sex parent.

9. Frequently Passes as Opposite Sex (6)

A. The client reported that he/she frequently passes as being of the opposite sex.

B. The client expressed feelings of shame and embarrassment about others' frequently perceiving him/her as being of the opposite sex.

C. The client expressed feelings of anger about others' perceiving him/her as being of the opposite sex.

D. The client reported that he/she has recently not heard any comments or remarks from others about being of the opposite sex.

E. The client has frequently passed as a member of the opposite sex because of his/her dress, preference for playing with members of the opposite sex, and participation in many games or activities that are typical of the opposite sex.

10. Insistence That He/She Was Born the Wrong Sex (7)

A. The parents reported that the client often insists that he/she was born the wrong sex.

B. In today's therapy session the client shared that he/she feels he/she was born the wrong sex.

C. The client has ceased making verbalizations about being born the wrong sex.

11. Disgust or Rejection of Sexual Anatomy (8)

A. In today's therapy session the client verbalized a disgust with or rejection of his/her sexual anatomy.

B. The client verbalized a desire to change his/her sexual anatomy.

C. The client has reduced the frequency of his/her critical and repulsive statements about his/her sexual anatomy.

D. The client has ceased making any critical or derogatory remarks about his/her sexual anatomy.

E. The client verbalized an acceptance of his/her sexual anatomy.

12. Physical/Sexual Abuse (8)

A. The client's confusion surrounding his/her sexual identity began around the time that he/she was physically abused.

B. The client's confusion surrounding his/her sexual identity began around the time that he/she was sexually abused.

C. The client's confusion surrounding his/her sexual identity has started to decrease as he/she works through his/her feelings surrounding the past abuse.

D. The client continues to be troubled by unresolved feelings of anger, hurt, and sadness about the past abuse.

INTERVENTIONS IMPLEMENTED

1. Build Therapeutic Trust (1)*

A. Today's therapy session focused on building the level of trust with the client through consistent eye contact, active listening, unconditional positive regard, and warm acceptance.

B. Listened closely to the client's concerns and reflected his/her feelings.

C. The therapy session was helpful in building the level of trust with the client.

* The numbers in parentheses correlate to the number of the Therapeutic Interventions statement in the companion chapter with same title in *The Child Psychotherapy Treatment Planner* (Jongsma, Peterson, and McInnis) by John Wiley & Sons, 2000.

D. The therapy session did not prove to be helpful in building the level of trust with the client as he/she remained guarded and resistant to talking about his/her sexual identity.

E. The client verbally recognized that he/she has trouble establishing trust with others because he/she often expects to be criticized or teased by others.

2. Explore Reasons for Opposite-Sex Identity (2)

A. Today's therapy session explored the client's reasons for his/her attraction to opposite-sex identity.

B. The therapy session was helpful in identifying the reasons or factors that have contributed to the client's attraction to an opposite-sex identity.

C. The therapy session did not produce insight into the factors contributing to the client's attraction to an opposite-sex identity.

D. A family therapy session was held to assess the dynamics within the family system that contributed to the emergence of the client's confusion surrounding his/her sexual identity.

3. Play-Therapy Techniques (3)

A. A psychoanalytic play-therapy session was held to explore the unconscious conflicts or core anxieties that contribute to the client's rejection of his/her gender identity.

B. Using a psychoanalytic play-therapy approach, the client's core conflicts and anxieties about his/her gender identity were identified and processed.

C. A child-centered play-therapy session was held to explore the client's sexual attitudes, and causes for the rejection of his/her gender identity.

D. The client was given unconditional positive regard and warm acceptance when expressing his/her thoughts and feelings about his/her gender identity.

E. The individual play-therapy sessions have helped the client work through the confusion surrounding his/her gender identity.

4. Cognitive Therapy Techniques (4)

A. Cognitive therapy techniques were employed to help the client identify the negative messages that he/she gives to himself/herself about sexual identity.

B. Today's therapy session helped identify the distorted cognitive messages that the client sends to self regarding his/her sexual identity.

C. The client was strongly encouraged to challenge the distorted or irrational thoughts that he/she had developed about his/her sexual identity.

5. Replace Negative Cognitions with Positive Self-Talk (5)

A. The client was encouraged to replace the negative cognitive messages regarding his/her gender identity with positive, realistic self-talk.

B. The client was encouraged to utilize positive self-talk as a means of decreasing his/her anxiety regarding gender identity and increase feelings of self-acceptance.

C. The cognitive therapy techniques have been helpful in revising the client's negative attitude regarding his/her sexual identity.

6. Confront Self-Disparaging Comments (6)

A. The client's self-disparaging comments about his/her gender identity and sexual anatomy were confronted and reframed in today's therapy session.

B. The client was helped to realize how the disparaging comments about his/her gender identity and sexual anatomy only reinforce his/her feelings of low self-esteem.

C. The client was challenged to cease making disparaging remarks about his/her gender identity and sexual anatomy around others as it only leads to his/her ostracization and feelings of alienation.

D. Reframed the client's disparaging remarks about his/her gender identity in an attempt to assist the client in perceiving himself/herself more positively.

7. Identify Positive Aspects of Sexual Identity (7)

A. The client was helped to identify the positive aspects of his/her own sexual identity.

B. The client was encouraged to exhibit the positive aspects of his/her own sexual identity around his/her peers.

C. The client reported that he/she gained a sense of acceptance from peers by sharing the positive aspects of his/her own sexual identity around others.

D. The client was given a homework assignment to identify the positive and negative aspects of his/her own sexual identity.

E. After completing the homework assignment, the client was encouraged to share the positive aspects of his/her own sexual identity with peers at school or in the neighborhood.

8. Mirror Exercise (8)

A. The client was instructed to perform a mirror exercise at home where he/she talks positively to self regarding sexual identity.

B. The client performed the mirror exercise and reported that it was helpful in increasing his/her feelings of self-esteem and self-worth.

C. The client reported that he/she followed through with performing the mirror exercise, but continues to experience feelings of low self-esteem regarding his/her sexual identity.

D. Processed the reasons for the client's failure to follow through with performing the mirror exercise.

9. Reinforce Positive Self-Descriptive Statements (9)

A. Today's therapy session reinforced the client's positive self-descriptive statements.

B. The parents were strongly encouraged to reinforce the client's positive self-descriptive statements at home.

C. The client was directed to verbalize at least one positive self-descriptive statement daily around others at school.

D. The client was encouraged to verbalize positive statements about self and others at school to help improve his/her peer relationships in this setting.

E. The client was given a homework assignment to record at least one positive self-descriptive statement daily in a journal.

10. Family Dynamics (10)

A. A family therapy session was held to explore the dynamics within the family system that reinforce or contribute to the client's gender identity confusion.

B. The family members were asked to list the stressors that have had a negative impact on the family.

C. The family therapy session revealed that the client has an overly enmeshed relationship with the opposite-sex parent.

D. The family therapy session revealed that the client has a distant and strained relationship with the same-sex parent.

E. The family members were asked to identify the things they would like to change within the family system.

11. Explore Parental Attitudes and Behaviors (11)

A. A therapy session was held with the parents to explore their attitudes and behaviors that may contribute to the client's sexual identity confusion.

B. Today's therapy session revealed how the parents' critical and disparaging remarks contribute to the client's sexual identity confusion.

C. The parent(s) were challenged and confronted to cease making critical and disparaging remarks about the client's sexual identity.

D. The parent(s) were encouraged to reinforce the positive aspects of the client's sexual identity.

E. The parent(s) verbally acknowledged the need to praise and reinforce the positive aspects of the client's sexual identity.

12. Identify Positive Traits Talents (12)

A. The client was assisted in developing a list of his/her positive traits, talents, and physical characteristics.

B. The client's positive traits, talents, and physical characteristics were reinforced in today's therapy session.

C. The parents were strongly encouraged to praise and reinforce the client's positive traits, talents, and physical characteristics.

D. The client was strongly encouraged to share his/her positive traits, talents, and physical characteristics with others to increase his/her self-esteem and feelings of belonging with peers.

13. Feelings of Hurt, Anger, or Distrust of Same-Sex Parent (13)

A. Today's therapy session explored for any feelings of hurt, anger, or distrust that the client may have toward the same-sex parent (or parent substitute).

B. Today's therapy session explored the factors that have contributed to the negative feelings between the client and same-sex parent.

C. Today's therapy session was helpful in identifying the root causes for the client's feelings of hurt, anger, and distrust toward the same-sex parent (or parent substitute).

D. The client verbalized feelings of anger and hurt about the same-sex parent's lack of involvement with him/her.

E. The client expressed feelings of anger and hurt about the same-sex parent's making derogatory or critical remarks about his/her sexual identity.

14. Increase Time Spent with Same-Sex Parent (14)

A. The same-sex parent was given a directive to increase time spent with the client in play and work activities.

B. The same-sex parent was given a homework assignment of performing a specific task with the client.

C. The client and the same-sex parent developed a list of tasks or activities that they would like to do together.

D. The opposite-sex parent was strongly encouraged to support and reinforce the development of the client's appropriate identification with his/her same-sex parent.

E. The opposite-sex parent was strongly encouraged to look for opportunities to reinforce the positive aspects of the client's relationship with his/her same-sex parent.

15. Assign "One-on-One" Exercise (15)

A. The "One-on-One" homework assignment from *The Brief Child Therapy Homework Planner* (Jongsma, Peterson, and McInnis) was assigned to increase the amount of quality time spent between the client and same-sex parent.

B. The client and same-sex parent reported that the "One-on-One" exercise helped facilitate a closer relationship between them.

C. The "One-on-One" exercise has helped the client feel more comfortable with his/her own sexual identity.

D. The client and his/her same-sex parent reported that they have spent little time together since being assigned the "One-on-One" homework assignment.

E. Processed the reasons why the client and same-sex parent have spent little quality time together.

16. Referral to Big Brother/Big Sister Program (16)

A. The client was referred to the Big Brother/Big Sister program to provide him/her with the opportunity to establish a close relationship with a same-sex adult.

B. The client expressed happiness about spending quality time with his/her Big Brother/Big Sister.

C. The client's involvement in the Big Brother/Big Sister program has helped to improve his/her self-image.

D. The client's Big Brother/Big Sister has proven to be a positive role model.

17. Conduct Family Therapy (17)

A. A family therapy session was held to explore the quality of the client's relationship with the same-sex parent.

B. The family therapy session revealed that the client has established a conflictual and strained relationship with the same-sex parent.

C. The client was given the opportunity to express his/her feelings of anger, hurt, and sadness about his/her conflictual relationship with the same-sex parent.

D. Today's family therapy session addressed the negative feelings between the client and his/her same-sex parent.

E. Today's family therapy session helped to resolve the negative feelings between the client and his/her same-sex parent.

18. Encourage Parental Positive Reinforcement (18)

A. The parents were strongly encouraged to provide frequent praise and positive reinforcement for the client's positive social behaviors.

B. The parents were strongly encouraged to praise and reinforce the client for dressing appropriately.

C. The parents were encouraged to praise and reinforce behaviors that would help build a positive gender identity for the client.

D. The parents were instructed to observe and record positive behaviors by the client between therapy sessions.

E. The client was strongly encouraged to engage in positive social behaviors that help to build a positive gender identity, increase confidence in self, and elicit parental support and acceptance.

19. Initiate Social or Play Activities (19)

A. The client was given the directive to initiate one social or play activity daily with same-sex peers.

B. The client was helped to identify a list of positive social or play activities that he/she could engage in with same-sex peers.

C. Role-playing and modeling techniques were utilized to teach the client effective ways to initiate social contacts.

D. The client successfully followed through with the directive to initiate at least one social or play activity daily with a same-sex peer.

E. The client failed to follow through with the directive to initiate at least one social or play activity daily with a same-sex peer.

20. Provide Positive Feedback (20)

A. The client was praised and reinforced in a more age-appropriate manner.

B. The client's positive social behaviors were praised and reinforced in today's therapy session.

C. The client was praised and reinforced for taking steps to establish friendships with same-sex peers.

D. The parents were given the directive to observe and record three to five positive social behaviors that the client engaged in with same-sex peers before the next therapy session.

E. The parents were strongly encouraged to reinforce the client for dressing in gender-appropriate clothing and engaging in positive social behaviors with his/her same-sex peers.

21. Assess Reasons for Desire to Cross-Dress (21)

A. Today's therapy session reviewed why the client's desire to cross-dress is related to times of high stress within the family system.

B. Explored whether the client's desire to cross-dress is related to times when he/she is feeling ignored by significant others.

C. Today's therapy session revealed that the frequency of the client's cross-dressing increases during times of stress within the family system and when he/she is feeling rejected or ignored.

D. The client expressed his/her desire to receive greater affirmation from the same-sex parent.

E. The client was encouraged to directly verbalize his/her need to spend increased time with parent(s), instead of meeting needs through cross-dressing.

22. List Positive Same-Sex Role Models (22)

A. The client was assigned the task of identifying his/her positive, same-sex role models.

B. Processed the reasons why the client admires and respects positive, same-sex role models.

C. The client was encouraged to engage in behaviors or activities similar to those of his/her positive, same-sex role models.

D. Reinforced the client's identification with the same-sex role model.

23. Assign "I Want to Be Like . . ." Exercise (23)

A. The client was assigned the "I Want to Be Like . . ." exercise from *The Brief Child Therapy Homework Planner* (Jongsma, Peterson, and McInnis) to structure positive role-model identification.

B. The client completed the homework assignment and was able to list several positive same-sex role models.

C. The client was able to identify the reasons why he/she respects or admires the same-sex role models.

D. The homework assignment helped promote the client's acceptance of his/her sexual identity.

E. After completing the homework assignment, the client was encouraged to engage in positive behaviors with same-sex peers.

24. Explore for Physical or Sexual Abuse (24)

A. The client's background was explored for a history of physical or sexual abuse that may have contributed to his/her gender confusion.

B. Today's therapy session revealed a history of physical abuse which has been a significant contributing factor to the client's gender confusion.

C. Today's therapy session revealed a past history of sexual abuse which has contributed to the client's gender confusion.

D. The client verbally denied ever being physically or sexually abused.

E. The client was given unconditional positive regard and warm acceptance in expressing his/her feelings about the past abuse.

GRIEF/LOSS UNRESOLVED

CLIENT PRESENTATION

1. Parent Death Reaction (1)*

A. The client presented as visibly upset and distressed over the recent loss of his/her parent.

B. Teachers, friends, and others have reported that the client is exhibiting various grief reactions such as anger, depression, and emotional lability around the recent loss of his/her parent.

C. The client indicated he/she cannot think of anything else but the death of his/her parent.

D. The client frequently expressed that he/she still cannot accept that this parental death really happened.

E. The client revealed that the feeling of being so alone and hopeless has been overwhelming for him/her since the parent's death.

F. The client has started to talk about the loss of his/her parent and has begun to accept consolation, support, and encouragement from others.

2. Termination of Parental Rights (2)

A. The client presented as sad and withdrawn after recently being told that his/her parents' rights are being terminated.

B. The client indicated that he/she refuses to believe that he/she will not see parents again.

C. Foster parents reported that the client is continually angry and upset since receiving the news of his/her parents' rights' being terminated.

D. The client has made progress in coming to terms with his/her parents' loss of their rights and has started to look forward to a new home and family.

3. Parental Incarceration Grief (3)

A. The client expressed feeling a big hole in his/her life since his/her parent went to prison.

B. The client reported being angry most of the time since his/her parent was incarcerated.

C. The client indicated that he/she has felt sad and embarrassed about the parent's imprisonment and has socially withdrawn from activities to avoid feeling more uncomfortable.

D. The client has begun to accept and adjust to parent's imprisonment and return to his/her normal level of functioning.

4. Grief Due to Geographic Move (4)

A. The client presented as depressed and focused on the loss of previous home and friends that have been left behind because of the geographic move.

B. The client reported feeling angry and upset all the time now at parents for their decision to move him/her away from his/her neighborhood and friends.

---

* The numbers in parentheses correlate to the number of the Behavioral Definition statement in the companion chapter with same title in *The Child Psychotherapy Treatment Planner* (Jongsma, Peterson, and McInnis) by John Wiley & Sons, 2000.

C. The parents indicated that the client is always sad and refuses to leave home except to go to school.

D. The client has started to accept the family's new location and is beginning to make new friends and involve himself/herself in other activities.

5. Parent Emotional Abandonment (5)

A. The client verbalized feeling abandoned emotionally since losing nearly all contact with his/her parent.

B. The client reported he/she has been cut off from nearly all contact with his/her other parent.

C. The client indicated he/she is devastated by the loss of nearly all meaningful contact with his/her parent.

D. The client has begun to openly grieve the emotional abandonment he/she has experienced from his/her parents.

6. Emotionally Upset (6)

A. The client presented in an upset, tearful, and distraught manner.

B. The client related that he/she is having a difficult time coming to terms with the recent loss he/she has experienced.

C. The client is gradually making progress in coming to terms and accepting his/her loss, as he/she reports crying less and not being as upset as before.

D. It appears the client is stuck in his/her grieving process and finding it difficult to move beyond being upset and distraught.

7. Social Withdrawal (7)

A. The client presents as very withdrawn and nonverbal around his/her past loss(es).

B. "I find it impossible to talk about," is one of the few verbalizations coming from the client regarding his/her past loss.

C. The client, with encouragement and support, has slowly moved from his/her withdrawn state and started to talk about the loss.

8. Angry/Tense (8)

A. Anger and tension dominate the client's affect, mood, and manner.

B. The client reports frequent verbal temper outbursts toward others and breaking things following the loss.

C. The client's anger is freely vented toward God, doctors, and others that "had a hand" in the loss.

D. There is a decrease in the client's anger as he/she acknowledges and explains that now he/she is feeling more hurt and sadness about the loss.

9. Guilty/Responsible (9)

A. The overall mood and manner of the client reflects a deep sense of guilt and responsibility for the recent loss.

B. The client reported those things that make him/her feel guilty and responsible for the loss.

C. The client is moving toward letting go of his/her guilt and accepting that he/she is not responsible for the loss.

D. To maintain control, the client appears to be stuck in his/her guilt and either unwilling or unable to move beyond this point in the process of grieving.

10. Avoidance of Loss (10)

A. The client presented with a high level of denial and strong resistance to acknowledging and accepting his/her loss.

B. The client's family system has a definite pattern of denial and nonacceptance of losses.

C. The client stated, "I don't believe this really happened; I won't accept this," and did not attend any part of the funeral process.

D. Cracks are starting to show in the client's denial as he/she is now believing the loss is real.

E. The client's denial has broken and he/she is now being overwhelmed with feelings of anger, hurt, and sadness.

INTERVENTIONS IMPLEMENTED

1. Establish Trust (1)*

A. Initial trust level was established with the client through the use of unconditional positive regard.

B. Warm acceptance and active listening techniques were utilized to establish the basis for a nurturing relationship with the client.

C. The client has formed a trust-based relationship with therapist and has started to express his/her feelings around the recent loss.

D. Despite the use of active listening, warm acceptance, and unconditional positive regard, the client remains hesitant to trust and begin sharing his/her feelings connected to the recent loss.

2. Identify Feelings around Loss (2)

A. The client was ask to write a letter to the lost loved one describing his/her feelings, desires, and wishes connected to that person.

B. The client read the letter that he/she had written to the lost loved one with appropriate affect and expression of feelings.

C. The client read the letter to the lost loved one with flat affect and showing no outward emotions either in his/her voice or facial expression.

3. Explore Story of Loss (3)

A. The client was asked to tell the story of his/her loss using photographs of the loved one.

B. The client told the story of his/her loss with appropriate affect.

* The numbers in parentheses correlate to the number of the Therapeutic Interventions statement in the companion chapter with same title in *The Child Psychotherapy Treatment Planner* (Jongsma, Peterson, and McInnis) by John Wiley & Sons, 2000.

    C. The client received affirmation and validation for the feelings he/she expressed in telling the story of the loss.

    D. The client told the story of the loss with little or no affect.

4. Employ Mutual Storytelling Technique (4)

    A. The client was engaged in a mutual storytelling exercise and encouraged to tell the story of his/her loss.

    B. The client readily told his/her story, which was interpreted for its underlying meaning.

    C. The client was told a story that used the same characters and settings as his/her story, but the new story wove in healthy ways to adapt to and resolve the loss.

    D. The client verbalized that the mutual storytelling technique was useful in giving him/her ways to cope with and resolve the loss.

5. Utilize "Before and After Drawing Technique" (5)

    A. Using the "Before and After Drawing Technique" (Cangelasi), the client was asked to tell the story of his/her loss through drawings of how he/she was before and then after the loss.

    B. The client explained the story told in his/her grief drawings, willingly filled in any gaps, and answered all questions that were asked.

    C. Feelings connected to the loss events were identified, processed, and validated.

    D. Drawing has opened the door to enable the client to tell the story of the loss and its effect on his/her life.

6. Use Puppets or Felt Figures (6)

    A. The client was encouraged to act out or tell the story of his/her loss using puppets or a felt board.

    B. The client acted out the story of his/her loss using puppets.

    C. The client used the felt board and figures to tell the story of the loss.

    D. The client was given positive verbal affirmation for sharing the story of his/her loss.

7. Read Books on Grief and Loss (7)

    A. The book *Where Is Daddy?* (Gogg) was read with the client.

    B. The book *Emma Says Goodbye* (Nystrom) was read with the client.

    C. The books about loss were discussed and processed with the client.

    D. The feelings expressed by the client during the readings and discussion of the book were mirrored, acknowledged, and validated.

    E. Through the reading of tho books, the client has gained an understanding of what the experience of loss is about and developed hope that he/she can work through it.

8. Teach Stages of Grieving Process (8)

    A. The parents were educated on the stages and process of grief and had their questions answered so they can better understand this process.

    B. It was emphasized with the family that grief is not a one-time event ("Just get over it") but an ongoing process.

C. All of the family members seem to have a better understanding of the grief process and, as a result, seem more capable of showing empathy and support toward one another.

D. Some family members are resistant to any new information about grief and are in denial about the power of its impact on people's lives.

9. Utilize Child-Centered Play Therapy (9)

A. Child-centered play therapy was utilized to help the client work through his/her loss.

B. When the client expressed a feeling within the child-centered play-therapy session, it was mirrored, reflected, and validated to him/her.

C. The client's feelings were reflected back to him/her in an affirming, nonjudgmental manner to promote his/her working through the grieving process.

D. The child-centered play-therapy approach has helped to support and encourage the client in working through the loss.

10. Employ Individual Play Therapy (10)

A. An individual play-therapy session was conducted with the client to help him/her express and work through feelings about the loss.

B. The client actively participated in the play-therapy session.

C. The feelings that were expressed through the client's play were affirmed and validated.

D. The supportive environment of the play-therapy sessions has helped the client express and work through many of the feelings surrounding his/her loss.

11. Use Art Therapy (11)

A. Various art-therapy techniques were used to provide the client with an opportunity to creatively express his/her feelings connected to the loss.

B. The client actively participated in the art therapy.

C. The client explained his/her artwork in detail, as requested.

D. The client's active participation in art therapy has helped him/her begin openly expressing feelings connected to the loss.

12. Use Art or Verbal Metaphor in Play Therapy (12)

A. The client was requested to talk about what his/her life was like prior to and after the loss using stories or drawings.

B. With encouragement, the client was able to talk about what his/her life was like prior to and after the loss.

C. The client was assisted in identifying the specific changes in his/her life that have occurred since the loss.

D. The feelings expressed by the client through his/her drawings or stories were mirrored, acknowledged, and validated.

13. Use "Five Faces" Technique (13)

A. The "Five Faces" technique (Jewett) was used to help the client move beyond his/her emotional block and become able to identify and express his/her feelings.

B. The client's ability to recognize feelings and express them has grown and been helpful in clarifying his/her many conflicting emotions connected to the grieving process.

C. The client continues to be blocked in his/her ability to identify and express grief-related feelings.

14. Explore Grief through Games (14)

A. The Goodbye Game and the Good Mourning Game were played with client to help him/her explore the process of grief.

B. The client received positive verbal reinforcement for disclosing his/her thoughts and feelings connected to his/her loss.

C. The client was resistive to using the therapeutic games as a springboard for expressing his/her thoughts and feelings related to the grief experience.

15. Identify/Clarify Feelings Connected to the Loss (15)

A. The role of feelings and the way they work were explained to the client.

B. The client was assisted in identifying, labeling, and expressing his/her feelings connected to the loss.

C. The client was supported with verbal affirmation and validation as he/she expressed feelings connected with the loss.

D. With assistance the client was able to identify, express, and work through his/her feelings connected to the loss.

16. Assign Grief Journal (16)

A. The client was ask to keep a daily grief journal to record his/her thoughts and feelings associated with the loss.

B. The client's grief journal was reviewed and significant disclosures of thoughts and feelings were supported and reinforced.

C. The client's grief journal was reviewed, but it revealed that the client continues to distance himself/herself from struggling with the pain of grieving.

D. The client has not followed through with recording his/her thoughts and feelings related to grief in a journal.

17. Support Group Referral (17)

A. The client was referred to and encouraged to attend a grief support group for adolescents.

B. The client's experience of attending a grief support group was processed and his/her continued attendance was supported and encouraged.

C. The client was resistive to a referral to a support group and has continued to refuse to attend such a group.

D. The client was once again encouraged to attend a grief support group even though he/she has been resistive to this idea in the past.

18. Read *Lifetimes* (18)

A. To help the client understand death more fully, the *Lifetimes* (Mellanie and Ingpen) book was read with him/her.

B. The client's questions that arose from the reading of the *Lifetimes* book were answered and supported.

C. The client's lack of questions was gently but firmly confronted as being an avoidance of grieving.

19. Arrange Contact with Experienced Griever (19)

A. The client was assisted in identifying some peer or adult he/she knows who has successfully worked through the grieving process and might be willing to talk with him/her about their experience.

B. The client was guided in developing a list of questions that he/she would like to have answered by the experienced person.

C. The client was encouraged to set a date to talk with the experienced griever either at a time outside of a session or within a conjoint session.

D. The client has followed through with talking with the experienced griever, and the therapist and client processed this positive experience within today's session.

20. Read *The Empty Place: A Child's Guide Through Grief* (20)

A. The book *The Empty Place: A Child's Guide Through Grief* (Temes) was used as a guide to help the client through the grief process.

B. The client was supported, guided, and reassured while moving through the stages of grief.

C. The client was encouraged to share the book *The Empty Place: A Child's Guide Through Grief* with parents to help them understand and support him/her in the grieving process.

21. Read *Don't Despair on Thursday*

A. Read *Don't Despair on Thursdays* (Moser) with the client.

B. Suggestions from the *Don't Despair on Thursdays* book were identified and processed with the client.

C. The client was assisted in selecting two ways to handle his/her grief feelings from the *Don't Despair on Thursdays* book, and plans were developed for the implementation into his/her daily life.

D. The client has reported positive results in using the suggestions from the *Don't Despair on Thursdays* book to cope with his/her feelings of grief.

22. Assign Interview with Clergy/Adult (22)

A. The client was asked to interview a clergyperson and an adult who has experienced a loss to learn about their experiences and how each has worked through it.

B. The client's interviews with the clergyperson and other adult were reviewed, with key elements of the experience being identified, and the message that "you will make it too" was reinforced.

C. The client failed to follow through with interviewing either a clergyperson or another experienced adult griever, and the assignment was given again.

23. Explore Thoughts of Guilt and Blame (23)

A. The client's thoughts and feelings of guilt and blame for the loss were explored.

B. The client's irrational thoughts and feelings were identified and replaced with more realistic ones.

C. The client's irrational thoughts and feelings regarding guilt and self-blame are no longer present.

24. Help Client Communicate Self-Blame for the Loss (24)

A. A Despart Fable was used with the client to help him/her begin expressing self-blame for the loss.

B. The client's active participation in the Despart Fable has assisted him/her in communicating the self-blame he/she feels for the loss.

C. The client resisted participation in the Despart Fable exercise as he/she did not know what to say.

D. The client has begun to openly express and communicate his/her feelings of self-blame for the loss.

25. Help Lift Self-Imposed Curse (25)

A. The therapist and client explored the client's belief in a self-imposed curse that makes him/her responsible for the death of the significant other.

B. The client was encouraged to ask the person who indicated that the death of the significant other was the client's fault to take the statement back.

C. A role-play phone conversation was done between the client and the deceased where the client had the opportunity to apologize for his/her behavior that "caused" the loss.

D. The client's unrealistic beliefs around the curse that caused the death of the significant other were confronted.

E. The client no longer believes that he/she is responsible for the death of the significant other through some curse phenomenon.

26. Create Absolution Rituals (26)

A. An absolution ritual was created for the client to assist him/her in resolving guilt and loss.

B. The client was asked for a commitment to implement and follow through with the ritual as created.

C. The ritual was monitored for its effectiveness and adjusted as required.

D. The absolution ritual seems to have been effective in reducing the client's feelings of guilt or blame for the loss.

27. List Positive Things about Deceased (27)

A. The client was asked to construct a list of all the positive things about the deceased and how he/she plans to remember each.

B. The list was processed with the client and each positive thing/memory was affirmed and the importance of remembering each was emphasized.

C. The client enjoyed the experience of listing positive memories about the deceased significant other.

D. The client was overwhelmed with emotion when talking about positive memories about the deceased significant other.

E. The client can now recall positive things about the deceased significant other without becoming overwhelmed with sadness.

28. Talk about Pictures and Other Mementos (28)

A. The client was asked to bring pictures and mementos of the deceased significant other to the therapy session.

B. The client followed through in bringing pictures and mementos of the deceased and he/she talked about the memories attached to each in an open, free manner, making little probing necessary.

C. The client had to be encouraged and prodded to talk about pictures and mementos that he/she brought as requested.

D. The client's grief appears to be lifting somewhat as he/she talks about positive memories attached to the deceased significant other.

29. Encourage and Support Appropriate Anger (29)

A. The client was encouraged and reminded in sessions to look angry when feeling angry, act angry, and then to put his/her anger into words.

B. The client's fear of looking and expressing anger was explored with him/her.

C. The client was supported and given positive verbal feedback when he/she acted angry and expressed it.

D. The client was confronted when he/she appeared to be feeling angry but acted otherwise.

E. The client's feelings of anger toward God, self, and others has diminished as he/she was able to express them freely.

30. Use Physical Techniques to Release Anger (30)

A. Various acceptable physical techniques (e.g., kneading clay or kicking a paper bag) were used to help the client release repressed angry feelings.

B. The exercise was processed and targets and causes for the anger were explored with the client.

C. The client only minimally participated in the physical techniques, despite encouragement and support's being given to him/her to do so.

D. The use of behavioral techniques has helped the client express and externalize his/her repressed angry feelings.

31. Prepare for An Apology/Asking Forgiveness (31)

A. The client was ask to either write a letter of apology or one asking for forgiveness from the deceased.

B. Role play was used with the client to practice asking for forgiveness or apologizing to the deceased.

C. Letters and role-play exercises have been successful at reducing the client's feelings of guilt.

32. Assign a Good-bye Letter (32)

A. The client was asked to write a good-bye letter or draw a good-bye picture to the deceased.

B. The client's completed letter or drawing was processed, and each feeling that he/she expressed or identified was affirmed.

C. Barriers that prevented the client from completing his/her letter or drawing were identified, processed, and resolved.

D. The client's completed letter or drawing indicates that he/she is making progress in the grieving process.

33. Process Visit to Grave of Loved One (33)

A. The client was prepared to make his/her first visit to the grave of the deceased loved one and selected the adult he/she would like to accompany him/her.

B. The selected adult was prepared to be supportive of and provide guidance for the client's visit to the gravesite.

C. The client followed through with visiting the grave of the deceased loved one, said good-bye, and left his/her letter or drawing at the gravesite.

D. The experience of visiting the gravesite of his/her loved one was processed with the client.

34. Teach Parents Supportive Methods (34)

A. The parents were taught various specific ways they could support and encourage the client in successfully working through the grief process.

B. The parents' efforts to show love, consolation, and provide comfort were affirmed and reinforced.

C. The parents have been resistant to increasing their behaviors that show comfort, consolation, and support to the client's grief.

D. The client has responded favorably to the parents' showing more support and empathy for his/her grief.

35. Assign Parents to Read Grief Books (35)

A. The client's parents were ask to read *Learning to Say Goodbye* (LeShan) to give them knowledge of the grieving process.

B. Accurate information that the parents gathered from their reading on the subject of grief was reinforced and any questions they had were answered.

C. The parents' unrealistic expectations about the grieving process were confronted and restructured into more healthy or appropriate expectations.

36. Conduct Family Session to Express Grief (36)

A. A family session was conducted in which each family member was encouraged to talk about his/her experience related to the loss.

B. Family members who found it impossible to talk about their grief feelings were reminded of the importance of doing so in order to work through the loss.

C. Family members were encouraged to talk more about the loss at appropriate times outside of sessions.

D. The client felt reassured and understood by virtue of other family members' sharing their feelings of grief connected to the loss.

37. Refer Parents to Grief Group (37)

A. The client's parents were referred and encouraged to attend a grief/loss support group.

B. The client's parents were open to the suggestion of attending a support group and have committed themselves to attending the next meeting.

C. The client's parents were resistant to the idea of attending a grief/loss support group and refused to follow through with this referral.

38. Encourage Involvement in Grieving Rituals (38)

A. The parents were encouraged to allow the client to be a part of all of the grieving rituals he/she requests to participate in.

B. The parents were directed to be sensitive, supportive, and comforting to the client during the grieving rituals he/she attends.

C. The various grieving rituals were explained to the client and he/she was given the choice of which he/she would like to attend.

D. The client's attendance at the funeral and other grieving rituals was beneficial in sharing grief with others and saying good-bye to the deceased.

39. Prepare Parents to Say Good-bye (39)

A. The biological parents were prepared to say good-bye to children they are losing custody of.

B. The parents were assisted in identifying and expressing their feelings around losing permanent custody of their children.

C. The parents were assisted in developing healthy, affirmative ways to say good-bye to the children they are losing custody of.

D. The parents selected a healthy, affirmative way to say good-bye to their children and they were assisted in developing plans to implement it.

E. Role play was used to give the parents exposure to saying good-bye to their children in a healthy, affirmative way.

F. Unresolved issues around having to say good-bye were addressed, processed, and resolved.

G. The parents have reached the point where they are ready to say good-bye to their children in a healthy, affirmative way.

40. Facilitate Good-bye Session (40)

A. A good-bye session was facilitated with the parents who were losing custody of their children so the parents could give an appropriate message of permission to each child to move on.

B. The parents were given affirmation and positive verbal feedback on their following through in saying good-bye to children in a positive, healthy way.

C. The good-bye session was a conflictual one in that the parents left the child feeling guilty for the parents' grief and sadness.

D. The parents have written a letter of good-bye and affirmation to their children over whom they have lost custody.

41. Create a Record of Life (41)

A. The client was asked to bring to a session pictures and other memorabilia that are associated with his/her life before and after the grief event.

B. The client was assisted in creating a book or album of his/her life.

C. The client's feelings associated with the loss were processed as they were expressed during the exercise of creating the album.

D. The client was able to select magazine pictures to put in his/her album that represented future hopes and plans, indicating a beginning resolution of grief.

42. "Create a Memory Album" Exercise (42)

A. The client was assisted in making a life book that reflected his/her past, present, and future following the exercise, "Create a Memory Album" from *The Brief Child Therapy Homework Planner* (Jongsma, Peterson, and McInnis).

B. A completed memory album was kept by the client and another was given to his/her current parents.

C. The client's parents affirmed the client's previous life experiences and accepted the memory album with interest.

D. The parents seemed anxious and resistive regarding the client's talking about his/her previous life experiences outside of the family.

43. Read "Petey's Journey Through Sadness" (43)

A. Read "Petey's Journey Through Sadness" from *The Brief Child Therapy Homework Planner* (Jongsma, Peterson, and McInnis) with the client in today's session.

B. The story was processed with the client and he/she was encouraged to share positive memories of his/her lost loved one.

C. The client's fears surrounding remembering the lost loved one were explored, addressed, and resolved using the story as an example.

D. The client talked freely about the story "Petey's Journey Through Sadness," but was unwilling to express positive memories of his/her lost loved one.

LOW SELF-ESTEEM

CLIENT PRESENTATION

1. Self-Disparaging Remarks (1)*

A. The client's deep sense of inferiority was reflected in frequent self-disparaging remarks about his/her appearance, worth, and abilities.

B. The lack of any eye contact on the client's part and negative self remarks are evidence of how little the client thinks of himself/herself.

C. The client reported feeling inferior to others and generally believes that he/she is a loser.

D. The client has stopped making self-critical remarks and even has begun to acknowledge some positive traits and successes.

2. Childhood Abuse/Neglect (1)

A. The client reported incidents of physical and emotional abuse which gave him/her the strong message of being worthless, unloved, and rejected.

B. The client provided numerous examples of how the parents always had negative things to say in his/her regard like, "You can't do anything right," and "If you could only be like your sister."

C. The client described his/her parents as being good people whom he/she loves but who have always been too busy to do things with him/her or attend school events he/she was a part of.

D. The client has started to make some connection between how he/she was treated by the parents as a child and how negatively he/she feels about himself/herself now.

3. Accepting Compliments (2)

A. The client acknowledged his/her problem of believing others when they say nice or complimentary things.

B. The parents reported that the client discounts any praise from them or others.

C. The client reported never hearing compliments from parents so now he/she is unsure how to respond to accolades from anyone.

D. The client has now begun to accept compliments at face value, feeling uncomfortable but good when these instances occur.

4. Refusal to Try New Experiences (3)

A. The client's pervasive failure expectation was reflected in his/her refusal to try new experiences.

B. The client reported being frustrated with his/her pattern of never trying any new experiences.

---

* The numbers in parentheses correlate to the number of the Behavioral Definition statement in the companion chapter with same title in *The Child Psychotherapy Treatment Planner* (Jongsma, Peterson, and McInnis) by John Wiley & Sons, 2000.

C. The client listed many experiences in which he/she experienced failure, but his/her perception was often slanted and distorted.

D. The client expressed that failure is his/her greatest fear.

E. The client has begun to take a few risks and try new experiences with encouragement and support.

5. Avoidant/Quiet (4)

A. The client presented in a quiet, avoidant manner.

B. The client reported that he/she avoids more than brief contact with others and usually has little to say in social situations with peers.

C. The parents reported that the client has always been shy with adults and peers.

D. The client has gradually started to withdraw less and is feeling less tense around others.

6. Cautious/Fearful (4)

A. The client presented with a frightened affect and a very cautious manner.

B. From the earliest times the client can remember, others have always frightened him/her and he/she always has been cautious not to upset anyone.

C. The client indicated that he/she is cautious and fearful of doing something wrong in social situations.

D. The client has started to be less cautious and now takes some carefully chosen social risks.

7. Pleasing/Friendly (5)

A. The client presented in a friendly, outgoing manner and seems eager to please others.

B. Everything was carefully checked out by the client to make sure what he/she is doing or saying is right or acceptable to others.

C. Past actions done to please others have gotten the client in trouble or left him/her feeling taken advantage of.

D. A noticeable decrease in the client's pleasing behaviors was observed as he/she is now starting to offer his/her thoughts and opinions more assertively.

8. Inability to Accept/Recognize Positive Traits (6)

A. The client denied having any talents or positive attributes that others would admire.

B. The client struggled to identify any positive traits or talents about himself/herself.

C. The client rejected all the identified positive traits pointed out to him/her by others.

D. The client was able to recognize and accept positive things about himself/herself.

9. Insecure/Anxious (7)

A. There was visible insecurity and anxiousness to the client's affect and manner.

B. The client described several instances in which he/she did not say or do anything in front of peers because of fear of ridicule and rejection.

C. The client reported feeling anxious and insecure at home and in all social/peer situations, after believing that others may not like him/her.

D. As the session progressed, the client became less anxious and more able to open up to the therapist.

E. The client reported feeling more self-confident when in the presence of peers.

10. Self-Defeating Behavior (8)

A. The client has often engaged in self-defeating behavior (i.e., drinking and sexual activity) to gain the acceptance of his/her peers.

B. The client identified that he/she found it easier to feel accepted by peers when he/she was using substances.

C. The client indicated that he/she has done various "bad acts" to gain the attention and acceptance of his/her peers.

D. The client has dropped most of his/her self-defeating behavior and has begun to work on accepting himself/herself.

11. Difficulty Saying "No" (9)

A. The client indicated he/she rarely says "no" to others out of fear of not being liked.

B. The client reported believing that he/she will not be liked unless he/she says "yes."

C. The client identified the paralyzing fear he/she experiences when saying "no" to others.

D. The client has worked on starting to say "no" to others to be more true to his/her real beliefs, values, feelings, or thoughts.

INTERVENTIONS IMPLEMENTED

1. Implement Psychoanalytic Play-Therapy (1)*

A. A psychoanalytic play-therapy approach was used which allowed the client to take the lead and explore his/her unconscious conflicts and fixations.

B. A psychoanalytic play-therapy approach was employed to establish trust with the client and assist him/her in letting go of negative thoughts, beliefs, and fears.

C. The client has been cooperative, but hesitant to build trust with the therapist or to take the lead in exploring his/her unconscious conflicts or fixations.

D. Psychoanalytic play-therapy approaches have helped the client build a level of trust with the therapist and begin to let go of his/her negative thoughts, beliefs, and fears.

2. Use Puppets to Build Self-Esteem (2)

A. Puppets were employed to assist the client in starting conversations and making friends to help build his/her self-esteem.

B. Puppets were used to give the client practice in asking for things he/she needs.

C. Puppets were used in a nondirect way to allow the client to create his/her own scenes for building a more positive sense of self-esteem.

D. Use of puppets has helped the client learn skills to raise his/her self-esteem and confidence.

* The numbers in parentheses correlate to the number of the Therapeutic Interventions statement in the companion chapter with same title in *The Child Psychotherapy Treatment Planner* (Jongsma, Peterson, and McInnis) by John Wiley & Sons, 2000.

3. Use Play-Doh to Relax Defenses (3)

A. Play-doh was used in a nondirect manner to help the client relax with the therapist and to open up avenues for personal self-expression.

B. The client's active involvement with the Play-doh has facilitated opportunities to enhance his/her self-esteem.

C. Negative self-talk that emerged in today's therapy session was gently confronted and remodeled.

D. The client's relaxed defenses and increased openness created by his/her use of Play-doh in session have resulted in a marked growth in his/her self-esteem.

4. Use Expressive Clay Technique (4)

A. An expressive clay technique was used to assist the client in expressing and communicating issues and to facilitate increasing his/her self-esteem.

B. The client actively worked with clay to increase his/her ability to express and communicate issues.

C. The client struggled with working with the clay and, despite assistance, was not able to express or communicate his/her issues.

D. The client's work with clay has facilitated his/her ability to express and communicate issues as well as increase his/her self-esteem.

5. Confront/Reframe Self-Disparaging Remarks (5)

A. The client's self-disparaging comments were confronted with the strong message that these comments were not an accurate reflection of reality.

B. The client's self-disparaging comments were realistically reframed and given to the client to replace the negative comments.

C. The client reported that he/she is more aware of his/her tendency to make self-disparaging remarks and has been more successful at reducing the frequency of this behavior.

6. Explore How Negative Feelings Are Acted Out (6)

A. The client was asked to construct a list of ways he/she sees him/herself expressing or acting out negative feelings about himself/herself.

B. The client's self-awareness was increased by exploring how he/she expresses or acts out negative feelings about self and how he/she could stop this habit.

C. It was consistently pointed out to the client in a warm, respectful manner when he/she was projecting a negative self-image.

7. Group Therapy Referral (7)

A. The client was referred to group therapy that is focused on building self-esteem.

B. Progress reports reflected that the client is actively taking part in group therapy and is slowly building some self-confidence.

C. The client's fear of social interaction was given as a reason for his/her refusal to attend group therapy.

8. Identify Parents' Critical Interactions (8)

A. In family sessions, critical interaction patterns were identified with the family and redirected to supportive, affirming interaction patterns.

B. A videotape of the family session was used to illustrate critical family interaction patterns.

C. Negative parenting methods were discussed with the parents, and new affirming methods were recommended.

D. The parents have become more aware of their disparaging parenting methods and reported implementation of more affirming child-guidance techniques.

9. Record Positive Aspects of Self (9)

A. The client was asked to identify one positive thing about himself/herself and record it in a journal.

B. The client's journal was reviewed and positive traits or accomplishments were identified, affirmed, and supported.

C. The client reported that he/she is feeling more positively about self and is more aware of his/her positive traits.

10. Develop Positive Self-Talk (10)

A. Positive self-talk techniques were taught to the client to assist in boosting his/her confidence and self-image.

B. Role play was used to practice positive self-talk techniques.

C. A commitment was elicited from the client to employ positive self-talk on a daily basis.

D. The positive self-talk technique has been effective in increasing the client's self-esteem.

11. Develop Affirmations List (11)

A. The client was assisted in developing a list of positive affirmations for himself/herself.

B. A commitment was elicited from the client to read the affirmation list three times.

C. The client reported that the regular reading of the self-affirmation list was beneficial in building self-esteem.

12. Use Positive Attitude Ball (12)

A. A Positive Attitude Ball (Childswork/Childsplay) was used to help the client identify and affirm positive things about himself/herself.

B. The positive things about the client that were identified through the use of the Positive Attitude Ball were verbally reinforced.

C. The client's statements that discounted the positive traits were confronted and the positive traits were verbally reaffirmed to him/her.

D. The client's identification of positive traits through the use of the Positive Attitude Ball has increased his/her self-esteem.

13. Reinforce Positive Statements (13)

A. The client's statements of self-confidence and identified positive things about self were verbally affirmed and supported.

B. The frequency of the client's positive self-descriptive statements has increased.

14. Play Therapeutic Games (14)

A. The UnGame (The UnGame Company) and The Thinking, Feeling, Doing Game (Creative Therapeutics) were played with the client to give him/her opportunities for self-disclosure.

B. Opportunities for feeling identification during games were seized to affirm the client's self-disclosure.

C. The client has become more adept at identifying and expressing his/her emotions.

15. Enhance Ability to Identify Feelings (15)

A. Feelings charts and cards were used to teach the client how to identify specific feelings.

B. The client was given positive verbal affirmation and reinforcement for identifying specific feelings during the session.

C. The client's resistance to identifying his/her feelings was confronted, addressed, and resolved.

D. Through the client's work with feelings charts and cards, he/she has developed the ability to identify specific feelings.

16. Assign Exercises from *The Building Blocks of Self-Esteem* (16)

A. The client was assigned exercises from the workbook *The Building Blocks of Self-Esteem* (Childswork/Childsplay).

B. The completed exercises from the self-esteem workbook were processed, with positive traits from each exercise being affirmed and reinforced.

C. The client validated each positive characteristic explored in the completed self-esteem building exercises to other adults (e.g., teachers, family, friends) and reported their responses.

D. The workbook exercises have helped to build the client's self-confidence and self-esteem.

17. Educate about Feelings Identification (17)

A. The client was educated in identifying, labeling, and expressing feelings.

B. The client was given a feeling list and then given various scenarios and asked to identify what the individual in the scenario might be feeling.

C. The client was asked to keep a daily feelings journal.

D. The client has become more adept at identifying and expressing his/her emotions.

18. Encourage Eye Contact (18)

A. The client's lack of eye contact was focused on and discussed with the client.

B. An agreement was obtained from the client to have regular eye contact with the therapist during sessions.

C. The client was confronted by the therapist when he/she avoided or failed to make eye contact.

D. The client reported an increase in the frequency of making eye contact with others outside of therapy sessions.

19. Broaden Eye Contact Experience (19)

A. The client was asked to make a commitment to increase eye contact with parents, teachers, and others.

B. The client's experience of making eye contact with all adults was processed, with feelings specific to this experience being identified.

C. The client reported an increase in the frequency of making eye contact with others outside of therapy sessions.

20. Negate Self-Critical Messages (20)

A. Read *Don't Feed the Monster on Tuesdays* (Moser) with the client and the ideas for handling self-critical messages were explored.

B. The client was assisted in identifying and implementing strategies for handling self-critical messages in daily life.

C. The client was helped to make a chart to record his/her progress in building self-esteem.

D. Monitoring, encouragement, and affirmation were provided for the client's progress in building self-esteem.

21. Identify Good Qualities about Self (21)

A. The client was asked to read *My Best Friend is Me* (Childswork/Childsplay) and then to make a list of his/her good qualities to process with the therapist.

B. The client's list of good qualities was processed and each quality was verbally affirmed and reinforced.

C. The client was instructed to read the list each morning and before bed.

D. The client's follow-through in reading the good quality list was monitored and redirection was given, if needed.

E. The client's list of positive qualities has helped him/her build a more secure sense of self-esteem.

22. Assign New Experience Exercises (22)

A. The client and parents were asked to complete the exercises "Dixie Overcomes Her Fears" and "Learn From Your Mistakes" from *The Brief Child Therapy Homework Planner* (Jongsma, Peterson, and McInnis).

B. The completed new-experience exercises were processed with the client and parents, with emphasis on identifying new experiences the client could try.

C. The client was helped to select and verbally commit to several new activities to try.

D. The client was monitored, supported, and encouraged to try new experiences.

E. The message that "failure is a part of the learning experience" was reinforced at regular intervals with the client.

F. The client has progressed to where he/she is willing to try new experiences and not be as afraid to fail.

23. Identify Emotional Needs (23)

A. The client was taught basic concepts of how to identify and verbalize his/her emotional needs.

B. Ways to increase the client's emotional needs' being met were explored.

24. Share Emotional Needs (24)

A. A family session was conducted in which the parents and the client exchanged and identified their emotional needs.

B. The client and family were educated in ways to be sensitive to others' needs and to ask for their own emotional needs to be met.

25. Utilize Therapeutic Stories (25)

A. *Dr. Gardner's Fairy Tales for Today's Children* (Gardner) was read and the client was helped to identify his/her feelings and needs.

B. Each of the fairy tales was processed with the client and he/she was assisted in identifying the feelings and needs of the characters in the stories.

C. The client was helped, encouraged, and supported in verbalizing his/her feelings and needs.

D. The client was given positive affirmation and reinforced for times when he/she verbally identified a feeling or need.

E. Through the use of *Dr. Gardner's Fairy Tales for Today's Children* and verbal affirmation and reinforcement, the client increased his/her ability to identify his/her needs and feelings.

26. Teach Assertiveness and Social Skills (26)

A. The client was asked to list situations in which he/she has had social difficulties or finds it hard to be assertive.

B. Difficult social situations which the client identified were role-played with him/her to teach assertiveness.

C. Behavioral rehearsal was utilized with the client to prepare him/her for facing the identified difficult social situations.

27. Face Challenging Situations (27)

A. The client was taught the "Pretending to Know How" (Thesis) and "The Therapist on the Inside" (Grigoryev) techniques for facing new and uncomfortable situations.

B. Techniques were rehearsed using two different situations that the client might face, and the client was asked to commit to using these techniques.

C. The experience of using "Pretending to Know How" and "The Therapist on the Inside" was processed and the client was asked to try these techniques on two additional situations/problems.

D. The client has successfully faced challenging situations using the new coping skills and has reported that his/her confidence is growing.

28. Assign *Good Friends Are Hard to Find* (28)

A. The parents were asked to read *Good Friends Are Hard to Find* (Fankel) with the client.

B. The parents were taught ways to help the client build and develop social skills using concepts from the Frankel book.

C. The client and parents were assisted in identifying suggestions/ideas from the Frankel book that could help increase the client's social skills.

D. The client's implementation and follow-through with the suggestions/ideas from the book have helped him/her begin to increase his/her social skills and confidence.

29. **Explore Incidents of Abuse (29)**

A. Possible incidents of physical, sexual, and emotional abuse were explored with the client.

B. The client was assisted in exploring how being a victim of abuse has affected his/her feelings about self.

C. The client's denial and resistiveness were explored and resolved so the client could connect past abuse with present negative feelings about self.

30. **Identify Distorted Beliefs (30)**

A. The client was asked to list his/her beliefs about self and the world.

B. The client's distorted, negative beliefs about self and the world were reframed.

31. **Develop Positive Messages (31)**

A. The client was helped to identify and develop more positive, realistic messages about himself/herself and the world.

B. New positive, realistic life messages were implemented by the client and used on a daily basis.

C. The client was confronted when he/she failed to make positive, realistic statements about self or life events.

D. The client reported that he/she has developed a more positive outlook about self and the world.

32. **Use Responsibilities to Aid Esteem (32)**

A. The client was helped to identify daily tasks the performance of which would increase his/her sense of responsibility and esteem.

B. The client's follow-through on daily tasks was monitored for consistency.

C. The client was given positive, verbal feedback for his/her follow-through on self-care responsibilities.

D. The client reported feeling better about himself/herself as he/she has become more active in performing daily responsibilities.

33. **Teach Parents 3 R's Technique (33)**

A. The 3 R's discipline technique was taught to the parents and they were encouraged then to read the book, *Raising Self-Reliant Children in a Self-Indulgent World* (Glenn and Nelson).

B. The parents were assisted in implementing discipline that is respectful, reasonable, and related (3 R's) to the misbehavior and coached to offer support, guidance, and encouragement as they followed through.

C. The parents have successfully implemented discipline that is respectful, reasonable, and related to the client's behavior.

34. Assign Telephone Contact about Accomplishment (34)

A. The client was given the homework assignment to initiate a phone conversation with the therapist and relate a recent accomplishment of his/hers.

B. The client was requested to initiate a phone call to the therapist to relate a recent accomplishment of his/hers.

C. The client received verbal praise, positive feedback, and compliments for his/her accomplishment.

D. The client was instructed in ways to receive and acknowledge praise, positive feedback, and compliments.

E. The feelings surrounding the experience of relating a recent accomplishment were processed with the client.

35. Use "Positive Thinking" Game (35)

A. The Positive Thinking Game (Childswork/Childsplay) was played with the client to promote healthy self-talk and thought patterns.

B. Processed the Positive Thinking Game experience with the client and identified specific ways to promote healthy self-talk and thought patterns.

C. The client was assisted in selecting and implementing several suggestions from the Positive Thinking Game into his/her daily life.

D. The client was monitored, guided, and encouraged to follow through with using new healthy self-talk and thought patterns in his/her daily life.

E. The parents were encouraged to play the Positive Thinking Game at home with the client several times per week.

36. Play "The Yarn Drawing" Game (36)

A. The client was asked to play The Yarn Drawing game (Leben) to help him/her gain a sense of empowerment.

B. The client actively participated in playing The Yarn Drawing Game, followed all the directives, and expressed satisfaction with the results.

C. The Yarn Drawing Game experience was processed and the empowerment gains achieved by the client were identified and reinforced.

D. The Yarn Drawing Game experience has helped the client become more willing to take risks with new experiences.

37. Utilize Projective Art Exercise (37)

A. A projective art exercise, "Magic Art" (Walker), was utilized with the client in today's session.

B. The client actively participated in the projective art exercise.

C. Key points of trust and risk from the projective art exercise were processed with the client.

D. The client's resistance to trying new experiences were explored before he/she was willing to participate in the Magic Art exercise.

38. Teach Acceptance of Compliments (38)

A. Neurolinguistic and reframing techniques were used to alter the client's self-messages to make him/her able to receive and accept compliments.

B. Role-play techniques were utilized to give the client opportunities to practice accepting compliments.

C. The client reported a positive experience with accepting compliments from others recently.

39. Positive Parenting Class Referral (39)

A. The parents were asked to attend a parenting class that focuses on the issues of "positive parenting."

B. The experience of positive parenting classes was processed along with key gains received.

40. Explore Parental Expectations (40)

A. Expectations that the parents hold for the client were explored and then affirmed where appropriate and adjusted when they were unrealistic.

B. The parents were educated in what are age-appropriate and realistic developmental expectations for the client and what are realistic parental expectations, given the client's abilities.

C. The parents were challenged in a respectful way when their expectations of the client seemed unrealistically high or age inappropriate.

D. The parents have adjusted their expectations to a more realistic level, given the client's developmental stage.

41. Increase Peer Group Activities (41)

A. The parents were presented with various options, like scouting, sports, music, etc., that could help boost the client's self-esteem, and they were encouraged to get him/her involved in at least one of them.

B. The role of extracurricular activities in building the client's self-esteem was explored, with positive aspects being identified.

C. The parents have followed through with enrolling the client in more peer group activities.

42. Identify Parents' Praise Opportunities (42)

A. The parents were assisted in identifying opportunities they could seize to praise, reinforce, and recognize positive things done by the client.

B. The parents were reminded of the importance of praise, reinforcement, and recognition in building the client's self-esteem.

C. Missed opportunities for praise, reinforcement, or recognition with the client were pointed out to the parents in family session.

D. Both the client and his/her parents report that the frequency of parental praise and recognition for the client's accomplishments has increased.

MEDICAL CONDITION

CLIENT PRESENTATION

1. Diagnosis of a Chronic, Non-Life-Threatening Illness (1)*

A. The client recently received a diagnosis of a chronic, non-life-threatening illness that will have a significant impact on his/her life.

B. The client presented as upset and worried after he/she received confirmation of having a chronic, but non-life-threatening medical condition.

C. The client was overwhelmed after he/she received the diagnosis of a chronic illness and the life changes it will require.

D. The client has started to accept his/her medical condition and has begun to make the required life changes.

2. Lifestyle Changes (1)

A. The client reported numerous lifestyle changes that need to be made in order to stabilize his/her medical condition.

B. The client is struggling with letting go of certain things in his/her lifestyle that stand in the way of treating his/her medical condition.

C. The client refused to consider making certain life changes that were recommended as part of his/her treatment.

D. Outside pressure from the family has moved the client to make the recommended life changes to improve his/her long-term physical health.

3. Diagnosis of an Acute, Life-Threatening Illness (2)

A. The client presented as very upset after he/she received a diagnosis of having an acute, life-threatening illness.

B. The client reported feeling an overwhelming sadness around having been diagnosed with an acute, life-threatening illness.

C. The client indicated that he/she has not told any of his/her friends of the diagnosis and its seriousness.

D. The client has begun to share his/her diagnosis and what it means with others close to him/her.

4. Diagnosis of a Terminal Illness (3)

A. The client reported with hesitation and difficulty his/her diagnosis of having a terminal illness.

B. The client failed to disclose his/her diagnosis of a terminal illness until he/she was asked.

---

* The numbers in parentheses correlate to the number of the Behavioral Definition statement in the companion chapter with same title in *The Child Psychotherapy Treatment Planner* (Jongsma, Peterson, and McInnis) by John Wiley & Sons, 2000.

C. The client indicated that he/she finds it impossible to talk about his/her diagnosis of a terminal illness.

D. The client has begun to openly acknowledge his/her diagnosis and its terminal nature.

5. Anxious/Sensitive (4)

A. The client presented with anxious feelings related to his/her serious medical condition.

B. The client reported that a discussion of anything related to his/her medical condition makes him/her feel anxious.

C. The client has developed some peace of mind about his/her serious medical condition.

6. Sad/Quiet (4)

A. The client presented in a sad, quiet manner.

B. The client found it very difficult to talk about his/her medical condition.

C. The client reported feeling overwhelming sadness around the loss of his/her health when the condition was diagnosed.

D. The client's sadness has decreased as he/she has been willing to talk more openly about the medical diagnosis and prognosis.

7. Social Withdrawal (4)

A. Recently the client has stopped associating with most of his/her friends.

B. The client reported that he/she has been spending all of his/her spare time alone.

C. The client appeared to be avoiding family and friends since learning of his/her medical condition.

D. Due to his/her particular medical condition, the client has seen no reason to interact or have relationships with others.

E. As the client has accepted his/her medical condition, he/she has begun to reconnect with others and receive their support.

8. Depression (4)

A. The client's mood has been depressed since his/her medical condition was confirmed.

B. The client presented in a depressed manner with low energy and little interest in life's activities.

C. As the client's depression has lifted he/she has started to have more energy and sees some hope in living with his/her medical condition.

9. Suicidal Ideation (5)

A. The client presented in a negative, despondent manner.

B. The client reported feeling very hopeless and helpless regarding the future due to his/her medical condition.

C. Suicidal thoughts and feelings seemed to dominate the client at the present time.

D. The client revealed a plan along with a backup plan to take his/her own life.

E. The client has gradually started to feel more hopeful and less despondent about his/her medical condition.

10. Denial (6)

A. The client presented as if there was nothing wrong with him/her despite evidence to the contrary.

B. The client reported that he/she did not agree with the seriousness of the condition as diagnosed by the physicians.

C. The client seemed to vacillate between accepting and denying the diagnosed medical condition.

D. The client refused to disclose or acknowledge having any medical condition.

E. The client's denial has started to lessen and he/she is beginning to talk about his/her condition in a realistic manner.

11. Resistive to Treatment (7)

A. The client presented in a resistive manner.

B. The client reported that he/she is not open to treatment of any kind for his/her medical condition.

C. The client's resistiveness to accepting treatment for his/her medical condition has had a deleterious effect on his/her general health.

D. The client has refused to cooperate fully with the recommended medical treatments.

E. The client has become more cooperative with medical treatment procedures.

INTERVENTIONS IMPLEMENTED

1. Gather History of Medical Condition (1)*

A. A history of the client's medical condition that included symptoms, treatment, and prognosis was gathered.

B. During the history-gathering process, the client was assisted in connecting feelings to aspects and stages of his/her medical condition.

C. A sketchy, vague history of the client's medical condition was gathered due to his/her unwillingness to provide specific information.

2. Obtain Additional Medical History (2)

A. Informed consent was obtained from the client so family and physician could be contacted for further information on his/her medical condition.

B. Additional information regarding the client's diagnosis, treatment, and prognosis was gathered from his/her physician.

C. Various family members contributed additional information when contacted on the client's medical condition and its progression.

D. The client refused to give consent to have either his/her physician or family members contacted about his/her medical condition.

---

* The numbers in parentheses correlate to the number of the Therapeutic Interventions statement in the companion chapter with same title in *The Child Psychotherapy Treatment Planner* (Jongsma, Peterson, and McInnis) by John Wiley & Sons, 2000.

3. Explore Client's Feelings regarding Medical Condition (3)

A. The client was assisted in identifying and verbalizing feelings connected to his/her medical condition.

B. The client was encouraged to recognize and express feelings related to the medical condition on a daily basis.

C. Instances of the client's recognizing, identifying, and expressing his/her feelings were affirmed and reinforced verbally.

D. The client was not open with his/her feelings regarding the current medical condition.

4. Explore Family's Feelings regarding Medical Condition (4)

A. Feelings associated with a family member's medical condition were explored and normalized for family.

B. Family sessions were conducted to help the family members clarify and share feelings they have experienced around the client's medical condition.

C. Family members were reminded that having a safe place to express feelings about the client's condition was helpful and healthy for all involved.

D. Family members expressed strong feelings of helplessness and fear of the client's medical condition's deteriorating in the future.

E. The client's siblings expressed feelings of anger and jealousy regarding the attention focused on the client's medical condition.

5. List Limitations Caused by Medical Condition (5)

A. The client was asked to list all changes, losses, and limitations that have resulted from his/her medical condition.

B. The client was assisted in making a list of his/her losses, changes, and limitations that resulted from the medical condition, due to his/her difficulty in connecting the two things.

C. The changes in the client's life brought on by the medical condition caused feelings of depression, frustration, and hopelessness.

6. Teach Stages of Grief (6)

A. The client was educated on the stages and process of grief.

B. The client was asked to identify the stages of the grief process the he/she has experienced.

7. Assign Books on Grief and Loss (7)

A. Several books on grief and loss were suggested to the client to read by himself/herself or with his/her parents.

B. Read *Don't Despair on Thursdays* (Moser) with the client to help him/her develop ideas for handling feelings of grief and loss.

C. Discussed and processed key ideas on grief and loss from the book with the client.

D. The client was assisted in identifying several ideas learned from reading the book and how he/she could utilize them to cope with his/her feelings of grief and loss.

E. The client was resistive to discussing anything from the book on grief and loss.

F. Ideas from the book have helped the client better cope with the feelings of grief and loss.

8. Keep a Grief Journal (8)

A. The benefits of keeping a grief journal were explained, identified, and reinforced with the client.

B. The client was asked to commit to keeping a daily grief journal to share in therapy sessions.

C. Daily grief journal material that the client has recorded was shared in sessions and entries were processed.

D. The client has not recorded his/her feelings on a daily basis and was reminded of his/her commitment to keep a grief journal.

9. Daily Mourning Time (9)

A. The client was educated in the value of mourning a loss.

B. Ways for the client to daily mourn loss were explored, with several being selected and developed for implementation.

C. The client was asked to commit to implementing his/her mourning ritual for a specific set amount of time daily and then get on with other daily activities.

D. The daily mourning ritual has been followed by the client and it has been effective in focusing grief feelings and increasing productivity during other times of the day.

E. The client has failed to follow through on implementing the daily mourning ritual and has avoided the grieving process.

F. Instead of focusing and limiting the intense grieving to specific times of the day, the client continues to be preoccupied with grief throughout the day.

10. Focus on Positive Life Aspects (10)

A. The client was assisted in listing all the positive aspects still present in his/her life.

B. The client was challenged to focus on the positive aspects of life which he/she identified rather than the losses associated with the medical condition.

C. Gentle confrontation was used when the client refocused on his/her losses rather than positive life aspects.

D. The client's focus on positive life aspects within sessions was reinforced.

11. Identify Spiritual Support Resources (11)

A. The client was assisted in identifying sources of spiritual support and how they could help him/her now.

B. The client was encouraged to actively utilize his/her identified spiritual resources and support on a daily basis.

C. The client has denied any interest in spiritual resources.

D. The client's spiritual faith is deep and is a significant source of strength and peace during this time of pain and stress.

12. Confront Denial of Need for Medical Treatment (12)

A. Gentle confrontation was used with the client regarding his/her denial of the seriousness of his/her condition and of the need for compliance with recommended treatment.

B. Denial was normalized as part of the adjustment process and barriers to acceptance of the need for treatment on the client's part were explored and addressed.

C. Despite gentle confrontation, the client continues to deny the seriousness of his/her condition and refuses to follow through with the recommended treatment.

D. The client's denial regarding the reality of the medical condition and the need for treatment has dissipated, resulting in consistent follow-through with medical recommendations.

13. Reinforce Acceptance of Condition (13)

A. The positive aspects of acceptance over denial of the medical condition were reinforced with the client.

B. The client's statements indicating acceptance of the condition were affirmed and reinforced.

C. Ambivalent statements by the client around his/her medical condition and its treatment were reframed to more positive ones and reinforced.

D. The client's denial regarding the reality of the medical condition and the need for treatment has dissipated, resulting in consistent follow-through with medical recommendations.

14. Explore Fears regarding Failing Health (14)

A. The client was asked to express his/her fears around failing health, death, and dying.

B. The fear of death and dying expressed by the client was explored and processed.

C. The concept of facing your fears was presented to and processed with the client.

D. The client was open in expressing his/her fears regarding death and dying and seems to have resolved these fears, resulting in peace of mind.

15. Normalize Anxious Feelings (15)

A. The client was assisted and supported in identifying and expressing feelings of anxiety connected to his/her medical condition.

B. The anxious and sad feelings identified around the condition by the client were affirmed and normalized.

C. The client was reminded of the value and benefit to his/her health and recovery of identifying and expressing feelings.

16. Assess/Treat Depression and Anxiety (16)

A. The client was assessed for level of depression and anxiety, and appropriate treatment was recommended.

B. It was determined that the client's level of depression was significant enough to merit focused treatment.

C. The client's anxiety was explored and appropriate interventions were implemented to assist the client in coping with these feelings.

D. The client was assisted in recognizing his/her depression and in beginning to express the feelings associated with it.

17. Support Group Referral (17)

A. The client was educated on the various types of support groups available in the community.

B. The client was referred to a support group of others living with the same medical condition.

C. The benefits of the support group experience were identified and reinforced with the client.

D. The client's experience with attending the support group was processed, and continued attendance was encouraged.

E. The client has failed to follow the recommendation of attending a support group.

18. Family Support Group Referral (18)

A. The purpose and benefits of attending a support group were identified and reinforced with the family.

B. Support group options were provided for the family.

C. The family was referred to a community support group associated with the client's medical condition.

D. The initial support group experience was processed with the family and continued attendance was encouraged and reinforced.

E. The family has not followed through with attending the recommended support group.

19. Monitor/Reinforce Treatment Compliance (19)

A. The client's compliance with the recommended medical treatment regimen was monitored.

B. The client's failure to comply with medical treatment recommendations was confronted and addressed.

C. Positive affirmation and encouragement were given to the client for his/her consistent follow-through on all aspects of the medical treatment regimen.

D. Despite gentle confrontation and encouragement, the client still fails to comply with the medical treatment recommendation for his/her medical condition.

20. Explore Factors Interfering with Treatment Compliance (20)

A. Misconceptions, fears, and situational factors were explored with the client for their possible interference with medical treatment compliance.

B. The client's misconceptions, fears, and other situational factors were resolved to improve his/her follow-through with recommended medical treatment.

C. Since making the connection between his/her fears and misconceptions and avoiding medical treatment, the client has started to cooperate fully and responsibly with his/her medical treatment.

D. The client's resistance to compliance with the medical treatment regimen continues to be a problem

21. Confront Defenses Blocking Medical Compliance (21)

A. All the client's defense mechanisms that block compliance with the medical regimen were confronted.

B. As defense mechanisms of manipulation and denial have been confronted, the client's compliance with the medical regimen has increased.

C. The client's defense mechanisms continue to block consistent compliance with the medical treatment regimen.

22. List Pleasurable Activities (22)

A. The client was asked to list all the activities that he/she has enjoyed doing.

B. The client's list of activities was examined for the ones that can still be enjoyed alone and with others.

C. The client was encouraged to start again involving himself/herself in these pleasurable activities on a regular basis.

D. In spite of encouragement, the client continues to resist engagement in pleasurable activities that he/she is capable of participating in.

23. Solicit Commitment to Pleasurable Activities (23)

A. The client was asked to make a verbal commitment to increase his/her activity level in pleasurable social and physical activities.

B. The client's involvement in activities was affirmed and reinforced.

C. The client's failure to keep his/her commitment to increase his/her activity level was gently confronted.

D. The client avoided the requested commitment by saying that he/she would give it a try and that's the best he/she could do.

E. In spite of encouragement, the client continues to resist engagement in pleasurable activities that he/she is capable of participating in.

24. Teach Relaxation Techniques (24)

A. Deep-muscle relaxation, deep breathing, and positive imagery techniques were taught to the client to enhance his/her ability to relax.

B. Behavioral rehearsal was utilized to give the client opportunity to practice each relaxation skill.

C. The client was reminded of the benefits of deep-muscle relaxation, deep breathing, and positive imagery, and he/she was encouraged to use each on a regular basis.

D. The client has implemented the relaxation techniques and reports positive reduction in stress and anxiety.

E. The client has failed to follow through with the implementation of relaxation techniques.

25. Utilize Biofeedback (25)

A. EMG biofeedback was utilized with the client to monitor, increase, and reinforce his/her depth of relaxation.

B. The use of biofeedback with the client has improved his/her overall depth of relaxation.

26. Develop Physical Exercise Routine (26)

A. The client was assisted in developing a plan for a daily physical exercise routine within the limits of his/her medical condition.

B. The benefits of daily physical exercise were identified and reinforced.

C. The physical exercise plan was implemented by the client along with a commitment to follow the plan on a daily basis.

D. The client's follow-through with daily exercise and commitment was monitored and re-inforced.

E. The client has not followed through with implementing any regular pattern of physical exercise.

27. Identify Distorted, Negative Thoughts (27)

A. The client was assisted in identifying his/her cognitive distortions that contribute to a negative attitude and hopeless feeling regarding his/her medical condition.

B. The connection between cognitive distortions and feelings of helplessness and negativity around the client's medical condition was established and made clear to him/her.

C. The client was resistive to identifying and in denial of engaging in cognitive distortion.

28. Teach Positive, Realistic Self-Talk (28)

A. The client was helped to generate a list of positive, realistic self-talk to replace the cognitive distortions and catastrophizing that accompany his/her medical condition.

B. The techniques of positive self-talk were taught to the client.

C. Role-play situations around the client's medical condition were utilized for the client to practice using positive self-talk.

D. The benefits of using positive self-talk reported by the client were reinforced.

29. Teach Healing Imagery (29)

A. Positive, healing imagery techniques were taught to the client.

B. The client practiced using healing imagery techniques in the session.

C. Plans for implementing positive imagery techniques were developed with the client.

D. The client was asked to make a commitment to use positive imagery techniques as planned.

E. The client reported consistent daily use of the positive healing imagery technique and has developed a positive mental attitude regarding the improvement in his/her medical condition.

30. Provide Accurate Medical Information (30)

A. The client was asked to develop a list of all questions he/she has concerning any aspect of his/her medical condition and treatment.

B. The client was given clear, accurate information in terms that were understandable on the causes, treatment, and prognosis for his/her medical condition.

C. The client's questions were answered in ways that he/she could understand.

D. After the use of role-playing and modeling to teach assertiveness, the client was encouraged to raise questions about his/her medical condition and treatment with his/her physician.

31. Information Resource Referral (31)

A. The parents and the client were given resource materials on the medical condition and Internet sites where further information is available.

B. Questions that resulted from the parents' and the client's reading were answered and processed.

C. The client's and parents' quest for information on the client's medical condition was encouraged and reinforced.

32. Identify Parents' Resources for Support (32)

A. The parents' sources of emotional support were probed and assessed.

B. The parents were asked to identify their sources of emotional support.

33. Encourage Parents' Obtaining Support (33)

A. The parents were assisted in identifying community resources for support.

B. Barriers to accepting support were explored with the parents and addressed.

C. The parents' need for support was identified and reinforced.

D. The parents have accepted their need for support and have followed through in making contact with potential resources for support.

34. Draw Out Parents' Fears (34)

A. The parents were encouraged to express their underlying fears around the client's possible death.

B. Empathy, affirmation, and normalization were used in responding to the fearful feelings that the parents verbalized.

C. The parents were given the reassurance of God's presence as the giver and supporter of life.

35. Explore Marital Conflict (35)

A. How the parents were dealing with the stress of the client's illness was explored with each individually.

B. The issue of increased conflicts between the parents due to medical condition was addressed.

C. Specific ways that each parent could be supportive and accepting of the other were identified.

36. Increase Family Members' Spirit of Tolerance (36)

A. In family sessions, a spirit of tolerance for individually different responses to stress was facilitated and encouraged between members.

B. Family members were reminded of each person's individual differences regarding internal resources and response styles in face of threat.

C. Tolerance was modeled to family members in sessions through active listening and warm acceptance of their feelings and thoughts.

37. Teach Power of Family's Involvement (37)

A. The family was educated in the potential healing power of members' involvement in all aspects of the client's care and recovery.

B. Assistance was provided to the family to help them make their care and home environment as warm, positive, kind, and supportive for the client as possible.

C. The family was provided with ongoing encouragement and reinforcement in providing warm, positive supportive care to the client.

MENTAL RETARDATION

CLIENT PRESENTATION

1. Subaverage Intellectual Functioning (1)*

A. The client has developed significant intellectual or cognitive deficits.

B. The results from the past intelligence testing revealed that the client's overall level of intellectual functioning lies in the Mild Mental Retardation range.

C. The results from the past intelligence testing revealed that the client's overall level of intelligence lies in the Moderate Mental Retardation range.

D. The results from the past intelligence testing revealed that the client's overall level of intelligence lies in the Severe Mental Retardation range.

E. The results from the past intelligence testing revealed that the client's overall level of intelligence lies in the Borderline range of functioning.

2. Impaired Academic Functioning (2)

A. The client has performed significantly below his/her expected grade and age levels in all academic areas.

B. The client's academic performance has been commensurate with his/her overall level of intelligence.

C. The client has performed academically below his/her expected grade and age levels, even when considering the results from the past intellectual testing.

D. Academically, the client has performed above his/her expected levels based on the results from the past intelligence testing.

3. Speech/Language Delays (2)

A. The results from the past speech/language evaluation demonstrated that the client has developed significant speech/language deficits.

B. The client's vocabulary and expressive language abilities are quite limited.

C. The client often has difficulty understanding what is being said to him/her because of his/her low receptive language skills.

D. The client displayed noticeable speech articulation problems during today's therapy session.

4. Poor Communication Skills (2)

A. The client has much difficulty communicating his/her thoughts and feelings in an effective manner because of his/her speech/language delays.

B. The client had much difficulty expressing his/her thoughts and feelings in today's therapy session.

---

* The numbers in parentheses correlate to the number of the Behavioral Definition statement in the companion chapter with same title in *The Child Psychotherapy Treatment Planner* (Jongsma, Peterson, and McInnis) by John Wiley & Sons, 2000.

C. The client had difficulty comprehending what was being discussed in today's therapy session because of his/her low receptive language abilities.

D. The client was able to communicate his/her thoughts and feelings in a simplistic but straightforward and effective manner in today's therapy session.

E. The client has demonstrated improvements in his/her ability to identify and express his/her basic thoughts and feelings.

5. Inadequate Self-Care (2)

A. The parents or caregivers reported that the client's self-care skills are very low.

B. The client has required a great deal of supervision when performing household chores or tasks at school.

C. The client has recently started to perform simple chores at home.

D. The client has recently performed his/her household chores or school responsibilities on a fairly consistent basis with prompting from caregivers.

6. Poor Personal Hygiene (2)

A. The parents or caregivers reported that the client's personal hygiene is often poor.

B. The client appeared unkempt during today's therapy session.

C. The client has a great deal of difficulty dressing himself/herself independently even when clothes have been preselected for him/her.

D. The client appeared neatly groomed and attired during today's therapy session.

E. The client has recently been dressing himself/herself independently.

7. Difficulty Following Instructions (3)

A. The client historically has had much difficulty comprehending and following instructions at home and school.

B. The parents and teachers reported that the client is capable of comprehending and following simple instructions, but has trouble following through with multiple or complex instructions.

C. The teachers reported that the client is best able to follow instructions when they are presented in simple terms and are given one at a time.

D. The parents and teachers reported that the client has shown improvement in following simple instructions on a consistent basis.

8. Short Attention Span (3)

A. The client has developed a short attention span and has difficulty staying focused for extended periods of time.

B. The client is easily distracted by extraneous stimuli and his/her own internal thoughts.

C. The client had trouble staying focused and often switched from one topic to another.

D. The client remained focused and was able to discuss important topics for a satisfactory length of time.

E. The client's attention span has improved in structured, low distraction settings where he/she receives supervision and greater individualized attention.

9. Memory Impairment (4)

A. The results from past intellectual and cognitive assessments have shown that the client has developed significant short- and long-term memory impairments.

B. The client has often had difficulty retaining or recalling what has been said to him/her because of his/her short-term memory deficits.

C. The client has had difficulty recalling significant past events because of his/her long-term memory deficits.

D. The client had demonstrated improvements in his/her everyday functioning by following a structured daily routine.

10. Concrete Thinking (5)

A. The client has much difficulty understanding psychological concepts because of his/her intellectual limitations and poor abstract reasoning abilities.

B. The client presented as very concrete in his/her thinking during today's therapy session.

C. The client's concrete thinking and poor abstract reasoning abilities have interfered with his/her problem-solving abilities.

D. The client demonstrated an understanding of basic psychological terms or concepts during today's therapy session.

E. The parents report that the client has demonstrated improvement in his/her ability to resolve or manage everyday, routine problems by following specific, concrete steps that are outlined for him/her.

11. Poor Social Skills (6)

A. The client has developed poor social skills and frequently engaged in immature or socially inappropriate behavior.

B. The client has often failed to pick up on important social cues or interpersonal nuances that are necessary to build and sustain meaningful relationships.

C. The client has started to develop the ability to differentiate between appropriate and inappropriate social behaviors.

D. The client displayed good social skills during today's therapy session.

12. Lack of Insight (7)

A. The client historically has shown very poor insight into the factors contributing to his/her emotional, behavioral, or interpersonal problems.

B. The client demonstrated a lack of insight into the factors contributing to his/her adjustment problems.

C. The client verbalized an awareness of the basic factors contributing to his/her adjustment problems, but had difficulty understanding the more complex factors.

13. Failure to Learn from Experience (7)

A. The client displayed a marked inability to learn from previous experiences or past mistakes because of his/her intellectual limitations.

B. The parents or caregivers reported that the client repeatedly makes many of the same mistakes, without appearing to learn from his/her experiences.

C. Parents or caregivers reported that the client has started to show mild improvement in his/her ability to learn from past experiences or mistakes.

D. The client does not commit as many of the same mistakes when he/she is placed in a highly structured setting with an established routine.

14. Low Self-Esteem (8)

A. The client's intellectual limitations and learning problems have been a significant contributing factor to his/her feelings of low self-esteem, inadequacy, and insecurity.

B. The client's low self-esteem has contributed to his/her hesitancy to try new tasks or apply himself/herself at school.

C. The client verbalized self-derogatory remarks when discussing his/her intellectual limitations or learning problems.

D. The client verbalized positive self-descriptive statements during today's therapy session.

E. The client has developed a healthy acceptance of his/her intellectual and cognitive limitations as evidenced by his/her ability to consistently verbalize feelings of self-worth.

15. Depression (8)

A. The client's intellectual deficits and academic struggles have contributed substantially to his/her feelings of depression.

B. The client appeared visibly sad when discussing his/her learning problems.

C. The client's feelings of depression have begun to decrease as he/she works toward gaining a greater acceptance of his/her intellectual limitations.

D. The client expressed feelings of happiness about his/her recent accomplishments at home and school.

E. The client's feelings of depression have decreased substantially.

16. Parents' Unrealistic Expectations (8)

A. The parents appeared to be in denial about the client's intellectual limitations.

B. The parents have developed unrealistic expectations of the client and have placed excessive pressure on him/her to function at a level that he/she is not capable of achieving.

C. The parents acknowledged that they have placed unrealistic expectations on the client to perform on a level that he/she is not capable of achieving.

D. The parents have started to adjust their demands on the client and are placing more realistic expectations on him/her.

E. The parents have gained an acceptance of the client's intellectual capabilities and have placed appropriate expectations on his/her functioning.

17. Parents' Overprotectiveness (8)

A. The parents have demonstrated a persistent pattern of overprotectiveness that interferes with the client's intellectual, emotional, and social development.

B. The parents became defensive when discussing how their overprotectiveness interferes with the client's growth and development.

C. The parents acknowledged that their overprotectiveness or infantilization of the client has interfered with his/her intellectual, emotional, and social development.

D. The parents have started to verbalize their expectations that the client assume household responsibilities and take care of his/her personal hygiene.

E. The parents' overprotectiveness has greatly diminished, and they have placed realistic expectations on the client.

18. Acting-Out Behaviors (9)

A. The client has demonstrated a persistent pattern of acting out when he/she becomes frustrated or upset because of his/her intellectual limitations or learning problems.

B. The client began to act in a silly and immature manner in today's therapy session when discussing his/her intellectual limitations or learning problems.

C. The client was helped to realize how he/she frequently begins to act out or engage in disruptive behaviors when frustrated or upset about not being able to perform a task.

D. The client has started to seek out help when frustrated about not being able to perform a task, instead of acting out or engaging in disruptive behaviors.

E. The client has demonstrated a significant reduction in the frequency of his/her acting-out or disruptive behaviors.

INTERVENTIONS IMPLEMENTED

1. Intellectual and Cognitive Assessment (1)*

A. A comprehensive intellectual and cognitive assessment was conducted to determine the presence of mental retardation and help gain greater insight into the client's learning strengths and weaknesses.

B. The findings from the current intellectual and cognitive assessment revealed the presence of Mild Mental Retardation.

C. The findings from the current intellectual and cognitive assessment revealed the presence of Moderate Mental Retardation.

D. The findings from the current intellectual and cognitive assessment revealed the presence of Severe Mental Retardation.

E. The findings from the current intellectual and cognitive assessment demonstrated that the client is currently functioning in the Borderline range of intellectual abilities.

2. Psychological Testing for Emotional/ADHD Factors (2)

A. The client received a psychological evaluation to assess whether emotional factors or ADHD are interfering with his/her intellectual functioning.

B. The findings from the psychological testing supported the presence of ADHD which is interfering with the client's intellectual and academic functioning.

C. The findings from the psychological testing revealed the presence of serious emotional problems that are interfering with the client's intellectual and academic functioning.

D. The findings from the evaluation did not support the presence of ADHD that could be interfering with the client's intellectual and academic functioning.

---

* The numbers in parentheses correlate to the number of the Therapeutic Interventions statement in the companion chapter with same title in *The Child Psychotherapy Treatment Planner* (Jongsma, Peterson, and McInnis) by John Wiley & Sons, 2000.

E. The findings from the psychological testing did not reveal any serious emotional problems that could be interfering with the client's intellectual and academic functioning.

3. **Neurological Examination/Neuropyschological Testing (3)**

A. The client was referred for a neurological examination and neuropsychological testing to rule out possible organic factors that may be contributing to the client's intellectual or cognitive deficits.

B. The findings from the neuropsychological evaluation revealed organic factors that may be contributing to the client's intellectual or cognitive deficits.

C. The findings from the neuropsychological evaluation did not reveal any organic factors that may be contributing to the client's intellectual or cognitive deficits.

4. **Give Evaluation Feedback (4)**

A. The client, parents, and school officials were given feedback from the intellectual and psychological testing.

B. The staff from the client's residential program were given feedback from the intellectual and psychological testing.

C. The client, parents, and school officials were given feedback from the neuropsychological testing.

D. The staff from the client's residential program were given feedback from the neuropsychological testing.

5. **Physical/Occupational Therapy Referral (5)**

A. The client was referred to physical and occupational therapists to assess for the presence of perceptual or sensory-motor deficits and determine the need for ongoing physical and/or occupational therapy.

B. The evaluation revealed significant perceptual or sensory-motor deficits and the need for ongoing physical and/or occupational therapy.

C. The evaluation did not reveal any significant perceptual or sensory-motor deficits or the need for ongoing physical and/or occupational therapy.

6. **Speech/Language Evaluation Referral (6)**

A. The client was referred for a comprehensive speech/language evaluation to assess possible deficits in this area and determine the need for speech/language therapy.

B. The comprehensive speech/language evaluation revealed a communication impairment and supported the need for speech/language therapy.

C. The comprehensive speech/language evaluation did not reveal a communication impairment or the need for ongoing speech/language therapy.

7. **Attend an Individualized Educational Planning Committee (IEPC) Meeting (7)**

A. An Individualized Educational Planning Committee meeting was held to determine the client's eligibility for special education services, to design educational interventions, and to establish goals.

B. The decision was made at the IEPC meeting that the client is eligible to receive special education services because of his/her intellectual or academic deficits.

C. The decision was made at the IEPC meeting that the client is not eligible to receive special education services.

D. Consulted with the client's parents, teachers, and other appropriate professionals about designing educational interventions to help the client achieve his/her academic goals.

E. The client's academic goals were identified at the IEPC meeting.

8. Design Effective Teaching Programs (8)

A. Consulted with the client, his/her parents, teacher, and other appropriate school officials about designing effective teaching programs or interventions that build on the client's strengths and compensate for his/her weaknesses.

B. The client's learning strengths and weaknesses were identified in the consultation meeting with the client, parents, teachers, and other appropriate school officials.

C. Consulted with the client, his/her parents, teachers, and other appropriate school officials about ways to maximize the client's learning strengths.

D. Consulted with the client, his/her parents, teachers, and other appropriate school officials about ways to compensate for the client's learning weaknesses.

9. Process Placement outside the Home (9)

A. Consulted with the client's parents, school officials, or mental health professionals about the need for placement in a foster home, group home, or residential program.

B. After consulting with the client's parents, school officials, or mental health professionals, the recommendation was made that the client should be placed in a foster home.

C. The recommendation was made that the client be placed in a group home or residential program to address his/her intellectual, academic, social, and emotional needs.

D. Placement of the client in a foster home, group home, or residential program was not recommended during the consultation meeting with parents, school officials, and mental health professionals.

10. Communication between Home and School (10)

A. The parents, teachers, and school officials were encouraged to maintain regular communication with each other via phone calls or written notes regarding the client's academic, behavioral, emotional, and social progress.

B. Consulted with the teachers and school officials about sending home daily or weekly progress notes informing the parents of the client's academic, behavioral, emotional, and social progress.

C. The client was informed of his/her responsibility to bring home daily or weekly progress notes, allowing for regular communication between parents and teachers.

D. The parents identified the consequences for the client's failure to bring home the daily or weekly progress notes from school.

11. Design Token Economy (11)

A. A token economy was designed for use in the classroom to improve the client's academic performance, impulse control, and social skills.

B. A token economy was designed for use in the residential program to improve the client's academic performance, impulse control, and social skills.

C. The client, parents, and teachers agreed to the conditions outlined in the token economy, and pledged to follow through with the implementation of the program.

D. The conditions of the token economy were explained to the client in terms that he/she could understand.

12. Praise Positive Behavior (12)

A. The parents were encouraged to provide frequent praise and positive reinforcement for the client's positive social behaviors and academic successes.

B. The parents praised the client's positive social behaviors and academic performance during today's therapy session.

C. The parents were assisted in identifying opportunities to praise the client's positive social behaviors and academic successes.

D. The client was strongly encouraged to engage in positive social behaviors and work hard to achieve academic goals to receive parents' approval and affirmation.

13. Design Reward System/Contingency Contract (13)

A. The client and parents were assisted in identifying a list of rewards to reinforce the client's adaptive or positive social behaviors.

B. A reward system was designed to reinforce the client's adaptive or positive social behaviors.

C. A contingency contract was designed to specify the negative consequences for the client's maladaptive or inappropriate social behaviors and the rewards for specified positive behaviors.

D. The conditions of the contingency contract were explained to the client in terms he/she could understand.

E. The client and parents verbally agreed to the terms of the reward system and/or contingency contract.

14. Educate Parents about Mental Retardation (14)

A. The client's parents were educated about the symptoms of mental retardation.

B. The therapy session helped the client's parents gain a greater understanding of the symptoms and characteristics of mental retardation.

C. The parents were given the opportunity to express their thoughts and feelings about raising a child with mental retardation.

D. The parents were given support in verbalizing their feelings of sadness, hurt, anger, or disappointment about having a child with mental retardation.

15. Assess Parents' Denial of Client's Intellectual Deficits (15)

A. A family therapy session was held to assess the parents' denial surrounding the client's intellectual deficits.

B. The parents' denial about the client's intellectual deficits was confronted and challenged so that they will begin to cooperate with the recommendations regarding placement and educational interventions.

C. The therapy session was helpful in working through the parents' denial surrounding the client's intellectual deficits, and they agreed to follow through with recommendations regarding placement and educational interventions.

D. The parents have remained in denial about the client's intellectual deficits and are opposed to following through with the recommendations regarding placement and educational interventions.

16. Assess Excessive Parental Pressure (16)

A. A family therapy session was held to assess whether the parents are placing excessive pressure on the client to function at a level that he/she is not capable of achieving.

B. The parents were asked to verbalize their expectations of the client's level of capabilities.

17. Confront Excessive Parental Pressure (17)

A. The parents were confronted and challenged about placing excessive pressure on the client to function at a level that he/she is not capable of achieving.

B. The parents acknowledged that they have placed unrealistic expectations and/or excessive pressure on the client to function at a level that he/she is not capable of achieving.

C. The parents agreed to cease placing excessive pressure on the client to perform at unrealistic levels.

D. The parents expressed resistance to the idea that they are placing excessive pressure on the client to function at unrealistic levels.

18. Assign Family Kinetic Drawing (18)

A. The client was asked to produce a family kinetic drawing to assess how he/she perceives his/her role in the family.

B. The client's family kinetic drawing was helpful in providing insight into how he/she perceives his/her role in the family.

C. The client's family kinetic drawing did not provide any insight into how he/she perceives his/her role in the family.

D. The evidence from the family kinetic drawing indicated that the client perceives himself/herself as being ostracized and isolated within the family.

E. The evidence from the family kinetic drawing indicated that the client experiences a sense of belonging and acceptance in his/her family.

19. Assess Parental Overprotectiveness (19)

A. The parent-child interactions were observed in today's therapy session to assess whether the parent's overprotectiveness or infantilization of the client interferes with his/her intellectual, emotional, or social development.

B. The client and parents were given a task to perform in today's therapy session to assess whether the parents are overprotective of the client.

C. The parents acknowledged that their pattern of overprotectiveness has interfered with the client's intellectual, emotional, and social development.

D. The therapy session was helpful in identifying various ways that the parents are overprotective of the client, and/or interfere with his/her intellectual, emotional, and social development.

E. The parents became defensive in today's therapy session when discussing their pattern of overprotectiveness.

20. Develop Realistic Parental Expectations (20)

A. Today's therapy session focused on helping the parents or caregivers develop realistic expectations of the client's intellectual capabilities and level of adaptive functioning.

B. The parents or caregivers were assisted in identifying a number of tasks that the client is capable of performing.

C. The therapy session helped the parents or caregivers identify several tasks that the client is not able to perform because of his/her intellectual deficits and level of adaptive functioning.

D. The parents or caregivers were instructed to provide supervision initially on tasks that they are not sure that the client is capable of performing.

E. The parents or caregivers have developed a good understanding of the client's intellectual capabilities and level of adaptive functioning.

21. Include Client in Family Outings (21)

A. The parents and family members were strongly encouraged to include the client in outings or activities on a regular basis.

B. A family therapy session was held to explore the family member's resistance or objections to including the client in some outings or activities.

C. The parents and family members pledged to include the client in regular family outings or activities.

D. The client and family members were assisted in identifying a list of outings or activities that they would enjoy doing together.

E. The parents and family members were confronted about their failure to include the client in many outings or activities.

22. Observe Positive Behavior (22)

A. The parents and family members were instructed to observe and record positive behaviors by the client between therapy sessions.

B. The parents were encouraged to praise and reinforce the client for engaging in the positive behavior.

C. The client was praised in today's therapy session for his/her positive behavior.

D. The client was strongly encouraged to continue to engage in the positive behavior to help improve his/her self-esteem, gain parents' approval, and receive affirmation from others.

23. Assign "You Belong Here" Exercise (23)

A. The client and parents were assigned the "You Belong Here" exercise from *The Brief Child Therapy Homework Planner* (Jongsma, Peterson, and McInnis) to promote feelings of acceptance and a sense of belonging in the family system, school setting, or community.

B. The client and parents were given the "You Belong Here" exercise to increase the client's responsibilities or involvement in activities at home, school, or community.

C. The "You Belong Here" exercise was assigned to help the parents develop a greater awareness of the client's intellectual capabilities and level of adaptive functioning.

D. The client and parents successfully completed the "You Belong Here" exercise, and he/she was encouraged to continue to engage in the responsible behaviors or social activities to further increase feelings of self-worth.

E. The client and parents failed to follow through and complete the "You Belong Here" exercise, and they were again challenged to do it.

24. Household Chore Assignment (24)

A. The client and family members developed a list of tasks or chores that the client is capable of performing at home.

B. The client was assigned a task to perform in the family to provide him/her with a sense of responsibility or belonging.

C. The client was given praise in today's therapy session for the successful completion of his/her assigned task or chore.

D. The client attempted to perform the assigned task or chore, but encountered difficulty when performing it.

E. The client failed to follow through with completing the assigned chore or task.

25. School/Residential Job Assignment (25)

A. Consulted with school officials about assigning a job to help build the client's self-esteem and provide him/her with a sense of responsibility.

B. Consulted with the staff at the residential program about assigning a job to help build the client's self-esteem and provide him/her with a sense of responsibility.

C. The client was given much praise in today's therapy session for being responsible in performing his/her job at school.

D. The client was given much praise in today's therapy session for being responsible in performing his/her job at the residential program.

E. Today's therapy session explored the reasons for the client's failure to comply with performing his/her job at school or the residential program.

26. Identify Components of Goal Accomplishment (26)

A. Today's therapy session identified periods of time when the client achieved success or accomplished a goal.

B. Today's therapy session was helpful in identifying the positive steps that the client took to successfully accomplish goals in the past.

C. The client was strongly encouraged to take steps similar to those that he/she had successfully taken in the past to accomplish present goals.

D. The therapy session revealed that the client achieved past success during periods of time when he/she received strong family support.

27. Teach Parents Behavior Management (27)

A. The parents were taught effective behavior management techniques to help decrease the frequency and severity of the client's temper outbursts, acting-out, and aggressive behaviors.

B. The parents were trained in the use of time out to manage the client's temper outbursts and aggressive behaviors.

C. The parents were instructed to remove privileges if the client engages in specific acting-out or aggressive behaviors.

D. The parents were challenged to follow through consistently with limits when the client displays temper outbursts, aggression, or acting-out behaviors.

E. The parents reported improvements in the client's behavior since they began consistently using time-outs and removal of privileges to deal with the client's temper outbursts, acting-out, and aggressive behaviors.

28. Utilize Natural Consequences (28)

A. The parents were instructed to utilize natural, logical consequences for the client's inappropriate social or maladaptive behaviors.

B. The parents were helped to identify natural, logical consequences for a variety of socially inappropriate or maladaptive behaviors.

C. The parents reported improvement in the client's behavior since they began using natural, logical consequences.

D. The therapy session revealed that the parents have not been consistent in following through or using natural, logical consequences to deal with the client's socially inappropriate or maladaptive behavior.

29. Establish Allowance/Finance Management (29)

A. The parents were assisted in establishing an allowance plan to increase the client's responsibilities at home and help him/her learn simple money management skills.

B. The client and parents established a budget whereby a certain percentage of the client's allowance money goes for both savings and spending.

C. The parents were encouraged to consult with schoolteachers about teaching the client basic money management skills.

D. The parents reported that the allowance plan has been successful in increasing the client's responsibilities around the home and teaching him/her simple money management skills.

E. The parents reported that, unfortunately, the allowance plan has not motivated the client to perform his/her household chores or responsibilities on a consistent basis.

30. Utilize Reward System to Improve Personal Hygiene (30)

A. The client and parents were assisted in identifying a list of rewards to be used to improve the client's personal hygiene and self-help skills.

B. A reward system was designed to help improve the client's personal hygiene and self-help skills.

C. The parents reported that the reward system has led to the desired improvements with the client's personal hygiene and self-help skills.

31. Implement "Activities of Daily Living" Program (31)

A. The parents were directed to use the reward system in the "Activities of Daily Living" program from *The Brief Child Therapy Homework Planner* (Jongsma, Peterson, and McInnis) to improve the client's personal hygiene and self-care skills.

B. The parents were strongly encouraged to praise and reinforce the client for improvements in his/her personal hygiene and self-care skills.

C. The parents reported that the "Activities of Daily Living" program has helped to improve the client's personal hygiene and self-care skills.

D. The parents reported that the client has demonstrated little improvement in his/her personal hygiene and self-care skills since utilizing the "Activities of Daily Living" program.

32. Teach Mediational/Self-Control Strategies (32)

A. The client was taught basic mediational and self-control strategies to help delay his/her need for immediate gratification and to inhibit impulses.

B. The parents were encouraged to establish a routine schedule for the client so that he/she postpones recreational or leisure activities until after completing his/her homework or household responsibilities.

C. The client was encouraged to utilize active listening skills and talk with significant others before making quick, hasty decisions about important matters or acting out without considering the consequences of his/her actions.

D. The client was helped to develop an action plan that outlined specific, concrete steps that he/she could take to achieve his/her identified long-term goals.

E. The client was helped to see the benefits of delaying his/her immediate need for gratification to achieve a longer-term goal.

33. Use Guided Imagery/Relaxation (33)

A. The client was trained in the use of guided imagery or deep-muscle relaxation techniques to help calm himself/herself and improve anger control.

B. The client and parents reported that the use of guided imagery and deep-muscle relaxation techniques has helped the client to calm himself/herself and control anger more effectively.

C. The client and parents reported little to no improvement with the use of guided imagery and deep-muscle relaxation techniques to help the client calm himself/herself down and control anger.

D. The client failed to utilize the guided imagery and deep-muscle relaxation techniques to help him/her control anger.

34. Reinforce Social Behaviors (34)

A. The client was educated about a variety of positive social behaviors.

B. A reward system was developed to reinforce specific, positive social behaviors.

C. The parents were strongly encouraged to look for opportunities to praise and reinforce any emerging positive social behaviors.

D. The client's positive social behaviors were praised during today's therapy session.

E. The client was given a homework assignment to practice a newly learned positive social skill at least three to five times before the next therapy session.

35. Teach Positive Social Skills (35)

A. Role-play and modeling techniques were used to teach the client positive social behaviors.

B. Mutual storytelling techniques using puppets were employed in the therapy session to teach the client positive social skills.

C. The client was able to correctly identify several positive social skills after engaging in the role-play or modeling exercises.

D. The client was instructed to practice a newly learned social skill that was taught to him/her through role playing, modeling, and mutual storytelling.

36. Participate in Special Olympics (36)

A. The client was encouraged to participate in the Special Olympics to help build his/her self-esteem.

B. The client and parents followed through with the recommendation to enroll the client in the Special Olympics.

C. The client expressed happiness about his/her participation and experiences in the Special Olympics.

D. The client and parents failed to follow through with the recommendation that the client participate in the Special Olympics.

37. Model Appropriate Expression of Emotions (37)

A. Puppets, dolls, and stuffed animals were used in today's individual play-therapy session to teach the client socially appropriate ways of expressing his/her emotions.

B. Puppets, dolls, and stuffed animals were used in today's individual play-therapy session to model socially appropriate ways to initiate and/or sustain conversations with others.

38. Teach Communication Skills (38)

A. The client was taught basic communication skills to improve his/her ability to express thoughts, feelings, and needs more clearly.

B. Role playing, modeling, and behavioral rehearsal techniques were used to teach the client effective ways to express his/her thoughts, feelings, and needs.

C. The client was taught the importance of displaying proper listening and maintaining good eye contact when communicating his/her thoughts and feelings with others.

D. The client was taught to utilize "I" messages to communicate his/her thoughts, feelings, and needs more clearly.

39. Educate Client about Emotions (39)

A. The client was helped to identify and label different emotions in today's therapy session.

B. Client-centered therapy principles were used to help the client identify and express his/her emotions.

C. The parents were encouraged to reflect the client's feelings at home to help him/her express his/her feelings more effectively.

D. The client has demonstrated improvements in his/her ability to identify and express his/her basic emotions since the onset of therapy.

40. Utilize Feelings Poster (40)

A. The Feelings Poster (Childswork/Childsplay, LLC) was utilized to help the client identify and express his/her emotions.

B. The Feelings Poster was used to educate the client about different emotions.

C. The Feelings Poster was used to help the client express his/her feelings about past separations or losses.

D. The Feelings Poster was used to help the client identify and express his/her emotions about a past traumatic event.

41. Express Emotions through Art (41)

A. The client was instructed in today's therapy session to first draw faces of basic emotions, and then was asked to share various times when he/she had experienced the different emotions.

B. The art therapy technique helped the client to identify and express different emotions.

C. An art therapy technique was employed, but the client had difficulty sharing times when he/she had experienced the different emotions in the past.

42. Conduct Filial Play Therapy (42)

A. A filial play-therapy session (i.e., parents present) was held to increase the parents' awareness of the client's thoughts and feelings.

B. A filial play-therapy session was held in an effort to strengthen the parent-child bond.

C. The filial play-therapy session helped the parents become more aware of the client's thoughts, feelings, and needs.

D. The parents were encouraged to be more interactive with the client during today's filial play-therapy session.

E. The filial play-therapy sessions have helped to create a stronger parent-child bond.

43. Utilize Child-Centered Play Therapy (43)

A. Child-centered play-therapy principles were used to help the client develop greater awareness of his/her unique thoughts, feelings, and needs.

B. The client was provided with unconditional positive regard in today's therapy session to build a level of trust and to support the client in the expression of his/her feelings.

C. The child-centered play-therapy sessions have helped the client develop an awareness of his/her unique interests and strengths.

D. Child-centered play-therapy principles were employed to strengthen the client's self-esteem and reinforce his/her self-worth.

44. Promote Acceptance of Intellectual Limits (44)

A. The client was helped to gain greater understanding and acceptance of the limitations surrounding his/her intellectual deficits and adaptive functioning.

B. A client-centered therapy approach was employed to reflect the client's feelings and move toward a greater acceptance of the limitations surrounding his/her intellectual deficits and adaptive functioning.

C. The client was helped to identify his/her unique strengths or interests as well as his/her individual weaknesses.

D. The client's self-worth was affirmed to help him/her come to a greater acceptance of the limitations surrounding his/her intellectual deficits and adaptive functioning.

45. Read *Don't Look at Me* (45)

A. *Don't Look at Me* (Sanford) was read to the client in today's therapy session to help him/her gain an acceptance of his/her limitations.

B. *Don't Look at Me* was read to the client in today's therapy session to help him/her develop an awareness of his/her own unique strengths or talents.

C. The client was able to relate to the main character in the book *Don't Look at Me* and shared times when he/she experienced feelings of inadequacy about his/her intellectual limitations or deficits.

D. The book *Don't Look at Me* was helpful in affirming the client's basic sense of self-worth.

46. Express Loss Fears through Art (46)

A. Art therapy techniques were utilized to help the client identify and verbalize his/her feelings related to issues of loss, separation, or abandonment by parental figures or key staff figures in residential programs.

B. The client was instructed to draw a picture reflecting his/her feelings about past losses, separations, or abandonment.

C. The client's artwork reflected feelings of sadness about past losses or separations.

D. The client's artwork did not provide any insight into his/her feelings about past losses, separations, or abandonment.

47. Refer for Medication Evaluation (47)

A. The client was referred for a medication evaluation to improve his/her impulse control and stabilize moods.

B. The client and parents agreed to follow through with a medication evaluation by a physician.

C. The client and parents have failed to follow through with seeking a medication evaluation to help improve the client's impulse control and stabilize his/her mood.

D. The client has been taking his/her psychotropic medication as prescribed.

E. The client has not complied with taking his/her psychotropic medication on a regular basis.

OPPOSITIONAL DEFIANT

CLIENT PRESENTATION

1. Negativistic/Hostile (1)*

A. The client presented in a negative, hostile manner.

B. The client was negative regarding all matters great or small and hostile to all of the therapist's responses.

C. The client expressed hostile defiance toward his/her parents.

D. The client has noticeably reduced his/her level of hostility and defiance toward most adults.

2. Acts As If Adults Are the Enemy (2)

A. The client voiced that he/she has seen parents and other adults who have authority as the enemy.

B. The client verbalized a "me-versus-them" attitude when referring to his/her interactions with most adults, especially those in authority.

C. The client has begun to see some adults, teachers, and even parents as possible allies as he/she has decreased his/her hostile attitude.

3. Argumentative (3)

A. The client's total mood was argumentative regarding even the most insignificant points.

B. There was an edgy, argumentative manner present in the client.

C. There was a marked decrease in the client taking issue with or arguing most points.

D. The client has reached a point where he/she is able to accept direction without arguing.

4. Unreasonable/Defiant (4)

A. The client presented with a strong sense of defiance toward rules or requests.

B. The client viewed all expectations of him/her as unreasonable and defied them.

C. The client has gradually become more reasonable and less defiant on small issues.

5. Annoyed/Irritated (5)

A. The client's mood was one of being annoyed with anyone who crosses him/her.

B. Being annoyed at everyone was the predominant mood of the client, coupled with irritation of all others who come in contact with him/her.

C. Overall, the client presented in a manner of being less annoyed with others and being somewhat tolerant of them.

D. The client is slowly coming to the point where he/she does not try to annoy others.

---

* The numbers in parentheses correlate to the number of the Behavioral Definition statement in the companion chapter with same title in *The Child Psychotherapy Treatment Planner* (Jongsma, Peterson, and McInnis) by John Wiley & Sons, 2000.

6. Blaming (6)

A. The client displayed an attitude of blaming others for his/her problems.

B. The client refused to take any responsibility for recent decisions and misbehavior, instead projecting it on to the parents and other authority figures.

C. The client carried the air that "I am not responsible or to blame for anything—it's all them."

D. The client has gradually started to take some responsibility for his/her decisions and behavior.

E. The client's general mood and manner reflect a noticeable decrease in blaming others for things that happen to him/her.

7. Lying (6)

A. The client continued to lie and to avoid responsibility for his/her actions/decisions, without any sign of shame or guilt.

B. The client appeared to be lying regarding how things were going for him/her.

C. There has been a noticeable decrease in the client's lying, and he/she is beginning to take some responsibility for his/her behavior.

8. Angry/Resentful (7)

A. The client presented in an angry, resentful, and generally uncooperative manner.

B. Anger predominated the client's mood, which was vented freely because "that's what he/she is paying for."

C. The client's overall manner was sullen and quiet, which covered a strong mood of anger and resentfulness.

D. The client's general mood and presentation reflected a noticeable decrease in anger and resentfulness.

9. Vindictive/Spiteful (8)

A. The client's mood was vindictive and spiteful toward all persons who he/she perceived as being "against me."

B. There was a vindictive, spiteful edge in the client's attitude toward all key figures in his/her daily life.

C. The client listed and vented acts of vengeance and spite he/she would to do to others.

D. The client has reduced his/her level of vindictiveness and spite toward others and has at times showed a little kindness in his/her speech.

10. Significant Impairments in Key Areas of Life (9)

A. The client reported impairments in his/her social, academic, and occupational functioning.

B. The client indicated that according to most people he/she was not doing well socially and academically, but it did not concern him/her.

C. The client's social and academic functioning have improved as he/she has taken responsibility for his/her actions and been less defiant.

INTERVENTIONS IMPLEMENTED

1. Build Trust (1)*

A. Initial level of trust was established with the client through use of unconditional positive regard.

B. Warm acceptance and active listening techniques were utilized to establish the basis for a trusting relationship.

C. The client seems to have formed a trust-based relationship and has started to share his/her feelings about conflictual relationships.

D. The client seems to have formed an initial trusting relationship and has started to disclose his/her thoughts and feelings.

2. Identify Oppositional Patterns (2)

A. The client's behavior patterns were explored to establish how he/she responds to rules and authority.

B. The client was willing and able to identify his/her oppositional patterns but did not perceive them as his/her problem.

C. The client's oppositional patterns were reviewed and pointed out with specific behavioral examples from his/her history.

3. Employ A.C.T. Model Play Therapy (3)

A. A.C.T. model play-therapy techniques were utilized to decrease the client's resistive behavior and to increase his/her prosocial behavior.

B. The client's feelings were acknowledged, limits were communicated, and prosocial and cooperative behavior was reinforced.

C. The client actively participated in today's A.C.T. play-therapy session.

D. The A.C.T. model of play therapy was explained to parents and they were informed of the client's progress.

E. The client's involvement in A.C.T. play therapy has resulted in a noticeable increase in his/her cooperative and prosocial behavior.

4. Employ Psychoanalytic Play-Therapy (4)

A. A psychoanalytic play-therapy approach was used to explore and gain an understanding of the client's unconscious conflicts and defiance.

B. The client actively participated in the psychoanalytic play-therapy sessions.

C. Psychoanalytic play therapy was utilized to interpret the client's resistance, transference issues, and/or core anxieties and to help him/her resolve conflicts.

D. The client's involvement in psychoanalytic play therapy has resulted in him/her showing more consistent prosocial behavior in his/her daily life.

---

* The numbers in parentheses correlate to the number of the Therapeutic Interventions statement in the companion chapter with same title in *The Child Psychotherapy Treatment Planner* (Jongsma, Peterson, and McInnis) by John Wiley & Sons, 2000.

5. Interpret Feelings in Play Therapy (5)

A. The client's feelings that emerged during play-therapy sessions were interpreted and then related to conflicts occurring in his/her daily life.

B. The client was taught the connection between feelings and behavior.

C. The parents were given feedback regarding the client's feelings expressed during play therapy and how they are connected to his/her behavior.

D. The client's connecting of his/her feelings with behavior has helped to decrease his/her daily conflicts.

6. Read "The Little Crab" (6)

A. The story of "The Little Crab" from *Stories For The Third Ear* (Wallas) was read and processed with the client and family.

B. "The Little Crab" metaphor was established with the family as a reference for change/growth.

7. Family Sessions Promote Respect/Cooperation (7)

A. Family sessions were held in which the key issues of mutual respect, cooperation, and conflict resolution were addressed and possible solutions were explored.

B. The family decided upon solutions to implement to change past patterns of unsuccessful conflict resolution, disrespect and uncooperativeness.

C. The family therapy sessions have been successful at reducing the level of tension between family members and increasing mutual respect and cooperation.

8. Play "Don't Be Difficult" Game (8)

A. The Don't Be Difficult game (Childswork/Childsplay) was played with the client to help decrease his/her uncooperative behavior and promote prosocial behavior.

B. The experience of playing the Don't Be Difficult game was processed with the client and positive gains were identified.

C. The client was asked to identify one prosocial behavior he/she learned from playing the Don't Be Difficult game to implement in his/her daily life.

D. The client's implementation of the selected prosocial behavior was supported, encouraged, and monitored for consistent follow-through.

9. Read *Everything I Do You Blame On Me*

A. The book *Everything I Do You Blame On Me* (Abern) was read and processed with the client.

B. By using the blaming story, the therapist helped the client to develop insight into his/her oppositional/defiant behaviors.

C. The client was asked to identify problem behaviors from the blaming story and state which ones match his/her own behavior.

D. The client was resistive to name any problem behaviors from the blaming story that matched his/her own behavior.

E. The client was firmly confronted about his/her problem behaviors that matched ones from the blaming story.

F. The client has developed more insight into his/her pattern of behavior from reading and processing the blaming story.

10. Verbalize Negative, Hostile Feelings (10)

A. An open, accepting, and understanding approach was utilized to encourage the client to express his/her negative, hostile feelings.

B. The causes for the client's angry and oppositional feelings were explored and he/she identified the perception that parents were unfair, overly controlling, and inclined toward favoritism for other siblings.

C. Negative and hostile feelings were normalized with the client to remove any barriers to verbalization of these feelings.

D. The client was taught about feelings with a special focus being placed on the negative, hostile ones.

11. Provide Paradoxical Interpretation for Behavior (11)

A. Negative, hostile, and defiant behaviors were processed and probed with the client.

B. The client was given paradoxical interpretations for his/her negative, hostile, and defiant behaviors.

C. Each identified negative, hostile, and defiant behavior was reframed for the client.

12. Teach Value of Respectfulness (12)

A. The therapist worked with the client to establish a framework for treating others in a respectful manner.

B. The client was asked to list negative consequences of not treating others with respect.

C. The client was taught the principle of reciprocity in relationships and asked to treat everyone with respect for the next week while observing respect received in return.

D. Role play was utilized to assist the client in practicing reciprocity principles in relating with others.

13. "If I Could Run My Family" Exercise (13)

A. The client was asked to complete the "If I Could Run My Family" exercise from *The Brief Adolescent Therapy Homework Planner* (Jongsma, Peterson, and McInnis), to explore the pro's and con's of control of the family.

B. The client was asked to identify the cons of being in control of the family, and each identified point was reinforced by the therapist.

C. The client's past pattern of disrespectful interactions was reviewed and negative results were reinforced.

D. The client reported several instances of switching from making complaints to making requests of others around him/her and also noted the positive results from this change.

14. Read *Winning Cooperation from Your Child* (14)

A. The parents were asked to read *Winning Cooperation from Your Child* (Wenning) and to gather key ideas from the book to process with the therapist.

B. Key ideas gathered from the parents' reading of the book were processed and ways to implement them were explored.

C. New suggestions for more effective ways to intervene with the client's problem behaviors were given to the parents.

D. The parents' resistiveness to the newly suggested ways to respond to the client's difficult behaviors was explored, processed, and resolved.

E. The parents' expanded knowledge of how to competently respond to difficult behaviors and the implementation of new methods have decreased their frustration and increased their effectiveness in dealing with the client's negative behaviors.

15. "Switching From Defense to Offense" Exercise (15)

A. The parents were asked to complete the "Switching From Defense to Offense" exercise from *The Brief Child Therapy Homework Planner* (Jongsma, Peterson, and McInnis) to help explore and establish new ways of intervening with the client.

B. New methods identified by the parents from the switching strategies exercise were refined and plans for implementation were made.

C. Role play was utilized with the parents to increase their confidence and to work out any bugs in the new intervention techniques.

D. The parents are responding positively to their switch from defensive to offensive parenting strategies, and the client's oppositional behaviors have diminished.

16. Play Therapeutic Game (16)

A. The Talking, Feeling, Doing Game (Gardner) was played with the client, during which he/she had numerous opportunities to express his/her feelings appropriately.

B. Playing the Talking, Feeling, Doing Game with the client has given him/her the opportunity to experiment with recognizing and expressing feelings.

C. The client has become more free to express his/her feelings in a respectful manner.

17. Teach Respectful Expression of Feelings (17)

A. The client was taught how to recognize and express his/her needs and feelings in a constructive, respectful way.

B. The client was asked to practice expressing his/her needs and feelings to the therapist in a constructive, respectful way.

C. The client was reminded of how his/her disrespectful manner of expressing feelings and wants had a negative impact on self and others.

D. The client and parents reported that the client is expressing his/her feelings and opinions in a more respectful manner.

18. Connect Feelings and Defiance (18)

A. The client's feelings associated with defiance were probed and connections between feelings and behaviors were established.

B. The client was asked to list any connections he/she saw between his/her feelings and his/her defiant behaviors.

C. The client's feelings of hurt or anger were explored as those that motivate the defiant, rebellious behavior.

D. As the client has expressed his/her feelings of hurt and frustration more openly, the oppositional and defiant behavior has diminished in intensity.

19. Employ Dominoes Demonstration (19)

A. Utilize a Domino Rally with the client to draw a visual representation of how feelings lead to behavioral events.

B. The client was taught the connection between feelings and behavioral events and then his/her history and the domino effect were used to illustrate and reinforce the point.

20. Complete "Filing a Complaint" Exercise (20)

A. The client was asked to complete the "Filing a Complaint" exercise from *The Brief Adolescent Therapy Homework Planner* (Jongsma, Peterson, and McInnis) to assist him/her in reframing complaints as requests.

B. The client was asked to identify the pro's and con's of complaints versus requests, with a focus on which is more respectful.

C. The client's past pattern of disrespectful interactions was reviewed and negative results were reinforced.

D. The client reported several instances of switching from making complaints to making requests of others around him/her and also noted the positive results from this change.

21. Videotape Destructive Interaction Patterns (21)

A. Videotaping was utilized in family sessions to help identify destructive patterns of interaction within the family.

B. The family was assisted in identifying destructive interaction patterns from viewing the video of a session and helped to develop new, respectful interactions through role play, role reversal, and modeling.

C. The family members reported an increase in respectful interaction between them and an increase in sensitivity to the pattern of disrespectful interaction that has been so prevalent in the past.

22. List Angry Feelings and Causes (22)

A. The client was asked to list all those people he/she feels angry with, complete with reasons for the anger.

B. The client was taught the negative effects of being too angry and how it can lead to behavioral problems.

C. The client was confronted when the reasons for his/her anger were unrealistic or self-serving.

D. The causes for the client's anger were more fully explored and steps were taken to resolve these angry feelings.

E. The client is beginning to resolve his/her angry feelings and this is reflected in more pleasant, cooperative behavior.

23. Assign Parents to Read *The Challenging Child* (23)

A. The parents were assigned to read chapters on defiant children from *The Challenging Child* (Greenspan).

B. The parents identified and processed key points gathered from their reading of *The Challenging Child*.

C. The parents were helped to identify and implement key concepts they learned from the assigned reading of *The Challenging Child* and processed them with the therapist.

D. The parents have expanded their understanding of defiant children and have implemented new key approaches in working with the client.

24. Teach Behavior Management Techniques (24)

A. The parents were asked to read *1-2-3 Magic: Training Your Preschoolers and Preteens to Do What You Want* (Phelan) and/or *8 Weeks to a Well-Behaved Child* (Windell) and then identify several new behavior management techniques.

B. The parents were assisted in selecting the best new behavior management techniques from the assigned readings to implement with the client.

C. The parents were helped to develop a plan to implement the new behavior management techniques.

D. Role play was used with the parents to help them gain experience and confidence in utilizing the new techniques.

E. The parents' implementation of the new techniques was monitored and encouragement and redirection were given to them.

F. The parents' consistent implementation of the behavior management techniques has improved their daily ability to manage the client's oppositional/defiant behaviors.

25. Play Checkers (25)

A. Checker rules were established by the client and the therapist and games were played with the client being confronted when he/she was violating or attempting to change the agreed-upon rules.

B. Importance of rules was reinforced with the client pointing out the chaos that would be present without them and the negative feelings that result when people break or bend rules.

26. Utilize "Tearing Paper" Exercise (26)

A. The family was assigned the "Tearing Paper" exercise and the guidelines were explained to them.

B. The family actively participated in the "Tearing Paper" exercise, following the guidelines set by the therapist.

C. The family members were observed and monitored as they participated in the assigned "Tearing Paper" exercise.

D. The exercise was processed with the family members as they cleaned up afterward and the positive feelings of releasing energy and doing an activity together without conflict were identified and reinforced.

27. Assign Parents *The Girls and Boys Book About Good and Bad Behavior* (27)

A. The parents were instructed to read *The Girls and Boys Book About Good and Bad Behavior* (Gardner) to promote conscience development and prosocial behavior.

B. Key concepts of the Gardner book were processed, identified, and reinforced with the client and parents.

C. The parents were helped to develop ways to use the key concepts from the Gardner book to promote the growth of the client's conscience.

D. The parents were encouraged to read the Gardner book weekly with the client.

E. The client has started to exhibit signs of developing a conscience in his/her daily behavior and increase in prosocial behavior.

28. Institute "Positive Consequences" (28)

A. Worked with the client's parents and teachers to develop "positive consequences" to administer when oppositional behavior occurs in the client.

B. The implementation of positive consequences has helped to reduce the client's oppositional behavior.

29. Teach Contingent Excommunication (29)

A. The parents were assisted in clarifying acceptable and unacceptable behavioral standards for the client and how to directly communicate them to him/her.

B. A system of "banishment from family" was established with the parents to be a significant consequence for unacceptable behavior.

C. The issue of not consistently following through with the temporary contingent banishment was addressed with the parents, with emphasis being given to reality of the client's past behavioral patterns of manipulation, and his/her utilization of "divide and conquer" methods.

30. Model Effective Child Interaction (30)

A. Healthy, respectful teen interaction techniques were modeled by the therapist for the parents in family session.

B. A videotape of family sessions was reviewed with the parents to examine the positive points of the therapist's teen interaction techniques.

C. The parents' unhealthy interaction patterns with the client were identified and they practiced replacing them with healthy interaction techniques the therapist had modeled in family session.

D. The parents and the client reported that their interaction at home was more pleasant, respectful, and productive.

31. Teach Parents Simplified Interactions (31)

A. The negative aspects of parental ororverbalization were reviewed with the parents, with special emphasis being placed on the amount of power they lose by doing so.

B. The parents were asked to list the client's nondestructive negative behaviors that they felt could be ignored, and then they were asked to start doing so.

C. The parents have become more aware of their tendency to try to reason too much with the client and have reduced their ororverbalizations.

32. Monitor Parents' Techniques (32)

A. The parents' use of new parenting techniques and interventions were monitored to encourage consistent use and to address any difficulties that were being experienced.

B. The parents were observed in waiting area and in family session effectively employing the new parenting techniques they had learned.

C. The parents were asked to describe how the use of new techniques and interventions were going, and lack of follow-through was addressed.

D. The parents report being pleased with the new techniques they are utilizing in their interaction with the client.

33. Assign Family a Mutual Task (33)

A. The family was assigned to make and complete a coat of arms, collage, or other task of mutual choosing together.

B. The family members were observed working on their task and were given feedback on using more constructive intervention behaviors.

C. The experience of completing the task was processed and cooperative, respectful interaction was reinforced with family members, and negative interaction was identified and redirected.

D. The experience of completing the mutual task was processed and the family was urged to use it as a beginning point for the family to cooperate more at home.

34. Implement "Do Something Different" Technique (34)

A. The "Do Something Different" technique was explained to the parents and possible ways for them to do something different were brainstormed.

B. The parents were assisted in selecting several of their ideas of ways to do something different, and plans were made for each to be used with the client.

C. Role play was used to give the parents experience, confidence, and feedback on using new responses to the client.

D. The parents' use of new responses was monitored for their effectiveness with the client.

E. The parents' consistent implementation of new responses has started to modify the client's oppositional behaviors.

35. Expose Parental Conflict (35)

A. In family session, conflict between the parents was uncovered, and the parents made a commitment to work conjointly on resolving the conflict.

B. The parents were confronted in family session on the conflicts present between them and shown the role these play in the client's oppositional behavior.

C. The parents worked in conjoint sessions to resolve the underlying conflicts present in their marriage.

36. Utilize Family System Approach (36)

A. A family system approach was utilized to identify family strengths and to use strengths to address areas of family dysfunction.

B. After normalizing dysfunction as a part of all families, the family members were able to identify specific dysfunctions in their family and begin to address them.

37. Teach Time-Out Procedures (37)

A. The parents were asked to list behaviors that are acceptable for the client and those that are unacceptable and that will result in time-out being implemented.

B. Behavioral limitations were given to the client in family session and explained briefly by the parents, complete with time-out consequences.

C. Behavioral parameters and components of the time-out consequence were developed with the parents.

D. The parents reported that the implementation of the time-out consequence has been successful at reducing the targeted negative behaviors.

38. Develop Behavior Modification Plan (38)

A. The parents were assisted in developing a behavior modification plan which included rewards for positive behavior and fines for negative behavior.

B. The parents' resistance to giving rewards for positive behavior was worked through so a behavior modification program could be developed and implemented.

39. Implement Behavioral Modification Plan (39)

A. The parents were given positive feedback on their follow-through on implementation and maintaining the behavioral modification program for the client.

B. The parents were confronted on their inconsistent follow-through on administering the behavioral modification plan they developed.

C. The parents were given support and encouragement in their efforts to implement and follow through on behavioral management/time-out program in the face of the client's strong resistance.

D. The parents report that the behavior modification plan is working smoothly and the client is responding favorably to the increase in targeted positive behavior.

40. Teach Barkley Method (40)

A. The parents were asked to view Barkley videos or read *Your Defiant Child* (Barkely and Benton) to gain an understanding of the Barkley approach.

B. The parents were asked to make a commitment to pursue this approach or not.

C. The family was assessed for having the strength and commitment to implement and follow through with the Barkley method.

41. Sculpt Family (41)

A. A family sculpture was created to depict the family members as they are, followed by sculpting the family members as they would like to be.

B. The family members were cooperative in sculpting themselves as they are but were unable to sculpt themselves in terms of how they would like to be.

42. Assess Family Interactions (42)

A. In family sessions, family interaction patterns were analyzed to locate points for possible intervention.

B. The analysis of interaction patterns was utilized to decide which intervention could be most appropriate for this family.

C. The experiential/strategic/structural intervention was implemented and embraced in the family with a commitment to follow through with what was prescribed.

PEER/SIBLING CONFLICTS

CLIENT PRESENTATION

1. Angry/Tense (1)*

A. The client described a pattern of frequent, intense conflict with peers and siblings.

B. The client appeared angry at everything and everybody and was not willing to be very cooperative in the counseling process.

C. The client denied responsibility for the frequent, overt verbal and physical fighting with both peers and siblings.

D. The level of anger and fighting between the client and siblings has decreased as they have actively worked with the therapist in session.

2. Competitive/Energetic (1)

A. There is an energetic and highly competitive nature to the client.

B. The client described him/herself as someone who loves a challenge and any type of competition.

C. The client's dialogue contains consistent references to "numero uno," "winners/losers," "top dog/low dog" in describing his/her relationship with peers and siblings.

D. The client reports that he/she has always competed and competed hard in everything.

E. The amount of competition between the siblings has started to decrease and they are getting along better and more cooperatively.

3. Projecting/Blaming (2)

A. The client displayed a propensity for blaming others for his/her problems.

B. The client refused to take any responsibility for the ongoing verbal and physical conflicts he/she has with peers and siblings.

C. The client viewed all problems or conflicts as the responsibility of others, not of himself/herself.

D. The client has slowly started to take responsibility for some of the conflicts he/she is involved with.

4. Parents' Unfairness/Favoritism (3)

A. The client reported that the parents always treat his/her siblings more favorably than they do him/her.

B. The client cited instances of his/her perception of parents' unfairness toward him/her.

C. The parents acknowledged that they find the other siblings easier to like than the client.

D. The client's complaints about unfairness and favoritism have started to decrease and his/her parents are beginning to be seen in a more favorable light.

---

* The numbers in parentheses correlate to the number of the Behavioral Definition statement in the companion chapter with same title in *The Child Psychotherapy Treatment Planner* (Jongsma, Peterson, and McInnis) by John Wiley & Sons, 2000.

5. Defiant/Vengeful (4)

A. The client presented in a vengeful, defiant manner.

B. The client reported a long list of people who have wronged or slighted him/her in some way and how he/she has gotten back at them.

C. The client's level of bullying has caused him/her to be constantly at odds with peers and siblings.

D. The client has gradually let go of some of his/her intimidation and vengeance and his started to have less conflict with peers and siblings.

6. Isolated/Intense (5)

A. The client presented as a lonely, isolated individual.

B. The client reported a history of aggressive relationships with peers which he/she has resolved by staying to himself/herself.

C. The client stated that he/she cannot get along with either peers or siblings without trouble so he/she chooses to stay to himself/herself.

D. Since taking part in the counseling process, the client has gradually started to relate at least superficially with others.

7. Impulsive/Intimidating (6)

A. The client showed a pattern of impulsiveness and intimidation within the session by not considering the consequences of his/her actions and by challenging the therapist.

B. The client described a pattern of relating with peers and siblings in an impulsive, intimidating manner.

C. The client reported a history of impulsive, intimidating actions toward peers that has caused him/her repeated social problems.

D. The client has gradually accepted that he/she is intimidating and this has been the reason for his/her conflicts with peers and siblings.

8. Aggressive/Mean (7)

A. The client seems to have an aggressive, mean manner in which he/she relates with others.

B. The client indicated that he/she has been involved in encounters which resulted in physical injuries to others.

C. No remorse appeared evident on the client's part for the painful way he/she treats others.

D. All responsibility for the client's aggressive, mean acts are laid on others or given great justification.

9. Insensitivity (7)

A. The client did not appear to be bothered by the ongoing conflicts he/she has with peers and siblings.

B. The hurtful impact on others of client's verbally hostile, aggressive behavior does not appear to have an affect on the client.

C. The client has started to understand the effect his/her conflictual behaviors have on others and his/her need to be more sensitive to them.

10. Fails to Respond to Praise/Encouragement (8)

A. Efforts to praise or encourage the client were rebuffed and negated.

B. The client indicated that he/she does not believe people when they say nice or encouraging things.

C. The client reported that he/she views praise as a way for people to try to "buy you off."

D. The client started to respond to and affirm the praise and encouragement he/she receives from others.

11. Parents' Hostility (9)

A. The client described instances from his/her childhood in which severe and abusive punishment resulted whenever he/she was blamed for negative behavior.

B. The client described how parents always unfavorably compared him/her with peers and siblings, leading to feelings of anger, inadequacy, and resentment.

C. The parents' style of relating to the client is rude and hostile.

D. The client's home environment appears to be highly competitive, where one sibling is often pitted against the other to outdo him/her in a given area and thus win the parents' praise.

E. The client has begun to understand how his/her attitude and behavior toward others are connected to parents' treatment of him/her in childhood.

F. The parents have begun to treat the client in a more respectful and less hostile manner.

INTERVENTIONS IMPLEMENTED

1. Build Trust and Express Feelings (1)*

A. Initial trust level was established with the client through the use of unconditional positive regard.

B. Warm acceptance and active listening techniques were utilized to establish the basis for a trust relationship with the client.

C. The client seems to have formed a trust relationship with the therapist and has started to share his/her feelings about conflictual relationships.

D. Despite the use of active listening, warm acceptance, and unconditional positive regard, the client appears to be hesitant to trust and to share his/her feelings and conflicts.

2. Explore Relationships and Assess Denial (2)

A. The client's perception of how he/she relates with siblings and peers was explored.

B. The client's degree of denial was found to be high regarding conflict and acceptance of responsibility for any part in it.

C. The client was open in acknowledging the high degree of conflict between the siblings and accepted responsibility for his/her part in the conflict.

---

* The numbers in parentheses correlate to the number of the Therapeutic Interventions statement in the companion chapter with same title in *The Child Psychotherapy Treatment Planner* (Jongsma, Peterson, and McInnis) by John Wiley & Sons, 2000.

3. Employ A.C.T. Model of Play Therapy (3)

A. A.C.T. model play-therapy sessions were conducted to acknowledge the client's feelings, communicate limits, and target appropriate alternatives to conflicts and aggression with peers/siblings.

B. Positive verbal affirmation was given to the client in A.C.T. play-therapy sessions when he/she displayed or verbalized appropriate alternatives to conflict and aggression with others.

C. The client willingly and actively participated in the A.C.T. play-therapy sessions.

D. The client's involvement in A.C.T. play-therapy sessions has helped him/her interact with peers and/or siblings with less conflict and aggression.

4. Employ Psychoanalytic Play Therapy (4)

A. A psychoanalytic play-therapy session was conducted to explore and understand the reasons for the client's intense conflicts with peers and/or siblings.

B. The client actively and freely participated in the psychoanalytic play-therapy sessions.

C. Transference issues that emerged in the psychoanalytic play-therapy sesions were worked through to resolution.

D. The client's feelings expressed during the psychoanalytic play-therapy sessions were interpreted and connected to his/her conflicts with peers and/or siblings.

E. The client's participation in psychoanalytic play therapy has reduced the frequency and intensity of his/her peer and/or sibling conflicts.

5. Interpret Feelings (5)

A. The client's feelings that emerged during the play-therapy session were interpreted to him/her and related to his/her conflicts with peers and/or siblings.

B. The client was assisted in increasing his/her understanding of the connection between feelings and his/her conflicts with peers and/or siblings.

C. The parents were informed of the feelings the client was expressing in play therapy and how they connected with his/her daily conflicts with peers and/or siblings.

D. The client's progress in connecting feelings with his/her peer/sibling conflicts has helped to reduce the daily frequency of conflict with peers and/or siblings.

6. Suggest Constructive Ways to Handle Conflicts (6)

A. Puppets were used to create scenarios to model and suggest to client constructive ways to handle conflicts with peers and/or siblings.

B. After each puppet scenario, the client was asked to identified how the conflict was constructively handled or resolved.

C. The client created several scenarios of conflict from his/her life using stuffed animals, to which the therapist suggested and modeled constructive ways of handling each one.

D. The client was encouraged to use the modeled means of reducing conflict in his/her daily life.

E. The client has used the suggested and modeled ways to handle conflicts constructively to decrease the amount of conflict in his/her own daily life.

7. Utilize the "Playing Baby" Game (7)

A. The Playing Baby game (Schaefer) from *101 Favorite Play Therapy Techniques* was explained to the parents, and plans were made to implement it with the client.

B. The parents have consistently and effectively implemented the Playing Baby game with the client.

C. The parents' failure to consistently use the Playing Baby game was addressed, processed, and resolved.

D. The parents' follow-through with using the Playing Baby game has reduced the level of conflict between the client and his/her siblings.

8. Utilize "Tearing Paper" Exercise (8)

A. The Tearing Paper exercise (Dawes) from *101 Favorite Play Therapy Techniques* was given and the guidelines explained to the family.

B. The family actively participated in the tearing paper exercise and followed all the guidelines set by the therapist.

C. The family was observed and monitored as they participated in the tearing paper exercise.

D. The tearing paper exercise was processed with the family members as they cleaned up and the positive feelings of releasing energy and doing activities without conflict were identified and reinforced.

9. Utilize "Stamping Feet" Method (9)

A. The Stamping Feet and Bubble Popping method (Wunderlich) from *101 Favorite Play Therapy Techniques* was used with the client to assist him/her in releasing feelings of anger and frustration.

B. The appropriate release of feelings of anger and frustration were emphasized with the client.

C. The client actively participated in the Stamping Feet and Bubble Popping method and the processing of it afterward.

D. Possible ways for the client to appropriately release angry feelings were explored and identified.

10. Teach Social Learning Techniques (10)

A. The parents and teachers were asked to identify all nonaggressive, cooperative, and peaceful behaviors of the client that they could praise and positively reinforce.

B. Role play and modeling techniques were used to show the parents and teachers how to ignore the client's nonharmful, aggressive behaviors and how to praise prosocial behaviors.

11. Teach an Understanding of Feelings (11)

A. The client was taught to identify basic feelings using a feelings chart.

B. Aggressive actions were focused on with the client to assist him/her in identifying how others might feel when they were the object of such actions.

C. The idea of how the client would like to be treated by others was explored, along with what he/she would need to do to make this possible.

12. "Negotiating a Peace Treaty" Exercise (12)

A. The client and the parents were asked to complete the "Negotiating a Peace Treaty" exercise from *The Brief Adolescent Therapy Homework Planner* (Jongsma, Peterson, and McInnis) to introduce the concept of negotiation.

B. The parents were asked to start negotiating key areas of conflict with the client.

C. Role-play sessions involving negotiation were used with the client and the parents to build their negotiating skills.

D. The positive aspects of negotiation versus winning and losing were identified and reinforced with the client.

13. Play "Helping, Sharing, and Caring" Game (13)

A. The Helping, Sharing, and Caring game (Gardner) was played with the client to expose him/her to feelings of respect for self and others.

B. The client was assisted in identifying how people feel when they show respect and receive respect from others.

C. The client was reminded of how others feel when they are treated in a rude, disrespectful manner.

D. The client reported success at more consistently showing respect for the feelings of others.

14. Read Gardner's Therapeutic Stories (14)

A. Therapeutic stories from *Dr. Gardner's Fairy Tales for Today's Children* (Gardner) were read with the client to help increase his/her awareness of feelings and to learn ways to cooperate with others.

B. Verbal affirmation and reinforcement were given to the client when he/she identified possible feelings of characters in the therapeutic stories.

C. The client was assisted in identifying ways that he/she could increase his/her cooperation with others and was asked to implement one in his/her daily life.

D. The client was redirected and verbally reinforced in implementing new cooperative behaviors.

E. Use of *Dr. Gardner's Fairy Tales for Today's Children* has helped the client increase his/her skills in identifying his/her feelings and cooperating with others.

15. Group Therapy Referral (15)

A. The client was referred to a peer therapy group to expand his/her social sensitivity and behavioral flexibility.

B. The client accepted the referral to group therapy and has been attending regularly.

C. The client reported that the group therapy experience has taught him/her to be more sensitive to the feelings of others.

D. The client has been resistive to group therapy and has not attended on a regular basis.

16. Play "Talking, Feeling, Doing" Game (16)

A. The Talking, Feeling, Doing game (Gardner) was played with the client to build and reinforce his/her awareness of self and others.

B. After playing the Talking, Feeling, Doing game the client began sharing more about him/herself and showing some sensitivity to others.

17. Play "Anger Control" Game (17)

A. The Anger Control game (Berg) was played with the client to expose him/her to new ways of handling aggressive feelings.

B. The client was asked to make a commitment to try one of the new ways to handle aggressive feelings that were learned through playing the Anger Control game.

C. The client has reported that he/she has successfully implemented new anger control techniques.

D. The client reported that he/she continues to have problems managing anger.

18. Play "Social Conflict" Game (18)

A. The Social Conflict game (Berg) was played with the client to introduce him/her to prosocial behavioral skills.

B. The client was asked to list all of the negative consequences that have resulted from his/her antisocial behaviors.

C. The client was reminded of the emotional and physical pain that his/her actions have caused others.

D. The client was assisted in identifying two positive consequences of showing respect and concern for others.

19. Behavioral Group Referral (19)

A. The client was asked to attend a behavioral contracting group that works to develop positive peer interactions.

B. The client's group goals for positive peer interaction were set and reviewed each week.

C. The client reported positive verbal feedback from peers on his/her interaction goals.

D. The client's positive gains in peer interaction were verbally reinforced and rewarded.

20. Facilitate Involvement in Cooperative Activities (20)

A. The benefits of involving the client in cooperative activities were discussed with the parents.

B. Options for cooperative activities were presented to the parents and they were asked to make a commitment to get the client involved.

C. The client was assisted in identifying positive gains he/she could make through participating in cooperative activities such as sports, music, and scouts.

D. The client's involvement in cooperative activities with peers has increased significantly since the parents have encouraged this activity.

21. Camp Referral (21)

A. The client was referred to a summer camp that focuses on building self-esteem and positive peer relationships.

B. The client was helped to identify a list of specific things he/she could do at camp to increase his/her self-esteem.

C. Gains in self-esteem and in peer relationships reported by the client as having been gained through the camp experience were affirmed and reinforced.

D. The client and his/her parents have not followed through on enrolling the client in a summer camp experience focused on building self-esteem and peer cooperation.

22. Read *Helping Your Child Make Friends* (22)

A. The parents were asked to read *Helping Your Child Make Friends* (Nevick) to gain ideas for helping the client build connections to peers.

B. The parents were assisted in identifying several suggestions from the book and in making plans to implement each of their selections.

C. The parents were affirmed, encouraged, and reinforced in their efforts to help the client build his/her social skills.

D. The parent's efforts to build the client's social skills have helped him/her begin to form new friendships.

23. "Joseph, His Amazing Technicolor Coat and More" Exercise (23)

A. The client was asked to complete the "Joseph, His Amazing Technicolor Coat and More" exercise from *The Brief Adolescent Therapy Homework Planner* (Jongsma, Peterson, and McInnis).

B. In processing the favoritism homework assignment, the client was assisted in identifying the negative and well as the positive aspects of being the parents' favorite child.

C. In processing the favoritism homework assignment, the client was reminded of the reality that even though nearly all the parents love their children, they may still have favorites.

24. Teach Open Responses to Praise and Encouragement (24)

A. The client was assisted in identifying how he/she responds to praise and encouragement from others.

B. The client's barriers to being open to positive feedback were identified.

C. New ways to respond positively to praise and encouragement were taught to the client.

D. Role play, modeling, and behavioral rehearsal were used to provide the client the opportunity to practice new accepting responses to praise and encouragement.

25. Teach Parents to Praise (25)

A. The parents were asked to list all the possible ways they might give verbal affection and appropriate praise to the client.

B. The parents' resistance to giving affection and praise to the client for expected behavior was addressed and resolved.

C. The parents were asked to chose three ways to give verbal affection and appropriate praise, and then were asked to implement each with the client when appropriate.

D. Affirmation and reinforcement was given to the parents for their reported use of verbal affection and praise with the client.

26. **Reduce Parental Aggression, Rejection, and Quarreling (26)**

   A. Parental patterns of aggression and rejection were identified in family session.

   B. The parents were assisted in removing acts to aggression and messages of rejection from their parenting.

   C. Various methods were modeled for the parents to respond to the client in a warm, firm, yet caring way.

   D. Parent messages of rejection were blocked and confronted in family sessions.

27. **Explore Rejection Experiences (27)**

   A. The client's rejection experiences with family and friends were probed.

   B. The client expressed numerous causes for his/her anger which were based in rejection by family and friends.

   C. The client denied any rejection experiences as being the basis for his/her anger.

28. **Read *How to End the Sibling Wars* (28)**

   A. The parents were asked to read *How to End the Sibling Wars* (Bienick) and to select several of the interventions to implement with their child.

   B. The parents were assisted in implementing chosen techniques from the assigned book and role play was utilized for the parents to increase their skills and confidence using the new techniques.

   C. The parents' resistance to trying new techniques was addressed and advantages of using new approaches was seeded with them.

29. **Read *Siblings Without Rivalry* (29)**

   A. The book *Siblings Without Rivalry* (Faber and Mazish) was assigned to the parents to read and process with the therapist.

   B. Based on their reading *Siblings Without Rivalry*, the parents identified two new ways to reduce rivalry and began implementing them in their family.

   C. The parents reported positive results from the new methods learned from reading *Siblings Without Rivalry* that they have implemented to decrease the level of rivalry in the family.

   D. The parents gave numerous excuses for their inconsistent use of new parenting methods and for the mixed results they experienced.

30. **Read *Between Parent and Child* (30)**

   A. The parents were asked to read the chapters "Jealousy" and "Children Who Need Professional Help" from *Between Parent and Child* (Ginott).

   B. The parents were assisted in identifying and changing key areas of the family structure to decrease the level of rivalry.

   C. The parents were reminded that the level of rivalry within their family system is destructive as they continue to work toward the level of a normal family interaction.

31. **Parenting Class Referral (31)**

   A. The parents were referred and encouraged to attend a support group.

   B. The parents reported attending a support group and receiving helpful feedback and encouragement.

   C. The parents offered several reasons for not yet attending a support group.

32. Utilize Behavior Modification Plan (33)

A. A behavior modification plan targeting cooperative sibling interaction was developed by the parents and the therapist for the client.

B. The parents were taught how to effectively implement and sustain a behavior modification program focused on reinforcing positive sibling interaction.

C. The parents' administration of the behavior modification plan was monitored, and encouragement was given to the parents to continue their work.

D. The parents were confronted when they failed to immediately reinforce positive interactions by the client.

E. The behavior modification plan focused on reinforcing positive sibling interaction has been successful in increasing such behaviors and reducing the sibling conflicts.

33. Conduct Evaluation Session (33)

A. The effectiveness of the behavior modification plan was reviewed with the client and the parents, with positive feedback given for implementing the contract.

B. Aspects of the behavioral modification contract focusing on reinforcing positive sibling interaction were modified with the client and the parents as expectations were unrealistically set too high.

C. The parents and the client were confronted on their lack of follow-through with the behavioral modification contract and resistance issues were addressed and resolved.

34. Assess Dynamics and Alliances Underlying Conflicts (34)

A. The dynamics and alliances present in the family were assessed in a family session.

B. A structural intervention was implemented with the family to create new, healthier alliances between the members.

C. Key dynamics that create and promote sibling conflict were confronted in the family.

35. Confront Disrespect and Teach Conflict Resolution Skills (35)

A. Family members' disrespectful interactions were highlighted and confronted in family session.

B. Conflict resolution skills were taught to the parents and siblings.

C. Role plays, behavioral rehearsal, and modeling were utilized with family members to teach effective conflict resolution skills and to give them each opportunities to practice these new skills themselves.

D. The family members have struggled to implement conflict resolution techniques as they give up easily and fall back to old patterns of arguing and verbal abuse.

36. Psychiatric/Psychological Evaluation Referral (36)

A. Options for a psychiatric or psychological evaluation were explained to the client and family.

B. The client was referred for a psychiatric evaluation.

C. The client was referred for a psychological evaluation.

D. The parents were asked to make a verbal commitment to follow through with the evaluation and report results back to the therapist.

37. Monitor Implementation of Assessment Recommendations (37)

A. The parents and the client were assisted in implementing the psychological/psychiatric evaluation's recommendations.

B. The importance of follow-through on the assessment recommendations for the client was emphasized with the parents.

C. The parents and the client were confronted for their inconsistent follow-through on the assessment recommendations.

D. The client and the parents reported following through on each of the recommendations of the evaluation and were given positive verbal affirmation for their efforts.

PHYSICAL/EMOTIONAL ABUSE VICTIM

CLIENT PRESENTATION

1. Confirmed Report of Physical Abuse by an Adult (1)*

A. The client's self-report of being assaulted by his/her parent has been confirmed by a Children's Protective Services worker.

B. The client's parent reported that the other parent has physically assaulted the client on more than one occasion

C. The client provided a detailed account of the assault by his/her parent and the resulting injuries.

D. The physical abuse reported by the client was reported to Children's Protective Services as required by mandatory reporting statutes.

2. Evidence of Victimization (2)

A. Bruises were evident on the client's body.

B. The client worked to explain away the injuries on his/her body, refusing to blame an adult for inflicting the injuries.

C. Past records of bruises and wounds revealed the extent of the client's victimization.

D. Since coming into treatment, the client has not reported receiving any bruises or wounds from his/her caregivers.

3. Fearful/Withdrawn (3)

A. The client appeared very fearful and withdrawn from others and avoids all but necessary interpersonal contacts.

B. Fear seems to dominate the client's contacts with others.

C. The client verbalized fear of further physical abuse by the caregiver.

D. Since establishing trust in counseling the client has started to be less fearful and withdrawn and a little more open about him/herself.

4. Closed/Detached (3)

A. The client presented in a closed and detached manner with little visible interest in others or things.

B. The client showed little interest in the counseling process and was careful not to reveal anything significant about him/herself.

C. The client seemed very closed and made a conscious effort to keep others at a safe distance and in the dark about him/herself.

D. Since establishing a relationship with the therapist, the client has started to be less fearful and more open about himself/herself.

---

* The numbers in parentheses correlate to the number of the Behavioral Definition statement in the companion chapter with same title in *The Child Psychotherapy Treatment Planner* (Jongsma, Peterson, and McInnis) by John Wiley & Sons, 2000.

5. Mistrustful/Anxious (3)

A. The client has a mistrustful, anxious manner when he/she interacts with others.

B. The client's body language and facial expressions seemed to indicate a high level of mistrust with others, especially adults.

C. The client reported a history of not being able to trust adults in his/her family because they rarely did what they said they would and often harmed him/her.

D. The client has begun to verbalize some connections between childhood pain and present attitudes of detachment and fear of others.

6. Low Self-Esteem (3)

A. The client's self-image seemed to be very low as he/she seldom made eye contact and frequently made self-disparaging remarks.

B. The client reported feeling worthless and unloved for as long as he/she can remember.

C. The client's experience in the accepting environment of counseling has started to boost his/her sense of self-esteem.

7. Angry/Aggressive (4)

A. The client has an angry, aggressive manner that is obvious to nearly everyone.

B. The client reported an increase in the frequency and severity of angry, aggressive behavior toward peers and adults.

C. Client projected the blame for his/her aggressive behaviors onto others.

D. The client described having a quick temper, which has resulted in his/her destroying many of his/her own possessions.

E. There has been a sharp decrease in the client's anger and aggressiveness since he/she started to disclose about his/her being physically and emotionally abused.

F. The client has begun to realize how his/her anger and aggression are the result of what he/she saw and experienced in his/her home as a child.

8. Recollections of the Abuse (5)

A. The client indicated he/she felt constantly haunted by the distressing memories of his/her past emotional and physical abuse.

B. The client reported that the memories of abuse intrude on his/her consciousness under a variety of circumstances.

C. The client described a chaotic childhood in which he/she was the victim of ongoing emotional and physical abuse.

D. The incidences of intrusive thoughts of the abuse has significantly diminished.

E. The client has begun to verbalize some connections between childhood pain and present attitudes of detachment and fear of others.

9. Strong Feelings When around Perpetrator (6)

A. The client indicated feeling intense anger and rage whenever he/she comes into contact with the perpetrator of his/her childhood abuse.

B. The caregivers have reported that the client becomes tearful and fearful immediately when the perpetrator of his/her childhood abuse is near.

C. The client expressed that he/she experiences mixed feelings of fear, anger, and rage whenever he/she encounters the perpetrator.

D. The client indicated he/she noticed that since talking in therapy, his/her feelings are not as intense or scary when he/she comes into contact with the perpetrator.

10. Depressed/Irritable (7)

A. The client presented with a depressed mood and manner that contained an irritable edge.

B. Between the client's depression and accompanying irritability, he/she was not willing or able to disclose about him/herself in counseling session.

C. The client reported a pattern of social withdrawal and detachment from feelings.

D. Since starting on antidepressant medication, the client's depression and irritability have decreased and he/she is beginning to self-disclose in counseling sessions.

11. Passive/Apathetic (7)

A. There was a strong passive, apathetic quality to the client that reflects little interest in what might happen to self or others.

B. Because of his/her apathetic, passive manner, the client showed little interest in the counseling process.

C. The client reported that as far back as he/she can remember he/she has not been concerned about what happens to him/her.

D. The client has exhibited less apathy and passivity since becoming more actively involved in therapy.

12. Regressive Behavior (8)

A. The client presented with numerous regressive behaviors such as baby talk and thumb sucking.

B. The client reported that he/she has begun to wet the bed since the abuse began.

C. Since beginning to share his/her physical and emotional abusive past, the client's regressive behaviors are reported to be decreasing.

13. Sleep Disturbance (9)

A. The client reported having difficulties with falling asleep, waking up frequently, and feeling tired and unrested in the morning.

B. The client indicated he/she has been experiencing frequent night terrors and recurrent nightmares.

C. The client has started to talk about the abuse he/she experienced in childhood and is now reporting less night terrors and more restful sleep.

D. The client has begun making connections between his/her sleeping difficulties and his/her history of being abused.

14. Running Away (10)

A. The client reported running away from home on several occasions to escape from the physical abuse.

B. It seems the client has used running away as an attempt to draw attention to the abusiveness in his/her home.

C. There has not been an incident of running away since the abuse of the client started to be addressed.

INTERVENTIONS IMPLEMENTED

1. Build Trust (1)*

A. A level of trust was built with the client through use of unconditional positive regard.

B. Warm acceptance and active listening techniques were used to establish trust with the client and thereby enable him/her to express feelings and facts around the abuse.

C. The client has formed a trust-based relationship that has increased his/her ability to express facts and feelings about the abuse.

D. Despite the use of unconditional positive regard, warm acceptance, and active listening, the client remains hesitant to share feelings and facts about the abuse.

2. Clarify Facts of the Abuse (2)

A. The client was assisted in clarifying and expressing the facts associated with the abuse.

B. Support and encouragement were given to the client to increase his/her level of disclosure of the facts around the abuse.

C. Even with support and encouragement being given to the client, he/she still had difficulty expressing and clarifying the facts about the abuse.

D. The client openly outlined the facts associated with the most recent incident of his/her being a victim of abuse.

3. Utilize Individual Play Therapy (3)

A. Individual play therapy was utilized to provide an environment that would give the client the opportunity to reveal facts and feelings surrounding the abuse.

B. The client willingly participated in the individual play-therapy session.

C. The client's play has been guarded and cautious during the play-therapy sessions, and he/she has avoided sharing any facts or feelings about the abuse.

D. Through the client's active participation in individual play-therapy sessions, he/she has begun to share some facts and feelings about the abuse.

4. Report Physical Abuse (4)

A. An assessment was conducted on the client to substantiate the nature and extent of the physical abuse.

B. The client was sent to a physician to confirm and document the physical abuse.

C. The physical abuse of the client was reported to the state child protection agency for further investigation.

D. The parents were notified about the client's revelation of physical abuse and that, as required by law, it has been reported to the state child protection agency for investigation.

---

* The numbers in parentheses correlate to the number of the Therapeutic Interventions statement in the companion chapter with same title in *The Child Psychotherapy Treatment Planner* (Jongsma, Peterson, and McInnis) by John Wiley & Sons, 2000.

5. Assess Veracity of Charges (5)

A. The client's family, physician, and criminal justice officials were consulted to assess the truthfulness of the client's allegations of physical abuse.

B. The truthfulness of the client's allegations regarding physical abuse was confirmed by his/her family, physician, and child protective services worker.

C. Consultation with the family, physician, and child protection service worker resulted in divided opinions regarding the veracity of the client's allegations of abuse.

6. Assess for Removal from Home (6)

A. The family environment was assessed to determine if it was safe for the client.

B. The family environment was determined to be unsafe for the client and he/she was moved to a safe, temporary placement outside the home.

C. After the family environment was assessed, a recommendation was made that a temporary restraining order be sought for the perpetrator.

7. Make Home Safe for Children (7)

A. The perpetrator agreed to move out of the home and not visit until the parents and protective service worker give their approval.

B. It was recommended to the nonabusive parent to seek a restraining order against the perpetrator.

C. The nonabusive parent was assisted in obtaining a restraining order and implementing it on a consistent basis.

D. The parent was monitored and supported for consistent implementation of "no contact" agreement between the perpetrator and the victim.

E. The parent was confronted on his/her inconsistent enforcement of restraining order to keep the perpetrator from the presence of the client.

8. Explore Expression of Feelings about Abuse (8)

A. The client's feelings toward the perpetrator were identified and explored.

B. Encouragement and support were given to the client as he/she was assisted in expressing and clarifying his/her feelings associated with the abuse experiences.

C. Even with support and encouragement, the client had difficulty clarifying and expressing any feelings about the abuse experiences.

D. The client expressed pain, anger, and fear as he/she told the story of the abuse.

9. Complete "My Thoughts and Feelings" Exercise (9)

A. The client was asked to complete and process the "My Thoughts and Feelings" exercise from *The Brief Adolescent Therapy Treatment Planner* (Jongsma, Peterson, and McInnis) to help him/her practice openness.

B. The client was reminded that openness leads to health and secrecy leads to staying sick.

C. The client's barriers to being more open were explored, identified, and removed.

D. The client was open in his/her expression of thoughts and feelings.

E. The client remains emotionally shut down and unwilling to express feelings openly.

10. Reassure Client of Protection (10)

A. The client was repeatedly reassured of concern and care of others in keeping him/her safe from further abuse.

B. The client was reassured by the parents and others that they were looking out for his/her safety.

C. The client's anxiety level seems to be diminished as he/she has accepted reassurance of safety.

11. Confront Denial of Family and Perpetrator (11)

A. Family sessions were conducted in which the family's denial of the client's abuse was confronted and challenged.

B. The perpetrator was asked to list all of his/her rationalizations for the abuse.

C. Confrontation was used to process the perpetrator's list of rationalizations for the abuse.

D. Confrontation was used with the perpetrator to break through his/her denial of abusing the client.

E. The use of confrontation and challenges has been effective in breaking through the perpetrator's denial and he/she is now taking ownership and responsibility for the abuse.

F. The perpetrator remains in denial of abusing the client in spite of confrontation and challenge to his/her rationalizations.

12. Confront Client Excusing Perpetrator Abuse (12)

A. The client was asked to create and process a list of reasons why he/she was abused by the perpetrator.

B. Each time the client made an excuse for the perpetrator's abuse he/she was confronted and reminded that he/she in no way deserved being abused.

C. The message was given to the client that even though he/she is not perfect the abuse was not deserved.

D. The client continued to excuse the perpetrator for the abuse and engaged in self-blame.

E. The client has begun to place clear responsibility for the abuse on the perpetrator and has discontinued self-blame.

13. Reassure That Abuse Not Deserved

A. The client was reassured that the physical abuse he/she received was in no way deserved no matter what he/she had done wrong, if anything.

B. The message of not deserving the abuse no matter what happened was consistently given to the client.

C. The client was educated regarding his/her deserving personal respect and controlled responses in punishment situations.

14. Reinforce Holding Perpetrator Responsible (14)

A. All statements by the client which hold the perpetrator responsible for the abuse were reinforced.

B. The client was asked to list all of the reasons why the perpetrator was responsible for the abuse.

C. The client was reminded that regardless of any misbehavior on his/her part it was still the perpetrator's fault for the abuse.

D. The client has consistently made statements putting responsibility for the abuse firmly on the perpetrator.

15. Confront Perpetrator about Abuse (15)

A. The client was prepared in order to build his/her confidence to confront the perpetrator with the abuse in a family session.

B. Role play was used with the client to provide him/her with experience in confronting the perpetrator.

C. Family sessions were conducted in which the parents and the client confronted the perpetrator with the abuse.

D. Confrontation of the perpetrator with the abuse was modeled by the parents in family sessions.

E. In the family session the client read a letter that he/she had written outlining the reasons why the perpetrator was responsible for the abuse.

16. Facilitate Perpetrator Apology (16)

A. The client was assessed as to his/her readiness to hear and accept an apology from the perpetrator.

B. The perpetrator's apology was processed for genuineness and level of honesty.

C. A family session was conducted in which the perpetrator apologized to the client and family for the abuse.

17. Counsel Parents on Boundaries (17)

A. The client's parents were counseled on what are and what are not appropriate discipline boundaries.

B. Past inappropriate disciplinary boundaries that allowed for abusive punishment were addressed and new appropriate boundaries established.

C. New appropriate boundaries for nonabusive, reasonable discipline were monitored for the parents' honoring and enforcing them.

D. The parents reported that they have successfully implemented disciplinary measures that are nonabusive and reasonable.

18. Perpetrator Group Referral (18)

A. The perpetrator attended and participated in the required effective parenting and anger management groups.

B. The gains made by the perpetrator in the group were monitored and reinforced.

C. The perpetrator was confronted on his/her noncompliance with attending required groups.

19. Perpetrator Psychological Evaluation/Treatment Referral (19)

A. The perpetrator was referred for a psychological evaluation.

B. The perpetrator cooperated with all aspects of the evaluation.

C. All treatment recommendations of the evaluation were given and explained to the perpetrator.

D. The perpetrator was asked to make a commitment to follow through on each of the treatment recommendations of the evaluation.

20. **Assess Parents' List of Appropriate Disciplines (20)**
A. The parents were asked to list all the acts of appropriate discipline they could envision.
B. The parents' list of appropriate disciplinary behavior was reviewed, with reasonable approaches being encouraged and reinforced.
C. The parents were monitored for their use of discipline techniques that reinforce reasonable, respectful actions and appropriate boundaries.
D. The parents were confronted and redirected when discipline was not reasonable and respectful.

21. **Construct Genogram That Identifies Abuse (21)**
A. A multigeneration family genogram was constructed with the family members.
B. The family members were assisted in identifying patterns of physical abuse from the multigenerational family genogram.
C. Ways to begin breaking the physically abusive family patterns were identified and implemented by family members.
D. The family members acknowledged that the pattern of multigenerational physical abuse is existent and vowed to stop this pattern within their own family.

22. **Assess Family Stress Factors (22)**
A. Family dynamics were assessed to identify stress factors and events that may have contributed to the abuse.
B. The family members were assisted in identifying effective ways to cope with stress in order to reduce the probability of abuse.
C. The family was directed to key community and professional resources that could assist in effectively coping with family stressors.
D. The family members were assisted in identifying steps to take to reduce environmental stressors that may contribute to the precipitation of violence.

23. **Evaluate Family for Substance Abuse (23)**
A. Family sessions were conducted to assess issues of substance use and abuse within the family.
B. The parents were referred for a substance abuse assessment.
C. The parents cooperated and completed the requested substance abuse assessments.
D. Efforts to assess the issue of substance abuse and use within the family were met with denial and resistance.

24. **Perpetrator Substance Abuse Treatment Referral (24)**
A. The perpetrator was referred to a substance abuse program.
B. The perpetrator successfully completed a substance abuse program and is now involved in aftercare.

C. The perpetrator was referred but refused to follow through on completing a substance abuse program.

25. Assign Letter to Perpetrator (25)

A. The client was asked to write a letter to the perpetrator expressing his/her feelings of hurt, fear, and anger.

B. The completed letter to the perpetrator was processed, providing the client with assistance and support in expressing the feelings connected to the abuse.

C. The client's inability to complete the assigned letter was explored with blocks being identified and processed.

D. The client was asked to write the letter expressing his/her feelings about the abuse to the perpetrator but refused to do so, saying that he/she did not want to feel those feelings again.

26. Assign Forgiveness Letter or Exercise (26)

A. The client was educated on the key aspects of forgiveness, with special emphasis being given to the power involved.

B. The client was asked to complete a forgiveness letter to the perpetrator while asserting the right to safety.

C. The client was given a forgiveness exercise to complete and to process in the next session.

D. The assigned letter of forgiveness was processed and the evident empowerment provided by the experience was reinforced.

27. Assign Letting-Go Exercise (27)

A. The potential benefits of the process of letting go of anger and hurt were explored with the client.

B. A letting-go exercise was assigned in which the client would bury an anger list about the perpetrator.

C. The letting-go exercise was processed with the client and feelings were identified and expressed.

D. The client struggles with letting go of feelings of hurt and anger and is not able to reach this goal as yet.

E. The client reports that he/she has successfully let go of his/her feelings of hurt and anger regarding being an abuse survivor.

28. Interrupt Anger and Aggression Triggered by Perpetrator (28)

A. Expressions of anger and aggression by the client were interpreted as triggered by feelings toward the perpetrator.

B. Displays of seemingly unrelated anger and aggression were reflected to the client as indications of how angry he/she must be toward the perpetrator.

C. The client's general displays of anger and aggression have diminished as he/she has developed insight into his/her feelings of anger focused on the perpetrator.

29. Reinforce Family Support and Nurture (29)

A. Family members were taught the importance of emotional support and nurturing to the client and how they each could provide it for him/her.

B. Positive reinforcement was given to family members for incidents of support and nurturing given to the client.

C. The family position that the client should forget the abuse now and move on was confronted and processed, with members being reminded of the client's need for ongoing support and nurturing in order to fully heal.

30. Identify a Basis for Self-Esteem (30)

A. The client's talents, importance to others, and spiritual value were reviewed with him/her to assist in identifying a basis for self-worth.

B. The client was asked to verbally affirm each of his/her positive strengths and attributes that were identified.

C. Positive self-talk was developed around the client's strengths and attributes that he/she could use on a daily basis to affirm himself/herself.

31. Formulate Future Plans (31)

A. The client was probed to determine what future plans he/she has developed.

B. The client was asked to complete the following sentence items: I imagine that ____, I will ____, I dream that someday ____, to assist and encourage the idea of future plans.

C. The client was encouraged to include interaction with peers and family as part of his/her future plans.

D. The client struggled to envision any future plans despite assistance and encouragement to do so.

32. Reinforce Positive Statements (32)

A. Every positive self-descriptive statement made by the client was affirmed and reinforced.

B. The client's negative statements about him/herself were confronted and reframed.

C. The pattern of the client making more positive than negative self-statements was recognized, reinforced, and encouraged to continue in that direction.

33. Reinforce Self-Worth (33)

A. Unconditional positive regard, genuine warmth, and active listening were used to reinforce the client's self-worth.

B. Large doses of praise for any accomplishment by the client were used to reinforce his/her self-worth.

C. The pattern of the client making more positive than negative self statements was recognized, reinforced, and encouraged to continue in that direction.

34. Encourage Participation in Activities (34)

A. The client was encouraged to actively participate in peer group interaction and extracurricular activities.

B. The client's excuses and barriers to increased social involvement were explored and removed.

C. Situations involving peer groups and extracurricular activities were role-played with the client to build his/her social skills and confidence level in social situations.

D. Despite encouragement and social skill building, the client remains resistant to peer group and extracurricular activity participation.

35. Identify Self-Protection Strategies (35)

A. Various actions for the client to take to protect himself/herself from future abuse were identified and reinforced.

B. Efforts were made to empower the client to take necessary steps to protect him/herself if the situation warranted it.

C. The client was "bombarded" with statements of empowerment regarding protecting him/herself.

36. Complete "Letter of Empowerment" Exercise (36)

A. The client was asked to complete the "Letter of Empowerment" exercise from *The Brief Adolescent Therapy Homework Planner* (Jongsma, Peterson, McInnis) to assist him/her in expressing thoughts and feelings around abuse.

B. Unconditional positive regard and active listening were used to help the client express his/her thoughts and feelings about the abuse.

C. Barriers and defenses of the client that prevent expression of thoughts and feelings about the abuse were identified, addressed, and removed.

D. Efforts to encourage the client to express thoughts and feelings about the abuse have not been effective, and the client remains closed regarding the abuse.

E. The client completed the "Letter of Empowerment" exercise and reported that it has helped him/her express his/her thoughts and feelings about the abuse.

F. The client has failed to complete the empowerment exercise and was redirected to do so.

37. Explore Loss of Trust in Adults (37)

A. The client was encouraged to express his/her loss of trust in adults.

B. The client was assisted in connecting his/her loss of trust to the perpetrator's abuse and others' failure to protect him/her.

C. The client rejected assistance in identifying and expressing loss of trust and stood firm that he/she still trusts adults.

38. Teach Discriminating Trust Judgments (38)

A. The client was educated in the process of making discriminating judgments of trusting people.

B. The client was assisted in identifying key factors that make some people trustworthy and those that make others untrustworthy.

C. Various scenarios of individuals were presented to the client to practice his/her trust-discrimination skills.

39. Teach Share-Check Technique (39)

A. The share-check technique was taught to the client to increase his/her skills in assessing an individual's trustworthiness.

B. Role-play situations were used with the client to build his/her skill and confidence in using the share-check technique.

C. The client was asked to make a commitment to using the share-check technique and reporting results of the experience.

D. The client reported success at using the share-check method of gradually building trust in others.

40. Victim Support Group Referral (40)

A. The benefits of the client attending a support group were identified and discussed.

B. The client was referred to a support group for teens who have been abused to decrease his/her feelings of being the only one in this situation.

C. The client's experience of attending a support group with the others who are in the same situation was processed.

D. The client indicated that he/she felt different from all the others in the support group.

E. The client reported feeling empowered and understood after having attended a support group of fellow survivors of abuse.

41. Assign Drawing Pictures of Self (41)

A. The client was asked to draw pictures that reflect how he/she feels about him/herself.

B. The client drew detailed pictures about how he/she feels about self.

C. With encouragement the client drew several vague, undetailed pictures of self.

D. The client willingly talked about each of the pictures he/she drew, identifying specific feelings about him/herself.

E. The client refused to do such "stupid, childish things" like drawing pictures.

42. Assign Drawing Faces of Self (42)

A. The client was asked to draw pictures of his/her own face before, during, and after the abuse occurred.

B. The client drew three faces in detail and, as the drawings were explained, the feelings that he/she had experienced.

C. The client attempted but could not draw the faces to reflect how he/she felt before, during, and after the abuse occurred.

43. Employ Child-Centered Play Therapy (43)

A. Child-centered approaches of genuine interest and unconditional positive regard were employed to provide the client with the supportive environment needed to resolve his/her feelings of fear, guilt, grief, and rage surrounding the abuse.

B. The feelings revealed during the play-therapy session were consistently reflected back to the client.

C. Consistent trust was communicated to the client that the direction of his/her play would promote the resolution of the fear and rage connected with his/her abuse.

D. The client's active participation in the child-centered play-therapy sessions has resulted in him/her beginning to resolve feelings surrounding the abuse.

44. Employ Psychoanalytic Play Therapy (44)

A. Psychoanalytic play-therapy principles were utilized to help the client overcome the feelings of fear, rage, guilt, and low self-esteem connected to the abuse.

B. The client was allowed to take the lead during today's therapy session in exploring the issues connected with the abuse.

C. The client's resistance, transference, and core depression were interpreted, using psychoanalytic play-therapy principles to assist him/her in overcoming the feelings of fear, guilt, rage, and low-self esteem connected to his/her abuse.

D. The use of psychoanalytic play therapy has helped the client begin to resolve the fear, guilt, rage, and low self-esteem issues connected to the abuse.

POSTTRAUMATIC STRESS DISORDER

CLIENT PRESENTATION

1. Traumatic Event (1)*

A. The client described a traumatic experience in which he/she had exposure to actual or threatened death.

B. The client described a traumatic experience that resulted in serious injury to self and/or others.

C. The client described a history of being physically and/or sexually abused.

D. The client was open and talkative about the traumatic event(s).

E. The client was guarded and reluctant to talk about the traumatic event(s).

2. Intrusive, Distressing Thoughts (2)

A. The client reported that he/she has experienced frequent intrusive, distressing thoughts or images about the traumatic event.

B. The client was visibly upset when describing the distressing images of the traumatic event.

C. The frequency and intensity of the client's intrusive, distressing thoughts or images have started to decrease as he/she works through his/her thoughts and feelings about the traumatic event.

D. The client denied experiencing any recent intrusive, distressing thoughts or images about the traumatic event.

3. Disturbing Dreams (3)

A. The client reported experiencing frequent nightmares or distressing dreams since the traumatic event first occurred.

B. The client has continued to be troubled by disturbing dreams associated with the trauma.

C. The client has experienced a mild reduction in the frequency of the disturbing dreams.

D. The client has not experienced any disturbing dreams about the traumatic event since the last therapy session.

4. Flashbacks, Hallucinations, Illusions (4)

A. The client reported experiencing numerous flashbacks, hallucinations, or illusions that the traumatic event is recurring.

B. The client experienced a flashback or hallucination during today's therapy session when discussing the traumatic event.

C. The frequency of the client's flashbacks, hallucinations, or illusions have started to decrease as he/she makes productive use of therapy.

D. The client denied experiencing any recent flashbacks, hallucinations, or illusions.

* The numbers in parentheses correlate to the number of the Behavioral Definition statement in the companion chapter with same title in *The Child Psychotherapy Treatment Planner* (Jongsma, Peterson, and McInnis) by John Wiley & Sons, 2000.

5. Intense Emotional Distress (5)

A. The client has experienced a significant amount of emotional distress and turmoil since the traumatic event first occurred.

B. The client was visibly distressed and upset when discussing the traumatic event.

C. The intensity of the client's emotional distress when discussing the traumatic event has started to diminish.

D. The client has been able to talk about the traumatic event without displaying a significant amount of emotional distress.

6. Strong Physiological Reaction (6)

A. The client reported that he/she often exhibits an intense physiological reaction (e.g., trembling and shaking, palpitations, dizziness, shortness of breath, sweating) when reminded of the traumatic event.

B. The client demonstrated a strong physiological reaction (e.g., trembling and shaking, shortness of breath, sweating) when discussing the traumatic event in today's therapy session.

C. The client's negative physiological reactions have started to decrease in intensity when talking about the traumatic event.

D. The client did not experience any negative physiological reaction when discussing the traumatic event.

7. Avoidance of Talking about Trauma (7)

A. The client has avoided conversations about the trauma and tries to also avoid thinking about it.

B. In an attempt to avoid the feelings associated with the trauma, the client has resisted talking about it.

C. The parents report that the client refuses to discuss the traumatic event.

D. The client's general avoidance of the subject of the trauma has waned and he/she is willing to discuss it briefly.

E. The client is now able to think about, talk about, and experience feelings about the trauma without fear of being overwhelmed.

8. Avoidance of Activities Associated with Trauma (8)

A. The client has avoided engaging in activities, going places, or interacting with people associated with the traumatic event.

B. The client acknowledged that he/she avoids activities, places, or people that remind him/her of the traumatic event because of the fear of being overwhelmed by powerful emotions.

C. The client has started to tolerate exposure to activities, places, or people that remind him/her of the traumatic event without feeling overwhelmed.

D. The client has returned to a pretrauma level of functioning without avoiding people or places associated with the traumatic event.

9. Limited Recall (9)

A. The client reported that he/she is unable to recall some important aspects of the traumatic event.

B. The client's emotional distress has been so great that he/she is unable to recall many details of the traumatic event.

C. The client has started to recall some of the important details of the traumatic event.

D. The client recalled most of the important aspects of the traumatic event.

10. Lack of Interest (10)

A. The client has displayed little interest in activities that normally brought him/her pleasure before the traumatic event.

B. The client has significantly reduced his/her participation in social or extracurricular activities since the traumatic event.

C. The client verbalized little to no interest in socializing or participating in extracurricular activities.

D. The client has started to participate in more social or extracurricular activities.

E. The client has participated in social or extracurricular activities on a regular, consistent basis.

11. Social Detachment (11)

A. The client has become more withdrawn since the traumatic event first occurred.

B. The client appeared aloof and detached in today's therapy session.

C. The client has started to socialize with a wider circle of peers.

D. The client has become more outgoing and interacts with his/her peers on a regular, consistent basis.

12. Emotionally Constricted (12)

A. The client has generally appeared flat and constricted in his/her emotional presentation since the traumatic event.

B. The client's affect appeared flat and constricted when talking about the traumatic event.

C. The client acknowledged that he/she is reluctant to share his/her deeper emotions pertaining to the traumatic event because of the fear of losing control of his/her emotions.

D. The client has started to show a wider range of emotions about the traumatic event in the therapy sessions.

E. The client has been able to express his/her genuine emotions about the traumatic event without feeling overwhelmed.

13. Pessimistic Outlook (13)

A. The client has developed a pessimistic outlook on the future and often feels overwhelmed by feelings of helplessness and hopelessness.

B. The client verbalized feelings of helplessness and hopelessness during today's therapy session.

C. The client has gradually begun to develop a brighter outlook on the future.

D. The client expressed a renewed sense of hope for the future in today's therapy session.

E. The client's willingness to assert himself/herself and assume healthy risks reflected his/her renewed sense of hope and feelings of empowerment.

14. Sleep Disturbance (14)

A. The client has experienced significant disturbances in his/her sleep pattern since the traumatic event.

B. The client reported having problems falling asleep.

C. The client has experienced frequent early morning awakenings.

D. The client reported recent improvements in his/her sleep.

E. The client reported experiencing a return to his/her normal sleep pattern.

15. Irritability (15)

A. The client has displayed irritability and moodiness since the trauma occurred.

B. The client's irritability has resulted in many incidents of verbal outbursts of anger over small issues.

C. The parents reported that the client reacts irritably to minor stimuli.

D. The client has become less irritable as the trauma is processed and underlying feelings are resolved.

16. Lack of Concentration (16)

A. The client has not been able to maintain concentration on schoolwork or other tasks.

B. The parents and teachers report that the client is having difficulty maintaining concentration since the traumatic event.

C. The client stated that his/her concentration is interrupted by flashbacks of the traumatic incident.

D. The client's concentration is becoming more focused as the feelings surrounding the trauma are resolved.

17. Hypervigilance/Mistrustfulness (17)

A. The client has developed a deep mistrust of others because of the traumatic event.

B. The client described himself/herself as being overly vigilant when he/she goes out into public places because of his/her fear of possible harm or danger.

C. The client appeared guarded and mistrustful during today's therapy session.

D. The client has slowly begun to develop trust and gained acceptance from several individuals.

E. The client's increased trust in others has helped to stabilize his/her mood and allowed him/her to work through many of his/her thoughts and feelings about the traumatic event.

18. Anxiety/Fearfulness (17)

A. The traumatic event has been a significant contributing factor to the client's high level of anxiety and fearfulness.

B. The client appeared visibly anxious and fearful when discussing the traumatic event.

C. The intensity of the client's anxiety and fearfulness has started to diminish when he/she talks about the traumatic event.

D. The client has demonstrated a marked decreased in the frequency and intensity of his/her anxious moods and fearfulness.

19. **Exaggerated Startle Response (18)**

A. The client has often displayed an exaggerated startle response when exposed to any sudden, unexpected stimuli.

B. The client displayed an exaggerated startle response in today's therapy session.

C. The client reported that he/she does not startle as easily or dramatically when exposed to unexpected stimuli.

20. **Symptom Duration over One Month (19)**

A. The symptoms that formed in reaction to the traumatic event have been present in the client for more than one month.

B. Although the traumatic event occurred many months ago, the symptom pattern has been present only for the past several weeks.

C. The parents reported that the client's symptoms seemed to have started immediately after the traumatic event several months ago.

D. The client's symptoms have been gradually improving since treatment began.

E. The client reported being free of all symptoms associated with the traumatic incident.

21. **Guilt (20)**

A. The client has been troubled by strong feelings of guilt since the traumatic event first occurred.

B. The client expressed feelings of guilt about surviving, causing, or not preventing the traumatic event.

C. The client has begun to work through and resolve his/her feelings of guilt about the traumatic event.

D. The client verbally denied experiencing any feelings of guilt about the traumatic event.

E. The client has successfully resolved his/her feelings of guilt about the traumatic event.

22. **Depression (20)**

A. The client reported experiencing a significant amount of depression and unhappiness since the traumatic event first occurred.

B. The client expressed strong feelings of sadness and hurt about the traumatic event.

C. The client's level of depression has begun to diminish as he/she works through many of his/her thoughts and feelings about the traumatic event.

D. The client did not appear sad or depressed when talking about the traumatic event

E. The frequency and intensity of the client's depressed moods have decreased significantly.

23. **Low Self-Esteem (20)**

A. The client's self-esteem has decreased significantly since the traumatic event.

B. The client verbalized feelings of low self-esteem, inadequacy, and insecurity.

C. The client has begun to take steps to improve his/her self-esteem and develop a positive self-image.

D. The client verbalized positive self-descriptive statements during today's therapy session.

E. The client has worked through many of his/her feelings surrounding the traumatic event and has developed a healthy self-image.

24. Angry Outbursts/Aggression (21)

A. The client described a persistent pattern of exhibiting intense outbursts of rage or becoming physically aggressive.

B. The client expressed strong feelings of anger and rage about the traumatic event.

C. The client has recently struggled to control his/her hostile/aggressive impulses.

D. The client was able to talk about the traumatic event with much less anger and resentment.

E. The frequency and severity of the client's angry outbursts and aggressive behaviors have decreased significantly.

INTERVENTIONS IMPLEMENTED

1. Build Therapeutic Trust (1)*

A. The focus of today's therapy session was on building the level of trust with the client through consistent eye contact, active listening, unconditional positive regard, and warm acceptance.

B. The client received unconditional positive regard and warm acceptance to help increase his/her ability to identify and express feelings connected to the traumatic event.

C. The therapy session was helpful in building the level of trust with the client.

D. The therapy session did not prove to be helpful in building the level of trust with the client as he/she remained guarded in talking about the traumatic event.

2. Explore Facts of Traumatic Event (2)

A. The client was gently encouraged to tell the entire story of the traumatic event.

B. The client was given the opportunity to share what he/she recalls about the traumatic event.

C. Today's therapy session explored the sequence of events before, during, and after the traumatic event.

3. Probe Emotional Reaction during Trauma (3)

A. Today's therapy session explored the client's emotional reaction at the time of the trauma.

B. The client was able to recall the fear that he/she had experienced at the time of the traumatic incident.

* The numbers in parentheses correlate to the number of the Therapeutic Interventions statement in the companion chapter with same title in *The Child Psychotherapy Treatment Planner* (Jongsma, Peterson, and McInnis) by John Wiley & Sons, 2000.

C. The client was able to recall the feelings of hurt, anger, and sadness that he/she had experienced during the traumatic incident.

D. The client was unable to recall the emotions that he/she experienced during the traumatic incident.

E. A child-centered therapy approach was used to explore the client's emotional reaction at the time of the traumatic incident.

4. Identify Negative Impact of Traumatic Event (4)

A. The client was asked how the traumatic event has negatively impacted his/her life.

B. The client's current level of functioning was compared to his/her pretrauma level of functioning.

C. The client identified various ways that the traumatic event has negatively impacted his/her life.

D. The client shared how the traumatic event has caused him/her to experience a considerable amount of emotional distress.

E. The client shared that the traumatic event has caused him/her to become more isolated and mistrustful of others.

5. Explore Effects of PTSD Symptoms (5)

A. Today's therapy session explored the effects that the PTSD symptoms have had on the client's personal relationships, functioning at school, and social/recreational life.

B. The client acknowledged that his/her erratic and unpredictable shifts in mood have placed a significant strain on his/her interpersonal relationships.

C. The client identified how the traumatic event has had a negative impact on his/her school functioning.

D. The client verbally recognized how he/she has become more detached and has engaged in significantly fewer social/recreational activities since the traumatic event.

6. Assess Anger Control (6)

A. A history of the client's anger control problems was taken in today's therapy session.

B. The client shared instances where his/her poor control of anger resulted in verbal threats of violence, actual harm or injury to others, or destruction of property.

C. The client identified events or situations that frequently trigger a loss of control of his/her anger.

D. The client was asked to identify the common targets of his/her anger to help gain greater insight into the factors contributing to his/her lack of control.

E. Today's therapy session helped the client realize how his/her anger control problems are often associated with underlying, painful emotions about the traumatic event.

7. Teach Anger Management Techniques (7)

A. The client was taught mediational and self-control strategies to help improve his/her anger control.

B. The client was taught guided imagery and relaxation techniques to help improve his/her anger control.

C. Role-playing and modeling techniques were used to demonstrate effective ways for the client to control anger.

D. The client was strongly encouraged to express his/her anger through controlled, respectful verbalizations and healthy physical outlets.

E. A reward system was designed to reinforce the client for demonstrating good anger control.

8. Teach Deep-Muscle Relaxation (8)

A. The client was taught deep-muscle relaxation methods along with deep breathing and positive imagery to induce relaxation and decrease his/her emotional distress.

B. The client reported a positive response to the use of deep-muscle relaxation methods and positive imagery techniques to help feel more relaxed and less distressed.

C. The client appeared uncomfortable and unable to relax when being instructed in the use of deep-muscle relaxation and guided imagery techniques.

9. Utilize EMG Biofeedback (9)

A. EMG biofeedback was utilized to help increase the depth of the client's relaxation.

B. The client seemed more relaxed after the use of EMG biofeedback to reduce the intensity of his/her emotional distress.

C. The client showed little to no improvement in his/her ability to relax through the use of EMG biofeedback.

10. Teach Relaxation Techniques to Help Induce Sleep (10)

A. The client was instructed to utilize relaxation techniques to help induce calm before attempting to go to sleep.

B. The client and the parents were encouraged to utilize the *Relaxation Imagery for Children* tape (Weinstock) to help the client induce calm before attempting to go to sleep.

C. The client and his/her parents were encouraged to use the *Magic Island: Relaxation for Kids* tape (Mehling, Highstein, and Delamarter) to help the client induce calm before attempting to go to sleep.

D. The client and parents reported that the relaxation tapes have been helpful to the client in inducing calm and allowing him/her to fall asleep much sooner.

E. The client reported that he/she has continued to have trouble falling asleep even after using the relaxation tapes.

11. Implement Systematic Desensitization (11)

A. An imaginal, systematic desensitization program, utilizing positive guided imagery, was designed to help reduce the client's emotional reactivity to the traumatic event.

B. The client verbally agreed to follow through with the implementation of the imaginal systematic desensitization program in therapy sessions.

C. The client reported that the use of imaginal systematic desensitization and positive guided imagery has helped to significantly reduce his/her emotional reactivity to the traumatic event.

D. The client reported a minimal reduction in his/her emotional reactivity to the traumatic event after use of imaginal systematic desensitization.

E. The client has not experienced a decrease in the reduction of his/her emotional reactivity to the traumatic event as a result of the use of the imaginal systematic desensitization program.

12. Explore Feelings Surrounding Traumatic Event (12)

A. Today's therapy session explored the client's feelings before, during, and after the traumatic event.

B. The client was given support and affirmation when retelling the story of the traumatic event.

C. The retelling of the traumatic incident helped to reduce the client's emotional distress.

D. The client has continued to exhibit a significant amount of emotional distress when telling the story of the traumatic event.

13. Identify Negative Self-Talk (13)

A. Today's therapy session identified how the client's negative self-talk and pessimistic outlook are associated with the trauma.

B. Today's therapy session focused on how the client's pessimistic outlook and strong self-doubts interfere with his/her willingness to take healthy risks.

C. A cognitive-behavioral therapy approach was utilized to identify the client's self-defeating thoughts.

14. Replace Distorted, Negative, Self-Defeating Thoughts (14)

A. The client was helped to replace his/her distorted, negative self-defeating thoughts with positive, reality-based self-talk.

B. The client was encouraged to make positive, realistic self-statements to decrease his/her emotional pain.

C. The client's distorted, negative self-defeating thoughts were challenged to help him/her overcome the pattern of catastrophizing events and/or expecting the worst to occur.

D. The client reported to experiencing increased calm by being able to replace his/her distorted, cognitive self-defeating thoughts with positive, reality-based self-talk.

15. Teach Gradual Approach to Avoided Stimuli (15)

A. The client was assisted in developing a plan to decrease his/her emotional reactivity by gradually approaching previously avoided stimuli that trigger thoughts and feelings associated with the trauma.

B. The client developed a hierarchy of steps that he/she can take to gradually approach the previously avoided stimuli that trigger thoughts and feelings associated with the trauma.

C. The client was trained in the use of relaxation, deep breathing, and positive self-talk prior to attempting to gradually approach the previously avoided stimuli.

D. The client reported that the use of relaxation, deep breathing, and positive self-talk has helped him/her gradually approach the previously avoided stimuli without experiencing a significant amount of distress.

E. The client failed to practice using the relaxation techniques and positive self-talk because of his/her fear of being overwhelmed by painful emotions.

16. Monitor Sleep Patterns (16)

A. The client was encouraged to keep a record of how much sleep he/she gets every night.

B. The client was trained in the use of relaxation techniques to help induce sleep.

C. The client was trained in the use of positive imagery to help induce sleep.

D. The client was referred for a medication evaluation to determine whether medication is needed to help him/her sleep.

17. Use Eye Movement Desensitization and Reprocessing (EMDR) (17)

A. The client was trained in the use of eye movement desensitization and reprocessing (EMDR) technique to reduce his/her emotional reactivity to the traumatic event.

B. The client reported that the EMDR technique has been helpful in reducing his/her emotional reactivity to the traumatic event.

C. The client reported partial success since our implementation of the EMDR technique to reduce emotional distress.

D. The client reported little to no improvement since implementation of the EMDR technique to decrease his/her emotional reactivity to the traumatic event.

18. Refer for Group Therapy (18)

A. The client was referred for group therapy to help him/her share and work through his/her feelings about the trauma with other individuals who have experienced traumatic incidents.

B. The client was given the directive to self-disclose at least once during the group therapy session about his/her traumatic experience.

C. The client's involvement in group therapy has helped him/her realize that he/she is not alone in experiencing painful emotions surrounding a traumatic event.

D. The client's active participation in group therapy has helped him/her share and work through many of his/her emotions pertaining to the traumatic event.

E. The client has not made productive use of the group therapy sessions and has been reluctant to share his/her feelings about the traumatic event.

19. Refer for Medication Evaluation (19)

A. The client was referred for a medication evaluation to help stabilize his/her mood and decrease the intensity of his/her angry feelings.

B. The client and parent(s) agreed to follow through with the medication evaluation.

C. The client was strongly opposed to being placed on medication to help stabilize his/her moods and reduce emotional distress.

20. Monitor Effects of Medication (20)

A. The client's response to the medication was discussed in today's therapy session.

B. The client reported that the medication has helped to stabilize his/her mood and decrease the intensity of his/her angry feelings.

C. The client reported little to no improvement in his/her mood or anger control since being placed on the medication.

D. The client reported that he/she has consistently taken the medication as prescribed.

E. The client has failed to comply with taking the medication as prescribed.

21. Hold Family Session to Facilitate Offering of Support (21)

A. A family therapy session was held to allow the client to express his/her feelings about the traumatic event in the presence of his/her family members.

B. A family therapy session was held to provide the family members with the opportunity to provide much-needed emotional support for the client.

C. The client responded favorably to the show of support from his/her family members.

D. Today's therapy session allowed all of the family members to express their feelings about the traumatic event.

E. Today's family therapy session explored the factors that interfere with the family members' ability to provide emotional support and nurturance for the client.

22. Inform Family Members about the Traumatic Event (22)

A. The family members were informed as to how the traumatic event impacted the client and his/her subsequent adjustment.

B. The client was given the opportunity to share how the traumatic event has impacted his/her adjustment and ability to cope.

C. The family members' denial about the impact of the traumatic event was challenged and confronted in today's therapy session.

D. The family members were given the opportunity to express their thoughts and feelings about how the traumatic event impacted the survivors.

23. Employ Child-Centered Play Therapy (23)

A. A child-centered play-therapy session was held to provide the client with the opportunity to identify and express his/her feelings surrounding the traumatic incident.

B. The client was offered unconditional positive regard and warm acceptance to help him/her identify and express his/her feelings surrounding the traumatic incident.

C. The feelings that were expressed in the client's play were reflected back to him/her in a nonjudgmental manner.

D. The child-centered play-therapy session reinforced the client's capacity for growth and ability to cope with the pain surrounding the traumatic event.

E. The play-therapy session has helped the client work through and resolve many of his/her painful emotions surrounding the traumatic incident.

24. Utilize Psychoanalytic Play Therapy (24)

A. A psychoanalytic play-therapy session was held to provide the client with the opportunity to express and work through his/her feelings surrounding the traumatic incident.

B. The client was allowed to take the lead in the psychoanalytic therapy session to help him/her begin to explore his/her painful emotions surrounding the traumatic incident.

C. The client's play reflected his/her feelings of anger, hurt, and sadness about the past traumatic incident.

D. The client's play in today's therapy session reflected the fear and vulnerability that he/she had experienced during the traumatic incident.

E. The client's feelings reflected in his/her play were interpreted and related to his/her feelings about the traumatic incident.

25. Use Mutual Storytelling Technique (25)

A. The mutual storytelling technique using puppets, dolls, and stuffed animals was employed to help the client identify and work through his/her feelings surrounding the past traumatic incident.

B. Using the mutual storytelling technique, the therapist created a story that modeled constructive steps that the client can take to protect himself/herself and feel empowered.

C. The client created a story through the use of puppets, dolls, and stuffed animals that reflected his/her emotions about the traumatic incident.

D. The client created a similar story to that of the therapists which reflected ways to protect self and feel empowered.

E. The mutual storytelling technique has been a helpful way for the client to not only express his/her feelings about the past traumatic incident, but also learn how to protect himself/herself and feel empowered.

26. Employ Art Therapy (26)

A. The client was provided with materials and asked to draw or paint a picture that reflected his/her feelings of the past trauma.

B. The client's artwork reflected his/her feelings of anger about the past traumatic incident.

C. The client's artwork reflected the fear, anxiety, and helplessness that he/she had experienced during the traumatic incident.

D. The client's drawings reflected his/her feelings of sadness and hurt about the past traumatic incident.

E. The content of the client's drawings was processed and he/she was given the opportunity to directly verbalize his/her feelings.

SCHOOL REFUSAL

CLIENT PRESENTATION

1. Reluctance or Refusal to Attend School (1)*

A. The client has demonstrated a persistent reluctance or refusal to attend school.

B. The client has missed a significant amount of school because of his/her separation anxiety and fearfulness about leaving home.

C. The client appeared visibly anxious in today's therapy session when discussing his/her return to school.

D. The client has recently started to attend school on a part-time basis.

E. The client has attended school on a regular, full-time basis.

2. Emotional Distress before Attending School (2)

A. The client and parents reported that he/she often exhibits a great deal of emotional distress before leaving home to attend school.

B. The client became visibly anxious and had difficulty separating from his/her parents in today's therapy session.

C. The intensity of the client's emotional distress before attending school in the morning has gradually started to diminish.

D. The client reported that he/she has recently been able to get ready for school in the morning without exhibiting any significant amount of emotional distress.

E. The client has consistently attended school without exhibiting distress before leaving home.

3. Emotional Distress after Arriving at School (2)

A. The parents and teachers reported that the client exhibits a significant amount of emotional distress after arriving at school.

B. The client has often requested that he/she either be allowed to call his/her parents or go home after arriving at school.

C. The intensity of the client's emotional distress after arriving at school has gradually started to diminish.

D. The client reported that he/she has recently been able to remain relaxed and calm after arriving at school.

E. The client has been able to remain relaxed and calm on a consistent basis after arriving at school.

4. Crying and Pleading (2)

A. The client has demonstrated a persistent pattern of crying and pleading to stay home before leaving for school in the morning.

---

* The numbers in parentheses correlate to the number of the Behavioral Definition statement in the companion chapter with same title in *The Child Psychotherapy Treatment Planner* (Jongsma, Peterson, and McInnis) by John Wiley & Sons, 2000.

B. The client has often cried and pleaded to go home after arriving at school.

C. The intensity and duration of the client's crying and pleading before leaving home or after arriving at school has gradually started to diminish.

D. The client reported that he/she has recently not exhibited any crying or pleading before leaving home or after arriving at school.

E. The client has attended school consistently without exhibiting any crying or excessive pleading.

5. Temper Tantrums (2)

A. The client has frequently exhibited intense temper tantrums before leaving home in the morning for school.

B. The client exhibited intense temper tantrums after arriving at school with the hope that he/she will be able to return home.

C. The frequency and intensity of the client's temper tantrums before leaving home or after arriving at school have gradually started to diminish.

D. The client has not exhibited any temper tantrums before leaving home or after arriving at school.

E. The client has attended school consistently without exhibiting any temper tantrums.

6. Somatic Complaints (3)

A. The parents reported that the client frequently makes somatic complaints (e.g., headaches, stomachaches, nausea) before leaving home to attend school.

B. School officials reported that the client often makes somatic complaints after arriving at school.

C. The client complained of not feeling well in today's therapy session when discussing his/her school attendance.

D. The frequency and intensity of the client's somatic complaints have recently started to diminish.

E. The client has demonstrated a significant reduction in the frequency and intensity of his/her somatic complaints.

7. Excessive Clinging/Shadowing (4)

A. The parents reported that the client often becomes very clingy when anticipating leaving home for school in the morning.

B. The client became very clingy in today's therapy session when asked to separate from his/her parents.

C. The intensity and duration of the client's clingy behavior before leaving home or after arriving at school has gradually started to diminish.

D. The client has recently been able to separate from his/her parents to attend school without exhibiting any excessive clinging or shadowing.

E. The client has consistently attended school without displaying any excessive clinging or shadowing of his/her parents.

8. Regressive Behaviors (4)

A. The client has often regressed and behaved in an infantile manner before separating from his/her parents to attend school.

B. The client spoke in a very regressive and immature manner in today's therapy session when discussing his/her school attendance.

C. The frequency of the client's immature and regressive behaviors has recently started to diminish.

D. The parents reported that the client has recently behaved in an age-appropriate manner before leaving home or after arriving at school.

E. The enmeshed family relationships have contributed to the emergence of the client's immature and regressive behaviors.

9. Family Enmeshment (4)

A. The client's enmeshed and overly dependent relationship with his/her parents has been a significant contributing factor to his/her reluctance or refusal to attend school.

B. The parents verbally recognized how they have reinforced the client's excessive dependency and in turn his/her reluctance to attend school.

C. The parents have encouraged the client to take steps to become more independent.

D. The parents have recently started to set limits on the client's overly dependent behaviors, excessive clinging, and temper tantrums.

E. The parents' improved ability to set limits on the client's overly dependent behaviors, excessive clinging, and temper tantrums has helped the client attend school on a full-time basis.

10. Negative Comments about School (5)

A. The parents and teachers reported that the client often verbalizes many negative comments about school.

B. The client verbalized several negative remarks about school during today's therapy session.

C. The frequency of the client's negative remarks about his/her school experiences or performance has recently started to decrease.

D. The client verbalized several positive remarks about school during today's therapy session.

E. The client has consistently been able to verbalize positive remarks about his/her school experiences or performance.

11. Unrealistic Fears or Worries (6)

A. The client has developed a persistent and unrealistic fear that some future calamity will separate him/her from his/her parents if he/she attends school.

B. The client shared his/her worry in today's therapy session about some future calamity separating him/her from his/her parents.

C. The client verbally recognized how his/her fear of some future calamity occurring is unrealistic and irrational.

D. The client has recently not verbalized any unrealistic fears or worries about a future calamity separating him/her from parents.

E. The client has ceased experiencing any unrealistic fears or worries about some calamitous event separating him/her from parents.

12. Separation/Loss (6)

A. The client has refused or been reluctant to attend school since experiencing a major separation or loss.

B. The client appeared visibly anxious and upset in today's therapy session when talking about the separation or loss.

C. The client was guarded and reluctant to discuss the past separation or loss.

D. The client was open and talkative about the past separation or loss in today's therapy session.

E. The client has been able to attend school on a regular, full-time basis since successfully working through many of his/her thoughts and feelings about the past separation or loss.

13. Traumatic Event (6)

A. The client has had difficulty attending school since experiencing a traumatic event.

B. The client appeared visibly anxious and upset in today's therapy session when talking about the traumatic event.

C. The client was guarded and reluctant to discuss the past traumatic event.

D. The client was open and talkative about the past traumatic event in today's therapy session.

E. The client has been able to attend school on a regular, full-time basis since successfully working through many of his/her thoughts and feelings about the past traumatic event.

14. Low Self-Esteem (7)

A. The client's low self-esteem and lack of confidence have been significant contributing factors to his/her fear of attending school.

B. The client expressed feelings of insecurity and strong self-doubts about his/her ability to succeed in school.

C. The client verbalized positive self-statements in today's therapy session about his/her ability to succeed in school.

D. The client's increase in school attendance has coincided with his/her increase in confidence and self-esteem.

E. The client has confidently attended school on a regular basis and usually talked about his/her school experiences in positive terms.

15. Fear of Failure or Ridicule (8)

A. The client's strong fear of failure and anxiety about his/her academic performance have been significant contributing factors to his/her reluctance or refusal to attend school.

B. The client has had problems attending school since experiencing failure, ridicule, or rejection.

C. The client's fear of failure or ridicule has recently started to decrease and he/she has been able to take healthy risks.

D. The client has consistently been able to apply himself/herself at school without experiencing any strong fear of failure or ridicule.

16. Shrinking from or Avoidance of Unfamiliar People (9)

A. The client has developed a persistent pattern of shrinking away from or avoiding contact with unfamiliar people in the school setting.

B. The client's social anxiety and fear of being ridiculed or scrutinized by others have been significant contributing factors to his/her school refusal.

C. In today's therapy session the client verbalized feelings of anxiety about interacting with unfamiliar people at school.

D. The client has started to feel more confident in interacting with unfamiliar people at school.

E. The client has successfully overcome his/her anxiety about interacting with unfamiliar people, and he/she socializes with others on a regular basis.

INTERVENTIONS IMPLEMENTED

1. Build Trust (1)*

A. The objective of today's therapy session was to establish trust with the client so that he/she can begin to identify and express feelings associated with his/her school attendance.

B. Attempts were made to build the level of trust with the client through consistent eye contact, active listening, unconditional positive regard, and warm acceptance.

C. The client's expression of thoughts and feelings during the therapy session was supported empathetically.

D. The therapy session was helpful in building a level of trust with the client.

E. The therapy session was not successful in establishing trust with the client as he/she remained guarded when discussing his/her thoughts and feelings about attending school.

2. Psychological Testing (2)

A. The client was referred for a psychological evaluation to assess the severity of his/her anxiety, depression, or gross psychopathology and to help gain greater insight into the underlying dynamics contributing to his/her school refusal.

B. The client was very guarded and reserved during the psychological testing.

C. The client appeared visibly anxious about taking part in the psychological testing.

D. The client approached the psychological testing in an honest, straightforward manner, and was cooperative with any test presented to him/her.

3. Psychoeducational Evaluation (3)

A. The client received a psychoeducational evaluation to rule out presence of a possible learning disability that may be contributing to his/her reluctance or refusal to attend school.

* The numbers in parentheses correlate to the number of the Therapeutic Interventions statement in the companion chapter with same title in *The Child Psychotherapy Treatment Planner* (Jongsma, Peterson, and McInnis) by John Wiley & Sons, 2000.

B. The client appeared anxious and seemed to lack confidence in his/her abilities during the psychoeducational evaluation.

C. The client was uncooperative during the psychoeducational evaluation and did not appear to put forth good effort.

D. Rapport was easily established with the client and he/she appeared motivated to do his/her best during the psychoeducational testing.

4. Give Evaluation Feedback (4)

A. The client and his/her family members were given feedback from the psychological testing.

B. The results from the psychological evaluation showed that the client is currently experiencing a mild/moderate/severe (circle one) amount of anxiety.

C. The results from the psychological testing revealed that the client is experiencing a mild/moderate/severe (circle one) amount of depression.

D. The results from the psychological testing revealed the presence of a severe psychiatric disorder.

E. The results from the psychoeducational evaluation revealed the presence of a learning disability that appeared to be contributing to the client's school refusal.

5. Implement *In Vivo* Systematic Desensitization (5)

A. Consulted with the client, parents, and school officials about designing and implementing an *in vivo* systematic desensitization program to help the client manage his/her anxiety and gradually attend school for longer periods of time.

B. The client and parents agreed to follow through with the implementation of the *in vivo* systematic desensitization program that allows the client to gradually attend school for longer periods of time.

C. The *in vivo* systematic desensitization program has helped the client attend school for gradually longer periods of time.

D. The *in vivo* systematic desensitization program has proved to be successful in allowing the client to return to school on a regular, full-time basis.

E. The client has not succeeded in attending school for the specified period of time because of his/her anxiety and difficulty separating from his/her parents.

6. Consult with Parents/School Officials (6)

A. Consulted with the parents and school officials to develop a plan to manage the client's emotional distress and negative outbursts after arriving at school.

B. An action plan was developed in today's therapy session to help the parents effectively separate from the client after arriving at school.

C. The parents were instructed to cease their lengthy goody-byes with the client after arriving at school.

D. The client was instructed to go to the principal's office to calm down if he/she begins to feel distressed after arriving at school.

E. The parents were instructed to reinforce the client's ability to calm himself/herself down after arriving at school.

7. Design/Implement Reward System/Contingency Contract (7)

A. The client and parents identified a list of rewards to be used to reinforce the client for attending school for increasingly longer periods of time.

B. A reward system was designed to reinforce the client for attending school for increasingly longer periods of time.

C. The client signed a contingency contract specifying the negative consequences for his/her failure to attend school for the specified period of time.

D. The client and parents verbally agreed to the terms of the contingency contract.

E. The reward system and/or contingency contract have helped the client attend school for increasingly longer periods of time.

8. Design/Implement Token Economy (8)

A. A token economy was designed to reinforce the client's school attendance.

B. The client, parents, and school officials agreed to the conditions outlined in the token economy program and agreed to follow through with their implementation.

C. The token economy has proven to be successful in increasing the client's school attendance.

D. The token economy, thus far, has not proven to be successful in increasing the client's school attendance.

9. Plan High-Success School Assignment (9)

A. Consulted with the client's teacher about planning an assignment that will provide him/her with an increased chance of success during the initial stages of treatment.

B. The teacher(s) were encouraged to give the client an assignment related to one of his/her interests.

C. The teacher(s) were encouraged to modify the length of the assignment to help decrease the client's anxiety.

D. The teacher(s) were encouraged to pair the client up with a friend or well-liked peer on a school assignment to help decrease his/her anxiety and provide him/her with the opportunity to achieve academic success.

10. Utilize Teacher's Aide/Positive Peer Attention (10)

A. Consulted with school officials about assigning a teacher's aide to the client to help reduce his/her fear and anxiety about attending school.

B. Recommendation was made that the client work with a teacher's aide to help address his/her learning problems.

C. Consulted with school officials about pairing the client with a positive peer role model to help him/her manage his/her fears and anxiety about attending school.

D. Recommendation was offered that the client be paired with a positive peer role model on a school assignment to help provide the client with a sense of acceptance and belonging at school.

E. The client reported that the support he/she has received from the teacher's aide or positive peer role model has helped to decrease his/her fear and anxiety about attending school.

11. Explore Negative Cognitive Messages (11)

A. Today's therapy session explored the irrational, negative cognitive messages that contribute to the client's anxiety and fear about attending school.

B. The client was helped to identify the irrational, negative cognitive messages that contribute to his/her anxiety and fear about attending school.

C. The client was strongly encouraged to challenge his/her irrational thoughts that contribute to his/her anxiety and fear about attending school.

12. Confront Irrational Fears (12)

A. Today's therapy session helped the client to realize that his/her fears about attending school are irrational or unrealistic.

B. A cognitive-behavioral therapy approach was used to help the client realize how his/her fears about attending school are irrational or unrealistic.

C. The client was helped to realize how his/her irrational or negative thinking is self-defeating and exacerbates his/her feelings of anxiety or depression.

13. Develop Positive Cognitive Messages (13)

A. The client was encouraged to use positive self-talk to help him/her reduce or cope with the anxiety or fear.

B. The client was strongly encouraged to replace his/her negative self-talk with positive cognitive messages that increase his/her self-confidence and reinforce his/her ability to cope with anxiety or fear about attending school.

C. The client reported that the use of positive cognitive messages has helped to increase his/her confidence while decreasing his/her anxiety and fearfulness.

D. The client has failed to follow through with using positive cognitive messages to help decrease his/her anxiety and fearfulness.

14. Teach Relaxation/Guided Imagery (14)

A. The client was taught relaxation techniques and guided imagery to help reduce his/her anxiety and fear about attending school.

B. The client reported a positive response to the use of relaxation or guided imagery techniques to help decrease his/her anxiety and fearfulness.

C. The client has failed to consistently use the relaxation or guided imagery techniques, and as a result has continued to experience anxiety and fearfulness about attending school.

15. Encourage Positive Self-Talk (15)

A. The client was encouraged to utilize positive self-talk as a means of managing his/her anxiety or fear before leaving to attend school.

B. The client was encouraged to utilize positive self-talk as a means of managing his/her anxiety or fear after arriving at school.

C. The client was directed to verbalize at least one positive statement about an accomplishment at school.

D. The client was given a homework assignment to record at least one positive school experience daily in a journal.

E. The client was encouraged to verbalize positive statements about others at school to help improve his/her peer relationships.

16. Develop Contingency Plan for Somatic Complaints (16)

A. Consulted with the parents and school officials to develop a contingency plan to manage the client's somatic complaints.

B. The parents and school officials were instructed to ignore the client's obvious psychosomatic complaints and redirect him/her to another task.

C. A contingency plan was developed where the client would go to the nurse's office at school and have his/her temperature taken to verify his/her illness before being allowed to call home.

D. The client was encouraged to use guided imagery and relaxation techniques to redirect his/her focus away from the somatic complaints.

17. Shift Focus from Physical Complaints to Emotional Conflicts (17)

A. Today's therapy session refocused the client's discussion away from physical complaints to emotional conflicts and the expression of feelings.

B. Today's therapy session helped the client realize how his/her somatic complaints are related to underlying emotional conflicts and painful emotions.

C. The client was helped to identify more effective ways to cope with stress and conflict to help reduce the chances of him/her developing somatic ailments.

D. The client was taught effective communication and assertiveness skills to help him/her communicate feelings more directly.

18. Teach Power of Secondary Gain (18)

A. Today's family therapy session helped the client and his/her parents develop insight into the secondary gain that the client receives from his/her physical illnesses and complaints.

B. The client and parents were helped to realize that the client's physical complaints and illnesses are aimed at eliciting nurturance and drawing the parents closer.

C. The client was helped to identify more effective ways to meet his/her needs instead of expressing somatic complaints.

D. The client gained the realization that he/she often develops psychosomatic ailments as a way to avoid stress and/or responsibilities at school.

E. The client was taught effective coping strategies to help him/her effectively deal with stress or demands at school.

19. Assess Family Dynamics (19)

A. A family therapy session was held to explore the dynamics within the family system that contribute to the emergence of the client's school refusal.

B. The family members were asked to list the stressors that have had a negative impact on the family.

C. The family members were asked to identify the things they would like to change within the family system.

20. Employ Family Sculpting (20)

A. The family sculpting technique was used to gain greater insight into the roles and behavior of each family member.

B. The client and family members were instructed to use the family sculpting technique to identify what positive changes they would like to see in the family.

C. The family sculpting technique showed how overly dependent the client is on his/her parent(s).

21. Assign Drawing of House (21)

A. In today's therapy session, the client was first asked to draw a picture of a house, then instructed to make up a story identifying what it is like to live in that house.

B. The art therapy technique (i.e., asking client to draw picture of a house) helped reveal insight into the family dynamics that contribute to the emergence of the client's school refusal.

C. The art therapy technique revealed how the client has developed an overly enmeshed relationship with one of his/her parents.

D. The art therapy technique helped to reveal how the client has developed a distant relationship with the disengaged parent.

E. The art therapy technique led to a discussion about how to increase the involvement of the disengaged parent.

22. Assign School Transport to Disengaged Parent (22)

A. The disengaged parent was asked to transport the client to school each morning.

B. The overly enmeshed parent was instructed not to be present when transporting the client to school.

C. The disengaged parent was instructed to play games or converse with the client while driving to school to help reduce his/her anxiety and fearfulness.

D. The therapist contacted the parent's employer to gain permission for the parent to adjust his/her work schedule to allow him/her to transport the client to school each morning.

23. Encourage Parents to Reinforce Autonomy (23)

A. The parents were strongly encouraged to praise and positively reinforce the client's autonomous behavior.

B. The parents were strongly encouraged to set limits on the client's overly dependent or regressive behavior.

C. The parents were encouraged to praise the client for attending school for the specified period of time.

D. The parents were encouraged to praise and reinforce the client for working alone on his/her school assignments.

E. The parent(s) were instructed to cease entering the classroom with the client in the morning.

24. Encourage Parents to Remain Calm (24)

A. Today's therapy session stressed the importance of the parents remaining calm and not communicating their anxiety to the client.

B. The parents were helped to realize how the client's anxiety increases when he/she perceives them as being anxious or apprehensive.

C. The parents were instructed to remain firm and clearly communicate the expectation that the client is expected to go to school when he/she becomes distressed and begs or pleads to stay home.

D. Role-playing and modeling techniques were used to teach the parents effective ways to manage the client's anxiety, fearfulness, or emotional distress.

E. The parents were instructed to verbalize confidence in the client's ability to manage his/her stress or anxiety at school.

25. Reinforce Positive Steps by Parents (25)

A. The parents were praised and reinforced for taking positive steps to help the client overcome his/her fear or anxiety about attending school.

B. The parents recognized that the combination of encouragement and consistent limit setting has helped the client attend school regularly.

C. The parents identified the positive steps they have taken to help the client attend school without exhibiting significant distress.

D. The parents were strongly encouraged to take the same steps to help the client continue to attend school on a regular basis.

26. Reinforce Parents' Limit Setting (26)

A. The parents were encouraged to set firm, consistent limits on the client's temper outbursts and manipulative behavior.

B. The parents were encouraged to set firm, consistent limits on the client's excessive clinging or pleading.

C. The parents acknowledged that they have been reluctant to set firm, consistent limits because of their desire to avoid dealing with the client's temper outbursts or heightened emotional distress.

D. The parents were informed that the intensity of the client's temper outbursts, pleading, or clinging will likely increase at first when they begin to set limits.

E. The parents were instructed to remain calm and firmly in control when they first begin to set limits on the client's temper outbursts, manipulative behavior, or excessive clinging.

27. Identify Times When Client Attended School (27)

A. Today's therapy session explored the days or periods of time when the client was able to attend school without exhibiting significant emotional distress.

B. The client was encouraged to use coping strategies similar to those that he/she had used in the past to attend school without displaying excessive fear or anxiety.

C. The client shared his/her realization that talking with other peers or school officials helped to decrease his/her anxiety and fearfulness after arriving at school.

D. Today's family therapy session revealed that the client has been able to attend school without exhibiting a significant amount of distress when the parents provide encouragement and set limits on his/her temper outbursts, manipulative behavior, or excessive clinging.

28. Teach Parents Anticipation of Stressors (28)

A. The parents were told to anticipate possible stressors or events (e.g., illness, school holidays, vacations) that might cause the client's fear and anxiety about attending school to reappear.

B. The parents were informed that the client may regress and exhibit more distress shortly before and after the next school break or holiday.

C. The client and parents were encouraged to use coping strategies that were successful in the past to help the client attend school, in the event that he/she regresses and experiences fear or anxiety about attending school in the future.

D. The client and parents identified potential stressors that may appear in the future that could impact the client's school attendance.

E. The client and parents identified coping strategies and developed a contingency plan that could help him/her cope with stress in the future.

29. Assign Parents to Write a "Letter of Encouragement" (29)

A. The parents were instructed to write a letter (assignment based on the "Letter of Encouragement" exercise from *The Brief Child Therapy Homework Planner* by Jongsma, Peterson, and McInnis) to the client that sends a clear message about the importance of attending school and reminding him/her of coping strategies that he/she can use to calm fears or anxieties.

B. The parents were instructed to place the "Letter of Encouragement" in the client's notebook so that he/she can read the letter at appropriate times during the school day when he/she begins to feel afraid or anxious.

C. The client reported that the parents' "Letter of Encouragement" helped him/her to calm down when beginning to feel anxious or afraid at school.

D. The "Letter of Encouragement" exercise helped the parents send a strong and clear message about the importance of attending school.

E. The parents failed to follow through with writing the "Letter of Encouragement" and were again asked to do it.

30. Identify Role of Enmeshed Parents (30)

A. Today's therapy session helped identify how the enmeshed or overly protective parents reinforce the client's dependency and irrational fear.

B. Today's therapy session explored the reasons why the enmeshed or overly protective parents have failed to set limits with the client's overly dependent and/or regressive behaviors.

C. The enmeshed or overly protective parents were helped to realize how they reinforce the client's excessive clinging or pleading when he/she begins to feel afraid.

D. The enmeshed or overly protective parents were taught more effective ways to deal with the client's overly dependent behaviors or irrational fears.

E. The parents were encouraged to redirect the client by engaging in activities or conversations that take his/her mind or attention off irrational fear.

31. Employ Paradoxical Intervention (31)

A. A paradoxical intervention was implemented to work around the family's resistance and to disengage the client from an overly protective parent.

B. The paradoxical intervention proved to be successful in working around the family's resistance and disengaging the client from the overly protective parent.

C. The paradoxical intervention helped increase the client's motivation to function more autonomously.

D. Processed the family's resistance in following through with the paradoxical intervention.

32. Assess Marital Dyad (32)

A. Today's therapy session assessed the marital dyad for possible conflict and triangulation that deflect the focus away from the discord and onto the client's symptoms.

B. Today's therapy session revealed that the client's separation anxiety and refusal to attend school appeared around the time when the parents began to experience marital conflict with one another.

C. The client verbalized his/her fear and anxiety about the parents' possibly getting a separation or divorce.

D. Recommendation was made that the parents pursue marital counseling.

E. The parents agreed to follow through with marital counseling to address their areas of conflict.

33. Explore Trauma History (33)

A. Today's therapy session explored whether the client's anxiety and fear about attending school are associated with a previously unresolved separation, loss, trauma, or realistic danger.

B. The assessment revealed that the client began to have trouble attending school after experiencing a significant separation or loss.

C. The assessment revealed that the client began having trouble attending school after experiencing a traumatic event.

D. The assessment revealed that the client began having trouble attending school after being exposed to a realistic danger.

34. Reinforce Expressing Feelings about Trauma (34)

A. The client was given encouragement and support in expressing his/her feelings associated with a past separation, loss, trauma, or realistic danger.

B. The client was helped to identify and clarify his/her feelings associated with a past separation, loss, trauma, or realistic danger.

C. Client-centered therapy principles were used to encourage and support the client in expressing his/her feelings surrounding a past separation, loss, trauma, or realistic danger.

D. The empty-chair technique was utilized to help the client express and work through his/her feelings associated with a past separation, loss, trauma, or realistic danger.

E. The client was encouraged to utilize a journal to express his/her thoughts and feelings associated with a past separation, loss, trauma, or realistic danger.

35. Assign Letter Writing about Trauma (35)

A. The client was assigned to write a letter to express his/her thoughts and feelings about a previous separation or loss.

B. The client was given the homework assignment of writing a letter to express his/her thoughts and feelings about a past traumatic or dangerous event.

C. Processed the content of the client's letter in today's therapy session.

D. The client's letter reflected strong feelings of anger about a past separation, loss, trauma, or realistic danger.

E. The client's letter reflected feelings of sadness, hurt, and vulnerability about a past separation, loss, trauma, or realistic danger.

36. Assign Letting-Go Exercise (36)

A. Explored whether the client was willing to perform a letting-go exercise in which a symbol of the past separation, loss, or trauma would be destroyed.

B. The client was assigned a letting-go exercise in which a symbol of the past separation, loss, or trauma was to be destroyed.

C. Processed the client's thoughts and feelings about the letting-go exercise.

D. The client identified the letting-go exercise as being helpful in releasing his/her feelings about a past separation, loss, trauma, or realistic danger.

E. The client stated that he/she was unable to perform the letting-go exercise because he/she does not feel ready to let go of his/her emotions surrounding the past separation, loss, trauma, or realistic danger.

37. Teach Assertiveness Skills (37)

A. The client was taught effective assertiveness skills to help reduce his/her social anxiety and/or fear of ridicule.

B. Role-playing techniques were used to teach the client effective assertiveness skills.

C. The client reported that the newly acquired assertiveness skills helped him/her feel relaxed and confident in different social situations.

D. The client reported that the newly acquired assertiveness skills have helped him/her overcome his/her fear of being ridiculed or embarrassed.

E. The client failed to practice the newly acquired assertiveness skills because of his/her fear of experiencing ridicule or rejection.

38. Play "Stand Up for Yourself" Game (38)

A. Played the Stand Up for Yourself game (Shapiro) to help establish rapport with the client.

B. Used the Stand Up for Yourself game to help teach the client effective assertiveness skills that can be used to help him/her feel more confident at school.

C. After playing the Stand Up for Yourself game, the client was able to identify several assertiveness and communication skills that will help him/her feel more confident and relaxed around others at school.

D. The client was given the homework assignment of practicing the assertiveness skills that he/she learned from playing the Stand Up for Yourself game.

E. The client reported that he/she was able to successfully practice the newly acquired assertiveness skills.

39. Encourage Participation in Peer Group Activities (39)

A. The client was strongly encouraged to participate in extracurricular or positive peer group activities at school to help him/her feel more comfortable and relaxed around others.

B. The client was assisted in developing a list of positive peer group activities that will help provide him/her with the opportunity to establish meaningful friendships at school.

C. The client verbalized an understanding of how his/her feelings of insecurity and inadequacy contribute to his/her reluctance to become involved in extracurricular or peer group activities at school.

D. The client reported that his/her recent participation in extracurricular or peer group activities helped him/her feel more comfortable and relaxed at school.

E. The client has continued to have problems separating from his/her parents and has not participated in any extracurricular or positive peer group activities.

40. Assign Time Spent with Peers (40)

A. The client was given a directive to spend a specified period of time with his/her peers after school or on weekends.

B. The client was helped to identify a list of activities that he/she would like to engage in with peers after school or on the weekends.

C. The client's increased involvement with peers after school or on weekends has helped him/her manage separations from his/her parents in a more adaptive manner.

D. The client has remained resistant to socializing with peers after school or on weekends because of his/her separation anxiety and fear of rejection or ridicule.

41. Assign Social Contact Initiatives (41)

A. The client was given the directive of initiating three social contacts per week with unfamiliar people or when placed in new social settings.

B. Role-playing and modeling techniques were utilized to teach the client appropriate ways to initiate conversations.

C. Processed the client's thoughts and feelings about initiating social contacts with unfamiliar people or when placed in new social settings.

D. The client followed through with the directive to initiate at least three social contacts per week.

E. The client failed to follow through with the directive to initiate at least three social contacts per week because of his/her social anxiety.

42. Read *Why Is Everybody Always Picking on Me?* (42)

A. The client was assigned to read *Why Is Everybody Always Picking on Me? A Guide to Understanding Bullies for Young People* (Webster-Doyle) to help teach him/her effective ways to deal with aggressive or intimidating peers at school.

B. Processed the content of the book *Why Is Everybody Always Picking on Me? A Guide to Understanding Bullies for Young People* in today's therapy session.

C. After reading the book, the client was helped to identify effective ways to deal with aggressive or intimidating peers at school.

D. The client was encouraged to practice the coping strategies that he/she learned from *Why Is Everybody Always Picking on Me? A Guide to Understanding Bullies for Young People.*

E. The client reported that the Webster-Doyle book has helped him/her effectively deal with aggressive or intimidating peers at school.

43. Utilize Child-Centered Play-Therapy Principles (43)

A. Child-centered play-therapy principles were utilized to help the client express his/her feelings and work through his/her fears about attending school.

B. The client was given unconditional positive regard and warm acceptance in expressing his/her feelings and worries about attending school.

C. The client's feelings and fears about attending school were reflected back to him/her in a nonjudgmental manner.

D. Reinforced the client's capacity to overcome his/her anxiety or fear about attending school.

E. The child-centered play-therapy principles have helped the client successfully work through his/her fear about attending school.

44. Employ Psychoanalytic Play Therapy (44)

A. Using a psychoanalytic play-therapy approach, the client was allowed to take the lead in exploring the unconscious conflicts or core anxiety that contribute to his/her school refusal.

B. Using a psychoanalytic play-therapy approach, the client's core conflicts and anxiety about attending school were identified and processed.

C. Processed and worked through the transference issues that emerged in today's therapy session.

D. Interpreted the client's feelings and fear expressed in his/her play and related them to his/her fear about attending school.

E. The psychoanalytic play-therapy sessions have helped the client work through and resolve the issues contributing to his/her school refusal.

45. Use Mutual Storytelling Technique (45)

A. The client actively participated in the mutual storytelling exercise.

B. Using the mutual storytelling technique, the therapist modeled effective ways for the client to overcome his/her anxiety or fear about attending school.

C. The client created a story using puppets, dolls, or stuffed animals that reflected his/her fear about attending school.

D. The client was helped to create a story using puppets, dolls, or stuffed animals that showed effective ways to cope with his/her fear or anxiety.

E. The client identified the mutual storytelling technique as being a fun and useful way to learn strategies on how to overcome his/her anxiety or fear about attending school.

46. Employ Art Therapy Techniques (46)

A. The client was instructed to draw a picture or create a sculpture reflecting what he/she fears will happen when he/she goes to school.

B. Processed the content of the client's artwork and discussed whether his/her fears about attending school are realistic or unrealistic.

C. The client's artwork reflected his/her fear about separating from parents to face stressors or responsibilities at school.

D. The client's artwork reflected his/her anxiety or fear about experiencing rejection or failure at school.

E. After completing his/her artwork, the client was helped to identify effective ways to overcome his/her fear about attending school.

47. Utilize Angry Tower Technique (47)

A. The Angry Tower technique (Saxe) was utilized in today's therapy session to help the client identify and express his/her underlying feelings of anger that contribute to his/her refusal to attend school.

B. The Angry Tower technique helped the client to openly identify the target(s) of his/her anger.

C. After playing the Angry Tower game, the client explored whether he/she would be willing to express his/her feelings of anger directly toward the target(s).

D. The therapeutic game led to a discussion about more effective ways for the client to express his/her feelings of anger.

E. The client and parents were instructed to play the Angry Tower game at home when the client is experiencing strong feelings of anger.

48. Refer Enmeshed Parent for Treatment (48)

A. The overly enmeshed parent was assessed for the possibility of having either an anxiety or depressive disorder that may be contributing to the client's refusal to attend school.

B. The client's overly enmeshed parent was referred for a medication evaluation to help decrease his/her anxiety or depression.

C. Recommendation was made that the overly enmeshed parent pursue individual therapy to help decrease his/her feelings of depression or anxiety.

D. The overly enmeshed parent followed through with seeking the medication evaluation.

E. The overly enmeshed parent followed up with pursuing individual therapy to decrease feelings of depression or anxiety.

49. Medication Evaluation Referral (49)

A. The client was referred for a medication evaluation to help decrease his/her anxiety or emotional distress.

B. The client and parents agreed to follow through with the recommendation to receive a medication evaluation.

C. The client was strongly opposed to being placed on medication to help stabilize his/her moods and/or decrease anxiety or fearfulness.

50. Monitor Medication Effects (50)

A. The client reported that he/she has been taking his/her medication as prescribed.

B. The client has not complied with taking his/her medication on a regular basis.

C. The client reported that the medication has helped to decrease his/her anxiety and emotional distress.

D. The client reported little to no improvement on the medication.

E. The client reported experiencing side effects from the prescribed medication.

51. Medical Examination Referral (51)

A. The client was referred for a thorough medical examination to rule out whether his/her health problems are genuine or psychosomatic in nature.

B. Consulted with the client's physician about the results from the medical examination.

C. The medical examination revealed that the client is experiencing genuine health problems, and he/she has subsequently been placed on medication and/or received appropriate treatment.

D. The medical examination did not reveal the presence of any genuine health problems; rather, the client's physical complaints appear to be psychosomatic in nature.

E. The client was encouraged to take the medication as prescribed for his/her genuine health problems.

SEPARATION ANXIETY

CLIENT PRESENTATION

1. Excessive Distress Anticipating Separation (1)*

A. The client has often exhibited a great deal of emotional distress when anticipating separation from his/her parents or major attachment figures.

B. The client became visibly upset and had difficulty separating from his/her parents in today's therapy session.

C. The client has gradually started to cope more effectively with separations and has not exhibited as much distress.

D. The client was able to separate from his/her parents or caregivers in today's therapy session without exhibiting any emotional distress.

E. The client has consistently been able to separate from his/her parents or caregivers without exhibiting emotional distress.

2. Crying and Pleading (1)

A. The parents reported that the client frequently begins to cry and plead to stay with them when anticipating separations.

B. The client had much difficulty separating from his/her parents or caregivers in today's therapy session and began to cry and plead to stay with them.

C. The intensity and duration of the client's crying and pleading behavior have gradually started to diminish.

D. The client was able to effectively separate from his/her parents or caregivers without crying or pleading.

E. The client has consistently been able to manage separations without crying or pleading to stay with the parents or caregivers.

3. Regressive Behaviors (1)

A. The parents reported that the client often regresses and behaves in an immature manner when anticipating separations from them.

B. The client regressed and displayed immature behaviors in today's therapy session when asked to separate from his/her parents/caregivers.

C. The frequency of the client's regressive or immature behaviors has gradually started to decrease.

D. The client was able to effectively separate from his/her parents/caregivers in today's therapy session without regressing or engaging in immature behaviors.

E. The client has ceased his/her pattern of engaging in regressive or immature behaviors when anticipating separations.

---

* The numbers in parentheses correlate to the number of the Behavioral Definition statement in the companion chapter with same title in *The Child Psychotherapy Treatment Planner* (Jongsma, Peterson, and McInnis) by John Wiley & Sons, 2000.

4. Temper Tantrums (1)

A. The parents reported that the client frequency displays intense temper outbursts when anticipating separations from them.

B. The client exhibited a temper tantrum in today's therapy session when asked to separate from his/her parents or caregivers.

C. The frequency and intensity of the client's temper tantrums around separation situations have gradually started to decrease.

D. The client was able to separate from parents/caregivers in today's therapy session without displaying a temper tantrum.

E. The client has demonstrated a significant reduction in the frequency and intensity of his/her temper tantrums around separation situations.

5. Unrealistic Worry about Possible Harm (2)

A. The client has experienced persistent and unrealistic worries about some possible harm befalling his/her parents/caregivers.

B. In today's therapy session the client expressed his/her worries about some possible harm befalling his/her parents/caregivers.

C. The frequency and intensity of the client's worries or anxiety about possible harm befalling his/her parents/caregivers has gradually started to diminish as he/she recognizes that the worries are unrealistic.

D. In today's therapy session the client did not verbalize any worries or fears about some possible harm befalling his/her parents/caregivers.

E. The client has overcome his/her excessive or unrealistic worries about some possible harm befalling his/her parents/caregivers.

6. Irrational Fear about Future Calamity (3)

A. The client has developed persistent and unrealistic fears that some future calamity will separate him/her from parents/caregivers.

B. The client expressed his/her fear in today's therapy session that some future calamity will separate him/her from parents/caregivers.

C. The client reported a slight reduction in the intensity of his/her fears about a calamitous event separating him/her from parents/caregivers.

D. The client did not express any irrational fears during today's therapy session.

E. The client has ceased experiencing his/her irrational fears about a future calamity separating him/her from parents/caregivers.

7. Emotional Distress after Separation (4)

A. The client has often exhibited a great deal of emotional distress after experiencing a separation from home or major attachment figure.

B. The client became visibly upset and protested vigorously after separating from his/her parents/caregivers in today's therapy session.

C. The client has gradually started to cope more effectively with separations and has not exhibited as much distress after separating from his/her parents/caregivers.

D. The client managed to separate from his/her parents/caregivers in today's therapy session without exhibiting an excessive amount of emotional distress.

E. The client has demonstrated a significant reduction in the intensity of his/her emotional distress after separating from home or major attachment figures.

8. Excessive Clinging (5)

A. The parents reported that the client often clings to them excessively when anticipating separations.

B. The client began to cling to his/her parents in today's therapy session when asked to separate from them.

C. The intensity and duration of the client's clinging has gradually started to diminish.

D. The client did not become clingy in today's therapy session when asked to separate from his/her parents/caregivers.

E. The client has consistently been able to manage separations effectively without exhibiting any excessive clinging.

9. Family Enmeshment/Overly Protective Parent(s) (5)

A. The client has established a highly enmeshed relationship with his/her parents which contributes to his/her separation anxiety.

B. The parents verbally recognized how their overprotectiveness reinforces the client's excessive dependency.

C. The parents have encouraged the client to become more independent and engage in play or socialize more often with peers.

D. The parents have reinforced the client's positive social behaviors and have set limits on his/her overly dependent behaviors.

E. The client has achieved a healthy balance between socializing with his/her peers and spending quality time with his/her parents and family members.

10. Nighttime Fears (6)

A. The client has demonstrated a significant amount of fearfulness and distress at night when it is time to separate from parents and sleep in his/her own room.

B. The client has often refused to sleep without the parents being present in the same room at night.

C. In today's therapy session the client verbalized his/her fears about sleeping alone.

D. The client's nighttime fears have gradually diminished and he/she has exhibited less distress when having to separate from the parents at bedtime.

E. The client has consistently slept in his/her own room at night without exhibiting any emotional distress or fearfulness.

11. Recurrent Nightmares (7)

A. The client has experienced frequent nightmares centering around the themes of separation from major attachment figures.

B. The client has often entered into his/her parents' room at night after experiencing a nightmare.

C. The client has continued to experience nightmares centering around the theme of separation.

D. The client has not experienced any recent nightmares.

E. The client reported that he/she has experienced a significant reduction in the frequency of his/her nightmares.

12. Frequent Somatic Complaints (8)

A. The client has expressed frequent somatic complaints when anticipating separations from home or major attachment figures.

B. The client expressed somatic complaints in today's therapy session after separating from his/her parents/caregivers.

C. The frequency and intensity of the client's somatic complaints have gradually started to decrease.

D. The client was able to separate from his/her parents in today's therapy session without voicing any somatic complaints.

E. The frequency and intensity of the client's somatic complaints have decreased significantly since the onset of treatment.

13. Traumatic Event History (9)

A. The client has had much difficulty separating from major attachment figures since experiencing a traumatic event.

B. The client verbally acknowledged that he/she has been more anxious and fearful since experiencing the traumatic event.

C. The client's separation anxiety has started to decrease since he/she began to express and work through his/her fears and painful emotions about the past traumatic event.

D. The client was guarded and reluctant to talk about the past traumatic event in today's therapy session.

E. The client was open and talkative about the past traumatic event in today's therapy session.

F. The client has demonstrated a significant reduction in his/her separation anxiety since working through many of his/her fears and feelings surrounding the past traumatic event.

14. Separation, Loss, Abandonment History (9)

A. The client has demonstrated a significant increase in separation anxiety since experiencing a major separation, loss, or abandonment.

B. The client appeared visibly anxious and upset in today's therapy session when talking about the past separation, loss, or abandonment.

C. The client was guarded and reluctant to talk about the past separation, loss, or abandonment in today's therapy session.

D. The client was open and talkative about the past separation, loss, or abandonment.

E. The client's separation anxiety has started to decrease as he/she works through his/her fears and feelings about the past separation, loss, or abandonment.

F. The client has successfully worked through his/her feelings about the past separation, loss, or abandonment and no longer exhibits any signs of separation anxiety.

15. Excessive Need for Reassurance (9)

A. The parents reported that the client seeks frequent reassurance about his/her safety and protection from possible harm or danger.

B. In today's therapy session the client sought reassurance from his/her parents about his/her safety.

C. The client has slowly started to calm himself/herself down and does not require as much reassurance as previously about his/her safety or protection from harm or danger.

D. The parents reported that the client seldom needs reassurance about his/her safety or protection from possible harm or danger.

16. Low Self-Esteem (10)

A. The client's low self-esteem and lack of confidence in himself/herself has contributed to his/her fears of being alone or participating in social activities.

B. In today's therapy session the client expressed strong feelings of inadequacy and insecurity about having to socialize with others or participate in social activities.

C. During today's therapy session the client expressed strong feelings or insecurity about separating from his/her attachment figures.

D. In today's therapy session the client verbalized confidence about his/her ability to socialize with others and participate in social activities.

E. The client has regularly participated in social activities without displaying any separation anxiety.

17. Excessive Shrinking from Unfamiliar or New Situations (11)

A. The client has displayed a pervasive pattern of withdrawing or shrinking away from unfamiliar people or new social situations.

B. In today's therapy session the client expressed feelings of anxiety and insecurity about having to interact with unfamiliar people or when placed in new social situations.

C. The client has gradually started to assert himself/herself more often in new social situations or when around unfamiliar people.

D. The client expressed increased confidence about his/her ability to socialize with unfamiliar people.

E. The client has consistently been able to converse or socialize with others in new social situations without displaying any separation anxiety.

INTERVENTIONS IMPLEMENTED

1. Psychological Testing (1)*

A. The client was referred for a psychological evaluation to assess the severity of his/her anxiety and help gain greater insight into the dynamics contributing to his/her symptoms.

B. The client was very guarded and reserved during the psychological testing.

---

* The numbers in parentheses correlate to the number of the Therapeutic Interventions statement in the companion chapter with same title in *The Child Psychotherapy Treatment Planner* (Jongsma, Peterson, and McInnis) by John Wiley & Sons, 2000.

C. The client appeared visibly anxious about taking part in the psychological testing.

D. The client was cooperative during the psychological testing and did not appear to be highly anxious.

2. Give Evaluation Feedback (2)

A. The family members were given feedback from the psychological testing.

B. The results from the psychological testing revealed that the client is experiencing a high level of anxiety.

C. The results from the psychological testing revealed that the client is experiencing a moderate amount of anxiety.

D. The results from the psychological testing revealed that the client is experiencing a mild amount of anxiety.

E. The results from the psychological testing did not reveal the presence of an anxiety disorder.

3. Build Therapeutic Trust (3)

A. The objective of today's therapy session was to establish trust with the client so that he/she can begin to identify and express his/her feelings.

B. Attempts were made to build the level of trust with the client through consistent eye contact, active listening, unconditional positive regard, and warm acceptance.

C. The client's expression of thoughts and feelings during the therapy session was supported empathetically.

D. The therapy session was helpful in building a moderate level of trust with the client.

E. The therapy session was not successful in establishing trust with the client as he/she remained guarded when discussing the factors contributing to his/her fears and anxiety.

4. Explore Origins of Fears (4)

A. Today's therapy session explored the origins and triggers of the client's fear of separation.

B. Today's therapy session assessed the strength of the client's fear of separation.

C. The therapy session helped identify the origins and triggers of the client's fear of separation.

D. The therapy session was not successful in identifying the origins or triggers of the client's fear of separation.

5. Explore Irrational Cognitive Messages (5)

A. Today's therapy session explored the irrational cognitive messages that produce the client's anxiety or fear about separation.

B. The client was helped to identify the irrational, negative cognitive messages that contribute to his/her anxiety and fears about separation.

C. The client was strongly encouraged to challenge the irrational thoughts that contribute to his/her anxiety and fears about separation.

6. Reality-Based Cognitive Messages (6)

A. To help cope with his/her anxiety and fears, the client was assisted in developing reality-based cognitive messages.

B. The client reported that the use of reality-based cognitive messages has helped to increase his/her confidence while decreasing his/her anxiety and fearfulness.

C. The client has failed to follow through with using reality-based cognitive messages to help decrease his/her anxiety and fearfulness.

D. The client was encouraged to use positive self-talk to increase his/her level of confidence.

E. The client was given a homework assignment to verbalize at least one positive self-statement around his/her peers.

7. Teach Fear Realization Improbability (7)

A. Today's therapy session helped the client realize how his/her fears about separation are irrational or unrealistic.

B. A cognitive-behavioral therapy approach was used to help the client realize how his/her fears about separation are irrational or unrealistic.

C. The client was helped to realize how his/her irrational or negative thinking is self-defeating and exacerbates his/her anxiety and fearfulness.

D. The client was helped to realize how the probability of his/her fears actually coming true are quite low.

E. The client was taught to replace his/her irrational or negative thinking with reality-based cognitive messages.

8. Teach Relaxation Techniques/Guided Imagery (8)

A. The client was taught relaxation techniques and guided imagery to help reduce his/her anxiety and fearfulness related to separations.

B. The client reported a positive response to the use of relaxation or guided imagery techniques to help decrease his/her anxiety and fearfulness.

C. The client has failed to use the relaxation or guided imagery techniques and as a result has continued to experience anxiety and fearfulness about possible harm or danger befalling his/her major attachment figures.

9. Encourage Positive Self-Talk (9)

A. The client was encouraged to utilize positive self-talk as a means of managing his/her anxiety or fears associated with separation.

B. The client was encouraged to utilize positive self-talk to increase his/her confidence about coping with separations.

C. The client was given a homework assignment to daily record in a journal at least one positive experience that occurred while away from his/her major attachment figures.

10. Use Biofeedback Techniques (10)

A. The client was trained in the use of biofeedback techniques to increase his/her relaxation skills and decrease the level of his/her anxiety.

B. The client was trained in the use of biofeedback techniques to improve his/her relaxation skills and decrease the frequency and intensity of his/her somatic ailments.

C. The client reported that the biofeedback techniques have helped to decrease his/her level of anxiety and fearfulness.

D. The client reported that the biofeedback techniques have helped to decrease the frequency and intensity of his/her somatic ailments.

E. The client reported that the biofeedback techniques have not been helpful in reducing his/her level of anxiety.

11. Encourage Parents' Limit Setting (11)

A. Counseled the parents about the importance of setting firm, consistent limits on the client's temper tantrums and/or excessive clinging or whining.

B. The parents acknowledged that they have been reluctant to set firm, consistent limits because of their desire to avoid dealing with the client's temper outbursts or heightened emotional distress.

C. The parents were instructed to remain calm and firmly in control when they first begin to set limits on the client's temper tantrums, excessive clinging, or whining.

D. The parents have become more firm and consistent in their limit setting.

12. Develop Reward System/Contingency Contract (12)

A. The client and parents identified a list of rewards to reinforce the client for managing separations from his/her parents without displaying excessive emotional distress.

B. A reward system was designed to reinforce the client for managing separations from his/her parents in a calm and confident manner.

C. The client signed a contingency contract specifying the negative consequences for his/her temper tantrums, excessive clinging, or whining that occur around separation points.

D. The client and parents verbally agreed to the terms of the contingency contract.

E. The reward system and/or contingency contract have helped the client manage separations from his/her parents without exhibiting excessive emotional distress.

13. Assign Time Spent in Independent Play (13)

A. The client was directed to spend gradually longer periods of time in independent play or with friends after school.

B. An action plan was developed to help the client spend gradually longer periods of time in individual play or with friends after school.

C. A reward system was designed and implemented to reinforce the client for spending gradually longer periods of time in independent play or with friends after school.

D. The parents were strongly encouraged to praise and reinforce the client for engaging in independent play or spending time with friends after school.

E. The client is spending more time away from parents/caregivers in independent peer group play.

14. Identify Past Successful Mechanisms (14)

A. Inquired into what the client does differently on days when he/she is able to separate from parents without displaying excessive clinging, pleading, crying, or protesting.

B. Today's therapy session was helpful in identifying the positive coping mechanisms that the client used in the past to successfully manage separations from his/her parents.

C. The client was strongly encouraged to use coping mechanisms similar to those that he/she used in the past to effectively separate from parents without displaying excessive clinging, pleading, crying, or protesting.

D. The client shared his/her realization that talking or playing with other peers helped to decrease his/her anxiety or fearfulness around separation points.

E. Today's family therapy session revealed that the client was able to manage separations effectively in the past when the parents provided encouragement and set limits on his/her temper tantrums, pleading, crying, protesting, or excessive clinging.

F. The client has begun using mechanisms currently that have been successful in the past.

15. Encourage Peer Group Activities (15)

A. The client was strongly encouraged to participate in extracurricular or positive peer group activities to help him/her feel more comfortable and relaxed around others.

B. The client was assisted in developing a list of extracurricular or positive peer group activities that will help provide him/her with the opportunity to establish meaningful friendships at school and in the neighborhood.

C. The client verbally recognized how his/her feelings of insecurity and inadequacy contribute to his/her reluctance to become involved in extracurricular or positive peer group activities.

D. The client reported that his/her recent participation in extracurricular or positive peer group activities has helped him/her cope more effectively with separations.

E. The client has continued to have problems separating from his/her parents/caregivers and has not recently participated in any extracurricular or positive peer group activities.

16. Teach Coping Skills via Behavioral Rehearsal/Role Play (16)

A. Behavioral rehearsal and role-playing techniques were utilized to help teach the client positive social skills and coping strategies to reduce his/her social anxiety.

B. The client was able to identify several positive social skills after engaging in the behavioral rehearsal and role playing exercises.

C. The client was able to identify several positive coping strategies that he/she can use to reduce his/her social anxiety.

D. After role playing in the therapy session, the client expressed a willingness to practice the newly learned social skills in his/her everyday situations.

E. The client was given the homework assignment to practice the newly learned social skills at least three to five times before the next therapy session.

17. Play "Draw Me Out" Game (17)

A. Played the Draw Me Out game (Shapiro) to help establish rapport with the client.

B. Played the Draw Me Out game to help the client overcome his/her shyness and communicate more effectively with peers.

C. After playing the Draw Me Out game, the client was able to identify several assertiveness and communication skills that will help him/her feel more confident and less anxious around peers.

D. The client was given the homework assignment of practicing the social or communication skills that he/she learned from playing the Draw Me Out game.

E. The client identified the Draw Me Out game as being helpful in reducing his/her social anxiety and shyness.

18. Assign Overnight Visit with Friend (18)

A. The client was given a directive to invite a friend for an overnight visit and/or set up an overnight visit at a friend's home.

B. The client was helped to identify positive coping strategies that he/she can use to reduce anxiety when spending the night at a friend's house.

C. The parents were strongly encouraged to praise and reinforce the client for having a friend sleep over at his/her house or spending the night at a friend's home.

D. The client was praised and reinforced for having a successful overnight visit.

E. Explored the client's fears that contribute to his/her reluctance to have an overnight visit with a friend.

19. Assign Task that Facilitates Autonomy (19)

A. The client and parents were helped to identify specific tasks that the client can perform to facilitate increased autonomy and provide him/her with a sense of empowerment.

B. The client was given the directive to perform a specific task to facilitate greater autonomy and increase his/her level of confidence.

C. The parents identified a specific chore that the client could perform at home to facilitate greater autonomy and provide him/her with a sense of empowerment.

D. The client was directed to write a school paper on a topic of interest without obtaining any assistance from the parents.

E. The client performed the assigned task and reported that it helped increase his/her level of confidence.

20. "Explore Your World" Exercise (20)

A. The client was assigned the "Explore Your World" exercise from *The Brief Child Therapy Homework Planner* (Jongsma, Peterson, and McInnis) to help foster greater autonomy and increase his/her time spent in independent play or activities outside of the home.

B. The client was assigned the "Explore Your World" exercise to help him/her tolerate separations from parents or attachment figures more effectively.

C. The client was assigned the "Explore Your World" exercise to help decrease the intensity of his/her fears about the surrounding environment being a foreboding or ominous place.

D. The client and parents reported that the "Explore Your World" exercise helped the client tolerate separations from the parents more effectively.

E. The client reported that the "Explore Your World" exercise helped to decrease the intensity of his/her anxiety and fearfulness.

21. Assign Weekly Outing for Parents (21)

A. The parents were instructed to go on weekly outings without the client to help him/her learn to tolerate separations more effectively.

B. The client was taught relaxation and deep breathing techniques to help reduce his/her separation anxiety while parents are away on their weekly outing.

C. The client was instructed to call a friend or play with siblings to help reduce his/her separation anxiety while parents are away on weekly outing.

D. The parents reported that they complied with the directive to go on a weekly outing without the client.

E. Explored the reasons for the parents' resistance to going on a weekly outing without the client.

22. **Shift Focus from Physical Complaints to Emotional Conflicts (22)**

A. Today's therapy session refocused the client's discussion away from physical complaints to emotional conflicts and the expression of feelings.

B. Today's therapy session helped the client realize how his/her somatic complaints are related to underlying emotional conflicts and painful emotions.

C. The client was helped to identify more effective ways to cope with stress and manage separations to help reduce the chances of him/her developing somatic ailments.

D. Role play and modeling techniques were utilized to help teach the client effective ways to communicate his/her feelings.

E. The client was taught effective communication and assertiveness skills to help him/her communicate feelings more directly.

23. **Teach Power of Insight into Secondary Gain (23)**

A. Today's family therapy session helped the client and his/her parents develop insight into the secondary gain that the client receives from his/her physical illnesses and complaints.

B. The client and parents gained the realization that the client's physical complaints and illnesses are often aimed at eliciting nurturance and drawing the parents closer.

C. The client was helped to identify more effective ways to meet his/her needs instead of developing somatic complaints.

D. The client gained the realization that he/she often develops psychosomatic ailments as a way to avoid stress and/or responsibilities.

E. The client was taught effective coping strategies to help him/her effectively deal with stress or demands that frequently occur when away from parents.

24. **Medical Examination Referral (24)**

A. The client was referred for a thorough medical examination to rule out whether his/her health problems are genuine or psychosomatic in nature.

B. Consulted with the physician about the results from the medical examination.

C. The medical examination revealed that the client has experienced genuine health problems and has subsequently been placed on medication and/or received appropriate treatment.

D. The medical examination did not reveal the presence of any genuine health problems; rather, the client's physical complaints appear to be psychosomatic in nature.

E. The client was encouraged to take the medication as prescribed for his/her genuine health problems.

25. Establish Contract to Sleep in Own Bedroom (25)

A. A contract was established to reinforce the client for being able to sleep in his/her own bedroom at night without exhibiting excessive distress or going into the parents' room at night.

B. The client and parents identified a list of rewards to reinforce the client for being able to sleep in his/her own bedroom at night.

C. A contingency contract was signed by the client and parents specifying the negative consequences of the client going into the parents' bedroom at night.

D. Assessed the parent-child relationship to identify the factors that contribute to the client going into the parents' bedroom at night.

E. The contract and reward system has proven to be effective in helping the client to sleep in his/her own bedroom at night without exhibiting excessive emotional distress.

26. Develop Nighttime Ritual (26)

A. The client and parents were helped to identify a ritual that they could perform at night to help alleviate the client's fears.

B. The client and parents were instructed to perform a ritual at night to help the client manage nighttime fears.

C. The client and parents reported that the nighttime ritual has helped to alleviate the client's fears.

D. The client has continued to be troubled by nighttime fears despite performing the nighttime ritual.

E. The client was praised and reinforced for taking positive steps to alleviate his/her nighttime fears.

27. Assess Family Dynamics (27)

A. A family therapy session was held to assess the dynamics that contribute to the emergence of the client's separation anxiety and fears.

B. The client and family members were asked to identify the stressors that have negatively impacted the family.

C. The client and family members were asked to identify the positive changes that they would like to see occur in the family.

D. The family therapy session was helpful in identifying the factors contributing to the emergence of the client's separation anxiety and fears.

E. The family members appeared guarded when discussing the possible factors that may contribute to the emergence of the client's separation anxiety and fears.

28. Assign House Drawing (28)

A. The client was instructed to draw a picture of a house and then create a story telling what it is like to live in that home.

B. Processed the content of the client's drawing and story to help assess family dynamics that contribute to the emergence of the client's separation anxiety.

C. The client's drawing and story were helpful in identifying the factors that contribute to his/her separation anxiety.

D. The client's drawing and story provided little insight into the family dynamics contributing to the emergence of the client's separation anxiety.

E. The client's drawing and story led to a discussion about the family dynamics that contribute to the client's separation anxiety.

29. Employ Family Sculpting Technique (29)

A. The family sculpting technique was employed to assess family dynamics and identify the roles and behaviors of each family member.

B. The family sculpting technique was helpful in identifying the family dynamics that contribute to the emergence of the client's separation anxiety.

C. The family sculpting technique was employed to help the family members identify the positive changes they would like to see occur within the family.

D. The family sculpting technique helped demonstrate how the client has established an overly dependent relationship on his/her parent(s).

E. The family sculpting technique provided little insight into the factors contributing to the emergence of the client's separation anxiety.

30. Counsel Family about Appropriate Boundaries (30)

A. Today's family therapy session focused on establishing appropriate parent-child boundaries.

B. The family members were counseled about the importance of establishing greater space and privacy.

C. The family members were helped to establish appropriate boundaries regarding space and privacy.

D. The family members were helped to establish rules regarding privacy in the bathroom and bedrooms.

E. Explored the factors contributing to the family members' resistance to respecting one another's space and privacy.

31. Identify Role of Overly Protective Parent (31)

A. The therapy session helped identify how the enmeshed or overly protective parent reinforces the client's dependency and irrational fears.

B. The overly protective parent acknowledged his/her role in reinforcing or maintaining the client's dependency and irrational fears.

C. The overly protective parent became defensive in today's therapy session when discussing his/her role in reinforcing the client's dependency and irrational fears.

D. Explored the reasons why the enmeshed or overly protective parent reinforces the client's dependency and irrational fears.

E. Explored the factors contributing to the enmeshed or overly protective parent's resistance to allowing the client greater autonomy.

32. Refer Enmeshed Parent for Treatment (32)

A. The overly enmeshed parent was assessed for the possibility of having either an anxiety or depressive disorder that may be contributing to the client's separation anxiety.

B. The client's parent was referred for a medication evaluation to help decrease his/her anxiety or depression.

C. Recommendation was made that the overly enmeshed parent pursue individual therapy to help decrease his/her feelings of depression or anxiety.

D. The overly enmeshed parent followed up with the medication evaluation.

E. The overly enmeshed parent followed up with pursuing individual therapy to decrease feelings of depression or anxiety.

33. Encourage Parents to Reinforce Autonomy (33)

A. The parents were strongly encouraged to provide praise and positive reinforcement for the client's autonomous behaviors.

B. The parents were strongly encouraged to set limits on the client's overly dependent behaviors.

C. The parents were encouraged to praise the client for engaging in independent play or socializing with friends.

D. The parents were encouraged to set limits on the client's attempts to enter into their room at night.

E. The parents were encouraged to send the client back to his/her bedroom at night.

34. Assign "Parents' Time Away" Exercise (34)

A. The parents were assigned the "Parents' Time Away" exercise from *The Brief Child Therapy Homework Planner* (Jongsma, Peterson, and McInnis) to help decrease the enmeshment between the client and them.

B. The "Parents' Time Away" homework assignment was given to the parents so that they can begin to take active steps toward helping the client function more independently.

C. The client was taught effective coping strategies to help him/her manage his/her anxiety or fears when the parents go away on their outing.

D. The parents reported that the homework assignment has helped the client to manage separations more effectively.

E. Explored the reasons for the parents' resistance to going away on weekly outings without the client.

35. Employ Paradoxical Intervention (35)

A. A paradoxical intervention was employed to work around the family's resistance and disengage the client from the overly protective parent.

B. The paradoxical intervention was successful in disengaging the client from the overly protective parent.

C. The parents failed to follow through with implementing the paradoxical intervention, and were encouraged to employ it before the next therapy session.

D. Explored the reasons for the parents' failure to follow through with the paradoxical intervention.

E. The paradoxical intervention helped to increase the client's motivation to function more autonomously.

36. Increase Time Spent with Disengaged Parent (36)

A. The disengaged or distant parent was strongly encouraged to spend more time with the client on a regular basis.

B. The disengaged or distant parent was directed to go on an outing with the client.

C. The disengaged or distant parent was instructed to assist the client with his/her homework.

D. The client and disengaged or distant parent were assigned to work on a project together around the home.

E. The increased time spent together by the client and disengaged parent has helped them develop a closer relationship.

37. Assess Marital Dyad (37)

A. Today's therapy session assessed the marital dyad for possible conflict and triangulation that deflects the focus away from the discord and onto the client's symptoms.

B. Today's therapy session revealed that the client's separation anxiety initially emerged around the time when the parents began to experience marital conflict with one another.

C. The client verbalized his/her fear and anxiety about the parents possibly getting a separation or divorce.

D. The recommendation was made that the parents seek marital counseling.

E. The parents agreed to follow through with marital counseling to address their areas of conflict.

38. Explore for Trauma History (38)

A. Today's therapy session explored whether the client's anxiety and fear about separation are associated with previously unresolved separation, loss, trauma, or realistic danger.

B. The assessment revealed that the client began to have trouble tolerating separations after experiencing a significant separation or loss.

C. The assessment revealed that the client began having trouble managing separations after experiencing a traumatic event.

D. The assessment revealed that the client began having trouble managing separations after being exposed to a realistic danger.

39. Probe Feelings about Painful Event (39)

A. The client was given encouragement and support in expressing his/her feelings associated with a past separation, loss, trauma, or realistic danger.

B. The client was helped to identify and clarify his/her feelings associated with a past separation, loss, trauma, or realistic danger.

C. Client centered therapy principles were used to encourage and support the client in expressing his/her feelings surrounding a past separation, loss, trauma, or realistic danger.

D. The empty-chair technique was utilized to help the client express and work through his/her feelings associated with a past separation, loss, trauma, or realistic danger.

E. The client was encouraged to utilize a journal to express his/her thoughts and feelings associated with a past separation, loss, trauma, or realistic danger.

40. Take Steps to Protect Client (40)

A. A family therapy session was held to discuss and identify the appropriate steps that need to be taken to protect the client and other children in the home from ongoing danger, abuse, or trauma.

B. An individual therapy session was held to help the client identify the appropriate steps that he/she can take to protect self from ongoing danger, abuse, or trauma.

C. Consulted with criminal justice officials and child protection case managers about implementing the necessary steps to protect the client and other children in the home from ongoing danger, abuse, or trauma.

D. Consulted with criminal justice officials and child protection case managers to determine whether the perpetrator should be removed from the home.

E. Recommendation was made that the perpetrator be removed from the home in order to protect the client and siblings from further danger, abuse, or trauma.

41. Design Letter about Past Trauma (41)

A. The client was given the homework assignment to write a letter to express his/her thoughts and feelings about a previous separation or loss.

B. The client was given the homework assignment of writing a letter to express his/her thoughts and feelings about a past traumatic or dangerous event.

C. Processed the content of the client's letter in today's therapy session.

D. The client's letter reflected strong feelings of anger about a past separation, loss, trauma, or realistic danger.

E. The client's letter reflected feelings of sadness, hurt, and vulnerability about a past separation, loss, trauma, or realistic danger.

42. Assign Letting-Go Exercise (42)

A. Explored whether the client was willing to perform a letting-go exercise in which a symbol of the past separation, loss, or trauma would be destroyed.

B. The client was assigned a letting-go exercise in which a symbol of the past separation, loss, or trauma would be destroyed.

C. Processed the client's thoughts and feelings about the letting-go exercise.

D. The client identified the letting-go exercise as being helpful in releasing his/her feelings about a past separation, loss, trauma, or realistic danger.

E. The client stated that he/she was unable to perform the letting-go exercise because he/she does not feel ready to let go of his/her emotions surrounding the past separation, loss, trauma, or realistic danger.

43. Utilize Child-Centered Play Therapy (43)

A. Child-centered play-therapy principles were utilized to help the client express his/her feelings and work through his/her fears about separation.

B. The client was given unconditional positive regard and warm acceptance in expressing his/her feelings and worries about facing separations.

C. The client's feelings and fears about separation were reflected back to him/her in a nonjudgmental manner.

D. Reinforced the client's capacity to overcome his/her anxiety or fears about separation.

E. The child-centered play-therapy principles have helped the client successfully work through his/her fears about separation.

44. Implement Psychoanalytic Play Therapy (44)

A. Using a psychoanalytic play-therapy approach, the client was allowed to take the lead in exploring the unconscious conflicts or core anxieties that contribute to his/her separation anxiety.

B. Using a psychoanalytic play-therapy approach, the client's core conflicts and fears about separation were identified and processed.

C. Processed and worked through the transference issues that emerged in today's therapy session.

D. Interpreted the client's feeling and fears expressed in his/her play and related them to his/her fears about separation.

E. The psychoanalytic play-therapy approach has helped the client work through and resolve the issues contributing to his/her separation anxiety.

45. Employ Mutual Storytelling Technique (45)

A. The client actively participated in the mutual storytelling exercise.

B. Using the mutual storytelling technique, the therapist modeled effective ways for the client to overcome his/her anxiety or fears about separation.

C. The client created a story using puppets, dolls, or stuffed animals that reflected his/her anxieties and fears.

D. The client was helped to create a story using puppets, dolls, or stuffed animals that showed effective ways to cope with his/her fear and anxiety.

E. The client identified the mutual storytelling technique as being a fun and useful way to find solutions to overcome his/her fears or anxieties.

46. Conduct Filial Play Therapy (46)

A. A filial play-therapy session was held to help develop a closer parent-child relationship between the client and the detached parent.

B. The client and detached parent actively participated in the mutual storytelling exercise.

C. Using a mutual storytelling technique, the client and detached parent were instructed to create a story using puppets, dolls, or stuffed animals to identify ways to reduce fear.

D. The client and detached parent were encouraged to use the mutual storytelling technique at home to help reduce the client's fears and anxieties when they begin to emerge.

E. The client and detached parent identified the mutual storytelling technique as being a fun and helpful way to create understanding and closeness between them.

47. Utilize Art Therapy Techniques (47)

A. The client was instructed to draw a picture or create a sculpture reflecting what he/she fears will happen upon separation from major attachment figures.

B. Processed the content of the client's artwork and discussed whether his/her fears about separation are realistic or unrealistic.

C. The client's artwork reflected his/her fears of some catastrophic event occurring when separated from major attachment figures.

D. The client's artwork reflected his/her fears of some possible harm or danger befalling self or others after separating from major attachment figures.

E. After completing his/her artwork, the client was helped to identify effective ways to overcome his/her fears about separation.

48. Teach Effective Communication Skills (48)

A. The client and parents were taught effective communication skills in today's therapy session.

B. Role-playing techniques were used to teach effective communication skills.

C. The client reported that the newly acquired communication skills have helped him/her feel more relaxed and confident in different social situations when away from parents.

D. The client was given the directive to practice his/her newly learned communication skills with peers at school and in the neighborhood.

E. The client failed to practice the newly acquired communication skills because of his/her resistance to separating from parents.

49. Play "Stand Up for Yourself" Game (49)

A. Played the Stand Up for Yourself game (Shapiro) to help establish rapport with the client.

B. Played the Stand Up for Yourself game to help teach the client effective assertiveness skills and thereby help him/her feel more confident at school after separating from parents.

C. After playing the Stand Up for Yourself game, the client was able to identify several assertiveness and communication skills that will help him/her feel more confident and relaxed around others after separating from parents.

D. The client was given the homework assignment of practicing the assertiveness skills that he/she learned from playing the Stand Up for Yourself game.

E. The client reported that he/she was able to successfully practice the newly acquired assertiveness skills.

50. Group Therapy Referral (50)

A. The client was referred for group therapy to improve his/her social skills and overcome social anxieties.

B. The client was agreeable to receiving group therapy to help improve his/her social skills and overcome social anxieties.

C. The client voiced his/her objection to being referred for group therapy to improve his/her social skills.

D. The client was given the directive to self-disclose at least two times in each group therapy session.

E. The client was encouraged to make positive self-statements or share significant life experiences in the group therapy sessions.

51. Medication Evaluation Referral (51)

A. The client was referred for a medication evaluation with a physician or psychiatrist to decrease his/her anxiety or emotional distress.

B. The client and parents agreed to follow through with the recommendation to receive a medication evaluation from a physician.

C. The client was strongly opposed to being placed on medication to help decrease his/her social anxiety or emotional distress.

52. Monitor Medication Effects (52)

A. The client reported that he/she has been taking his/her medication as prescribed.

B. The client has not complied with taking his/her medication on a regular basis.

C. The client reported that the medication has helped to decrease his/her anxiety and emotional distress.

D. The client reported little to no improvement on the medication.

E. The client reported experiencing side effects from the prescribed medication.

SEXUAL ABUSE VICTIM

CLIENT PRESENTATION

1. Self-Report of Sexual Abuse (1)*

A. The client reported that he/she has been sexually abused.

B. The client was guarded and evasive when being questioned about whether he/she has ever been sexually abused.

C. The client has previously reported being sexually abused, but has since recanted these earlier statements.

D. The client has verbally denied being sexually abused, although there is other evidence to suggest that he/she has been abused.

2. Physical Signs of Sexual Abuse (2)

A. The medical examination revealed physical signs of sexual abuse.

B. The medical examination did not reveal any physical signs of sexual abuse.

3. Strong Interest about Sexuality Issues (3)

A. The client has displayed a strong interest in or curiosity about issues related to sexuality since his/her sexual victimization.

B. The client exhibited a strong interest in or curiosity about issues related to sexuality in the therapy session.

C. The client's strong interest in or curiosity about issues related to sexuality has masked deeper feelings of sadness, hurt, and helplessness about his/her own sexual victimization.

D. The client has demonstrated less of a preoccupation with issues related to sexuality since addressing his/her own sexual abuse issues.

4. Advanced Knowledge of Sexuality (3)

A. The client has developed an advanced knowledge of sexuality for a child his/her age.

B. The client has developed an advanced knowledge of sexuality because of his/her past sexual victimization.

C. The client spoke about sophisticated sexual behaviors in today's therapy session.

D. The client has developed an age-appropriate knowledge of sexuality.

5. Sexualized Behaviors (4)

A. The client has displayed highly sexualized behaviors with his/her family members, other adults, and peers.

B. The client has engaged in inappropriate sexual behavior with younger or same-aged children.

* The numbers in parentheses correlate to the number of the Behavioral Definition statement in the companion chapter with same title in *The Child Psychotherapy Treatment Planner* (Jongsma, Peterson, and McInnis) by John Wiley & Sons, 2000.

C. The client's past sexual victimization has contributed to his/her highly sexualized behaviors.

D. The client has engaged in sexualized behaviors with others in an attempt to meet his/her dependency needs.

E. The client has not engaged in any recent sexual behaviors.

6. Sexual Themes in Play/Artwork (4)

A. The parent(s) and teachers reported that sexual themes often emerge in the client's play or artwork.

B. Sexual themes appeared in the client's play during today's therapy session.

C. The client's artwork reflected a strong sexual preoccupation.

D. The client has recently engaged in sexualized play with his/her peers.

E. Sexual themes have not appeared in the client's recent play or artwork.

7. Recurrent and Intrusive Recollections of Sexual Abuse (5)

A. The client has experienced recurrent, intrusive, and distressing recollections of the past sexual abuse.

B. The client has reexperienced intrusive and distressing recollections of the past sexual abuse after coming into contact with the perpetrator and/or having exposure to sexual topics.

C. The client denied being troubled any longer by intrusive recollections of the sexual abuse.

8. Recurrent Nightmares (5)

A. The client has experienced recurrent nightmares of the past sexual abuse.

B. The client reported that he/she continues to be troubled by recurrent nightmares of the past sexual abuse.

C. The client has reexperienced nightmares of the sexual abuse since coming into contact with the perpetrator and/or being exposed to sexual topics.

D. The client stated that he/she is no longer troubled by nightmares of the past sexual abuse.

9. Dissociative Flashbacks, Delusions, or Hallucinations (6)

A. The client reported experiencing dissociative flashbacks of the past sexual abuse.

B. The client reported experiencing delusions and hallucinations related to the past sexual abuse.

C. The client reported reexperiencing dissociative flashbacks, delusions, or hallucinations since coming into contact with the perpetrator and/or being exposed to sexual topics.

D. The client stated that dissociative flashbacks, delusions, or hallucinations have ceased.

10. Anger and Rage (7)

A. The client expressed strong feelings of anger and rage about the past sexual abuse.

B. The client has exhibited frequent angry outbursts and episodes of rage since the onset of the sexual abuse.

C. The frequency and intensity of the client's angry outbursts have decreased since he/she has felt more secure and started to work through his/her feelings about the sexual abuse.

D. The intensity of the client's anger has decreased whenever he/she talks about the past sexual abuse.

E. The client has demonstrated a reduction in the frequency and intensity of his/her angry outbursts and episodes of rage.

11. Disturbance of Mood and Affect (8)

A. The client has experienced frequent and prolonged periods of depression, anxiety, and irritability since the sexual abuse occurred.

B. The client appeared visibly depressed when talking about the sexual abuse.

C. The client appeared anxious when talking about the sexual abuse.

D. The client's moods have gradually started to stabilize as he/she works through his/her feelings of sadness, anxiety, insecurity, and anger about the past sexual abuse.

E. The client's moods have stabilized and he/she reports no longer being troubled by frequent or prolonged periods of depression, anxiety, or irritability.

12. Regressive Behaviors (9)

A. The client has engaged in frequent regressive behaviors (e.g., thumb sucking, baby talk, bed wetting) since the onset of the sexual abuse.

B. The client exhibited regressive behaviors in today's therapy session when he/she began talking about the past sexual abuse.

C. The client has engaged in more regressive behaviors since being removed from his/her home.

D. The client was able to talk about sexual abuse issues in today's therapy session without engaging in any regressive behaviors.

E. The client has demonstrated a significant reduction in the frequency of his/her regressive behaviors.

13. Fearfulness/Distrust (10)

A. The client stated that he/she has felt strong feelings of fearfulness and a marked distrust of others since being sexually abused.

B. The client's fearfulness has slowly started to diminish and he/she has begun to establish trust with significant others.

C. The strong support from family and individuals outside the family has helped to decrease the client's fearfulness and distrust.

D. The client has successfully worked through many of his/her feelings surrounding the sexual abuse and has established close, trusting relationships with significant others.

14. Social Withdrawal (10)

A. The client has become significantly more withdrawn from others since the onset of the sexual abuse.

B. The client appeared detached and withdrawn in today's therapy session when the topic of the sexual abuse was being discussed.

C. The client acknowledged that he/she has become more withdrawn because of his/her feelings of low self-esteem and distrust of others.

D. The client has started to become more assertive and outgoing in interactions with family members, other adults, and peers.

15. Family Denial (10)

A. The family members present in today's therapy session stated that they do not believe that the client was sexually abused.

B. The client's family members are currently divided as to whether to believe the client's report that he/she has been sexually abused.

C. The client's family members acknowledged that the sexual abuse has occurred, but have minimized the importance of the issue or the impact that it has had on the client.

D. The denial in the family system about the sexual abuse has ceased.

16. Family Secrecy (10)

A. The client and family members have been secretive about the sexual abuse and until recently have not disclosed it to any individuals or agencies outside of the family.

B. Today's therapy session revealed that key family member(s) remain unaware of the sexual abuse.

C. Therapy has helped to eliminate the secrecy within the family about the sexual abuse.

17. Inappropriate Parent-Child Boundaries (10)

A. The inappropriate parent-child boundaries within the family system have been one of the significant contributing factors to the emergence of the sexual abuse.

B. The parents have established very weak and inappropriate parent-child boundaries.

C. The parent(s) have started to take active steps to establish appropriate parent-child boundaries.

D. Therapy has helped to establish appropriate parent-child boundaries and generational lines in the family to greatly minimize the risk of sexual abuse ever occurring in the future.

18. Feelings of Guilt and Shame (11)

A. The client expressed strong feelings of guilt and shame about the past sexual abuse.

B. The client has continued to experience strong feelings of guilt and shame about the past sexual abuse, despite being given reassurance that he/she is not responsible for the sexual abuse.

C. The client's feelings of guilt and shame have started to decrease as he/she now recognizes that the perpetrator is responsible for the sexual abuse.

D. The client has successfully worked through and resolved his/her feelings of guilt and shame about the past sexual abuse.

19. Low Self-Esteem (11)

A. The client expressed strong feelings of low self-esteem and insecurity about the past sexual abuse.

B. The client's self-esteem has started to improve as he/she works through his/her feelings about the past sexual abuse.

C. Strong family support has helped to increase the client's self-esteem.

D. The client verbalized several positive self-descriptive statements during today's therapy session.

INTERVENTIONS IMPLEMENTED

1. Building Trust (1)*

A. The focus of today's therapy session was on building the level of trust with the client through consistent eye contact, active listening, unconditional positive regard, and warm acceptance.

B. The therapy session was helpful in building the level of trust with the client.

C. The therapy session did not prove to be helpful in building the level of trust with the client as he/she remained guarded in talking about the sexual abuse.

2. Expression of Feelings (2)

A. The client was given encouragement and support to tell the entire story of the sexual abuse and to express his/her feelings experienced during and after the abuse.

B. The client described the sequence of events before, during, and after the sexual abuse incidents, but neither showed nor talked of any feelings.

C. Client-centered principles were used to encourage and support the client in expressing his/her feelings surrounding the past sexual abuse.

D. The parent(s) were encouraged to allow the client opportunities at home to express his/her thoughts and feelings about the sexual abuse.

3. Report Sexual Abuse (3)

A. The sexual abuse was reported to the appropriate child protection agency.

B. Criminal justice officials have been informed of the sexual abuse.

C. The client has been referred for a medical examination to determine whether there are any physical signs of the sexual abuse and/or evaluate any health problems that may have resulted from the sexual abuse.

D. The client and family members were supportive of the sexual abuse being reported to the appropriate child protection agency or criminal justice officials.

E. The client and family members objected to the sexual abuse being reported to the appropriate child protection agency or criminal justice officials.

4. Veracity of Sexual Abuse Charges (4)

A. Consulted with child protection case manager and criminal justice officials to assess the veracity of the client's sexual abuse charges.

B. Consulted with the physician who examined the client to assess the veracity of the sexual abuse charges.

---

* The numbers in parentheses correlate to the number of the Therapeutic Interventions statement in the companion chapter with same title in *The Child Psychotherapy Treatment Planner* (Jongsma, Peterson, and McInnis) by John Wiley & Sons, 2000.

C. Consultation with the child protection case managers, criminal justice officials, and physician has provided strong support for the client's reports that he/she has been sexually abused.

D. Consultation with the child protection case managers, criminal justice officials, and physician has provided inconclusive evidence as to whether the client has been sexually abused.

E. Consultation with the child protection case managers, criminal justice officials, and physician has provided little or no support for the client's reports that he/she has been sexually abused.

5. Consultation to Develop Appropriate Treatment Interventions (5)

A. Consulted with the criminal justice officials and child protection case managers about developing appropriate treatment interventions.

B. Consulted with the client's physicians about developing appropriate treatment interventions.

C. After consulting with the child protection case managers, criminal justice officials, and physician, the recommendation was made that the client should receive individual therapy to address the sexual abuse issues.

D. The consultation meeting with the child protection and criminal justice officials produced the recommendation that family therapy be mandatory.

E. After consulting with the child protection case managers and criminal justice officials, it was determined that the perpetrator be required to participate in his/her own therapy.

6. Reveal Sexual Abuse to Family (6)

A. A conjoint therapy session was held to reveal the sexual abuse to key family member(s) or caregiver(s).

B. A family therapy session was held to eliminate the secrecy about the client's sexual abuse.

C. A conjoint therapy session was held to reveal the nature, frequency, and duration of the sexual abuse to key family member(s) and/or caregiver(s).

7. Remove Perpetrator from Home (7)

A. Consulted with criminal justice officials and child protection case managers to determine whether the perpetrator should be removed from the home.

B. Recommendation was made that the perpetrator be removed from the home in order to protect the client and siblings from future occurrences of sexual abuse.

C. The perpetrator was court-ordered to leave the home and not be allowed any contact with the client and/or family member(s).

D. The perpetrator was required to leave the home, but will be allowed supervised visitation with the client and/or family member(s).

E. Recommendation was made that the perpetrator be allowed to remain in the home under the conditions that he/she agrees to and follows through with treatment.

8. Protect Client and Other Children (8)

A. Consulted with criminal justice officials and child protection case managers about implementing the necessary steps to protect the client and other children in the home from future sexual abuse.

B. A family therapy session was held to discuss and identify the appropriate steps that need to be taken to protect the client and other children in the home from future sexual abuse.

C. An individual therapy session was held to provide the client with the opportunity to identify what steps he/she feels need to occur in order to feel safe.

9. Consider Placement of Client (9)

A. Consulted with criminal justice officials and child protection case managers to assess whether it is safe for the client to remain in the home or if he/she should be removed.

B. The decision was made that the client be allowed to remain in the home, while the perpetrator was required to leave.

C. The decision was made to allow the client to continue living in the home because it was felt that the nonabusive parent would take the necessary steps to protect him/her from further sexual abuse.

D. Recommendation was made that the client be placed in a foster home to ensure his/her protection from further sexual abuse.

E. Recommendation was made that the client be placed in a residential treatment program to ensure his/her protection from further sexual abuse and provide treatment for his/her emotional/behavioral problems.

10. Confront Denial within Family System (10)

A. The family members' denial about the impact of the sexual abuse was confronted and challenged so that they can begin to provide the support the client needs in order to make a healthy adjustment.

B. The family members' denial of the sexual abuse was strongly challenged and responsibility for the sexual abuse was placed on the perpetrator.

C. The therapy session was helpful in working through the family members' denial surrounding the sexual abuse, and they agreed to follow through with the necessary treatment and support.

D. The therapy session was not successful in working through the family members' denial about the sexual abuse.

11. Empower Client (11)

A. Today's therapy session sought to empower the client by reinforcing the steps necessary to protect himself/herself.

B. Today's therapy session sought to empower the client by praising and reinforcing his/her decision to report the sexual abuse to the appropriate individuals or agencies.

C. The client was strongly encouraged to contact a child protection "hotline," police, or the therapist if he/she is ever sexually abused in the future.

D. The client was helped to identify a list of safe places where he/she can go if feeling at risk of sexual abuse.

E. The client was taught effective assertiveness and communication skills to help him/her stand up for himself/herself and feel safe.

12. Establish Boundaries within Family System (12)

A. The family members were counseled about establishing appropriate parent-child boundaries to ensure the protection of the client and other children in the home from further sexual abuse.

B. The family members were counseled about establishing appropriate adult-child boundaries regarding privacy, physical contact, and verbal content.

C. An assessment of the family system revealed weak and blurred parent-child boundaries.

D. Today's therapy session sought to strengthen the roles and responsibilities of the non-abusive parent in enforcing appropriate privacy, physical contact, verbal content, and adult-child boundaries.

13. Explore Stress Factors or Precipitating Events (13)

A. Today's therapy session explored the stress factors or precipitating events that contributed to the emergence of the sexual abuse.

B. Today's therapy session explored the family dynamics that have contributed to the emergence of the sexual abuse.

C. Today's therapy session was helpful in identifying the stress factors or precipitating events that contributed to the emergence of the sexual abuse.

D. Today's therapy session identified several family dynamics that have contributed to the emergence of the sexual abuse.

E. The family members were taught positive coping strategies and effective problem-solving approaches to help them manage stress and overcome the identified problems.

14. Detail Where Abuse Occurred in Home (14)

A. The client was given an assignment to draw a diagram of the house where the sexual abuse occurred, indicating where everyone slept, to provide greater insight into the factors or precipitating events that led up to the sexual abuse.

B. The client recounted the story of the sexual abuse as he/she shared the diagram of the house where the sexual abuse occurred.

C. The client's drawing of the diagram where the sexual abuse occurred was helpful in identifying the precipitating events leading up to the sexual abuse.

D. The client shared a diagram of the house where the sexual abuse occurred but was guarded in talking about the details or the precipitating events that led up to the sexual abuse.

E. The client refused to complete the assignment of drawing a diagram of where the sexual abuse occurred.

15. Assign Family Kinetic Drawing (15)

A. The client was instructed to produce a family kinetic drawing to help assess the dynamics that possibly contributed to the emergence of the sexual abuse.

B. The client's family kinetic drawing provided insight into the family dynamics that have contributed to the emergence of the sexual abuse.

C. The client's family kinetic drawing produced little to no insight into the factors contributing to the emergence of the sexual abuse.

D. The client's completion of the family kinetic drawing led to a productive discussion about his/her family relationships.

16. Assign House Drawing (16)

A. The client was asked to draw a picture of a house, then create a story describing what it is like to live in that home.

B. Processed the client's drawing and story to help assess his/her family dynamics.

C. The client's drawing and story reflected his/her feelings of anxiety and fearfulness about the past sexual abuse.

D. The client's drawing and story reflected his/her feelings of anger about the past sexual abuse.

E. The client's feelings were reflected as expressed in the drawing and story, and these feelings were related then to his/her feelings about the past sexual abuse.

17. Construct Family Sex Abuse Genogram (17)

A. The client and family members constructed a multigenerational family genogram that identified the history of sexual abuse within the family.

B. The construction of the multigenerational family genogram helped the client to realize that other family members have been sexually abused and that he/she is not alone.

C. The construction of the multigenerational family genogram helped the perpetrator recognize the cycle of repeated boundary violations within the extended family.

D. The construction of a multigenerational family genogram helped the family members voice their commitment to taking the necessary steps to end the cycle of sexual abuse within their family.

18. Assign Letter to Perpetrator (18)

A. The client was given a homework assignment to write a letter to the perpetrator and bring it to the following therapy session for processing.

B. The client expressed strong feelings of sadness, hurt, and disappointment in his/her letter to the perpetrator.

C. The client expressed strong feelings of anger about the sexual abuse in his/her letter to the perpetrator.

D. The client expressed a willingness to share the letter directly with the perpetrator.

E. After processing the letter, the client reported that he/she is not ready to share his/her thoughts and feelings about the sexual abuse directly with the perpetrator.

19. Employ Art Therapy to Express Feelings toward Perpetrator (19)

A. Art therapy techniques (e.g., drawing, painting, sculpting) were employed to help the client identify and express his/her feelings toward the perpetrator.

B. The client made productive use of the therapy session and was able to express strong feelings of anger toward the perpetrator in his/her artwork.

C. The client's artwork reflected feelings of sadness, anger, hurt, and disappointment that he/she experiences in regard to his/her relationship with the perpetrator.

D. The client appeared uncomfortable and had difficulty expressing his/her feelings toward the perpetrator through art.

20. Utilize Angry Tower Technique (20)

A. The Angry Tower technique (Saxe) was used to help the client express his/her feelings of anger about the past sexual abuse.

B. The client vented strong feelings of anger toward the perpetrator while playing the Angry Tower game.

C. Using the Angry Tower technique, the client expressed strong feelings of anger toward the nonabusive parent for failing to protect him/her from the sexual abuse.

D. The Angry Tower technique has helped the client to express and work through his/her feelings of anger surrounding the past sexual abuse.

21. Utilize Art Therapy to Express Impact on Life (21)

A. The client was instructed to create a drawing or sculpture that reflected how the sexual abuse has impacted his/her life and feelings about himself/herself.

B. The client made productive use of the art therapy session and was able to vividly express how the sexual abuse has impacted his/her life and feelings about self.

C. The client's artwork reflected how the sexual abuse has caused him/her to feel small, helpless, and vulnerable.

D. The client's artwork reflected his/her feelings of guilt and shame about the sexual abuse.

E. The client appeared uncomfortable and had difficulty in expressing through his/her artwork how the sexual abuse has impacted his/her life or feelings about self.

22. Play the "Talking, Feeling, Doing" Game (22)

A. The Talking, Feeling, Doing game was utilized during the initial stage of therapy to help establish rapport with the client.

B. The Talking, Feeling, Doing game proved to be helpful in allowing the client to express his/her feelings about the past sexual abuse.

C. After playing the Talking, Feeling, Doing game, the client was able to talk about how the sexual abuse has affected his/her life.

D. While playing the Talking, Feeling, Doing game the client expressed feelings of sadness about how the sexual abuse has impacted his/her personal and family life.

E. After playing the Talking, Feeling, Doing game, the client was encouraged to express to other family members and supportive individuals his/her thoughts and feelings about the past sexual abuse.

23. Give "You Are Not Alone" Exercise (23)

A. The client was given the "You Are Not Alone" exercise from *The Brief Child Therapy Homework Planner* (Jongsma, Peterson, and McInnis) to help him/her express feelings connected to the sexual abuse and decrease feelings of guilt and shame.

B. The client reported that he/she found the "You Are Not Alone" exercise helpful in reducing his/her feelings of guilt, shame, anger, and fear.

C. The "You are Not Alone" exercise helped the client talk about how the sexual abuse has impacted his/her life.

D. The client did not follow through with completing the "You Are Not Alone" exercise and the assignment was given again.

E. Read the "You Are Not Alone" story in today's group therapy session to facilitate a discussion among group members about how the sexual abuse has impacted their lives.

24. Teach Guided Fantasy and Imagery Techniques (24)

A. Guided fantasy and imagery techniques were taught to help the client identify and express his/her thoughts and feelings associated with the sexual abuse.

B. The client reported a positive response to the use of guided fantasy and imagery techniques to help him/her identify his/her thoughts, feelings, and unmet needs associated with the sexual abuse.

C. Guided fantasy and imagery techniques were used, but the client still had difficulty identifying and expressing his/her thoughts, feelings, and unmet needs associated with the sexual abuse.

25. Solicit Support from Family Members (25)

A. The family members were encouraged to provide emotional support and nurturance for the client to help him/her cope with the sexual abuse.

B. Today's therapy session was successful in eliciting support and nurturance for the client from the other family members.

C. An individual therapy session was held with the nonabusive parent to explore the factors contributing to his/her resistance to provide emotional support and nurturance for the client.

D. A family therapy session was held with the siblings to explore their reluctance to provide emotional support and nurturance for the client.

E. The parent(s) were instructed to provide frequent praise and positive reinforcement to the client to help him/her build self-esteem and feel accepted in the family system.

26. Facilitate Time Spent with Non-Abusive Parent (26)

A. The disengaged, nonabusive parent was directed to spend more time with the client in leisure, school, or household activities.

B. The client and disengaged, nonabusive parent were assisted in identifying a list of activities that they would like to perform together.

C. The client verbalized his/her need to spend greater time with the disengaged, nonabusive parent in leisure, school, or household activities.

D. The disengaged, nonabusive parent verbalized a commitment to spend increased time with the client.

E. Today's therapy session explored the factors contributing to the distant relationship between the client and nonabusive parent.

27. Read *Allies in Healing* (27)

A. The client's parents and significant others were assigned to read *Allies in Healing* (Davis) to assist them in understanding how they can help the client recover from the sexual abuse.

B. The client's parents followed through in reading *Allies in Healing* and found it helpful in identifying ways that they can help the client recover from the sexual abuse.

C. The parents have failed to start reading *Allies in Healing,* and were again encouraged to do so to help them understand how they can help the client recover from the sexual abuse.

28. Confront Perpetrator (28)

A. The perpetrator's denial of the sexual abuse was confronted.

B. The client was helped to prepare to confront the perpetrator about the sexual abuse.

C. The client confronted the perpetrator about how the sexual abuse has negatively impacted his/her life and feelings about self.

D. The perpetrator was confronted about minimizing the significance of the sexual abuse.

E. The perpetrator was confronted with the facts of the sexual abuse, but continued to deny sexually abusing the client.

29. Conduct Apology Session (29)

A. The perpetrator was helped to prepare to apologize to the client and other family members about the sexual abuse.

B. The perpetrator apologized to the client and family members for the sexual abuse.

C. The perpetrator listened appropriately to the client and family members' expressions of anger, hurt, and disappointment about the sexual abuse, and then offered a sincere apology.

D. A decision was made to postpone the apology session because the perpetrator does not appear ready to offer a sincere or genuine apology to the client and family members.

30. Sexual Offender's Group Referral (30)

A. The perpetrator was referred to a sexual offender's group to address his/her inappropriate sexual behaviors.

B. The perpetrator was required by the legal system to attend a sexual offender's group.

C. The perpetrator has consistently attended the sexual offender's group.

D. The perpetrator has failed to consistently attend the sexual offender's group.

E. The perpetrator has been an active participant in the sexual offender's group, and stated that it has helped him/her identify the factors contributing to his/her inappropriate sexual behaviors.

31. Read *Out of the Shadows* (31)

A. The family members were assigned to read *Out of the Shadows* (Carnes) to expand their knowledge of sexually addictive behaviors.

B. The family members read *Out of the Shadows,* and found it helpful in expanding their knowledge about sexually addictive behaviors.

C. The family members have failed to read *Out of the Shadows,* and were again encouraged to do so to expand their knowledge of sexually addictive behaviors.

32. Assign Forgiveness Letter/Forgiveness Exercise (32)

A. The client was given a homework assignment to write a forgiveness letter to the perpetrator and bring it to the following session for processing.

B. The client's letter reflected his/her readiness to offer forgiveness to the perpetrator and/or significant family member(s).

C. The client verbalized his/her forgiveness to the perpetrator and/or significant family member(s) in today's therapy session.

D. After processing the client's letter, it was evident that the client is not ready to offer forgiveness to the perpetrator and/or significant family member(s).

33. Employ Child-Centered Play Therapy (33)

A. A child-centered play-therapy approach was utilized to help the client begin to identify his/her feelings surrounding the past sexual abuse.

B. The client was given unconditional positive regard, warm acceptance, and support while working through his/her feelings surrounding the past sexual abuse in today's play-therapy session.

C. The client's feelings were reflected as expressed in his/her play, and these feelings were then related to his/her feelings about the past sexual abuse.

D. The child-centered play-therapy sessions have helped the client begin to express his/her feelings about the past sexual abuse.

E. The child-centered play-therapy sessions have helped the client work through many of his/her feelings surrounding past sexual abuse.

34. Implement Psychoanalytic Play Therapy (34)

A. Using a psychoanalytic play-therapy approach, the client was allowed to take the lead in exploring and expressing his/her feelings surrounding the past sexual abuse.

B. The client's feelings were interpreted as expressed in his/her play and these feelings were related to his/her feelings about the past sexual abuse.

C. Transference issues that arose in the client's play were processed and worked through.

D. The client has been able to express his/her feelings about the past sexual abuse through the medium of play, but the client has been resistant to openly talk directly about his/her thoughts and feelings.

E. The psychoanalytic play-therapy sessions have helped the client work through many of his/her thoughts and feelings surrounding the past sexual abuse.

35. Utilize Mutual Storytelling Technique (35)

A. The client actively participated in the mutual storytelling exercise.

B. The mutual storytelling technique was used to model constructive steps that the client can take to protect himself/herself and feel more empowered.

C. The client created a story using puppets, dolls, or stuffed animals that reflected his/her feelings of helplessness and vulnerability.

D. The client was helped to create a story using puppets, dolls, or stuffed animals that taught him/her steps that he/she could take to feel safe and protected.

E. The client identified the mutual storytelling technique as being helpful in learning how to protect himself/herself.

36. Employ "Feelings and Faces" Exercise (36)

A. The "Feelings and Faces" exercise from *The Brief Child Therapy Homework Planner* (Jongsma, Peterson, and McInnis) was used to help the client express his/her myriad of emotions surrounding the past sexual abuse.

B. The client reported that the "Feelings and Faces" exercise helped him/her identify and express his/her different emotions about the sexual abuse.

C. After completing the "Feelings and Faces" exercise, the client was able to express his/her different emotions about the sexual abuse to family members or significant others.

D. The client failed to complete the "Feelings and Faces" exercise and was instructed to do it again.

37. Use Mutual Storytelling Technique with Nonabusive Parent (37)

A. The mutual storytelling technique was used in today's filial play-therapy session to help establish a closer relationship between the nonabusive parent and the client.

B. Using a mutual storytelling technique, the client was able to share his/her feelings about the past sexual abuse in the presence of the nonabusive parent.

C. Using a mutual storytelling technique, the nonabusive parent was helped to identify the client's feelings about the past sexual abuse.

D. The nonabusive parent was encouraged to give empathy and support for the client's expression of feelings about the past sexual abuse.

E. The client and nonabusive parent were encouraged to use the mutual storytelling technique to strengthen their relationship.

38. Employ Color-Your-Life Technique (38)

A. The Color-Your-Life technique (O'Connor) was employed to help the client identify and verbalize his/her feelings about the sexual abuse.

B. Using the Color-Your-Life technique, the client expressed strong feelings of sadness and hurt about the past sexual abuse.

C. The Color-Your-Life technique helped the client identify and express his/her feelings of anger about the past sexual abuse.

D. The Color-Your-Life technique helped the client identify how the past sexual abuse made him/her feel anxious, fearful, and helpless.

E. The results of the Color-Your-Life technique reflected the client's ambivalent feelings toward the perpetrator.

39. Encourage Positive Peer Group/Extracurricular Activities (39)

A. The client was encouraged to participate in positive peer group or extracurricular activities to improve his/her self-esteem and gain a sense of acceptance.

B. The client developed a list of positive peer group or extracurricular activities that will provide him/her with the opportunity to establish friendships and improve self-esteem.

C. The client reported that his/her participation in positive peer group or extracurricular activities has helped him/her improve self-esteem and gain a sense of acceptance.

D. The client acknowledged that his/her feelings of low self-esteem and shame have contributed to his/her reluctance to become involved in positive peer group or extracurricular activities in the past.

40. List Supportive People (40)

A. The client was asked to develop a list of resource people outside of the family whom he/she can turn to for support, guidance, and affirmation.

B. The client was given a homework assignment to seek support or guidance from at least one individual outside of his/her family before the next therapy session.

C. The client reported that he/she has benefitted from receiving support, guidance, and affirmation from individuals outside of his/her family.

D. The support that the client has received from resource people outside of the family has helped him/her cope with the trauma of the sexual abuse.

E. The client has been hesitant to turn to the resource people outside of the family for support, guidance, or affirmation because of his/her mistrust.

41. Survivor Group Referral (41)

A. The client was referred to a survivor group with other children to assist him/her in realizing that he/she is not alone in having experienced sexual abuse.

B. The client was given the directive to self-disclose at least once during the group therapy session.

C. The client's participation in the survivor group with other children has helped him/her realize that he/she is not alone in experiencing sexual abuse.

D. The client has actively participated in the survivor group therapy sessions and verbalized many of his/her feelings about the past sexual abuse.

E. The client has offered support to other members of the survivor group when they have shared their thoughts and feelings about their own sexual abuse experiences.

42. Assign Readings (42)

A. Read *A Very Touching Book* (Hindman) to the client in today's therapy session to help him/her verbalize feelings about the past sexual abuse and identify steps that he/she can take to feel protected or empowered.

B. Read the book *I Can't Talk About It* (Sanford) to help the client verbalize his/her feelings about the past sexual abuse.

C. Read the book *It's Not Your Fault* (Jance) to reinforce that the client is not responsible for the sexual abuse.

D. The key concepts from the assigned readings were processed with the client.

E. The assigned reading(s) helped the client to identify and express his/her feelings about the past sexual abuse.

43. Read *My Body Is Mine, My Feelings Are Mine* (43)

A. Read the book *My Body Is Mine, My Feelings Are Mine* (Hoke) in the therapy session to help the client identify appropriate and inappropriate forms of touching.

B. Read *My Body Is Mine, My Feelings Are Mine* to teach the client about body safety.

C. After reading the book, the client was able to identify appropriate and inappropriate forms of touching.

D. After reading the book, the client was able to identify ways to protect himself/herself.

E. The parents were assigned to read the book *My Body Is Mine, My Feelings Are Mine* at home with the client to teach him/her about body safety.

44. Connect Painful Emotions to Sexualized Behavior (44)

A. The therapy session was helpful in identifying for the client how underlying, painful emotions (e.g., fear, hurt, sadness, anxiety) are related to the emergence of the client's sexualized or seductive behaviors.

B. The client acknowledged that his/her sexualized or seductive behaviors are associated with underlying painful emotions arising from the past sexual abuse.

C. A client-centered therapy approach was utilized to help the client make a connection between his/her underlying, painful emotions and his/her sexualized or seductive behaviors.

D. Role-playing and modeling techniques were used to demonstrate appropriate ways for the client to express his/her underlying painful emotions.

E. The client was helped to identify more appropriate ways to express his/her painful emotions and meet his/her needs instead of through sexualized or seductive behaviors.

45. Use Anatomical Dolls (45)

A. Anatomically detailed dolls were used to assess whether the client has been sexually abused.

B. Anatomically detailed dolls or puppets were used to allow the client to tell and show how he/she was sexually abused.

C. Caution was exercised to not lead the client's description about the past sexual abuse.

D. Through the use of anatomically detailed dolls, the client was able to identify how he/she was sexually abused.

E. The use of anatomically detailed dolls helped the client verbalize his/her feelings about the past sexual abuse.

46. Play Kids in Court Game (46)

A. Played the Kids in Court game in the therapy session to help the client prepare for his/her testimony in court.

B. The client reported that the Kids in Court game helped reduce some of his/her anxiety about testifying in court.

C. After playing the Kids in Court game, the client reviewed effective strategies that he/she can use to alleviate anxiety about testifying in court.

D. The nonabusive parent was encouraged to provide strong support and encouragement for the client before he/she testifies in court.

47. Assess Parents' Psychiatric/Substance Abuse Problem (47)

A. The client's parent(s) were assessed for the possibility of having a psychiatric disorder and/or a substance abuse problem.

B. The client's parent(s) agreed to seek substance abuse treatment.

C. The client's parent(s), because of their denial, have refused to seek substance abuse treatment.

D. The parent(s) were referred for a psychiatric evaluation and therapy to address their psychiatric disorder.

E. The parent(s) refused to comply with the recommendation to seek a psychiatric evaluation and/or therapy.

48. Medication Evaluation (48)

A. The client was referred for a medication evaluation to help stabilize his/her mood.

B. The client and parents agreed to follow through with a medication evaluation by a physician.

C. The client verbalized strong opposition to being placed on medication to help stabilize his/her mood.

49. Monitor Effects of Medication (49)

A. The client's response to the medication was discussed in today's therapy session.

B. The client reported that the medication has helped to stabilize his/her moods.

C. The client reported little to no improvement in his/her mood since being placed on the medication.

D. The client reported that he/she has consistently taken the medication as prescribed.

E. The client has failed to comply with taking the medication as prescribed.

F. The client was encouraged to report the side effects to the prescribing physician and/or psychiatrist.

SLEEP DISTURBANCE

CLIENT PRESENTATION

1. Emotional Distress about Sleep (1)*

A. The parents indicated that the client has difficulty falling asleep and makes repeated demands to sleep with them.

B. The parents reported the client becomes emotionally distressed about his/her difficulty to fall or remain asleep.

C. The client's incessant crying and leaving his/her bed has caused the parents to exceed their frustration tolerance level.

D. The new strategies implemented by the parents and designed to reduce the client's distress have helped the client fall and stay asleep.

2. Demands Made on Parents about Sleep (2)

A. The parents stated that they can only remember a few times that the client went to sleep without him/her making a long list of demands upon them.

B. The client's demands at bedtime have caused the parents to become sleep deprived and extremely frustrated.

C. The parents reported a nightly listing of demands made by the client before he/she eventually falls asleep.

D. The parents indicated that now the client falls asleep without difficulty or demands and remains asleep most nights.

3. Distress about Frightening Dreams (3)

A. The parents indicated the client experiences frightening dreams that result in awakening, crying, heart racing, and then a fear of returning to sleep.

B. The client reported details of dreams that caused him/her distress as the dreams involve threats to him/herself or significant others.

C. The client's frightening dreams have caused him/her to get very few good nights of rest, and therefore he/she is often tired and very irritable, which has negatively affected his/her school performance.

D. The parents reported that the client is experiencing fewer frightening dreams and is getting more nights of uninterrupted good rest.

4. Walking in Apparent Sleep State (4)

A. Parents reported that the client has repeatedly been found in a sleep state, walking about their house at different hours of the night.

B. The parents expressed concern over the client's sleep-state walking around the house.

---

* The numbers in parentheses correlate to the number of the Behavioral Definition statement in the companion chapter with same title in *The Child Psychotherapy Treatment Planner* (Jongsma, Peterson, and McInnis) by John Wiley & Sons, 2000.

C. The client's walking about in an apparent sleep state has negatively affected parents sleep and increased their fear about not being able to keep him/her safe.

D. The client indicated that he/she cannot remember walking about in a sleep state, although parents tell him/her that it has happened.

E. The parents reported that the client has not had an incident of walking around in a sleep state for several months.

5. Abrupt Panicky Awakening without Dream Recall (5)

A. The parents reported that the client frequently awakens abruptly with screaming and intense anxiety that they cannot comfort easily.

B. The client indicated he/she cannot recall any part of the dreams from which he/she awakens with screaming.

C. The intense anxiety and autonomic arousal caused by the client's unrecalled dreams have made him/her afraid to go to sleep at night.

D. The frequency of the client's abrupt awakening with panicky screaming has decreased as the client and parents have started addressing various issues in the family.

6. Prolonged Sleep or Excessive Day Napping (6)

A. The client's prolonged sleep pattern has not resulted in him/her feeling rested but instead very tired.

B. The parents indicated that the client's prolonged sleep at night and excessive daytime napping still leaves him/her continually tired.

C. Even though he/she sleeps a lot, the client still indicated he/she feels tired all the time.

D. The parents indicated that the client has started to nap less and feel more rested and refreshed after his/her nighttime sleep.

INTERVENTIONS IMPLEMENTED

1. Assess Presleep and Sleep Patterns (1)*

A. Both the client's presleep and sleep patterns were explored with parents and client.

B. The client's presleep and actual sleep patterns were assessed and key points for intervention were identified.

C. Strategies for intervening at the identified key points of the client's sleep behavior pattern were developed with the parent's assistance and plans for implementation were made.

D. The parents' implementation of the strategies to aid the client's sleep induction were monitored, with redirection and encouragement being given as needed.

E. The client's sleep patterns have become more regular and less disturbing to the family routine.

---

* The numbers in parentheses correlate to the number of the Therapeutic Interventions statement in the companion chapter with same title in *The Child Psychotherapy Treatment Planner* (Jongsma, Peterson, and McInnis) by John Wiley & Sons, 2000.

2. Assign Record of Sleep and Caregiver's Responses (2)

A. The parents were given a form and asked to chart data related to the client's presleep activity, sleep time, awakening occurrences, and the caregiver's response to the child.

B. The parents' failure to consistently record data on the sleep behavior and response form was addressed and a commitment to do the charting thoroughly was elicited from them.

3. Assess Presleep and Sleep Activity (3)

A. The client's presleep and sleep activity record was reviewed and assessed for overstimulation, caregiver reinforcement, and contributing stressors.

B. The assessment of the record was shared with the parents noting incidents of overstimulation, caregiver reinforcement, and high stress.

C. Strategies to reduce the overstimulation, caregiver reinforcement, and contributing stressors were explored with parents.

D. The reduction in overstimulation, caregiver reinforcement, and stressors has resulted in a more consistent and less disturbed sleep pattern for the client.

4. Assess Role of Daily Stressors (4)

A. The parents and client were assisted in identifying the daily stressors in the client's life.

B. The role of the identified stressors in the interruption of the client's sleep was assessed.

C. The parents and the client were helped to make connections between daily stressors and how they interrupt the client's sleep.

D. The parents were assisted in developing and implementing ways to decrease the client's daily level of tension.

E. The decrease in daily tension in the client has improved his/her pattern of sleep.

5. Assess Level of Family Conflict (5)

A. Met with the family to assess the level of conflict and tension present in the family unit.

B. Family members were asked to identify conflicts and areas of tension they saw present in the family.

C. From the assessment, interventions were developed and implemented with the family to reduce the level of conflict and tension that was present and negatively affecting the client's sleep.

D. The family was helped to recognize the connection between the conflict and tension in the family and the client's sleeping difficulties.

E. Resolving some of the family conflicts and decreasing the tension present has helped to improve the client's quality and pattern of sleep.

6. Assess Role of Depression (6)

A. The client's level of depression was assessed as a possible cause of his/her sleep disturbance.

B. The assessment concluded that a definite connection exists between the client's depression and his/her sleep disturbance and recommended that the depression should be addressed in therapy.

C. The assessment concluded that depression does not play a significant role in the client's sleep disturbance.

D. The assessment strongly recommended that the client's depression should be treated as the primary problem, as the sleep disturbance was a result of it.

7. Explore Recent Traumatic Events (7)

A. Recent traumatic events were explored with the client to determine the extent of their effect on his/her sleeping.

B. No recent traumatic events were uncovered that could be the cause of the client's disturbed pattern of sleep.

C. The client's sleep disturbance seems to be greatly affected by the recent traumatic events in his/her life.

D. The client and parents have reported less sleep disturbance since he/she has started processing recent traumatic events.

8. Probe Disturbing Dreams (8)

A. The client's disturbing dreams were probed for their possible relationship to life stressors.

B. The probing of client's disturbing dreams established a connection between them and present stressors in his/her life.

C. No connection could be established between the client's disturbing dreams and stressors in his/her life.

D. The client has begun to address his/her life stressors and now is experiencing less disturbing dreams.

9. Explore for Sexual Abuse (9)

A. The issue of whether the client had been the victim of sexual abuse was gently explored.

B. The exploration of sexual abuse with the client uncovered several incidents where he/she was a victim of abuse.

C. The exploration of sexual abuse with client and his/her parents failed to uncover any past incidents of abuse.

D. The client was referred to a specialized program for victims of sexual abuse.

E. Given the ongoing nature of the sexual abuse, the abuse was reported to the state's child protection services.

10. Medical Evaluation Referral (10)

A. The client was referred to a physician to rule out any physical and/or pharmacological causes for the sleep disturbance.

B. The client and parents followed through with the referral to the recommended physician.

C. The parents signed releases so that the physician could share information from the assessment with the therapist.

D. The results of the physician's assessment were reviewed and processed with the client and his/her parents.

E. The physician's assessment indicated that there was no physical or pharmacological cause for the client's sleep disturbance.

11. Encourage Parents to Set Limits (11)

A. The parents were assisted in identifying specific areas where they were vulnerable to the client's manipulative behaviors.

B. The parents were helped to develop and implement ways to set firm limits on the client's manipulative behaviors.

C. Role plays and behavioral rehearsal techniques were used to build the parents' skill and confidence in implementing the new firm behavioral limits.

D. The parents were monitored on their consistent implementation of the new firm limits and given encouragement and redirected as needed.

E. The client's manipulative behaviors have decreased as the parents have consistently followed through with setting new firm behavioral limits.

12. Establish Bedtime Routine (12)

A. The parents and the client were educated regarding the benefits of establishing a consistent bedtime routine for the client.

B. The parents and the client were assisted in developing a step-by-step bedtime routine that they could consistently and firmly implement.

C. The developed bedtime routine was role-played in a family session by the parents and client.

D. The parents' implementation of the client's bedtime routine was monitored and adjusted as needed.

E. The bedtime routine and its consistent implementation has reduced the stress and chaos of client's nightly ritual.

13. Assess Marital Dyad (13)

A. Met with the parents to assess the level of stress that is present in their marital relationship.

B. The parents were assisted in exploring the possible impact their marital conflict has on the client's sleep behavior.

C. The parents were given a referral for marital counseling.

D. The parents' follow-through and progress in marital therapy was monitored, with progress being affirmed.

E. The parents have worked to decrease the level of stress in their relationship, which has alleviated many of the client' sleep problems.

14. Conduct Family Sessions to Reduce Tension (14)

A. Family sessions were conducted to explore and identify conflicts and areas of tension present within the family.

B. The conflicts identified by family members were processed and resolved in the family therapy session.

C. In the family therapy session, members agreed upon ways to reduce the tension present in the family.

D. The reduction in family conflict and tension has helped to improve the client's sleeping pattern.

15. Assign Record of Bedtime Routine (15)

A. The parents were asked to keep a written record of the client's adherence to the bedtime routine, and to bring the record for review at a future therapy session.

B. The record kept by the parents was reviewed and consistent implementation of the bedtime routine was verbally reinforced.

C. The parents' failure to adhere to routine revealed by the record review was processed and redirected.

D. Keeping the record has helped the parents become more consistent in implementing the bedtime routine.

16. Reinforce Calming Sleep-Induction Routine (16)

A. The benefits of consistently sticking to the calming sleep-induction routine were identified and reinforced with the client.

B. Verbal reinforcement was given to client for his/her consistent adherence to a calming sleep-induction routine.

C. The client was gently redirected and encouraged to adhere consistently to the calming sleep-induction bedtime routine.

D. The client's adherence to the calming sleep-induction routine has improved the quality and quantity of his/her sleep.

17. Utilize Play-Therapy Techniques (17)

A. Client-centered play-therapy techniques were utilized to help the client express and resolve his/her feelings and emotional conflicts.

B. A psychoanalytic play-therapy approach was used to access the client's emotional conflicts and to explore healthy ways to resolve them.

C. The client took an active role in the play-therapy session.

D. Play-therapy techniques have helped the client explore and resolve his/her emotional conflicts.

18. Interpret Play-Therapy Behavior (18)

A. The client's play-therapy behavior was interpreted as a reflection of his/her feelings toward family members.

B. The client embraced the interpretation of his/her play-therapy behavior as a reflection of his/her feelings toward family members.

C. The client rejected the interpretation of his/her play-therapy behavior as a reflection of his/her feelings toward parents.

D. The client accepted the interpretation of his/her play-therapy behavior and identified feelings he/she had toward specific family members.

19. Assess Fears of Being Alone (19)

A. The nature, severity, and origin of the client's fear of being alone in the bedroom were explored with the client.

B. The client was assisted in identifying all the reasons for his/her fears.

C. As the client has explored and faced his/her fear of being alone, the fear has been reduced.

20. Explore Level of Anxiety (20)

A. The client's general level of anxiety was explored in depth.

B. It was determined by the assessment that the client's level of anxiety did not warrant specialized treatment.

C. The exploration of the client's general level of anxiety indicated that focused treatment would be recommended.

D. Based on the exploration of the client's anxiety, a shift will be made to focus on the anxiety first and the sleep disturbance at a later time.

21. Teach Positive Self-Talk (21)

A. The client's irrational fears were identified and confronted.

B. The client was taught the technique of positive, realistic self-talk and assisted in developing ways that he/she could implement it with his/her irrational fears.

C. Role play and behavioral rehearsal were utilized to give the client the opportunity to practice positive, realistic self-talk on his/her fears.

D. The client was given encouragement and verbal affirmation when he/she utilized positive self-talk on his/her fears.

E. The client's use of positive, realistic self-talk has helped to diminish the impact of the fear on his/her sleep.

22. Teach Relaxation Skills (22)

A. The client was trained in deep-muscle relaxation skills both with and without the use of an audiotape.

B. The client practiced deep-muscle relaxation to increase his/her ability to use the skill to induce sleep.

C. The client's use of deep-muscle relaxation was monitored, with positive affirmation being given to him/her for using the skills on a consistent basis to induce sleep.

D. Consistent use of the deep-muscle relaxation exercises has helped the client more effectively to cope with his/her fears and anxieties.

23. Train in Use of Relaxation Tapes (23)

A. The client was trained to use relaxation tapes to calm himself/herself as a preparation for sleep.

B. The client made a commitment to using the tapes on a nightly basis as part of his/her preparation for sleep.

C. The client's follow-through on using the relaxation tapes to induce the sleep was monitored and redirection was given as needed.

D. The client's consistent use of the relaxation tapes in preparation for sleep has improved his/her ability to fall and stay asleep.

24. Administer Electromyographic Biofeedback (24)

A. Electromyographic (EMG) biofeedback was administered to the client to train and reinforce his/her successful relaxation response.

B. The client's response to electromyographic biofeedback was assessed and monitored for its effectiveness.

C. The client reported being able to relax more consistently and effectively since the EMG training, which has resulted in an improvement in his/her quality of sleep.

25. Medication Evaluation Referral (25)

A. The client's need for antidepressant medication was discussed with the client's parents.

B. An evaluation for antidepressant medication was arranged for the client.

C. The client and parents cooperated and completed the evaluation for antidepressant medication.

D. The parents and client were asked to make a verbal commitment to follow through on all of the recommendations of the medication evaluation.

26. Monitor Medication Compliance (26)

A. The client's need to take the medication consistently as prescribed was explained and reinforced to the client and his/her parents.

B. The client and parents were asked to report any side effects to the prescribing psychiatrist or to therapist.

C. The client's medication was monitored for is effectiveness and for any possible side effects.

D. The client and parents were monitored for the client's taking the medication consistently as prescribed.

E. The medication seems to have had a positive impact on the client's sleep pattern.

F. The medication has not been effective in improving the client's sleep pattern.

SOCIAL PHOBIA/SHYNESS

CLIENT PRESENTATION

1. Lack of Eye Contact (1)*

A. The parents and teachers reported that the client displays very little eye contact during his/her social interactions with others.

B. The client displayed poor eye contact during today's therapy session.

C. The client demonstrated satisfactory to good eye contact with individuals who he/she feels comfortable around, but exhibits poor eye contact with unfamiliar people.

D. The client maintained good eye contact during today's therapy session.

E. The parents and teachers reported that the client consistently maintains good eye contact.

2. Quiet and Reserved (1)

A. The client reported a history of being quiet and reserved in the majority of his/her social interactions.

B. The client was very quiet in today's therapy session and initiated few conversations.

C. The client often does not respond to overtures from other people.

D. The client has started to appear more at ease in the therapy sessions, as evidenced by the increased number of conversations that he/she initiates.

E. The client was much more open and talkative in today's therapy session.

3. Shyness/Social Anxiety (2)

A. The client described himself/herself as being shy and anxious in many social situations.

B. The client appeared anxious (e.g., hand tremors, lack of eye contact, fidgeting, restless, stammering) and inhibited during today's therapy session.

C. The client's social anxiety has gradually started to diminish, and he/she reported of feeling more at ease in his/her conversations with others.

D. The client reported feeling confident and relaxed in the majority of his/her recent social interactions.

E. The client has interacted socially with his/her peers on a regular, consistent basis without excessive fear or anxiety.

4. Avoidance of Unfamiliar People (2)

A. The client has consistently avoided contact with unfamiliar people.

B. The client expressed feelings of anxiety about interacting with unfamiliar people.

C. The client has started to initiate more conversations with unfamiliar people.

D. The client has initiated social contacts with unfamiliar people on a consistent basis.

---

* The numbers in parentheses correlate to the number of the Behavioral Definition statement in the companion chapter with same title in *The Child Psychotherapy Treatment Planner* (Jongsma, Peterson, and McInnis) by John Wiley & Sons, 2000.

5. Withdrawal in New Social Situations (2)

A. The parents and teachers reported that the client usually withdraws from others in social situations.

B. The client verbalized feelings of anxiety about interacting with others when placed in new social settings.

C. The client has recently started to assert himself/herself in new social settings.

D. The client has interacted with others in new social situations on a regular, consistent basis.

6. Social Isolation/Withdrawal (3)

A. The client described a persistent pattern of withdrawing or isolating himself/herself from most social situations.

B. The client acknowledged that his/her social withdrawal interferes with his/her ability to establish and maintain friendships.

C. The client has gradually started to socialize with a wider circle of peers.

D. The client has become more outgoing and interacted with his/her peers on a regular, consistent basis.

7. Excessive Isolated Activities (3)

A. The client has spent an excessive or inordinate amount of time involved in isolated activities, instead of socializing with peers.

B. The client verbalized an understanding of how his/her excessive involvement in isolated activities interferes with his/her chances of establishing friendships.

C. The client reported spending less time in isolated activities and has started to seek out interactions with his/her peers.

D. The client has achieved a healthy balance between time spent in isolated activities and social interactions with others.

8. No Close Friendships (4)

A. The client described a history of having few to no close friendships.

B. The client does not have any close friends at the present time.

C. The client expressed feelings of sadness and loneliness about not having any close friends.

D. The client has begun to take steps (e.g., greet others, compliment others, make positive self-statements) to try to establish close friendships.

E. The client has now established close friendships at school and/or in the community.

9. Enmeshed Family Relationships (4)

A. The client has established an enmeshed relationship with his/her parents which interferes with his/her opportunities to socialize with peers.

B. The parents verbally recognized how they reinforce the client's excessive dependency at the expense of establishing peer friendships.

C. The parents have encouraged the client to become more independent.

D. The parents have reinforced the client's positive social behavior and set limits on overly dependent behavior.

E. The client has achieved a healthy balance between socializing with his/her peers and spending time with family members.

10. Overly Rigid Parents (4)

A. The parent's rigid and strict enforcement of rules and boundaries has decreased the opportunities that the client has to socialize with his/her peers.

B. The client expressed frustration about the parents being overly rigid and not allowing many opportunities for him/her to socialize with others.

C. The client effectively asserted himself/herself with parents and requested that he/she be given the opportunity to socialize more with peers.

D. The parents verbally recognized the need to loosen the rules and boundaries to allow for increased opportunities for the client to socialize with his/her peers.

E. The parents have established appropriate and fair boundaries that allow the client to spend time with peers and fulfill his/her responsibilities at home and school.

11. Hypersensitivity to Criticism/Rejection (5)

A. The client has been very hesitant to become involved with others for fear of being met by criticism, disapproval, or perceived signs of rejection.

B. The client described a history of experiencing excessive or undue criticism, disapproval, and rejection from parental figures.

C. The client acknowledged that he/she tends to overreact to the slightest sign of criticism, rebuff, or rejection and subsequently withdraws from other people.

D. The client has begun to tolerate criticism or rebuff from others more effectively.

E. The client has continued to interact with others even in the face of criticism, disapproval, or perceived slights from others.

12. Excessive Need for Reassurance (6)

A. The client has been very reluctant to become involved with others unless he/she receives strong signs of assurance that he/she is liked or accepted.

B. The client has often sought reassurance from others in order to feel positive about himself/herself.

C. The client has started to reassure himself/herself with positive self-talk instead of turning excessively to others for approval and affirmation.

D. The client has achieved a healthy balance between affirming self and seeking affirmation from others.

13. Reluctance to Take Risks (7)

A. The client has been reluctant to engage in new activities or take personal risks because of the potential for embarrassment or humiliation.

B. The client verbalized a desire to engage in new activities or take healthy risks to help improve his/her self-esteem and develop friendships.

C. The client has started to take healthy risks in order to find enjoyment, build self-esteem, and establish friendships.

D. The client has engaged in new activities and assumed healthy risks without excessive fear of embarrassment or humiliation.

14. Negative Self-Image (8)

A. The client's negative self-image and lack of confidence have interfered with his/her ability to establish friendships.

B. The client verbalized several self-derogatory remarks and compared himself/herself unfavorably to others.

C. The client shared his/her viewpoint of self as being socially unattractive.

D. The client's increased confidence in self has helped him/her be more outgoing.

E. The client has consistently verbalized positive statements about himself/herself in the presence of others.

15. Poor Social Skills (8)

A. The client has established poor social skills and presents as socially immature.

B. The client has lacked awareness and sensitivity to the social cues and interpersonal nuances that are necessary to build positive peer friendships.

C. The client has started to develop an awareness of the social skills needed to build meaningful friendships.

D. The client has displayed good social skills in his/her recent interactions with peers and adults.

E. The client has developed a number of essential social skills that have enhanced the quality of his/her interpersonal relationships.

16. Lack of Assertiveness (9)

A. The client historically has much difficulty asserting himself/herself in social situations where it is indicated.

B. The client has generally avoided any social situations that involve the potential for conflict.

C. The client is beginning to assert himself/herself more often instead of withdrawing from interpersonal problems or conflicts.

D. The client has recently asserted himself/herself in an effective manner during conflict with others.

17. Family History of Excessive Criticism (9)

A. The client reported a history of receiving undue or excessive criticism from his/her family members.

B. The client appeared sad, anxious, and upset when describing the criticism that he/she has received from family members in the past.

C. The parents acknowledged that their overly harsh or critical remarks have contributed to the client's social anxiety, timidity, and low self-esteem.

D. The client asserted himself/herself with the parents about their making overly critical remarks and asked them to cease making derogatory remarks in the future.

E. The parents have increased the frequency of their positive statements toward the client and refrained from making any overly critical or hostile remarks about the client.

18. Physiological Distress (10)

A. The client's social anxiety has been manifested in his/her heightened physiological distress (e.g., increased heart rate, profuse sweating, dry mouth, muscular tension, and trembling).

B. The client appeared visibly anxious (i.e., trembling, shaking, sweating, tense, and rigid) when talking about his/her social relationships.

C. The client reported that he/she has recently experienced less physiological distress when interacting with others.

D. The client has been able to consistently interact with other people in a variety of social settings without experiencing any physiological distress.

INTERVENTIONS IMPLEMENTED

1. Psychological Testing (1)*

A. A psychological evaluation was conducted to assess the severity of the client's anxiety and help provide greater insight into the dynamics contributing to the emergence of his/her shyness and social anxiety.

B. The client was cooperative during the psychological testing and provided insight into the factors contributing to his/her social anxiety or shyness.

C. The client appeared highly anxious and was difficult to engage during the psychological testing.

2. Psychoeducational Evaluation (2)

A. The client received a psychoeducational evaluation to rule out the presence of a possible learning disability that may be contributing to his/her social withdrawal in the school setting.

B. The client was cooperative during the psychoeducational evaluation and appeared to put forth his/her best effort.

C. The client's low self-esteem and feelings of insecurity appeared to interfere with his/her performance during the psychoeducational evaluation.

3. Speech/Language Evaluation Referral (3)

A. The client was referred for a comprehensive speech/language evaluation to rule out a possible impairment that may contribute to his/her social withdrawal.

B. The client was accepting of the need for a comprehensive speech/language evaluation.

C. The comprehensive speech/language evaluation revealed the presence of a speech/language impairment that contributes to the client's social withdrawal.

D. The comprehensive speech/language evaluation did not reveal the presence of a speech/language impairment that may contribute to the client's social withdrawal.

---

* The numbers in parentheses correlate to the number of the Therapeutic Interventions statement in the companion chapter with same title in *The Child Psychotherapy Treatment Planner* (Jongsma, Peterson, and McInnis) by John Wiley & Sons, 2000.

4. Evaluation Feedback (4)

A. The client and his/her parents were given feedback on the findings from the psychological evaluation.

B. The psychological testing results confirmed the presence of an anxiety disorder that contributes to the client's shyness and social withdrawal.

C. The psychological testing results indicated that the client is experiencing a significant amount of depression that is contributing to his/her social withdrawal.

D. The psychoeducational evaluation results revealed the presence of a learning disability that contributes to the client's lack of confidence and social withdrawal in the school setting.

E. The psychoeducational evaluation results did not reveal the presence of a learning disability that may contribute to the client's social withdrawal.

5. Build Trust (5)

A. The focus of today's therapy session was on building the level of trust with the client through consistent eye contact, active listening, unconditional positive regard, and warm acceptance.

B. Unconditional positive regard and warm acceptance helped the client increase his/her ability to identify and express feelings.

C. The therapy session was helpful in building the level of trust with the client, as he/she became more open and relaxed.

D. The session was not helpful in building the level of trust with the client, who remained quiet and reserved in his/her interactions.

6. Design *In Vivo* Systematic Desensitization Program (6)

A. A systematic desensitization program was designed to help decrease the client's social anxiety and increase the frequency and duration of social contacts.

B. The client and parents verbally agreed to follow through with the implementation of the systematic desensitization program.

C. The client and parents followed through with the implementation of the systematic desensitization program, and reported a reduction in the client's social anxiety.

D. The client and parents partially followed through with the systematic desensitization program, and reported a minimal reduction in social anxiety.

E. The client and parents failed to follow through with the implementation of the systematic desensitization program, and as a result the client did not experience a decrease in the reduction of his/her social anxiety.

7. Develop Reward System/Contingency Contract (7)

A. A list of rewards was developed to reinforce the client for initiating social contacts and/or engaging in leisure/recreational activities with peers.

B. A reward system was designed to reinforce the client for initiating social contacts and/or engaging in leisure/recreational activities with peers.

C. The client signed a contingency contract specifying the rewards for increasing his/her social contacts and/or negative consequences for failing to initiate the agreed-upon number of social contacts.

D. The client has recently increased his/her social contacts and successfully met the goals of the reward system.

E. The client failed to follow through with the conditions outlined in the contingency contract and did not increase his/her social contacts.

8. Teach Guided Imagery/Relaxation (8)

A. The client was taught guided imagery and deep-muscle relaxation techniques to help decrease his/her social anxiety.

B. The client consistently practiced the guided imagery and deep-muscle relaxation techniques at home between the therapy sessions.

C. The client reported a positive response to the use of guided imagery or deep-muscle relaxation techniques to help decrease his/her social anxiety.

D. The client reported that the guided imagery and deep-muscle relaxation techniques have not been helpful in reducing his/her social anxiety.

9. Utilize Positive Self-Talk (9)

A. The client was encouraged to utilize positive self-talk as a means of managing his/her social anxiety or fears.

B. Role-playing and modeling techniques were used to teach the client positive self-talk to reduce social anxiety or fears.

C. The client reported that the use of positive self-talk between the therapy sessions helped to reduce his/her social anxiety.

D. The client reported that he/she tried to use positive self-talk, but still felt overwhelmed by his/her social anxiety.

E. The client failed to follow through with utilizing positive self-talk as a means of reducing his/her social anxiety or fears.

10. Initiate Daily Social Contact (10)

A. The client was given the directive to initiate one social contact per day.

B. The client followed through with the directive to initiate at least one social contact per day.

C. The client partially followed through with the directive to initiate one social contact per day.

D. The client failed to follow through with the directive to initiate one social contact per day.

E. Role-playing and modeling techniques were utilized to teach effective ways to initiate social contacts.

11 Role Play Social Skills (11)

A. Behavioral rehearsal, modeling, and role-playing techniques were used to teach the client positive social skills and appropriate ways to initiate conversations with others.

B. The client was able to identify several positive social skills after engaging in the behavioral rehearsal and role-playing exercises.

C. After role playing in the therapy session, the client expressed a willingness to practice the newly learned social skills in his/her everyday situations.

D. The client reported that he/she recently practiced the social skills that were taught through role playing.

E. The client did not follow through with practicing many of the social skills that were modeled in the previous therapy session.

12. Assign "Greeting Peers" Exercise (12)

A. The client was given the "Greeting Peers" exercise from *The Brief Child Therapy Homework Planner* (Jongsma, Peterson, and McInnis) to reduce social isolation and help him/her begin to take steps toward establishing peer friendships.

B. The client successfully completed the "Greeting Peers" exercise and was reinforced for initiating social contacts.

C. The client partially completed the "Greeting Peers" exercise, initiating contact with some peers socially, but it was an anxiety-producing experience for the client.

D. The client did not follow through in completing the "Greeting Peers" exercise, and the assignment was given again.

13. Reinforce Social Behavior (13)

A. The parents were strongly encouraged to praise and reinforce any emerging positive social behavior.

B. The client's positive social behavior was praised during today's therapy session.

C. The client was asked to list some positive social behavior that he/she exhibited.

14. Identify Similarities with Peers (14)

A. The client was assisted in developing a list of similarities between himself/herself and his/her peers.

B. The client was assisted in developing a list of activities that he/she could engage in with peers.

C. The client was encouraged to share his/her interests with peers who have similar interests.

15. Participate in Peer Group Activities (15)

A. The client was strongly encouraged to participate in extracurricular or positive peer group activities to provide opportunities to establish meaningful friendships.

B. The client was assisted in developing a list of or positive peer group activities that will provide him/her with the opportunity to establish meaningful friendships.

C. The client verbalized an understanding of how his/her feelings of insecurity and inadequacy contribute to his/her reluctance to become involved in positive peer group activities.

D. The client reported to recently participating in positive peer group activities.

E. The client denied participating in any recent extracurricular or positive peer group activities.

16. Assign Overnight Visit with Friend (16)

A. The client was given the homework assignment to either invite a friend for an overnight visit and/or set up an overnight visit at the friend's home.

B. The client was given the opportunity to express and work through his/her fears and anxiety about inviting a friend for an overnight visit or setting up an overnight visit at a friend's home.

C. The client complied with the directive to have an overnight visit with a friend, resulting in some anxiety but also pride of accomplishment.

D. The client failed to set up an overnight visit with a friend.

17. Assign Journal of Social Experiences (17)

A. The client was asked to keep a journal of his/her positive and negative social experiences between therapy sessions.

B. The positive and negative social experiences that the client listed in his/her journal were processed.

C. The positive social behaviors that the client displayed in the recent past were reinforced.

D. The client failed to develop a list or keep a journal of his/her positive and negative social experiences.

18. Assign "Show Your Strengths" Exercise (18)

A. The client was assigned the "Show Your Strengths" exercise from *The Brief Child Therapy Homework Planner* (Jongsma, Peterson, and McInnis) to help identify his/her strengths or interests that could be used to initiate social contacts and establish friendships.

B. The client successfully completed the "Show Your Strengths" exercise and felt good about sharing the results with peers, as they were receptive.

C. The client did not follow through with completing the "Show Your Strengths" exercise and was asked again to work on it.

D. The client reported that the "Show Your Strengths" exercise helped to increase his/her self-esteem and confidence.

E. The client reported that sharing his/her strengths with others helped him/her to feel accepted by peers at school or in the neighborhood.

19. Explore Past Successful Social Experiences (19)

A. Today's therapy session explored past social situations where the client was able to interact without excessive fear or anxiety.

B. The client was helped to identify the positive coping mechanisms that he/she had used in the past to reduce his/her anxiety or fearfulness in social settings.

C. The client was helped to realize how he/she felt more comfortable and less anxious in the past when he/she exercised good social skills.

D. The client was helped to identify the positive social skills that he/she used in the past to feel more comfortable and relaxed around others.

E. The client was strongly encouraged to utilize successful coping strategies from the past that had helped to reduce his/her social anxiety.

20. Contact School Officials about Socialization (20)

A. School officials were contacted about ways to increase the client's socialization (e.g., write for school newspaper, tutor a more popular peer, pair the client with another popular peer on classroom assignment).

B. The school officials agreed to assign tasks or activities that will enable the client to socialize with peers.

C. The consultation with school officials was helpful in increasing the client's socialization with his/her peers.

21. Give Feedback on Negative Social Behavior (21)

A. The client was given feedback on his/her negative social behaviors that interfere with his/her ability to establish and maintain friendships.

B. The client appeared defensive when given feedback on his/her negative social behaviors.

C. The client responded favorably to constructive criticism about his/her negative social behaviors and identified more appropriate social behaviors that will help him/her establish and maintain friendships.

D. The client was helped to realize how his/her avoidance of eye contact interferes with his/her chances of interacting with others.

22. Teach Assertiveness Skills (22)

A. The client was taught effective assertiveness skills to help communicate his/her thoughts, feelings, and needs more openly and directly.

B. Role-playing techniques were used to teach effective assertiveness skills.

C. The client reported that the newly acquired assertiveness skills helped him/her feel more confident in social situations.

D. The client failed to use assertiveness skills that were recently taught.

E. The client acknowledged that his/her fear of rejection contributes to his/her lack of assertiveness.

23. Play "Draw Me Out" Game (23)

A. The Draw Me Out game (Shapiro) was played in the therapy session to help the client overcome his/her shyness and communicate more effectively with peers.

B. After playing the Draw Me Out game, the client was able to identify effective ways to manage or overcome his/her shyness and social anxiety.

C. After playing the Draw Me Out game, the client was able to identify several effective communication skills.

D. The client was given the directive to practice the newly learned social and communication skills that he/she had learned from playing the Draw Me Out game.

E. The client identified the Draw Me Out game as being helpful in increasing his/her confidence in social situations.

24. Assign Reading on How to Deal with Aggressive Peers (24)

A. *Why Is Everybody Always Picking On Me? A Guide to Understanding Bullies for Young People* (Webster-Doyle) was read to the client in the therapy session to teach him/her effective ways to deal with aggressive or intimidating peers.

B. The client and parents were instructed to read *Why Is Everybody Always Picking On Me? A Guide to Understanding Bullies for Young People* at home to teach the client effective ways to deal with aggressive or intimidating peers.

C. The content of the assigned book on aggressive behavior was processed.

D. The client was able to identify several effective ways to deal with aggressive or intimidating peers after reading *Why Is Everybody Always Picking On Me? A Guide to Understanding Bullies for Young People.*

E. The client was instructed to practice the skills that he/she learned from reading the assigned book on aggressive behavior, when the opportunity arises.

25. Play "Stand Up for Yourself" Game (25)

A. The Stand Up for Yourself game (Shapiro) was played in the therapy session to teach the client effective assertiveness skills.

B. The Stand Up for Yourself game was played to help establish rapport with the client during the initial stages of therapy.

C. After playing the Stand Up for Yourself game, the client was able to identify several effective assertiveness skills.

D. The client was instructed to practice the newly learned assertiveness skills at least three times before the next therapy session.

E. The client identified the Stand Up for Yourself game as being helpful in increasing his/her assertiveness with peers.

26. Explore History of Traumas (26)

A. The client's background was explored for a history of rejection experiences, harsh criticism, abandonment, or trauma that may have contributed to the client's low self-esteem and social anxiety.

B. The client developed a time line where he/she identified significant historical events, both positive and negative, that have occurred in his/her background.

C. The client identified a history of abandonment and/or traumatic experiences that coincided with the onset of his/her feelings of low self-esteem and social anxiety.

D. Exploration of the client's background did not reveal any significant rejection or traumatic experiences that contributed to the onset of his/her social anxiety.

27. Probe Feelings Associated with Traumas (27)

A. The client was given the opportunity to express his/her feelings about past rejection experiences, harsh criticism, abandonment, or trauma.

B. The client was given empathy and support in expressing his/her feelings about past rejection experiences, harsh criticism, abandonment, or traumatic events.

C. The client was instructed to use a journal to record his/her thoughts and feelings about past rejection experiences, harsh criticism, abandonment, or trauma.

D. The empty-chair technique was employed to facilitate the client's expression of feelings surrounding past rejection experiences, harsh criticism, abandonment, or trauma.

E. The client was instructed to draw pictures that reflect his/her feelings about past rejection experiences, harsh criticism, abandonment, or trauma.

28. Explore Family Dynamics/Stressors (28)

A. A family therapy session was held to explore the dynamics within the family system that contribute to the client's feelings of anxiety and insecurity.

B. The client and family members were asked to list the stressors that have had a negative impact on the family and contributed to the client's feelings of anxiety and insecurity.

C. The client and family members were asked to identify the things that they would like to change within the family.

D. The therapy session was helpful in identifying the family dynamics that have contributed to the client's feelings of anxiety and insecurity.

E. The therapy session did not reveal any significant stressors within the family system that have contributed to the client's feelings of anxiety and insecurity.

29. Explore Overly Protective Parenting (29)

A. The therapy session explored how the overly protective parents reinforce the client's dependency and social anxiety.

B. The parents were encouraged to engage in social activities (e.g., go out on a date together) independent of the client.

C. The parents followed through with the recommendation to engage in social activities independent of the client.

D. The parents failed to follow through with the recommendation to socialize with others independent of the client.

E. The parents verbally recognized how their overprotectiveness reinforces the client's excessive dependency on them.

30. Encourage Limits on Dependent Behavior (30)

A. The parents were strongly encouraged to reinforce the client's steps toward greater independence.

B. The parents were challenged to set limits on the client's overly dependent behaviors (e.g., immature whining and complaining, shadowing parents in social settings).

C. The client was encouraged to engage in independent activities outside of the home and/or away from parents.

D. The client followed through with the recommendation to engage in independent activities outside of the home.

E. The client failed to follow through the recommendation to engage in independent activities outside of the home.

31. Teach Parents to Ignore Oppositional Behavior (31)

A. The parents were instructed to ignore occasional and mild oppositional or aggressive behaviors by the client (unless they become too intense or frequent) during the initial stages of treatment so as not to extinguish emerging assertive behaviors.

B. The parents were helped to identify times when it is best to ignore mild oppositional or aggressive behavior versus times when it is appropriate to set limits for more intense oppositional or aggressive behavior.

32. Teach Power of Secondary Gain (32)

A. A family therapy session was held to explore whether the client achieves any secondary gain from his/her social anxiety and withdrawal.

B. The client and parents were assisted in identifying the secondary gain(s) that are achieved from the client's social anxiety and withdrawal.

C. The therapy session was helpful in showing how the client's social withdrawal reduces his/her social anxiety in the short run and maintains a close relationship with his/her parents.

D. The client verbally recognized how his/her social withdrawal and unwillingness to take healthy risks prevents him/her from experiencing rejection, but also interferes with chances to establish friendships.

E. The family therapy session failed to identify any secondary gain that is achieved from the client's social anxiety and withdrawal.

33. Assess Parents' Mental Health (33)

A. The parent(s) were evaluated for the presence of a possible anxiety or affective disorder that may contribute to the client's shyness and social anxiety.

B. The client's mother was referred for a medication evaluation and/or individual therapy to address her anxiety or affective disorder.

C. The client's father was referred for a medication evaluation and/or individual therapy to address his anxiety or affective disorder.

D. The client's parent agreed to follow through with the medication evaluation.

E. The client's parent agreed to follow through with individual therapy to address the anxiety or affective disorder.

34. Assess Parent-Child Dyad (34)

A. The parent-child dyad was explored in today's therapy session to determine whether the parents are placing unrealistically high standards on the client.

B. The parents were helped to recognize how their unrealistically high standards for the client contribute to his/her anxiety and feelings of insecurity.

C. The client's parents were resistant to the interpretation that they are placing unrealistically high standards on the client.

D. The parents were helped to identify more realistic expectations for the client.

E. The client was taught effective assertiveness and communication skills to help him/her assert self with parents about their placing unrealistically high standards on him/her to perform.

35. Teach Parents Reasonable Expectations (35)

A. The parents were taught about what are reasonable expectations for the client's developmental level.

B. The parents acknowledged that their expectations have been unreasonable, and agreed to adjust them to a more realistic level.

C. The factors that contributed to the parents' unrealistically high standards were explored.

D. The parents became defensive and resistant when discussing how their unrealistically high standards create anxiety and feelings of insecurity for the client.

36. Employ Child-Centered Play Therapy (36)

A. Child-centered play-therapy principles were used to help the client overcome his/her social anxieties and feel more confident in social situations.

B. The client was given unconditional positive regard and warm acceptance while expressing his/her feelings of anxiety and insecurity.

C. The client's feelings expressed in his/her play were reflected and related to his/her fears, anxieties, and insecurities in everyday social situations.

D. The child-centered play-therapy sessions have affirmed the client's capacity for self-growth and reinforced his/her ability to overcome social anxiety.

E. The child-centered play-therapy sessions have helped the client overcome his/her social anxiety and feel more confident in social situations.

37. Utilize Psychoanalytic Play Therapy (37)

A. Using a psychoanalytic approach, the client was allowed to take the lead in the play-therapy session to explore the etiology of his/her unconscious conflicts.

B. The client's unconscious conflicts and core anxieties were brought to the surface in today's psychoanalytic play-therapy session.

C. Processed and worked through the transference issues that emerged in the play-therapy session.

D. The client's fears and anxieties reflected in his/her play were interpreted and related to his/her feelings in many social situations.

E. The psychoanalytic play-therapy sessions have helped the client resolve and work through the issues related to his/her social phobia or shyness.

38. Utilize Ericksonian Play-Therapy Technique (38)

A. An Ericksonian play-therapy technique was used whereby the therapist spoke through a "wise doll" (or puppet) to an audience of other dolls or puppets to teach the client positive social skills.

B. The client identified the puppet play or storytelling technique as being an enjoyable and beneficial ways to learn about positive social skills.

C. After finishing the story, the client was helped to identify positive social skills that were taught by the "wise doll."

D. The client was encouraged to practice the social skills he/she learned from the "wise doll" in his/her everyday social situations.

E. The client was given the homework assignment to practice at least one positive social skill each day that was taught by the "wise doll."

39. Use Storytelling Technique (39)

A. The therapist used puppets, dolls, and stuffed animals to create stories that modeled positive social skills.

B. The therapist used puppets, dolls, and stuffed animals to create a story that modeled appropriate ways to introduce self and greet others.

C. Using puppets, dolls, or stuffed animals, the therapist created a story that taught the importance of making positive statements about self and others in everyday social situations.

D. A storytelling technique using puppets, dolls, and stuffed animals was used to model ways for the client to appear more confident and assured of self in social situations.

E. The client was given the directive to practice at least one positive social skill daily that was taught in the stories using puppets, dolls, and stuffed animals.

40. Employ Art Therapy (40)

A. Art therapy was employed to help establish rapport and develop a trusting relationship with the client.

B. The art therapy sessions have been helpful in establishing rapport and building a trusting relationship with the client.

C. The client has actively participated in the art therapy sessions.

D. The client's drawings or artwork have helped provide insight into the factors contributing to his/her social phobia or shyness.

E. The art therapy sessions have helped the client begin to open up and verbally share his/her insecurities and fears.

41. Assign Artwork Reflecting Social Anxieties (41)

A. The client was instructed to draw a picture or create a sculpture that reflects how he/she feels around unfamiliar people or when placed in new social settings.

B. After finishing his/her drawing or sculpture, the client was able to discuss his/her insecurities around unfamiliar people or in new social situations.

C. The client's artwork reflected his/her fears about embarrassing or humiliating himself/herself in front of others.

D. The client's artwork reflected his/her fears about being ignored or rejected by others.

E. The client's artwork led to a discussion about what he/she can do to feel more comfortable around unfamiliar people or in new social situations.

42. Assign Drawing of Symbols of Positive Attributes (42)

A. The client was instructed to draw objects or symbols on a large piece of paper or poster board that symbolized his/her positive attributes.

B. After identifying his/her positive attributes, the client discussed how he/she can use his/her strengths to establish peer friendships.

C. The client was asked to share his/her strengths or interests with peers three to five times during the next week.

D. The client reported that the art assignment helped him/her feel more positive about self.

43. Group Therapy Referral (43)

A. The client was referred for group therapy to improve his/her social skills.

B. The client was supportive of the recommendation to participate in group therapy to help improve his/her social skills.

C. The client voiced his/her objection to being referred for group therapy to improve his/her social anxiety.

44. Assign Self-Disclosure in Group Therapy (44)

A. The client was given the directive to self-disclose at least two times in each group therapy session.

B. The client complied with the directive to self-disclose at least two times in today's group therapy session.

C. The client failed to follow through with the directive to self-disclose at least two times in today's therapy session.

D. The client was encouraged to make positive self-statements or share positive life experiences in the group therapy sessions.

45. Medication Evaluation Referral (45)

A. The client was referred for a medication evaluation with a physician to decrease his/her anxiety or emotional distress.

B. The client and parents agreed to follow through with the recommendation to receive a medication evaluation from a physician.

C. The client was strongly opposed to being placed on medication to help decrease his/her social anxiety or emotional distress.

46. Monitor Medication Effects (46)

A. The client reported that the medication has helped to decrease his/her anxiety and stabilize moods.

B. The client reports little to no improvement on the medication.

C. The client has not complied with taking his/her medication on a regular basis.

D. The client reported experiencing side effects from the prescribed medication.

SPECIFIC PHOBIA

CLIENT PRESENTATION

1. Persistent and Unreasonable Fear (1)*

A. An immediate anxiety response has been exhibited by the client each time he/she encountered the phobic stimulus.

B. The client reported that the strength of his/her phobic response has been increasing in the past several months.

C. The client described the level of fear he/she experiences around the phobic stimulus as paralyzing.

D. The client indicated that the phobia has been a recent occurrence but has quickly become very persistent and unreasonable.

E. As the client has become engaged in therapy, there has been a decrease in the intensity and frequency of the phobic response.

2. Avoidance and Endurance of Phobia (2)

A. The client reported that his/her avoidance of the phobic stimulus has caused major interference in his/her normal daily routines.

B. The client indicated that the intensity of his/her anxiety around the phobic stimulus has resulted in marked personal distress.

C. The client questioned whether or not he/she would ever be able to resolve the phobia.

D. The client has progressed to the point where the phobic stimulus does not create interference in his/her normal daily routines or cause him/her marked distress.

3. Sleep Disturbance (3)

A. The client reported that his/her sleep has been disturbed by frequent dreams of the feared stimulus.

B. The client indicated his/her disturbed sleep pattern has started to affect his/her daily functioning.

C. The client's sleep has improved as he/she has worked toward resolving the feared stimulus.

4. Dramatic Fear Reaction (4)

A. The client indicated that at the slightest mention of the phobic stimulus he/she has a dramatic fear reaction.

B. The client's reaction to the phobic stimulus is so dramatic and overpowering that it is difficult to calm him/her down.

C. The client reported that his/her reaction to the phobic stimulus is rapidly becoming more and more dramatic.

---

* The numbers in parentheses correlate to the number of the Behavioral Definition statement in the companion chapter with same title in *The Child Psychotherapy Treatment Planner* (Jongsma, Peterson, and McInnis) by John Wiley & Sons, 2000.

D. There has been a marked decrease in the client's dramatic fear reaction to the phobic stimulus since he/she has started to work in therapy sessions.

5. Parental Reinforcement (5)

A. The parents have catered to the client's fear and have thus reinforced and increased it.

B. The parents' own fears seemed to be projected onto and acted out by the client.

C. The parents have worked to curb their reaction to the client's fears, which has resulted in a marked decrease in the client's level of fear.

INTERVENTIONS IMPLEMENTED

1. Build Trust (1)*

A. An initial level of trust was established with the client through the use of unconditional positive regard.

B. Warm acceptance and active listening techniques were utilized to establish the basis for a trusting relationship.

C. The client has formed a trust-based relationship and has begun to express his/her fearful thoughts and feelings.

D. Despite the use of active listening, warm acceptance, and unconditional positive regard, the client remains hesitant to trust and to share his/her thoughts and feelings.

2. Assess Client's Fear (2)

A. The history of the development of the client's phobic fear was gathered.

B. The range of stimuli for the client's fear was discussed in depth and assessed.

C. Times and instances when the client was free from the fear while in the presence of the phobic stimulus were explored.

D. It was clear from the assessment of the client's phobic fear that he/she becomes overwhelmed and virtually paralyzed when in the presence of the phobic stimulus.

3. Construct Anxiety Hierarchy (3)

A. The client was directed and assisted in constructing a hierarchy of anxiety-producing situations.

B. The client was successful at identifying a range of stimulus situations that produced increasingly greater amounts of anxiety.

4. Teach Progressive Relaxation (4)

A. The client was taught progressive relaxation methods.

B. Behavioral rehearsal was utilized to increase the client's mastery of the relaxation methods.

C. The client was successful at developing relaxation using the deep-muscle and guided imagery methods.

* The numbers in parentheses correlate to the number of the Therapeutic Interventions statement in the companion chapter with same title in *The Child Psychotherapy Treatment Planner* (Jongsma, Peterson, and McInnis) by John Wiley & Sons, 2000.

D. The client was instructed to continue to practice the deep-muscle relaxation methods as a homework assignment.

5. Use Biofeedback (5)

A. EMG biofeedback techniques were utilized to facilitate the client's relaxation skills.

B. The client achieved deeper levels of relaxation from the EMG biofeedback experience.

6. Teach Guided Imagery (6)

A. Guided imagery techniques were taught to the client to enhance relaxation.

B. The when and where of putting guided imagery to use was discussed with the client.

C. A plan for implementation was developed and the client was asked to make a commitment to utilize the techniques in the identified circumstances.

7. Utilize Systematic Desensitization (7)

A. A systematic desensitization procedure was utilized to reduce the client's phobic response.

B. The desensitization procedure produced a marked decrease being observed in the client's phobic response.

C. The client reported that his/her level of anxiety has been reduced significantly since the implementation of the systematic desensitization procedures.

8. Assign *In Vivo* Desensitization (8)

A. An *in vivo* desensitization experience was assigned to the client in which he/she had graduated contact with his/her phobic stimulus.

B. The exercise "Gradually Facing a Phobic Fear" from the *Brief Adolescent Therapy Homework Planner* (Jongsma, Peterson, McInnis) was assigned to the client to help prepare him/her to directly face the phobic fear.

C. The client's successful *in vivo* encounter with the phobic stimulus was processed, and the client was asked to repeat the encounter again.

9. Draw Fear-Producing Stimuli (9)

A. The client was assigned to draw three things and/or situations that cause him/her to be fearful.

B. Processed the client's drawings of his/her fear-producing stimuli.

C. The client completed the drawings but refused to process them.

D. The drawing assignment has helped the client begin to talk more openly about his/her fears.

10. Employ Child-Centered Play-Therapy (10)

A. Child-centered play-therapy approaches of unconditional positive regard and displaying trust in the client's capacity were used to increase his/her ability to handle fearful encounters.

B. The client's feelings were reflected back to him/her in a nonjudgmental manner to help build his/her confidence in handling fearful encounters.

C. The use of unconditional positive regard has not helped the client feel more confident in handling his/her fearful encounters.

D. The use of client-centered play-therapy techniques has helped to increase the client's abilities to handle fearful encounters.

11. Interpret Play-Therapy Feelings (11)

A. The client was helped to identify and interpret his/her feelings.

B. The client's feelings were interpreted and related back to his/her fearful experiences in specific situations.

C. The client struggled to see connections between his/her feelings and fearful encounters.

D. The client's progress in seeing a relationship between his/her feelings and specific fearful experiences has helped to resolve his phobic reaction.

12. Employ Psychoanalytic Play Therapy (12)

A. A psychoanalytic play-therapy approach was used to explore the client's core issues and gain an understanding of any unconscious conflicts, fixations, or core anxieties.

B. The client willingly participated in the psychoanalytical play-therapy session.

C. The client was resistive and uncooperative with the psychoanalytic play-therapy approach.

D. The client's active work with the psychoanalytic play-therapy sessions has helped him/her make progress in resolving issues related to his/her phobic fear.

13. Employ Stimulus Desensitization Interventions (13)

A. A session was conducted with the client in which he/she was surrounded with pleasant pictures, readings, and storytelling related to the phobic stimulus situation.

B. The client remained calm and relaxed while the phobic stimulus situation was depicted in pictures, informational material, and storytelling.

C. The client's ability to face the phobic fear was affirmed and his/her ability to cope was reinforced.

14. "Maurice Faces His Fears" Exercise (14)

A. The client was assigned to read "Maurice Faces His Fears" from *The Brief Child Therapy Homework Planner* (Jongsma, Peterson, and McInnis) to help him/her identify fears and their origins.

B. The identified fears and their origins were further explored, clarified, and affirmed.

C. Strategies were developed to help the client cope with his/her fears that were identified using the facing fear story.

D. The client's identification of his/her fears and their origin has helped him/her develop coping strategies for dealing with them.

15. Use of Humor (15)

A. Situational humor, jokes, riddles, and stories about the phobic stimulus were used to decrease the client's tension and seriousness regarding the fear.

B. The client was asked to start each day by telling the parents a joke, riddle, or silly story about the phobic stimulus.

C. A humorous side was pointed out for each issue/fear the client raised.

16. Use Narrative Approach (16)

A. The client was assigned to write out the story of his/her fears.

B. The client acted out the story he/she wrote about his/her fears.

C. The client's story was processed after he/she acted it out.

D. The client was assisted in writing effective coping resolutions to the story that he/she could implement in future phobic situations.

E. The strategies developed using the narrative approach have helped reduce the client's fears in his/her daily life.

17. Utilize Neurolinguistic Programming on Nightmares (17)

A. Using a neurolinguistic approach, the client described his/her dreams and then drew a picture of how he/she would like them to end.

B. The client cooperated with the instructions given to retell the dream and squeeze a hand like a remote control device when the dream story becomes especially scary, changing the ending to a pleasant one.

C. The client repeated the revised story of the dream three times as instructed by the therapist.

D. The client was assigned to put a picture of the desired ending to the dream under his/her pillow at night.

E. The client's cooperation with the neurolinguistic treatment approach has resulted in a significant reduction in the frequency of the client's nightmares.

18. Create a "Stuffed Animal Team" (18)

A. The client was assisted in creating a "stuffed animal team" (Slekman) to help him/her find ways to cope with his/her fear.

B. The client was asked to introduce each stuffed animal team member and say what he/she liked about them and then identify how each team member would suggest the client respond to his/her fear.

C. The client was helped to select one of the healing suggestions offered to implement in coping with his/her fear.

D. The client was encouraged and monitored in his/her implementation of the chosen strategy to overcome his/her phobic fear.

E. The client's use of the suggested strategies from the stuffed animal team has helped reduce the level of fear he/she experiences.

19. Obtain Updates and Reinforce Progress (19)

A. The client was asked to give updates on his/her fearful experience with incidents that occurred between sessions and how he/she handled them.

B. The client received feedback, coaching, and positive reinforcement for facing his/her fearful situations.

C. The client has vaguely reported fearful situations he/she has encountered.

D. The client's weekly reports have reflected consistent progress in his/her overcoming phobic fears.

20. Assign "Line Down the Middle of the Page" Exercise (20)

A. The client was assigned the "Line Down the Middle of the Page" exercise (Conyer) to assist him/her in identifying his/her fears.

B. The client completed the listing of good and bad things exercise and his/her identified fears were clarified and confirmed.

C. The client was assisted in elaborating on his/her fears after completing the listing exercise.

D. The client's identification of his/her fears has helped to form and implement strategies to begin reducing them.

21. Construct "Worry Can" (21)

A. The client was given instructions on how to create a "worry can" to serve as a receptacle for his/her identified anxiety-producing stimuli.

B. The client was encouraged to make a list of his/her worries, cut each item out, and put each in a "worry can."

C. The client was instructed to share the contents of his/her "worry can" with significant adults in his/her life.

D. The contents of the "worry can" were ceremonially burned with the client to symbolically put an end to the his/her worries.

E. The client's completion of the "worry can" exercise has helped to significantly reduce the intensity and frequency of his/her daily worries.

22. Prescribe Symptom Enactment (22)

A. The client was given the prescription of acting out his/her symptom daily at a specific time and in specific ways.

B. The client was asked to make a commitment to following through on the prescription as prescribed.

C. The client's follow-through was monitored and effective utilization was affirmed and reinforced.

D. The client reported that the symptom enactment procedure has helped him/her reduce his/her phobic fear.

23. Play Game Close to Phobic Object (23)

A. A game of the client's choice was played with him/her in the presence of the "feared" object.

B. The experience of being close to a feared object was processed, with positive reinforcement being given to the client for his/her accomplishment.

24. Enlist Family Support (24)

A. In family session, the parents were taught various ways to give support to the client when he/she experienced his/her phobic fear, and they were encouraged not to give support when he/she panicked or failed to face fear.

B. The parents' implementation of the support intervention strategy was monitored with them receiving support, encouragement, and as necessary, redirection to the client.

C. The client has been more successful at encountering the phobic stimulus situation since the parents have reinforced the client's encounters.

25. Identify Family Phobic Reinforcement (25)

A. The parents were assisted in identifying the ways in which they reinforce the client's phobia.

B. The family was assisted in identifying ways that each member could reinforce the client's success at overcoming the phobia.

C. The parents were confronted when they were observed reinforcing the client's fear.

26. Assess Family Members Modeling Fear (26)

A. Family members were assessed for their own phobic fear responses that teach the client to be afraid.

B. Family members were confronted on their own phobic fear responses that reinforce the client's phobic fear.

C. Family members were taught new ways of responding to their phobic stimulus situations that would not reinforce the phobic fear.

D. The family members who continue to experience phobic fear of their own were referred for individual counseling to treat this condition.

27. Probe Symbolic Meanings of Phobic Situation (27)

A. The possible symbolic meaning of the client's phobic stimulus was probed and discussed.

B. Selected interpretations of the phobic stimulus were offered to the client and each was processed with him/her.

28. Clarify/Differentiate Present Fear from Past Pain (28)

A. The client was asked to list his/her present fears and also past emotionally painful experiences that may be related to current fear.

B. The client was assisted in clarifying and separating his/her present irrational fears from past emotional/painful experiences.

C. Since the client was successful at separating past emotionally painful experiences from the present, he/she has reduced phobic fears.

29. Reinforce Expression of Feelings about Trauma (29)

A. The positive value of expressing feelings was emphasized with the client.

B. Using active listening and unconditional positive regard techniques, the client was encouraged to express his/her feelings regarding the past painful experiences.

C. Gentle questioning was used with the client to help him/her start sharing feelings from the past.

D. Feelings that the client shared regarding past painful experiences were affirmed and supported.

30. Link Past Pain with Present Anxiety (30)

A. The connection the client was making between his/her past emotional pain and present anxiety was pointed out.

B. When talking about his/her present fear the client was reminded of how he/she connected it to his/her past emotional pain.

C. Since the client was successful at separating past emotionally painful experiences from the present, he/she has reduced phobic fears.

31. Separate Real versus Imagined Threats (31)

A. The client was asked to make a list of all his/her fears, then put an asterisk by the ones that he/she believed were without question rational and reasonable.

B. The client was helped to differentiate and make clear distinctions between real and imagined dangerous situations that produce fear.

C. The client was confronted when he/she was observed in session talking as if an irrational fear was reasonable and acceptable.

32. Teach Cognitive and Behavioral Coping Strategies (32)

A. The client was taught various cognitive and behavioral coping strategies (e.g., diversion, deep breathing, positive self-talk, and deep-muscle relaxation) to implement when experiencing his/her fears.

B. Role play and behavioral rehearsal were used to give the client the opportunity to build his/her skills and confidence in using the phobic fear-coping strategies.

C. The client was helped to develop specific plans to implement the cognitive/behavioral coping strategies to overcome the phobic fear.

D. The client's implementation of the cognitive/behavioral strategies was encouraged and monitored.

E. The client's effective implementation of the cognitive/behavioral strategies has helped control his/her level of phobic fear reaction.

33. Use Goal-Oriented Metaphor (33)

A. The *Blammo-Surprise! Book* (Lankton) was read with the client to give him/her a goal-oriented metaphor to help alleviate his/her fear.

B. The client's use of the goal-oriented metaphor was monitored for effectiveness.

C. The parents were taught the power of metaphors and asked to read the *Blammo-Surprise! Book* with the client nightly at bedtime.

34. Teach Use of "Therapist on the Inside" (34)

A. The client was introduced to the strategy "The Therapist on the Inside" (Grigoryev) in *101 Favorite Play Therapy Techniques*, and the details of implementation were gone over carefully.

B. The client was asked to commit to implementing the internalized therapist strategy in face of the phobic fear in everyday life, and to report the results.

C. The internalized therapist strategy was monitored with adjustments being made and with the client's positive implementations being reinforced.

35. Identify Disturbed Schemas and Automatic Thoughts (35)

A. The client was asked to list all thoughts, ideas, etc., that he/she has before a panic attack.

B. Using the client's list of anxiety-producing thoughts, he/she was assisted in identifying all distorted schemas and automatic thoughts that precede and contribute to his/her anxiety response.

36. Revise Core Schemas and Replace Negative Talk (36)

A. Cognitive restructuring was used to teach the client how to revise his/her core schemas.

B. The client was assisted in developing positive, realistic self-talk to replace negative, distorted messages.

C. Role play and behavioral rehearsal were used to give the client an opportunity to implement positive, realistic self-talk in coping with his/her fear.

D. The client was confronted when parts of old schemas or distorted, negative messages appeared in his/her thought processing.

E. The cognitive restructuring has been successful at reducing the client's phobic fear response.

37. Monitor and Coach Use of Coping Techniques (37)

A. The client was coached and encouraged in his/her use of positive self-talk, progressive relaxation, guided imagery, and deep-breathing techniques in his/her daily life.

B. The client was assisted in developing his/her skills in using positive self-talk and deep-breathing exercises in his/her daily life.

C. The client has consistently improved his/her skills and use of and mastery of anxiety-reducing techniques.

38. Verbally Reinforce Progress (38)

A. The progress that the client has achieved in overcoming his/her phobic fear was reviewed and verbally reinforced.

B. The client was asked to list all circumstances in which he/she was successful at encountering the phobic stimulus situation, and the success was reinforced.

SPEECH/LANGUAGE DISORDERS

CLIENT PRESENTATION

1. Low Expressive Language Test Results (1)*

A. The results from the speech/language evaluation showed that the client's expressive language abilities are significantly below his/her expected level.

B. The results from the speech/language evaluation showed that the client's expressive language abilities are moderately below his/her expected level.

C. The results from the speech/language evaluation showed that the client's expressive language abilities are mildly delayed.

D. The results from the speech/language evaluation did not reveal any significant problems with the client's expressive language abilities.

2. Expressive Language Deficits Manifested (2)

A. The client's expressive language deficits are manifested in his/her limited vocabulary, frequent errors in tense, and difficulty recalling words or producing sentences of developmentally appropriate length or complexity.

B. The client had difficulty communicating his/her thoughts and feelings in today's therapy session because of his/her limited vocabulary.

C. The speech/language pathologist reported that the client has difficulty recalling words or producing sentences of developmentally appropriate length or complexity.

D. The client's expressive language abilities have recently begun to improve since he/she began receiving speech/language services.

E. The speech/language services have helped to improve the client's expressive language abilities up to the expected level.

3. Low Receptive Language Test Results (3)

A. The results from the speech/language evaluation showed that the client's receptive language abilities are significantly below his/her expected level.

B. The results from the speech/language evaluation showed that the client's receptive language abilities are moderately below his/her expected level.

C. The results from the speech/language evaluation showed that the client's receptive language abilities are mildly delayed.

D. The results from the speech/language evaluation did not reveal any significant delays in the client's receptive language abilities.

4. Receptive Language Deficits Manifested (4)

A. The client's receptive language deficits are manifested in his/her difficulty understanding simple words or sentences, and certain types of words such as spatial terms or longer, complex statements.

---

* The numbers in parentheses correlate to the number of the Behavioral Definition statement in the companion chapter with same title in *The Child Psychotherapy Treatment Planner* (Jongsma, Peterson, and McInnis) by John Wiley & Sons, 2000.

B. The client had difficulty understanding key concepts in today's therapy session because of his/her receptive language deficits.

C. The client had difficulty following and comprehending multiple, complex directions because of his/her receptive language deficits.

D. The speech/language pathologist reported that the client's receptive language abilities have started to improve.

E. The speech/language pathologist reported that the client has improved his/her receptive language abilities to his/her expected level.

5. Academic Problems Due to Expressive/Receptive Language Deficits (5)

A. The client's expressive language deficits have interfered with his/her academic performance.

B. The client's receptive language deficits have interfered with his/her academic performance.

C. The client acknowledged that he/she is often reluctant to ask questions or seek out help in the classroom because of his/her speech/language problems and fear that he/she will appear "stupid" in the eyes of peers.

D. The client's academic performance has started to improve since he/she began receiving speech/language services.

E. The client has improved his/her academic performance to his/her level of capability.

6. Communication Problems Due to Expressive/Receptive Language Deficits (5)

A. The speech/language pathologist and teacher(s) reported that the client has difficulty communicating his/her thoughts and feelings because of his/her language delays.

B. The client had difficulty verbalizing his/her thoughts and feelings in today's therapy session because of his/her language deficits.

C. The client had difficulty identifying and expressing his/her emotions because of his/her language deficits.

D. The client has started to become more communicative in the classroom since he/she began receiving speech/language services.

E. The client communicated his/her thoughts and feelings in an effective manner in today's therapy session.

7. Speech Articulation Problems (6)

A. The client has been diagnosed by a speech/language pathologist as having a significant speech articulation problem.

B. The client displayed speech articulation problems during today's therapy session.

C. The speech/language pathologist reported that the client has trouble producing the following letter sounds: ____, ____, ____, ____ (fill in the blank).

D. The client's speech articulation problems did not interfere with his/her ability to communicate thoughts and feelings in an effective manner during today's therapy session.

E. The client has achieved mastery of the expected speech sounds that are appropriate for his/her age and dialect.

8. Stuttering (7)

A. The client and parents reported that the client stutters in many social situations.

B. The client began to stutter in today's therapy session when talking about emotionally laden or anxiety-producing topics.

C. The client reported that his/her stuttering increases when he/she feels anxious or insecure.

D. The client did not stutter in today's therapy session.

E. The client's stuttering has ceased and he/she is able to speak fluently and at a normal rate on a regular, consistent basis.

9. Low Academic Performance Due to Articulation/Stuttering (8)

A. The client's deficits in speech sound production or fluency have interfered with his/her academic performance.

B. The client acknowledged that he/she is reluctant to ask questions or seek out help in the classroom because of his/her speech articulation problems.

C. The client acknowledged that he/she is reluctant to ask questions or seek out help in the classroom because of his/her fear of stuttering.

D. The client's academic performance has started to improve since he/she began receiving services for his/her speech articulation problems.

E. The client's academic performance has started to improve since he/she began to receive speech/language services for his/her stuttering problems.

10. Communication Problems Due to Articulation/Stuttering (8)

A. The client's speech articulation problems have interfered with his/her ability to communicate his/her thoughts and feelings in an effective manner.

B. The client's stuttering interferes with his/her ability to communicate effectively.

C. The client has started to be more communicative with others since he/she began receiving services for his/her speech articulation problems.

D. The client has started to be more communicative with others since he/she began receiving speech/language services for his/her stuttering problem.

E. The client was open and communicative in today's therapy session.

11. Selective Mutism (9)

A. The parents reported that the client refuses to speak in certain social situations.

B. School officials reported that the client refuses to speak at school.

C. The client refused to speak in today's therapy session.

D. The client has gradually started to speak more often in a wider circle of social situations.

E. The client spoke with the therapist for the first time in today's therapy session.

F. The client's selective mutism has been eliminated, and he/she regularly communicates with others in a variety of social situations.

12. Social Withdrawal (10)

A. The client's expressive language deficits have contributed to his/her social withdrawal and lack of assertiveness in many social settings.

B. The client's receptive and expressive language deficits have contributed to his/her social withdrawal and lack of assertiveness in many social settings.

C. The client's speech articulation problems have contributed to his/her withdrawal and lack of assertiveness in many social settings.

D. The client's fear of stuttering has contributed to his/her social withdrawal and lack of assertiveness in many social settings.

E. The client has recently started to socialize more with his/her peers.

13. Anxiety about Speech Problems (10)

A. The client appeared anxious when discussing his/her speech/language problems in today's therapy session.

B. The client reported that his/her anxiety increases significantly when he/she has to speak in social situations.

C. The client's high anxiety level has contributed to his/her problems with stuttering.

D. The client appeared at ease when discussing his/her speech/language problems during today's therapy session.

E. The client's improved speech/language abilities have coincided with a reduction in his/her level of anxiety.

14. Low Self-Esteem (10)

A. The client's speech/language problems have contributed to his/her feelings of low self-esteem, inadequacy, and insecurity.

B. The client expressed feelings of inadequacy and insecurity about his/her speech/language problems during today's therapy session.

C. The client acknowledged that he/she has a tendency to give up easily on many school assignments because of his/her difficulty understanding key concepts or terms.

D. The client verbalized positive self-statements during today's therapy session about his/her improved speech/language abilities.

E. The client has gained a healthy acceptance of his/her speech/language problems, and actively participates in many discussions at home, school, and with peers.

15. Acting-Out, Aggressive, and Negative Attention-Seeking Behaviors (11)

A. The client has displayed a recurrent pattern of engaging in acting-out, aggressive, or negative attention-seeking behaviors when he/she begins to feel insecure or frustrated about his/her speech/language problems.

B. The client expressed feelings of anger and frustration about his/her speech/language problems during today's therapy session.

C. The client expressed feelings of anger, hurt, and sadness about the teasing or criticism that he/she has received from peers about his/her speech/language problems.

D. The frequency and severity of the client's acting-out, aggressive, and negative attention-seeking behaviors have gradually started to decrease as the client is learning more effective ways to cope with his/her speech/language problems.

E. The client has ceased his/her pattern of engaging in acting out, aggressive, and negative attention-seeking behaviors when feeling frustrated about his/her speech/language problems.

INTERVENTIONS IMPLEMENTED

1. Speech/Language Evaluation (1)*

A. The client was referred for a speech/language evaluation to assess the presence of a disorder and determine his/her eligibility for special education services.

B. The findings from the speech/language evaluation showed that the client is eligible to receive speech/language services.

C. The findings from the speech/language evaluation showed that the client does not meet the criteria for a speech/language disorder and is not eligible to receive special education services.

2. Psychoeducational Evaluation (2)

A. The client received a psychoeducational evaluation to assess his/her intellectual abilities to rule out the presence of other possible learning disabilities.

B. The client was cooperative during the psychoeducational evaluation and appeared motivated to do his/her best.

C. The client was uncooperative during the psychoeducational evaluation and did not appear to put forth good effort.

D. The findings from the psychoeducational evaluation revealed the presence of a specific learning disability.

E. The findings from the psychoeducational evaluation did not reveal the presence of a specific learning disability.

3. Psychological Testing (3)

A. The client received a psychological evaluation to determine whether emotional factors or ADHD are interfering with his/her speech/language development.

B. The client approached the psychological testing in an honest, straightforward manner, and was cooperative with any requests presented to him/her.

C. The client was uncooperative and resistant to engage during the evaluation process.

D. The findings from the psychological testing revealed the presence of ADHD, which has interfered with the client's development.

E. The findings from the psychological testing revealed the presence of underlying emotional problems, which have interfered with the client's speech/language development.

4. Neurological Examination/Neuropsychological Examination Referral (4)

A. The client was referred for a neurological evaluation to rule out the presence of organic factors that may be contributing to the client's speech/language problem.

B. The client received a neuropsychological evaluation to rule out the presence of organic factors that may be contributing to the client's speech/language problem.

C. The findings from the neurological examination revealed the presence of organic factors that have interfered with the client's speech/language development.

* The numbers in parentheses correlate to the number of the Therapeutic Interventions statement in the companion chapter with same title in *The Child Psychotherapy Treatment Planner* (Jongsma, Peterson, and McInnis) by John Wiley & Sons, 2000.

D. The findings from the neuropsychological examination revealed the presence of organic factors that have interfered with the client's speech/language development.

E. The findings from the neurological and/or neuropsychological evaluation did not reveal the presence of any organic factors that may be contributing to the client's speech/language development.

5. Referral for Hearing/Medical Examination (5)

A. The client was referred for a hearing examination to rule out a possible hearing problem that may be interfering with his/her speech/language development.

B. The client was referred for a medical examination to rule out possible health problems that may be interfering with his/her speech/language development.

C. The findings from the hearing examination revealed the presence of a hearing loss that has interfered with the client's speech/language development.

D. The findings from the medical examination revealed the presence of health problems that have interfered with the client's speech/language development.

E. The findings from the hearing and/or medical examinations did not reveal the presence of any hearing or health problems that have contributed to the client's speech/language development.

6. Attend IEPC Meeting (6)

A. The client's IEPC meeting was held with the parents, teachers, speech/language pathologist, and school officials to determine the client's eligibility for special education services, to design educational interventions, to establish speech/language goals, and to outline emotional issues that need to be addressed in counseling.

B. The recommendation was made at the IEPC meeting that the client receive special education services to address his/her speech/language deficits.

C. It was decided at the IEPC meeting that the client is not in need of special education services because he/she does not meet the criteria for a speech/language disorder.

D. The IEPC meeting was helpful in identifying specific speech/language goals.

E. The IEPC meeting was helpful in identifying emotional issues that need to be addressed in therapy.

7. Consultation about Intervention Strategies (7)

A. Consulted with the client, parents, teachers, and speech/language pathologist about designing effective intervention strategies that build on the client's strengths and compensate for his/her weaknesses.

B. The client, parents, teachers, and speech/language pathologist identified several learning or personality strengths that the client can use to improve his/her speech/language abilities.

C. The consultation meeting with the client, parents, teachers, and speech/language pathologist identified the client's weaknesses and intervention strategies that he/she can utilize to overcome his/her speech/language problems.

8. Referral to Private Speech/Language Pathologist (8)

A. The client was referred to a private speech/language pathologist for extra assistance in improving his/her speech/language abilities.

B. The client and parents followed through with the recommendation to work with a private speech/language pathologist.

C. The client and parents failed to follow through with the recommendation to contact a private speech/language pathologist.

D. The client's speech/language abilities have improved since he/she began working with the private speech/language pathologist.

E. The client's work with the speech/language pathologist has helped him/her manage or overcome the stuttering problem.

9. Maintain Communication between Home and School (9)

A. The parents, teachers, and speech/language pathologist were encouraged to maintain regular communication with each other via phone calls or written notes regarding the client's speech/language development.

B. The client's teachers were asked to send home daily or weekly progress notes informing the parents about the client's academic progress, particularly in regard to his/her speech/language development.

C. The speech/language pathologist was encouraged to send home regular progress reports informing the parents of the client's progress in speech/language therapy.

10. Educate Parents about Speech/Language Disorder (10)

A. The client's parents were educated about the signs and symptoms of the client's speech/language disorder.

B. The therapy session helped the client's parents gain a greater understanding of the signs and symptoms of the client's speech/language disorder.

C. The parents were given the opportunity to express their thoughts and feelings about their child's speech/language disorder.

D. The parents were given support in verbalizing their feelings of sadness about the client's speech/language disorder.

11. Encourage Parental Positive Reinforcement (11)

A. The parents were encouraged to provide frequent praise and positive reinforcement regarding the client's speech/language development.

B. The parents were encouraged to praise the client for his/her efforts in attempting to master new speech sounds.

C. The parents were strongly encouraged to praise and positively reinforce the client for achieving his/her speech/language goals.

D. The parents were encouraged to praise and reinforce the client for speaking up and asserting himself/herself in new social situations.

E. Explored the reasons for the parents' resistance in offering praise and positive reinforcement to the client.

12. Parent's Denial of Speech/Language Problem (12)

A. A family therapy session was held to assess the parents' denial surrounding the client's speech/language problem.

B. The parents' denial about the client's speech/language problem was confronted and challenged so that they will begin to cooperate with the recommendations regarding placement and interventions for the client.

C. The therapy session was helpful in working through the parents' denial surrounding the client's speech/language problems, and they agreed to follow through with the recommendations regarding placement and interventions.

D. The parents have remained in denial about the client's intellectual deficits and are opposed to following through with the recommendations regarding placement and educational interventions.

13. Design Reward System for Speech (13)

A. Consulted with the speech/language pathologist about designing a reward system to reinforce the client for achieving his/her goals in speech therapy and mastering new speech behaviors.

B. The client and parents were helped to develop a list of possible rewards that could be used to reinforce the client for achieving his/her speech therapy goals.

C. The reward system has helped the client achieve his/her goals in speech therapy.

14. Assign "Home-Based Reading and Language Program" (14)

A. The "Home-Based Reading and Language Program" from *The Brief Child Therapy Homework Planner* (Jongsma, Peterson, and McInnis) was utilized to help build the client's vocabulary.

B. The client was instructed to read to the parents for 15 minutes, 4 times weekly, and then retell the story to them to help build his/her vocabulary.

C. The "Home-Based Reading and Language Program" was employed to help the client feel more comfortable and confident in verbalizing his/her thoughts and opinions.

D. The client and parents were encouraged to utilize the reward system outlined in the "Home-Based Reading and Language Program" to maintain the client's interest and motivation in improving his/her expressive and receptive language skills.

E. The client and parents reported that the "Home-Based Reading and Language Program" has helped the client feel more confident in expressing his/her thoughts and opinions.

15. Client Verbalize Feelings about Family Outing (15)

A. The client and his/her family were given the directive to go on a weekly outing, and afterward have the client share his/her thoughts and feelings about the outing to increase his/her expressive and receptive language abilities.

B. The parents reported that the client's retelling of the weekly outing has helped him/her feel more confident in expressing his/her thoughts and feelings.

C. The parents were instructed to provide frequent praise and positive reinforcement to the client for retelling the story of the family outing.

D. The client and parents were instructed to use the "Tell All About It" program from *The Brief Child Therapy Homework Planner* (Jongsma, Peterson, and McInnis) to help the client increase his/her confidence in expressing his/her thoughts and feelings.

E. The "Tell All About It" program was utilized to increase the parents' support and involvement with the client's speech/language development.

16. Assign Parents to Sing Songs (16)

A. The parents were instructed to sing songs with the client to help him/her feel more comfortable with his/her verbalizations in the home.

B. The parents reported that the exercise of singing songs along with the client has helped the client feel more comfortable and confident in verbalizing his/her thoughts and feelings at home.

C. The parents reported that singing songs along with the client has helped the client feel less anxious about his/her speech/language problems.

17. Confront Excessive Parental Pressure (17)

A. A family therapy session was held to assess whether the parents are placing excessive or unrealistic pressure on the client to "talk right."

B. The parents were confronted and challenged about placing excessive or unrealistic pressure on the client to "talk right."

C. The parents acknowledged that they have placed excessive or unrealistic pressure on the client to overcome his/her speech/language problems.

D. The parents agreed to cease placing excessive pressure on the client to "talk right."

E. The parents became defensive in the therapy session when they were confronted about placing excessive or unrealistic pressure on the client to speak clearly or fluently.

18. Teach Parents Realistic Expectations (18)

A. Today's therapy session focused on helping the parents develop realistic expectations of the client's speech/language development.

B. The parents were encouraged to communicate regularly with the speech/language pathologist to help them develop more realistic expectations about the client's speech/language development.

C. The parents were encouraged to consult with the speech/language pathologist about exercises at home that may help facilitate the client's speech/language development.

D. The parents have developed realistic expectations of the client's speech/language development.

19. Observe Parent-Child Interactions (19)

A. The parent-child interactions were observed in today's therapy session to assess how the family communication patterns affect the client's speech/language development.

B. Today's family therapy session revealed how the parents and family members often speak for the client when he/she begins to feel anxious about speech/language problems.

C. Today's family therapy session revealed how the parents often speak and fill in the pauses for the client when he/she begins to stutter.

D. Today's therapy session revealed how the client seldom takes the lead in initiating conversations among family members.

E. Today's therapy session revealed how the parents and family members often make critical remarks about the client's speech/language problems.

20. Assess Parents Speaking for Client (20)

A. Today's therapy session explored whether the parents often speak or fill in the pauses for the client to protect him/her from feeling anxious or insecure about speech.

B. The parents acknowledged that they often speak or fill in the pauses for the client to protect him/her from feeling anxious or insecure about the speech/language problems.

C. The parents agreed to cease speaking or filling in the pauses when the client begins to feel insecure.

D. The client reported that he/she has started to feel more confident and less anxious since the parents ceased their practice of speaking or filling in the pauses for him/her.

E. Explored the reasons for the parents' resistance to cease speaking or filling in the pauses for the client when he/she begins to feel anxious or insecure.

21. Encourage Client to Initiate Conversation (21)

A. The parents were strongly encouraged to allow the client to take the lead more often in initiating and sustaining conversations.

B. The client and parents were instructed to spend 10 to 15 minutes together on a daily basis where the client takes the lead in initiating and sustaining conversations.

C. A reward system was designed to reinforce the client for initiating conversations at home.

D. The factors that contribute to the client's resistance to initiate or sustain conversations at home were explored.

E. The client and parents reported that he/she has taken the lead more often in initiating and sustaining conversations.

22. Teach Communication Skills (22)

A. The client and parents were taught effective communication skills (e.g., active listening, reflecting feelings, "I" statements) to facilitate the client's speech/language development.

B. Role-playing techniques were used to teach the client effective communication skills.

C. The parents were encouraged to use active listening skills and reflect the client's feelings to help facilitate his/her speech/language development.

D. The client was taught to utilize "I" messages to communicate his/her thoughts, feelings, and needs more clearly and effectively.

23. Develop Acceptance of Limitations (23)

A. Today's therapy session helped the client and parents develop an understanding and acceptance of the limitations surrounding the client's speech/language disorder.

B. The client and parents were given support in expressing their feelings about the limitations surrounding the client's speech/language disorder.

C. The parents were seen in today's therapy session to help them express and work through their feelings of sadness about the client's speech/language disorder.

D. The client and parents have gained a healthy understanding and acceptance of the limitations surrounding the client's speech/language disorder.

24. Gently Confront Withdrawal (24)

A. The client was gently confronted about his/her pattern of withdrawing in social settings to avoid experiencing anxiety about his/her speech/language problems.

B. The reasons for the client's pattern of withdrawing in social settings were explored.

C. The client was taught effective communication and assertiveness skills to help him/her feel more confident and less anxious in social settings.

D. The client acknowledged that he/she often withdraws in social settings to avoid experiencing criticism or ridicule about his/her stuttering.

E. The client acknowledged that he/she often withdraws in social settings to avoid feeling embarrassed or anxious about his/her speech articulation problems.

25. Assign One Comment in Classroom (25)

A. The client was assigned the task of contributing at least one comment to the classroom discussion each day to increase his/her confidence in speaking before others.

B. The client reported that the homework assignment of contributing at least one comment to classroom discussion per day has helped increase his/her confidence in speaking before others.

C. The reasons were explored for the client's failure to follow through with contributing at least one comment to classroom discussion per day.

D. A reward system was utilized to reinforce the client for contributing at least one comment during classroom discussion per day.

26. Assign Show-and-Tell (26)

A. The client was assigned the task of sharing his/her toys or personal objects during show-and-tell time at school to increase his/her expressive language abilities.

B. The client reported that his/her participation in show-and-tell at school has helped increase his/her confidence in expressing self around others.

C. The reasons were explored for the client's resistance to participate in show-and-tell at school.

D. The parents and teachers were strongly encouraged to praise and reinforce the client for sharing his/her toys or personal objects during show-and-tell.

27. Teach Positive Coping Mechanisms (27)

A. The client was taught deep breathing and muscle relaxation techniques to help him/her cope with frustration surrounding speech/language problems.

B. The client was encouraged to utilize positive self-talk to help him/her cope with frustration surrounding speech/language problems.

C. The client was taught cognitive restructuring techniques to help him/her cope with frustration surrounding speech/language problems.

D. The client reported that the positive coping mechanisms (e.g., deep breathing and muscle relaxation techniques, positive self-talk, cognitive restructuring) have helped to decrease his/her frustration with speech/language problems.

E. The client reported experiencing little or no reduction in the level of his/her anxiety or frustration through the use of relaxation techniques, positive self-talk, or cognitive restructuring.

28. Teach Self-Control Strategies (28)

A. The client was taught deep breathing and relaxation techniques to inhibit the impulse to act out or engage in negative attention-seeking behaviors when encountering frustration with his/her speech/language problems.

B. The client was encouraged to utilize positive self-talk when encountering frustration with his/her speech/language problems, instead of acting out or engaging in negative attention-seeking behaviors.

C. The client was taught mediational, self-control strategies (e.g., "stop, look, listen, and think") to inhibit the impulse to act out or engage in negative attention-seeking behaviors when encountering frustration with speech/language problems.

D. The client was taught cognitive restructuring techniques to help him/her inhibit the impulse to act out or engage in negative attention-seeking behaviors when encountering frustration with speech/language problems.

E. The client reported that the self-control strategies have helped him/her cope with frustrations surrounding speech/language problems and reduce the frequency of his/her acting out or negative attention-seeking behaviors.

29. Assign "Shauna's Song" (29)

A. The client was assigned to read "Shauna's Song" from *The Brief Child Therapy Homework Planner* (Jongsma, Peterson, and McInnis) to help him/her identify and express feelings of insecurity about speech/language problems.

B. The client's responses to the review questions from the short story, "Shauna's Song," were processed.

C. The client and parents were assigned to read "Shauna's Song" to help the client develop an awareness and acceptance of speech/language problems.

D. The client reported that the story, "Shauna's Song," helped him/her realize how he/she withdraws when feeling anxious about speech/language problems.

E. The client reported that the story "Shauna's Song" helped him/her identify personal strengths that can be used to gain acceptance in peer group or school settings.

30. Utilize Child-Centered Play-Therapy Principles (30)

A. Child-centered play-therapy principles were utilized to help the client face and work through his/her insecurities regarding speech/language problems.

B. The client was given unconditional positive regard and warm acceptance in expressing his/her insecurities about speech/language problems.

C. The client's insecurities about speech/language problems were reflected back to him/her in a nonjudgmental manner.

D. The client's capacity to face and work through his/her insecurities regarding speech/language problems was reinforced.

E. The client-centered play-therapy principles have helped the client successfully face and work through his/her insecurities regarding speech/language problems.

31. Use Mutual Storytelling Technique (31)

A. The client actively participated in the mutual storytelling exercise.

B. Using the mutual storytelling technique, the therapist modeled effective ways for the client to manage his/her insecurities and frustrations surrounding speech/language problems.

C. The client created a story using puppets, dolls, or stuffed animals that reflected his/her insecurities and frustrations about speech/language problems.

D. The client was helped to create a story using puppets, dolls, or stuffed animals that showed effective ways to cope with his/her frustrations surrounding speech/language problems.

E. The client identified the mutual storytelling technique as being a fun and useful way to manage his/her frustrations surrounding speech/language problems.

32. Implement Systematic Desensitization with Metronome (32)

A. Consulted with the client, parents, and speech/language pathologist about designing and implementing a systematic desensitization program where a metronome is introduced and gradually removed to slow the client's rate of speech and help him/her control stuttering.

B. The client and parents agreed to follow through with the implementation of the systematic desensitization program using a metronome.

C. The systematic desensitization program has helped slow the client's rate of speech and helped him/her control stuttering.

D. The systematic desensitization program has not yet proven to be helpful in controlling the client's stuttering.

33. Teach Anxiety-Reduction Techniques (33)

A. The client was taught deep breathing and relaxation techniques to decrease his/her anticipatory anxiety in social settings and help control stuttering.

B. The client was encouraged to utilize positive self-talk when experiencing anticipatory anxiety in social settings to help control stuttering.

C. The client was taught cognitive restructuring techniques to help decrease his/her anticipatory anxiety in social settings and control stuttering.

D. The client reported that the anxiety-reduction techniques have helped to decrease his/her anticipatory anxiety in social settings.

34. Assign Three Social Contacts per Day (34)

A. The client was given the homework assignment of initiating three social contacts per day with peers to help him/her face and work through anxieties and insecurities related to stuttering.

B. Role-playing and modeling techniques were utilized to teach the client appropriate ways to greet peers and initiate conversations.

C. The "Greeting Peers" exercise from *The Brief Child Therapy Homework Planner* (Jongsma, Peterson, and McInnis) was utilized to help increase the frequency of the client's social interactions with peers and help him/her face and work through anxieties and insecurities related to stuttering.

D. The "Greeting Peers" exercise has helped reduce the client's social isolation and enabled him/her to face and work through anxieties related to his/her stuttering problem.

E. The client reported that the "Greeting Peers" exercise has helped him/her increase social contacts and overcome anxieties associated with his/her stuttering problem.

35. Design Oral Reading Program (35)

A. Consulted with the speech/language pathologist and teachers about designing a program in which the client orally reads passages of increasing length or difficulty in the classroom.

B. The client's anxieties and insecurities about reading in the classroom were processed.

C. The client was given much praise and positive reinforcement for reading passages in the classroom.

D. A reward system was designed to reinforce the client for reading in the classroom.

E. The client has experienced increased confidence in his/her ability to verbalize thoughts and feelings since he/she began orally reading passages in the classroom.

36. Design *In Vivo* Desensitization Program (36)

A. A speech/language pathologist was consulted about designing an *in vivo* desensitization program to help the client overcome anxiety associated with stuttering.

B. The client was trained in the use of deep-muscle relaxation techniques, as part of the *in vivo* desensitization program, to help decrease his/her anxiety associated with stuttering.

C. The *in vivo* desensitization program has helped to decrease the client's anxiety associated with his/her stuttering problem.

D. The client reported that the *in vivo* desensitization program has helped to decrease the frequency and intensity of his/her stuttering.

E. Thus far, the *in vivo* desensitization program has not proven to be successful in reducing the client's anxiety related to his/her stuttering problem.

37. Use Role-Playing and Positive Coping Strategies (37)

A. Role playing was used in today's therapy session to model effective ways for the client to extinguish anxiety that triggers stuttering in various social settings (e.g., reading in front of class, talking on phone, introducing self to unfamiliar peer).

B. The client was trained in the use of cognitive restructuring techniques to extinguish his/her anxiety that triggers stuttering in various social settings.

C. The client was strongly encouraged to utilize positive self-talk as a means of reducing his/her anxiety that frequently triggers stuttering in various social settings.

D. The client reported that the role-playing exercises were helpful in reducing his/her anxiety.

E. The client reported that the cognitive restructuring techniques and positive self-talk helped to extinguish his/her anxiety that triggers stuttering.

38. Use Psychoanalytic Play-Therapy Approaches (38)

A. Using a psychoanalytic play-therapy approach, the client was allowed to take the lead in exploring the unconscious conflicts or core anxieties that contribute to his/her selective mutism.

B. A psychoanalytic play-therapy approach was utilized to help the client work through his/her feelings surrounding past loss, trauma, or victimization that have contributed to the emergence of selective mutism.

C. Interpreted the client's feelings and fears expressed in his/her play and related them to the emergence of his/her selective mutism.

D. The psychoanalytic play therapy approaches have helped the client work through and resolve the issues contributing to the emergence of the selective mutism.

39. Assess Family Dynamics (39)

A. A family therapy session was held to assess the dynamics that contribute to the client's refusal to speak in some situations.

B. The family members were asked to list the stressors that have had a negative impact on the family.

C. The family members were asked to identify the things that they would like to change within the family system.

D. The family therapy session was helpful in identifying the factors that contribute to the client's refusal to use speech in some situations.

40. Explore Past Loss, Trauma, or Victimization (40)

A. Today's therapy session explored the client's background for a possible history of loss, trauma, or victimization that may have contributed to the onset of his/her selective mutism.

B. Today's therapy session revealed how the client's selective mutism emerged after he/she experienced a significant loss or traumatic event.

C. An individual play-therapy session was held to help the client begin to express and work through his/her feelings about the past loss, trauma, or victimization.

41. Employ Ericksonian Play-Therapy Technique (41)

A. An Ericksonian play-therapy technique was employed whereby the therapist spoke through a "wise doll" (or puppet) to an audience of other dolls or puppets to teach the client effective ways to cope with past loss, trauma, or victimization.

B. An Ericksonian play-therapy technique was utilized to help establish rapport with the client.

C. The client identified the Ericksonian play-therapy technique as being a fun and useful way to learn how to cope with past loss, trauma, or victimization.

42. Employ Art Therapy (42)

A. An art therapy approach was used in the early stages of therapy to help establish rapport and allow the client to begin to express his/her feelings through artwork.

B. The art therapy sessions have helped the client begin to work through his/her feelings.

C. The client's artwork revealed insight into the factors contributing to the emergence of selective mutism.

D. Processed the content of the client's artwork and related it to the emergence of his/her selective mutism.

E. The art therapy sessions have helped the client establish trust with the therapist so that now he/she has begun to directly verbalize his/her thoughts and feelings.

43. Medication Evaluation (43)

A. The client was referred for a medication evaluation to help stabilize his/her moods.

B. The client was referred for a medication evaluation to address his/her symptoms of ADHD that interfere with speech/language development.

C. The client and parents agreed to follow through with the medication evaluation.

D. The client and parents voiced their opposition to medication being used to stabilize moods and/or address symptoms of ADHD.

E. The client and parents were strongly encouraged to maintain regular communication with the psychiatrist or prescribing physician to monitor the effectiveness of the medication.